THE KALMAR WAR 1611–1613

Gustavus Adolphus's First War

Michael Fredholm von Essen

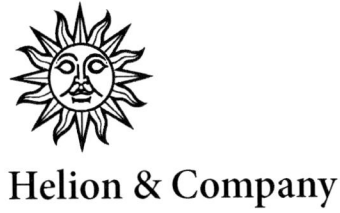

Helion & Company

Helion & Company Limited
Unit 8 Amherst Business Centre
Budbrooke Road
Warwick
CV34 5WE
England
Tel. 01926 499 619
Email: info@helion.co.uk
Website: www.helion.co.uk
Twitter: @helionbooks
Visit our blog http://blog.helion.co.uk/

Published by Helion & Company 2023
Designed and typeset by Serena Jones
Cover designed by Paul Hewitt, Battlefield Design (www.battlefield-design.co.uk)

Text © Michael Fredholm von Essen 2023
Illustrations © as individually credited
Colour artwork by Sergey Shamenkov © Helion & Company 2023
Colour flag illustrations by Lesley Prince © Helion & Company 2023
Maps drawn by George Anderson © Helion & Company 2023

Illustrations attributed to Army Museum, Stockholm, are reproduced under the Creative Commons license and derived from the website https://digitaltmuseum.se. Illustrations attributed to Royal Armoury, Stockholm, or Skokloster Castle are reproduced under the Creative Commons license and derived from the website http://emuseumplus.lsh.se. Illustrations attributed to History Museum, Stockholm, or Economy Museum – Royal Coin Cabinet/SHM, Stockholm, are reproduced under the Creative Commons license and derive from the website https://samlingar.shm.se. Other illustrations are reproduced under GNU Free Documentation License (GNU FDL), coupled with the Creative Commons Attribution Share-Alike License, or derived from the author's personal collection. Photographs attributed to Medström and Medström/Publisher Produktion reproduced with the permission of this publisher. The photographs of the Drabant Guards at Vadstena are reproduced with the permission of Stefan Ingesson and Adam Ingesson. Every reasonable effort has been made to trace copyright holders and to obtain their permission for the use of copyright material. The author and publisher apologise for any errors or omissions in this work, and would be grateful if notified of any corrections that should be incorporated in future reprints or editions of this book.

ISBN 978-1-804510-06-3

British Library Cataloguing-in-Publication Data.
A catalogue record for this book is available from the British Library.

All rights reserved. No part of this publication may be reproduced, stored in a retrieval system, or transmitted, in any form, or by any means, electronic, mechanical, photocopying, recording or otherwise, without the express written consent of Helion & Company Limited.

For details of other military history titles published by Helion & Company
Limited, contact the above address, or visit our website: http://www.helion.co.uk

We always welcome receiving book proposals from prospective authors.

Contents

Chronology	iv
Introduction	xvi
Dramatis Personae	xviii
Prologue: The Two Kings	xxii
1: The Origin of the Kalmar War	31
2: Tactical Doctrines	42
3: The Danish Military Establishment	46
4: The Norwegian Military Establishment	94
5: The Swedish Military Establishment	100
6: The Outbreak of War	159
7: The Siege of Kalmar	183
8: The Offensive Against the River Göta Älv Castles	198
9: The Battle for Kalmar	201
10: The West Coast	217
11: Norway and Lapponia	219
12: The Invasion of Ösel	223
13: The Winter Campaign	225
14: The Summer Campaign	243
15: Gustavus Adolphus's Response	261
16: The Overland Offensive Towards the Swedish Heartland	267
17: The Naval Expedition Towards Stockholm	273
18: Operations into Norway	279
19: The Treaty of Knäred	283
Colour Plate Commentaries	290
Further Reading	297
Bibliography	299

Chronology

All dates are Old Style (OS).

1611

9 February	Danish Council of the Realm authorises war against Sweden.
28 February	King Christian directs the Hanseatic League to cease all trade with Sweden.
3–5 March	King Christian orders mobilisation throughout Norway.
4 March	King Christian orders the governor of Trondheim, Steen Bille, to prepare for an invasion of Sweden.
6 March	Naval squadron under Jørgen Daa is ordered to blockade Elfsborg Castle to cut the Swedish sea lines of communications in the Skagerrak Strait and North Sea.
10 March	Naval squadron first under Gabriel Kruse, then Erik Urne, is ordered to blockade Kalmar to cut the Swedish sea lines of communications in the southern Baltic Sea.
31 March	King Charles appoints Hans Claesson Bielkenstierna admiral, ordering him to assemble the Swedish main fleet at Älvsnabben, a natural harbour in the southern Stockholm Archipelago.
4 April	King Christian signs the declaration of war on Sweden. Governor General Enevold Kruse of Norway and his commanders write to the King, reporting that they are unable to raise the requested number of men and asking him to instead send them enlisted foreign infantry to augment the Norwegian forces. Meanwhile, Danish armies assemble.
6 April	King Christian's herald brings the Danish declaration of war to Jönköping, Sweden.
11 April	Admiral of the Realm Mogens Ulfeldt is ordered to set out with the Danish main fleet.
24 April	King Christian arrives in Christianopel and assumes command of the army there.
28 April	King Christian angrily responds to Governor General Kruse that the Norwegians should not make suggestions and demands but instead follow orders.
29 April	Planned date for King Charles to lead the Swedish main army out of Örebro, but he procrastinates and delays the march.

CHRONOLOGY

1 May	On the planned date for Denmark's initiation of hostilities, King Christian leads his army across the border, and his advance guard disperses the Swedish cavalry company there.
3 May	King Christian reaches Kalmar, and Swedish cavalry sallies out to harass the Danes. Planned date for King Christian's enlisted German units to arrive by ship in Scania, but they do not arrive on time.
4 May	King Christian lays siege to Kalmar town and castle.
5 May	Swedes at Kalmar again sally out to harass the Danes, and King Christian is almost hit by falconet fire. Sweden formally issues the reciprocal declaration of war on Denmark.
6 May	Danish siege artillery is delivered at Kalmar. King Charles orders Governor Anders Larsson of Reval, Estonia, to invade the Danish island of Ösel. (Having received the order in July, Larsson sent Swedish units to occupy the island.)
7 May	Danish artillery at Kalmar is in position; new planned date for King Charles to lead the main army out of Örebro.
8 May	King Charles orders Colonel Jacob Tomasson to invade the Norwegian province of Härjedalen with peasant levies from the Swedish province of Dalecarlia.
9 May	King Charles orders his governor of Lapponia, Baltzar Bäck, to invade the Norwegian province of Jämtland and sends an open letter to the peasants of Härjedalen and Jämtland, urging them to renounce Danish rule. Belatedly, the King marches out of Örebro on the way to Kalmar.
13 May	Danes at Kalmar commence mining operations against the town walls.
17 May	Swedish warship *Obekant* is sunk at Kalmar by Danish artillery fire.
18 May	King Charles reaches Jönköping; Swedes sally out from Kalmar.
19 May	Danes at Kalmar attempt to attack the Swedish warships of the Kalmar Squadron with a burner but fail.
22 May	On the western front, Danes under Steen Maltesen Sehested attempt to storm Elfsborg Castle; Swedish warship *Sankt Per* is sunk at Kalmar by Danish artillery fire.
23 May	Swedish inshore vessels unsuccessfully attack Danish squadron at Elfsborg, and King Charles leaves Jönköping. At night, Swedes again sally out from Kalmar, where the Danes have abandoned the mining operations due to the loss of both mining engineers.
23–24 May	Swedes from the Elfsborg Squadron attempt to carry out a surprise attack by night on Daa's squadron with rowing boats, but Danes repulse the attack.
25 May	Port Admiral Godske Lindenow, with the Danish squadron that blockades Elfsborg, orders the annexation of the Swedish islands off the River Göta Älv Estuary. Danes at Kalmar again attempt to attack the Swedish warships of the Kalmar Squadron with a burner but fail.
26 May	King Charles reaches Vetlanda.
27 May	King Christian successfully storms Kalmar town.
28 May	King Charles reaches Högsby. The following day (29 May), he learns of the fall of Kalmar town.

THE KALMAR WAR

31 May	On the western front, Gert von Rantzau spearheads a Danish offensive towards Nya Lödöse.
1 June	Sehested follows Rantzau's advance guard towards Nya Lödöse.
3 June	Sehested reaches Elfsborg Castle, skirmishes with the garrison, steals some cattle, and retreats to Kungsbacka. King Charles reaches Ålem.
7 June	Sehested returns across the border and, the following day (8 June), builds a fortified camp at Frölunda.
9 June	Sehested continues towards Nya Lödöse; King Charles reaches Ryssby.
10 June	King Christian leaves Kalmar and sails to Christianopel to bring reinforcements.
11 June	King Charles's advance guard reaches Kalmar, which results in a cavalry skirmish. Duke Philip of Glücksburg and Gert von Rantzau make a demonstration against Elfsborg Castle but without success. Jesper Matsson Cruus evacuates Nya Lödöse and withdraws to the north.
12 June	King Charles and the Swedish main army reach Kalmar, and Danish cavalry sorties from Kalmar town in force but is pushed back inside. Sehested burns Gothenburg and sends Albert Skeel to take possession of the abandoned town of Nya Lödöse. King Christian orders Sehested to abandon the western campaign and instead march to Växjö, and King Charles orders Cruus to march to Kalmar. (In a later order, he is countermanded to shadow Sehested during his expected march to Kalmar.)
13 June	Encountering four Swedish infantry companies in a fortified position behind a stream, Skeel chooses not to push on further.
16 June	Sehested moves his entire army into Nya Lödöse.
18–21 June	Swedes unsuccessfully attempt to evict Danes from Kvarnholm Island outside Kalmar.
22 June	Sehested receives King Christian's order (from 12 June) to abandon the western campaign and instead march to Växjö. Norwegian raiding party is reported in Dalecarlia which prevents the Dalecarlians from marching to Kalmar in support of King Charles.
23 June	Swedes manage to bring a few hundred reinforcements under Captain Lars Brink into Kalmar Castle.
24 June	Swedes raid the Danish depot on Stensö Peninsula, capturing a boyer from Stralsund.
25 June	Godske Lindenow's squadron arrives to reinforce the Danish army and fleet elements at Kalmar. Sehested reaches Varberg and receives orders to send Gert von Rantzau and his men to Kalmar.
26 June	Gustavus Adolphus takes Christianopel. Danes at Kalmar carry out a failed sortie. Sehested sends Jørgen Lunge with a corps against Frölunda, but it is soon halted by a Swedish unit the following day (27 June).
29 June	Receiving King Christian's order to march by way of Christianopel to join him at Kalmar, Sehested prepares to move his army to the eastern front. Having captured some cattle, Lunge returns to Varberg with his corps.

CHRONOLOGY

30 June	Swedish inshore fleet under Anders Cordell arrives to the Kalmar region, breaking through Peder Nielsen's attempt to block their approach.
1 July	At Kalmar, Swedes take up positions on Svinö Island, from which they engage Danish ships with artillery fire. Sehested sets out on the march to Kalmar; soon, Cruus follows him on a more direct road across Småland (and, as will be shown, indeed arrives at Kalmar before Sehested).
2 July	Swedes land on Stensö Peninsula, but Danes evict them after stiff combat.
5 July	Swedish cavalry under Måns Stierna again raids Christianopel.
7 July	King Christian arrives on Stensö Peninsula by sea with reinforcements, including Gert von Rantzau.
8 July	Danes at Kalmar town sally out against King Charles's Swedes in a minor raid. During the afternoon, Bielkenstierna brings the Swedish main fleet to Kalmar.
10 July	Bielkenstierna attacks Erik Urne's squadron at Kvarnholm Island, forcing him to retreat, which enables supplies to be brought into Kalmar Castle.
13 July	King Charles orders Bielkenstierna to attack Urne's and Lindenow's squadrons to the south of Kalmar, but Bielkenstierna is in the process of salvaging the sunken warships.
14 July	King Charles appoints Colonel Per Hammarskiöld commandant of Kalmar Castle. In Norway, the newly mobilised army refuses to leave camp, and many refuse to swear loyalty to the governor general, Enevold Kruse.
15 July	King Charles sends reinforcements into Kalmar Castle.
16 July	Cruus reaches Kalmar with the Västergötland army.
17 July	King Charles attempts to retake Kalmar town, but, in the intense fighting, the town is set on fire and destroyed. The King fails to dislodge the Danes but does insert Christer Some as new governor at Kalmar Castle. On the western front, Nils Silfverbielke, commandant of Elfsborg Castle, storms Kungsbacka in Danish Halland, burning the town, having first devastated the Norwegian territories north of Gothenburg.
18 July	Sehested's infantry arrives at Kalmar by sea, joining forces with King Christian's army in the battle for Kalmar.
19 July	Fighting at Kalmar gradually ends, and King Charles fails to retake the town. In the evening, Admiral Mogens Ulfeldt reaches the northern part of the Kalmar Strait from his previous operations area at Gotland.
20 July	Entire units desert from the freshly mobilised Norwegian army.
21–22 July	Danish fleets attempt to blockade the Swedish main fleet at Kalmar, but it breaks out during the night.
23 July	King Christian offers battle with his entire army outside the Swedish camp, but King Charles refuses battle, instead retreating during the night and establishing a new camp at Ryssby.

THE KALMAR WAR

25 July	Jacob De la Gardie, King Charles's commanding general on the eastern side of the Baltic, unites Novgorod County with the Kingdom of Sweden.
27 July	Christer Some orders seven of the remaining 11 exposed Swedish vessels at Kalmar Castle to be burned.
29–30 July	Danes subject Kalmar Castle to intensive artillery bombardment.
30 July–2 Aug	King Christian attacks the camp at Ryssby but without success.
2 August	Christer Some initiates negotiations with the Danes.
3 August	Christer Some surrenders Kalmar Castle.
4 August	Christer Some writes to Johan Ulfsparre, the commandant at Borgholm, advising him to surrender as well.
5 August	King Christian sends a trumpeter to Öland to demand the island's surrender.
7 August	Öland local officials surrender to King Christian, who sends four companies to the island. Ulfsparre withdraws his men into Borgholm Castle.
8 August	King Christian crosses to Öland, preparing to lay siege to Borgholm Castle, but Ulfsparre surrenders Borgholm Castle in return for free departure.
12 August	King Charles sends a letter to King Christian, challenging the Danish King to single combat to conclude the war. Öland swears fealty to King Christian.
14 August	King Christian scornfully turns down the Swedish King's challenge and insults King Charles by calling him a fool and claiming the war as already won.
15 August	King Charles responds to King Christian's insulting letter. Following a bungled attempt to invade northern Sweden from Jämtland, Norwegian commander Jens Bielke abandons the provinces of Jämtland and Härjedalen and retreats towards Trondheim.
19 August	Gert von Rantzau moves against the Swedish camp at Ryssby but is defeated and almost captured.
20 August	Two Swedish cavalry banners raid the Danes at Kalmar then retreat to Ryssby. Late in the day, King Christian leads the army towards Ryssby, arriving and building a camp the following day (21 August).
22 August	Bielke reaches Trondheim; Swedish units occupy both Jämtland and Härjedalen.
22–23 August	Skirmishes take place between Danes and Swedes at Ryssby.
28 August	King Christian returns to Kalmar with his field army.
2 September	Ulfeldt's fleet defeats Admiral Jacob Gottberg in a skirmish at the northern promontory of Öland, in which Gottberg loses the warship *Röda Lejonet*. Afterwards, Ulfeldt sails to Kalmar while Gottberg returns to Älvsnabben.
8 September	King Charles orders Jöran Claesson Uggla to reinforce the Västergötland border with Norway and the town of Nya Lödöse. Soon after, Silfverbielke again sets out to raid Halland.
11 September	King Christian rides to Christianopel. Soon after, his men move into winter quarters in Blekinge and Scania.
14 September	Ulfeldt's fleet returns to Copenhagen.

CHRONOLOGY

19 September	King Charles reluctantly orders some exhausted units into winter quarters.
21 September	Knud Brahe and Ulrich Sandberg defeat Silfverbielke, who falls into Danish captivity.
26 September	King Christian returns to Denmark with the main fleet; Gustavus Adolphus crosses the Kalmar Strait to Öland.
6 October	King Charles appoints Olof Stråle commandant of Elfsborg Castle to replace the captured Silfverbielke.
7 October	Borgholm Castle surrenders to Gustavus Adolphus, who takes possession the following day.
16 October	King Charles and Gustavus Adolphus (recently back from Öland) leave the camp at Ryssby and set out by sea to Nyköping.
30 October	King Charles dies from natural causes.
19 November	Scanian and Halland Banners are sent home from the Halland border, being replaced by enlisted cavalry units.
27 November	Danish longboats under Captain Jens Munk raid the roadstead off Elfsborg, damaging a Swedish ship.
2 December	Johan van Monickhouen sets out from Stockholm, bound for the Dutch Republic, to enlist soldiers. Ultimately, he cannot pass through the Danish blockade of Skagerrak Strait, so must proceed overland.
6 December	King Christian orders Jørgen Daa to return to Copenhagen for the winter.
26 December	Parliament in Nyköping recognises Gustavus Adolphus as King of Sweden.

1612

7 January	Steen Laxmand, commandant of Bohus Castle, sends part of the garrison on a short-time raid into Västergötland.
11–15 January	Gustavus Adolphus travels from Nyköping to Västervik, on the way to Ryssby, preparing for a surprise attack on Kalmar.
14 January	King Christian crosses the Danish Strait.
15 January	King Christian marches into Halmstad with reinforcements.
16 January	King Christian sends a raiding party under Lieutenant Knud Gyldenstjerne of the Ribe Banner into south-western Småland. Mistaking the raiders for a major Danish army, Governor Böllja reports a Danish offensive towards Jönköping to Gustavus Adolphus, who receives the report on the road to Ryssby. In response, the Swedish King orders Duke John of Östergötland and Field Marshal Cruus to Småland to delay the Danes.
20 January	Nils Stiernskiöld notifies Gustavus Adolphus that Kalmar is now so strongly fortified that a surprise attack is impossible. Having assembled a corps on Småland's southern border, Breide Rantzau moves into Småland.
21 January	Having ravaged south-western Småland, Gyldenstjerne returns to Halmstad. The same day, Duke John reaches Jönköping while King Christian assembles an army at Varberg.

THE KALMAR WAR

21–24 January	Breide Rantzau ravages Småland, burns Växjö, and assaults nearby Kronoberg Castle over the ice-covered lake that protects it. His men fail to take the castle but do burn its barn.
23 January	Danes defeat and disperse Erik Jönsson's cavalry banner near Kalmar.
24 January	Gustavus Adolphus arrives in Ryssby.
25 January	Rantzau retreats towards Scania because of a sudden thaw. King Christian sets out with the main army from Varberg, aiming for Gullberg Castle.
26 January	Early in the morning, King Christian's Danes reach and unsuccessfully attempt to storm Gullberg Castle, ably defended by Lady Emerentia Pauli. Abandoning the assault, King Christian instead occupies Nya Lödöse.
27 January	Duke John joins forces with Cruus south of Falköping.
28 January	Gustavus Adolphus sets out from Ryssby towards Växjö.
29 January	King Christian attempts, but fails, to destroy with artillery fire the Swedish warships put up at Elfsborg Castle for the winter.
30 January	Abandoning the attempt against Elfsborg Castle, King Christian returns to Nya Lödöse; he orders his men to ravage the province of Västergötland.
31 January	Gustavus Adolphus writes to Bäck, ordering him to cease any unnecessary violence in occupied Jämtland and Härjedalen and instead protect the people now under his rule.
1 February	King Christian leads his army into Västergötland.
3 February	Gustavus Adolphus reaches Växjö.
5 February	Gustavus Adolphus moves into Danish Scania.
7 February	King Christian burns Skara.
8 February	Gustavus Adolphus burns Vä.
9 February	King Christian leaves Skara and retreats towards the west.
10 February	Danish gain victory in a skirmish between Danish and Swedish cavalry patrols at Vånga in Västergötland.
11 February	In Scania, Gustavus Adolphus and some of his men rest in Vittsjö upon their retreat towards Småland.
11–12 February	Anders Bille defeats Gustavus Adolphus in a night battle at Vittsjö; Gustavus Adolphus falls through the ice but is saved. Around the same time, Breide Rantzau overwhelms the Swedish bridgehead at Osby; surviving Swedes flee north to reestablish a defensive line at the border.
12 February	Retreating south from his raid into Västergötland, King Christian crosses the River Göta Älv into Norwegian territory to avoid Duke John and Cruus's attempt to intercept the retreating Danish army.
13 February	Having left Stiernskiöld in command of the defensive line at the border, Gustavus Adolphus arrives in Jönköping farther to the north. King Christian reaches Bohus Castle, where he remains until 19 February.
17–19 February	Swedish units under Duke John and Cruus enter Halland.
20 February	Duke John and Cruus take and burn Varberg town, avoiding Varberg Castle.

CHRONOLOGY

21 February	Duke John and Cruus defeat King Christian at Kölleryd, near Varberg.
26 February	Cruus reaches Nya Lödöse.
27 February	Cruus retakes Nya Lödöse. Afterwards, he thoroughly ravages Bohuslän in revenge for the previous Danish and Norwegian atrocities, burning Kungahälla and Uddevalla in the process.
12 March	Gustavus Adolphus sends an open letter to the Norwegians, encouraging them to throw off Danish rule.
21 March	Jørgen Daa sets out with a naval squadron bound for the River Göta Älv Estuary.
24 March	Two Danish warships set out to patrol the Baltic Sea, and Gustavus Adolphus orders Baltzar Bäck, governor of Lapponia, to bring his men to Stockholm to defend against an expected Danish landing.
1 April	On or around this day, Admiral Jacob Beck sets out with a naval squadron to blockade Kalmar and Öland.
8 April	In anticipation of the departure of the Swedish fleet, Gustavus Adolphus imposes sanctions on those German mercantile centres that provide supplies to Denmark and pay the Sound Toll to the Danish Crown.
9 April	Faced with Danish naval supremacy in the River Göta Älv Estuary after the arrival of Admiral Daa's Skagerrak Squadron, Gustavus Adolphus orders the crews and cannons of the Swedish warships there to be sent to Stockholm and the ships to be cleared of gear and scuttled so as to deny them to the Danes.
17 April	The first two Swedish warships in Stockholm ready to set out.
28 April	Danish vanguard units march towards the River Göta Älv Estuary.
29 April	Boats from Öland capture a Danish boyer from Ystad loaded with beer, bound for Kalmar. In response, three Danish yachts from Kalmar with 140 soldiers set out and manage to retake the boyer.
1 May	Danes under Major Peter von Heinemark and Captain Holger Rosencrantz storm the fortified Swedish camp at Ryssby, but the Swedes under Jacob Jacobsson Snakenborg Bååt have already established a new fortified position at Ålem.
2 May	King Christian sets sail on the *Victor*, with Lindenow's squadron of the main fleet from Helsingør in the Danish Strait, towards Elfsborg Castle.
5 May	King Christian disembarks his men near Elfsborg Castle, establishes a fortified camp nearby, and personally reconnoitres the enemy stronghold.
6 May	King Christian lays siege to Elfsborg Castle.
7–8 May	During the night, two Danish warships take up positions in the estuary between Elfsborg and Gullberg castles, cutting communications between them.
8 May	Danes open a canal that empties Elfsborg Castle's moat of water.
12 May	Danish siege batteries at Elfsborg Castle are ready for action.
13 May	Danes at Elfsborg Castle take outer defences at Skinner's Rock.
15 May	King Christian demands that Olof Stråle surrender Elfsborg Castle.
17 May	Danes explode a mine under one of Elfsborg Castle's walls.

THE KALMAR WAR

19 May	Gert von Rantzau reaches Kalmar to take command of the Danish eastern army.
22 May	Danes commence intensive artillery bombardment of Elfsborg Castle, take Skinner's Rock, and then attempt to storm the castle, during which defenders accidentally set one of their own towers on fire. In the east, Gert von Rantzau marches out of Kalmar to attack Ålem, which the Swedes abandon. Danes burn Ålem.
23 May	Stråle surrenders Elfsborg Castle in return for free departure the following day. Danish main fleet arrives off Kalmar.
24 May	Stråle's men march out, and King Christian assumes control over Elfsborg Castle.
26 May	Gustavus Adolphus asks Duke John to assume command in the war against Denmark and Norway so that he can sail to Finland to assume command in the war in Muscovy.
28 May	Danes move against Gullberg Castle.
29 May	Danes commence artillery bombardment of Gullberg Castle.
30–31 May	Gert von Rantzau successfully lands on Öland.
31 May	King Christian demands the surrender of Gullberg Castle, and the new commanders of Gullberg accept to surrender in exchange for free departure.
1 June	Gullberg Castle's garrison departs. Gert von Rantzau's Danes defeat Hammarskiöld's Swedes on Öland and surround Borgholm Castle.
6 June	King Christian marches into Västergötland.
6–7 June	During the night, Rantzau finally manages to deploy his siege artillery against Borgholm Castle.
7 June	Richard Clerck's squadron sets out from Älvsnabben, bound for Gotland. Arriving at Mariestad, Gustavus Adolphus learns of the loss of Elfsborg and Gullberg castles and postpones the voyage to the eastern front.
12 June	Rantzau's siege artillery breaches the walls of Borgholm Castle.
13 June	Hammarskiöld surrenders Borgholm Castle against the right to free departure, a promise that the Danes only keep in part. Having sailed around Gotland, without encountering any Danish warships, Clerck's squadron returns to Älvsnabben. At Gärdhem, King Christian learns that the Swedish King stands at Nybro, so he moves to confront the Swedes.
14 June	King Christian's army arrives at Nybro but finds the Swedish camp abandoned.
15 June	Retreating in the face of superior Danish numbers, Gustavus Adolphus reaches Höjentorp, north-east of Skara. King Christian rides into Lidköping but finds the town abandoned. As a result, the Danish King orders a general retreat but is now pursued by the Swedish King, who has gathered reinforcements.
20–27 June	Rantzau and his army depart from Öland and return to Kalmar to prepare for an offensive towards the north.
24 June	King Christian retreats beyond Alingsås.

CHRONOLOGY

25 June	Gustavus Adolphus marches into Alingsås. Danish main fleet at Kalmar, under Ulfeldt, sets out bound for Danzig. Rantzau begins the offensive towards the north.
28 June	Danes demolish Gullberg Castle.
29 June	Having retreated all the way to Gullberg, King Christian establishes a camp for his army there. Embarking upon the long-planned offensive towards the north, Rantzau reaches Högsby, where he disperses a Swedish corps under Colonel Jesper Cruus.
1 July	Ulfeldt's fleet arrives in Danzig.
2 July	Finding no Swedish warships, Ulfeldt's fleet departs from Danzig. Rantzau continues the march towards the north. Gustavus Adolphus moves into Jönköping.
5 July	Having abandoned the pursuit of the Danish King, Gustavus Adolphus orders Hammarskiöld to send his cavalry to the royal army and then use his infantry and levies to delay Rantzau's army. Duke John reaches Jönköping and prepares to defend Östergötland by erecting a line of abatis at Kisa. Rantzau reaches Målilla.
6 July	Rantzau reaches Vimmerby. Failing to find supplies, he soon retreats to Kalmar, abandoning the objective to join forces with King Christian at Jönköping.
10 July	King Christian sets out from Gullberg, bound for Jönköping. Soon after, Danish units from Elfsborg Castle and Norwegian units from Uddevalla move north against Brätte in Västergötland. Having circled Gotland on its way from Danzig, Ulfeldt's fleet lands at Västervik, intending to establish a supply depot there.
12 July	Gustavus Adolphus begins the march from Jönköping towards Eksjö.
14 July	Having already suffered a determined attack by Hammarskiöld, during which the town of Västervik caught fire, the Danish supply vessels abandon the port. Reaching Vetlanda, Gustavus Adolphus learns that King Christian is on his way towards Jönköping. Colonel Johan van Monickhouen sets sail from the Dutch Republic, bound for Norway, with an infantry regiment enlisted on behalf of Sweden.
15 July	Gustavus Adolphus reaches Repperda, from which he sends a reconnaissance force against the Danes. Having already abandoned the offensive, Rantzau's army reaches Vimmerby.
16 July	Gustavus Adolphus defeats Rantzau's men in a skirmish at River Em, near Målilla.
17 July	Gustavus Adolphus defeats Rantzau's men in a skirmish at Emmenäs.
18 July	Rantzau is back in Högsby. Swedish main fleet sets out from Älvsnabben, sailing south towards the seas off Västervik, where the Danish main fleet was operating until recently. In Norway, Monickhouen's Dutch ships pass Trondheim.
19 July	Monickhouen's Dutch regiment lands at Stjørdal, east of Trondheim.
20 July	Having taken major damage from a severe storm, Swedish main fleet returns to Älvsnabben. Pursuing Rantzau's army in its retreat towards Kalmar, Gustavus Adolphus reaches Högsby. Finding that Rantzau had escaped the Swedish envelopment, the Swedish King turns back to relieve Jönköping.

THE KALMAR WAR

23 July	King Christian, with the main army, finally reaches Jönköping, whose defenders burn the outskirts of the town to deny cover to the Danes.
24 July	News about the Danish King's arrival and, more importantly, his lack of siege artillery reaches Gustavus Adolphus. Swedish main fleet again sets out from Älvsnabben in search of the Danish fleet; however, the same day, the Danish main fleet returns to Copenhagen by way of Kalmar, which it passes on 25 July.
26 July	Swedes under the local game warden, Mickel Jönsson of Tenhult, defeat Albert Skeel in a skirmish at Rogberga. King Christian receives news (from captured Swedish prisoners) about Rantzau's retreat and orders a general retreat towards Halmstad.
27 July	Swedes under Sven Krååk defeat a Danish raiding party from Blekinge near Madesjö, Småland.
29 July	Danish fleet returns to Copenhagen, where it arrives one or two days later (30–31 July).
29 July–6 Aug	Swedish main fleet operates in the bay of Danzig, capturing several merchantmen.
31 July	Gustavus Adolphus reaches Jönköping with the Swedish field army.
2 August	Alexander Ramsay's, George Sinclair's, and George Hay's companies of enlisted Scots in Swedish service set out from Scotland.
8 August	King Christian returns to Copenhagen by way of Halmstad.
10 August	Having searched in vain for the Danish main fleet, the Swedish main fleet returns to Älvsnabben.
11 August	King Christian sets out from Copenhagen with the Danish main fleet in an attempt to attack Stockholm by sea.
16–20 August	Having reached Kalmar on the previous day, King Christian embarks several army units there.
19 August	Ramsay's, Sinclair's, and Hay's companies of enlisted Scots land at Romsdal, Norway.
24–25 August	King Christian's fleet is in Danzig.
26 August	Norwegian peasant levies defeat Ramsay's and Sinclair's Scots at Kringen, massacring the survivors.
31 August	Skirmishes take place between Danish and Swedish longboats in the Stockholm Archipelago. Swedes withdraw to Vaxholm, and Monickhouen arrives in Stockholm with his Dutch regiment.
2–4 September	Continuing skirmishes take place between Danish and Swedish naval units in the Vaxholm area.
4 September	King Christian gives up the attempt to take Stockholm. The Danish fleet sets out on its voyage back to Copenhagen but is delayed by contrary winds.
6 September	Gustavus Adolphus, in Jönköping, learns of the Danish fleet off Stockholm. In Madesjö, west of Kalmar, Krååk defeats a Danish raiding party from Kalmar.
8 September	Monickhouen attacks the Danish fleet with 500 men embarked on boats and burners, but the Danes discover the attempt, which fails.
9 September	Gustavus Adolphus arrives in Stockholm.
10 September	Danish fleet finally manages to leave the Stockholm Archipelago.

13 September	King Christian leaves his fleet off Bornholm, hands over command to Ulfeldt, lands at Ystad, and travels the rest of the distance overland.
17 September	King Christian is back in Copenhagen.
18 September	Discouraged by his failure to bring the war into Sweden's core territories, King Christian agrees to peace negotiations.
1 October	Gustavus Adolphus instructs Duke John to move his men into Västergötland to repulse a late September incursion into Dal by Lunge, supported by Norwegian units.
14 October	Admiral Clerck is ordered to convoy merchantmen with supplies on their way from Germany to Sweden.
29 November	Negotiations for peace begin in Knäred.

1613

19 January	The Treaty of Knäred concludes the war.

Introduction

The present book aims to describe and analyse the Kalmar War of 1611–1613 between Sweden and the united Kingdoms of Denmark and Norway. This was the last war in which Denmark–Norway successfully exercised its military might against Sweden, which, in the final stages of the confrontation, was ruled by the young Gustavus Adolphus, who inherited the war from his father.

The war derived from rivalry between the Danish and Swedish Crowns, yet disputes were primarily mercantile in origin. Since Denmark controlled the strait between the Baltic Sea and the North Sea, Sweden sought alternative trade routes. One was found through the sparsely populated Arctic North: Lapponia, named after the indigenous Lapps, or Sami people. In 1607, King Charles IX of Sweden declared himself 'King of the Lapps' and sent men to collect taxes in what by tradition was regarded as Norwegian territory. This was an option enabled by the 1595 Treaty of Teusina between Sweden and Muscovy. Unfortunately for Sweden, this was a time when the Swedish army was heavily engaged on the eastern front, again facing off against Muscovy and the Polish–Lithuanian Commonwealth in Livonia, Estonia, Finland, and indeed in Muscovy itself. Taking advantage of Sweden's commitments in the east, King Christian IV of Denmark and Norway in 1611 declared war upon Sweden and invaded Swedish territory from the south.

Combat operations also took place along the Swedish–Norwegian border and elsewhere in the Baltic region, on land and on sea. Both sides used mercenaries enlisted on the Continent in addition to national units. Sweden also employed Scottish and Dutch privateers and enlisted Dutch and Scottish expeditionary forces that landed in Norway. Nonetheless, Denmark ultimately conquered several key Swedish fortresses. However, the Danish thrust against the Swedish heartland failed, and the Kalmar War was the last time when Denmark successfully defended its control of the southern Baltic Sea against Sweden.

The principal commander on the Swedish side was the young Gustavus Adolphus, who later rose to prominence in the Thirty Years' War. The losses in the Kalmar War proved to Gustavus Adolphus that the Swedish army was becoming obsolete and needed thorough modernisation. As a result, the Kalmar War was the catalyst that prompted Gustavus Adolphus to reform the Swedish army, which in turn set Sweden on the path to become a regional great power.

While the Kalmar War soon was overshadowed by the subsequent Thirty Years' War and even in Scandinavia received comparatively little scholarly attention, the conflict gave rise to many local legends. Stories about the war were told and retold, sometimes as far away as in Scotland. Besides, Denmark controlled access to the Continent during the conflict, which the Danish Crown used to its advantage by disseminating propagandistic newsletters and leaflets. Soon, oral tales began to merge with the information in the printed newsletters, and they grew in the retelling. The result was a large corpus of legends that ultimately diffused into the annals of local and even national history. Most of the best stories about the war cannot be confirmed by contemporary archive records, and the researcher faces great difficulties in disentangling myth from fact. Although it is disappointing to remove so many stirring tales, the effort must be done. Even so, some may yet, despite the best of intentions, have slipped through the net and made it into the present book.

At the time of the war, some of the belligerent powers followed different calendars. The Gregorian calendar, named after the sixteenth-century Pope Gregory XIII, who introduced it, had been developed as a correction to an observed error in the old Julian calendar. The visible result of the correction was that the date was advanced 10 days; that is, 4 October 1582 was followed by 15 October 1582. France and the Holy Roman Empire changed calendar on this date, as did most Catholic nations. However, many Protestant countries, including Sweden, initially objected to adopting a Catholic innovation. They retained the Julian calendar, which, for this reason, differed from the one used in Catholic nations and at present. Old Style (OS) and New Style (NS) are terms commonly used with dates to indicate that the calendar convention used at the time described is different from that in use at present. Unless noted otherwise, the dates given here will be OS since the events described primarily took place in Sweden, Denmark, and Norway, all of which used the OS.

An attempt has been made to include, in addition to English-language translations, the original names in Danish, Norwegian, Swedish, Finnish, German, and other relevant languages where it seems important to do so for reasons of clarity. However, since neither language had a codified system of spelling at the time, the forms used are not necessarily those used today. Still, anybody with a working knowledge of the language should be able to identify the word forms employed. The same goes for personal names, which were then spelled in a variety of ways. Moreover, names and titles were long and cumbersome, and we often do not know which of several given names an individual preferred.

Dramatis Personae

Denmark

Ernest Louis (1587–1620), Duke of Saxe-Lauenburg. Military entrepreneur.
George (1582–1641), Duke of Brunswick and Lüneburg. Military entrepreneur and grandson of King Christian II of Denmark.
Philip (1584–1663), Duke of Schleswig-Holstein-Sonderburg-Glücksburg (hence shortened to 'Duke of Glücksburg'). Commander of the enlisted cavalry of the Duchies and grandson of King Christian III of Denmark.
Ahlefeldt, Godske von (c. 1570–c. 1625), lieutenant colonel. Veteran of Dutch and, from 1601 to 1605, Swedish service, in which he served as commandant of Pernau, Estonia.
Bielke, Jens (1580–1659), commander of Norwegian levies and one of the major landowners in Norway.
Bille, Anders Steensen (1578–1633), cavalry captain. Commander of the Scanian Banner of the retinue of nobles.
Bille, Steen Jensen (1565–1629), *lensmand* in Trondheim, Härjedalen, and Jämtland, as well as a scholar, former diplomat, and translator of hymns.
Daa, Claus (1579–1641), lieutenant and, in 1612, promoted to captain of the Aalborg Banner. Distant relative of Jørgen Daa.
Daa, Herluf Trolle (1565–1630), admiral. Son of Jørgen Daa in an early marriage. Widely known as a disreputable character involved in endless legal battles and corrupt practices, he nonetheless enjoyed King Christian's trust.
Daa, Jørgen (d. 1619), admiral. Commander of the navy's Skagerrak Squadron. Although not as disreputable as his son, he was similarly known for unscrupulous legal battles.
Hagen, Benedict Bernd von (c.1570–1611 or more likely 1612), captain. Veteran of Dutch service and military entrepreneur.
Heinemark, Peter von (fl. 1604–1616), major (*Wachtmeister*). Dutch veteran also known as Pieter Heymarck.
Hundemark, Peder Clausen (d. 1611), captain.
Krabbe, Tage (1553–1612), cavalry captain. *Lensmand* in Halmstad and commander of the Halland Banner.
Kruse, Enevold (1554–1621), governor general of Norway. Commandant of Akershus Castle.

Kruse, Gabriel Christophersen (d. 1647), navy captain. Distant relative of Enevold Kruse.

Laxmand, Steen Madsen or **Maltesen** (d. 1615), commandant of Bohus Castle and *lensmand* in Bohuslän. Veteran of Continental wars, diplomat, and experienced naval officer.

Lindenow, Godske Christophersen (d. 1612), Port Admiral in Copenhagen.

Lunge, Jørgen (1577–1619), captain. Veteran of Dutch service and the Anglo–Spanish War of 1585–1604, in which he ultimately served as a major. Back in Denmark, King Christian, in 1605, ordered him to raise an enlisted regiment for the Duchy of Brunswick-Lüneburg. He was promoted to Danish colonel in 1612 and to commandant of Elfsborg Castle and Grand Marshal of the Realm in 1616.

Nielsen, Peder (d. 1622), navy captain. Commander of the Kalmar Flotilla.

Parsow, Tessen von (1572–1614), colonel. Veteran officer, scholar, and military entrepreneur from Mecklenburg who had fought in numerous wars, including against the Ottoman Empire.

Pentz, Marquard von (1570/1575–1627), cavalry captain and ultimately colonel. Enlisted officer from Mecklenburg.

Rantzau, Breide (1556–1618), colonel. Governor of Copenhagen and sometime corps commander in Scania.

Rantzau, Gert von (1558–1627), major general and soon afterwards field marshal. Wealthy military entrepreneur and younger brother of Breide Rantzau.

Rosencrantz, Holger (1589–1647), captain. Officer of the King's Regiment, in which he commanded an enlisted Dutch company.

Sehested, Claus Maltesen (1558–1612), governor of Ösel and *lensmand* in Arensburg, the island's primary castle.

Sehested, Steen Maltesen (1553–1611), Grand Marshal of the Realm and field marshal. Veteran of Dutch service, experienced colonel 'of the House', which meant that he received waiting pay from the Danish Crown, and elder brother of Claus Maltesen Sehested.

Sinclair, Andrew or **Anders** (1555–1625), captain. Naturalised Danish nobleman originally from Scotland.

Skeel, Albert (1572–1639), captain. Commandant of Ribe Castle and commander of the Ribe Banner of the retinue of nobles, he had previously served as a court functionary, navy captain on King Christian's voyage to the North Cape in 1599, and vice admiral during the King's interrupted voyage to Norway in 1600.

Skeel, Jørgen (1578–1631), lieutenant of the Aarhus Banner of the retinue of nobles and promoted to cavalry captain during the war. Younger brother of Albert Skeel.

Ulfeldt, Mogens (1569–1616), Grand Admiral of the Realm and admiral of the main fleet. Known for his loyalty to King Christian, whom he had accompanied both to the North Cape in 1599 and England in 1606.

Urne, Erik Axelsen (1570–1631), navy captain and promoted to admiral in 1611. Commander of the first squadron of the main fleet and an experienced mariner who, among other journeys, had participated in King Christian's voyage to the North Cape in 1599.

Sweden

Charles Philip (1601–1622), Duke of Södermanland, Närke, and Värmland. Son of King Charles IX and younger brother of Gustavus Adolphus.

John (1589–1618), Duke of Östergötland. Youngest son of the late King John III and cousin of Gustavus Adolphus.

Bååt, Bo Gustavsson (d. 1629), governor of Kalmar.

Bååt, Jacob Jacobsson Snakenborg (1560–1627), admiral of the Kalmar Squadron and, from 1612, colonel of the Småland cavalry and infantry. Commandant of Kalmar Castle and distant relative of Bo Gustavsson Bååt.

Banér, Nils Gustavsson (1589–1614), cavalryman of probably Gustavus Adolphus's Life Banner. Son of a senior noble executed for treason by King Charles.

Banér, Per Gustavsson (1588–1644), cavalryman of probably Gustavus Adolphus's Life Banner. Elder brother of Nils Banér.

Bielkenstierna, Hans Claesson (1574–1620), admiral. Veteran naval officer who had fought against privateers and blockade breakers in several wars.

Böllja, Sten Claesson (d. 1641), cavalry captain. Commander of the Uppland Banner and governor of Jönköping.

Bonde, Carl (1581–1652), governor of Dalecarlia and, from 1613, Mountain County (Bergslagen). Veteran of the 1605 Battle of Kircholm in Livonia.

Bonde, Ulf (1585–1657), colonel of infantry in Västergötland, Värmland, and Dal. Younger brother of Carl Bonde.

Clerck, Richard Jacob (d. 1625), admiral. Veteran Scottish naval officer and master shipwright who was in Dutch service before he settled in Sweden. He may have called himself 'Jacob' before 1611 and is in Swedish historiography known as Richard Clerck the Elder (to distinguish him from his nephew of the same name).

Cruus, Jesper Andersson (1576–1647), colonel. Veteran of the wars on the eastern front against the Commonwealth.

Cruus, Jesper Matsson (1576 or 1577–1622), field colonel in Västergötland and field marshal. Veteran of the wars on the eastern front against the Commonwealth and in Muscovy and distant relative of Jesper Andersson Cruus.

Gottberg, Jacob (fl. 1594–1614), admiral. Born the son of a Pomeranian goldsmith, he went into Swedish service in 1593 and soon acquired a reputation as a talented naval officer.

Gyllenstierna, Göran Nilsson (1575–1618), Grand Admiral of the Realm.

Hammarskiöld, Per (Peder) Michaelsson (c. 1560–1646), colonel of cavalry in Småland and captain of the Småland Banner. In 1611, commandant of first Kalmar Castle and then Borgholm Castle. Veteran of the wars on the eastern front against the Commonwealth and in Muscovy.

Hård, Olof Larsson, af Segerstad (1555–1630), colonel of infantry in Småland. A former admiral and governor of Kalmar.

Krååk, Sven Håkansson (1570–1663?), captain. Småland veteran of the wars on the eastern front who had risen from the ranks.

Krakow, Mårten (1538? –1616), commandant of first Gullberg and then, in May 1612, Vaxholm Castle.

Monickhouen, Johan (Jean) van (d. 1614), colonel. A Dutchman since at least 1608 in Swedish service, he was a qualified military engineer and siege specialist who first served in Livonia. His name was often spelled 'Johan von Mönnichhofen'.

Pauli, Emerentia Pålsdotter (1585–1648), Mårten Krakow's wife and auxiliary commandant of Gullberg Castle.

Rosenhane, Johan Göransson (1571–1624), colonel of cavalry in Västergötland.

Silfverbielke, Nils Bengtsson (fl. 1580–1640), admiral and sometime castle commandant.

Some, Christer (*c.* 1565–1618), colonel general and field marshal. Veteran of the wars on the eastern front against the Commonwealth and in Muscovy.

Stierna, Göran Månsson (d. 1617), colonel. Governor of Kronoberg and Jönköping Counties.

Stierna, Måns Pedersson (d. 1622), cavalry captain. Distant relative of Göran Månsson Stierna.

Stiernskiöld, Nils (1583–1627), colonel. Veteran of the wars on the eastern front against the Commonwealth and in Muscovy who, in 1610, was so badly wounded by an exploding cannon that, for three years, he could only walk with crutches.

Stråle, Olof Andersson (1578–1648), commandant of Elfsborg Castle. Based on his previous experiences, more of a diplomat and administrator than a soldier.

Prologue: The Two Kings

Christian IV, King of Denmark and Norway

Crowned King of Denmark and Norway upon reaching maturity in 1596, **Christian IV** (1577–1648; r. 1588–1648) of the House of Oldenburg had high hopes of establishing his lands as the leading state in northern Europe.

The King of Denmark was the ruler of several quite different domains. He was King of Denmark, which comprised Jutland, the Danish islands of Zealand, Fyn, and Lolland, and the Scanias. Denmark was commonly referred to as 'the Kingdom'. He was also King of Norway since the crowns of Denmark and Norway were united in a personal union under one king. In addition, he was the suzerain of Schleswig-Holstein, which extended south of Jutland to the River Elbe in the vicinity of Hamburg. While the King of Denmark personally owned about half of Schleswig-Holstein, much of the rest belonged to the Duke of Holstein-Gottorp, with whom there was considerable friction. Moreover, Holstein was a duchy within the Holy Roman Empire, which gave it the rights and duties of other Imperial domains. In addition, there were several other, formally independent counties and enclaves in the area, all of which depended on the King of Denmark. Schleswig-Holstein and the adjoining enclaves were commonly referred to as 'the Duchies'. Finally, the King of Denmark had also obtained, by inheritance, sovereignty over Oldenburg and Delmenhorst, two German counties west of Bremen and the River Weser. These two possessions were commonly referred to as 'the Counties'. King Christian styled himself, in the antiquarian style popular at the time, 'King of Danes, Norwegians, Vandals, and Goths, Duke of Schleswig, Holstein, Stormarn, and Dithmarschen, and Count of Oldenburg and Delmenhorst'.

Denmark remained an elective monarchy. Upon succeeding to the throne, King Christian had to sign an accession charter (Danish: *håndfæstning*, 'handbinding'; German: *Manifest*), which curtailed the monarch's power. Yet the King frequently found means to work around these limitations. When he at first found it difficult to gain the support of the Council of the Realm, which was dominated by the nobility, for a war against Sweden, he threatened that, if the Council did not authorise it, he would declare war in his capacity as the Duke of Holstein and gain the fruits of war alone.

King Christian spoke Danish, German, Latin, French, and Italian. German was the language most commonly used at court and the language of his mother. Nonetheless, he wrote personal letters in Danish.

PROLOGUE: THE TWO KINGS

King Christian IV, with his characteristic braid in front of his right ear. (Pieter Isaacszoon, 1612)

King Christian was keenly interested in magnifying the glory and power of Danish kingship. He was particularly keen on developing the navy, which he considered his personal possession. King Christian led a number of building projects, including those of several churches, castles, and the Copenhagen Arsenal.

King Christian was also a man who loved life and amorous affairs. He was married to Anne Catherine of Brandenburg, a daughter of Joachim Frederick, Elector of Brandenburg and Regent to the Duchy of Prussia. Among their numerous children was his eventual successor, Frederick III. Yet King Christian also fathered many children with a series of mistresses. In an age not known for moderation, King Christian's many romantic liaisons and numerous children were notable, so too was his capacity for drinking.

Charles IX, King of Sweden, and His Son Gustavus Adolphus

Charles IX (1550–1611; r. 1599–1611) of the House of Vasa was the youngest son of King Gustavus I. When King Gustavus died in 1560, Charles received a duchy that encompassed most of the provinces of Södermanland and Närke and parts of Västmanland and Västergötland. At age 15, he was put in command of the Swedish artillery for the conquest of Varberg Castle during the Nordic Seven Years' War (1563–1570). Three years later, he joined his elder brother John in the rebellion that overthrew their half-brother, King Erik XIV. In response, King Erik challenged Charles to single combat, but, for various reasons, the duel never took place.

Charles's elder brother then assumed the throne as King John III (1537–1592; r. 1569–1592). There was much rivalry within the House of Vasa. King John had a son, Sigismund, who in 1587 was elected King of Poland and accordingly ruler of the Polish–Lithuanian Commonwealth. With the death of King John in 1992 from natural causes, Sigismund inherited the Swedish throne. Duke Charles, Sigismund's uncle, was appointed regent in the King's absence. However, Sigismund was a Catholic while Sweden had become a Lutheran country. Moreover, Duke Charles regarded himself as better qualified than his nephew to rule Sweden.

Duke Charles accordingly rose against King Sigismund. In 1598, King Sigismund led an expedition to Sweden. Duke Charles ultimately defeated King Sigismund's Polish–Swedish army at Stångebro on 25 September 1598. Sigismund had to withdraw, losing most of his remaining Swedish supporters in the process. In 1599, Duke Charles called a parliament in Jönköping, which duly declared Sigismund deposed from the Swedish throne and confirmed the Duke as regent. The Duke then explained his views on the succession order to the remaining members of the Swedish branch of the House of Vasa, after which a parliament in Norrköping in 1604 recognised Duke Charles as King of Sweden. From 1607 onwards, he styled himself, in the antiquarian style popular at the time, 'King of Swedes, Goths, Vandals, Finns, Karelians, Lapps in Northern lands, Cajanians, and Estonians in Livonia'.

PROLOGUE: THE TWO KINGS

King Charles IX. (Gripsholm Castle)

Gustavus Adolphus, 1610 or 1611. (Gold medal, possibly by Ruprecht Miller; photo: Gabriel Hildebrand, Economy Museum – Royal Coin Cabinet/SHM, Stockholm)

The King was married twice, from 1579 with Mary of the Palatinate, with whom he had six children. After her death, he married Christina of Holstein-Gottorp, with whom he had three children, including their son Gustavus Adolphus.

Both as a man and ruler, King Charles was unpredictable and ruthless. He was also suspicious, vindictive, unforgiving, and prone to violence. There was a streak of insanity in the House of Vasa, but King Charles seems to have not succumbed to it, even though he, like his father and brothers, displayed signs of psychopathy. He frequently regarded those who spoke out against him as traitors, for which he sentenced them to death. His reign was characterised, if not by terror, at least by fear. Yet King Charles was also an efficient and meticulous planner and skilful politician who successfully played out different groups within parliament against each other. In religion, King Charles leaned towards Calvinism, which did not prevent him from displaying the Lutheran facade required to become King of Sweden.

King Charles fell victim to a stroke in the summer of 1609. He never fully recovered and died in Nyköping on 30 October 1611.

Gustavus Adolphus (1594–1632; r. 1611–1632), Grand Duke of Finland, Duke of Estonia, and Duke of Västmanland, was still a very young man when the Kalmar War broke out. Inexperienced and still untested in warfare, he nonetheless soon grew into the truly charismatic commander who, in later years, would put his stamp on European affairs. Although the real character of Gustavus Adolphus is difficult to separate from the personality cult that, because of his later military successes, was built around his person already in his lifetime and even more so after his death, many contemporary eyewitnesses have given evidence that he was well liked, even admired, by most of those who met him, whether nobles or commoners.

Gustavus Adolphus was generally friendly and in a good mood. He had a sense of humour, made jokes, and enjoyed social events such as banquets and dances. Like his father, Gustavus Adolphus had a temper and sometimes reacted with anger. However, unlike his father, grandfather, and most uncles, he was not cruel or vindictive and did not physically violate those who displeased him. Although Gustavus Adolphus trusted his own counsel and would not allow himself to be ruled by others, he was cooperative and would listen to their opinions and advice.

Highly educated in both the sciences and humanities, Gustavus Adolphus was also well versed in languages. In addition to Swedish, German, and probably some Finnish (the three predominant languages of the Swedish

PROLOGUE: THE TWO KINGS

Axel Oxenstierna, 1626.
(Jacob Heinrich Elbfas;
photo: Medström)

kingdom), he spoke Latin, Italian, French, and Dutch. He understood Spanish, English, and Scots and knew some Polish and Russian.[1] He was trained in philosophy and jurisprudence, read and was influenced by the Dutch jurist Hugo Grotius (1583–1645), and (in striking contrast to many other rulers then and later) grounded his arguments in these disciplines when speaking before the Council or parliament. Yet Gustavus Adolphus was also genuinely pious. God ruled over life and death, and the best that mankind, even a man born to kingship, could aim for was to do his duty in accordance with his Christian conscience, even if this conflicted with reasons of state.[2]

In war, Gustavus Adolphus led from the front, sharing the labours and risks with his men. He encountered the Dutch model of warfare (more on

---

1 Nils Ahnlund, *Gustav Adolf den store* (Stockholm: Aldus/Bonniers, 1963), pp.22–23.

2 Sven Lundkvist, 'Verklighetsuppfattning och verklighet: En studie i Gustav II Adolfs handlingsramar', in R. Sandberg (ed.), *Studier i äldre historia tillägnade Herman Schück 5/4 1985* (Stockholm: Festschrift, 1985), pp.227–41.

which later) already as a child. John of Nassau, one of the chief architects of the Dutch model, served in Sweden in 1601–1602. Given command of the Swedish field army in Livonia, he provided some ideas on how to reform organisation and tactics. Gustavus Adolphus, then eight years old, met John at least once, upon his departure from Sweden. Five years later, in 1607, Gustavus Adolphus first met his future major general, Dodo von Innhausen und zu Knyphausen, who previously had been in Dutch service and thoroughly knew the Dutch model. In 1608, 14 years old, Gustavus Adolphus spent two months of training in the Dutch model under the mentorship of Jacob De la Gardie (1583–1652), who himself had been trained in its use in the Dutch Republic while he served as a colonel there. This ended Gustavus Adolphus's formal military training. However, he continued to read and observe, and, moreover, the outbreak of the Kalmar War in 1611 obliged him henceforth to assume a leading role in warfare.

Gustavus Adolphus was not afraid of delegating important tasks to others. He trusted his advisors. He particularly relied on his chancellor ever since 1612, the 11-years-older Axel Oxenstierna (1583–1654). Gustavus Adolphus allowed Lord High Chancellor Oxenstierna to develop the state machinery as needed, without fear that the Chancellor might conspire against him. Indeed, Sweden at the time of Gustavus Adolphus's ascension to the throne can be said not yet to have had a machinery of state. Without Oxenstierna, it is unlikely that the country would have remained a functioning state after the Kalmar War nor within a few years emerged as a great power.

PROLOGUE: THE TWO KINGS

Map 1. Denmark, Norway, and Sweden.

THE KALMAR WAR

Map 2. Provinces of the main theatre of operations (Author's map)

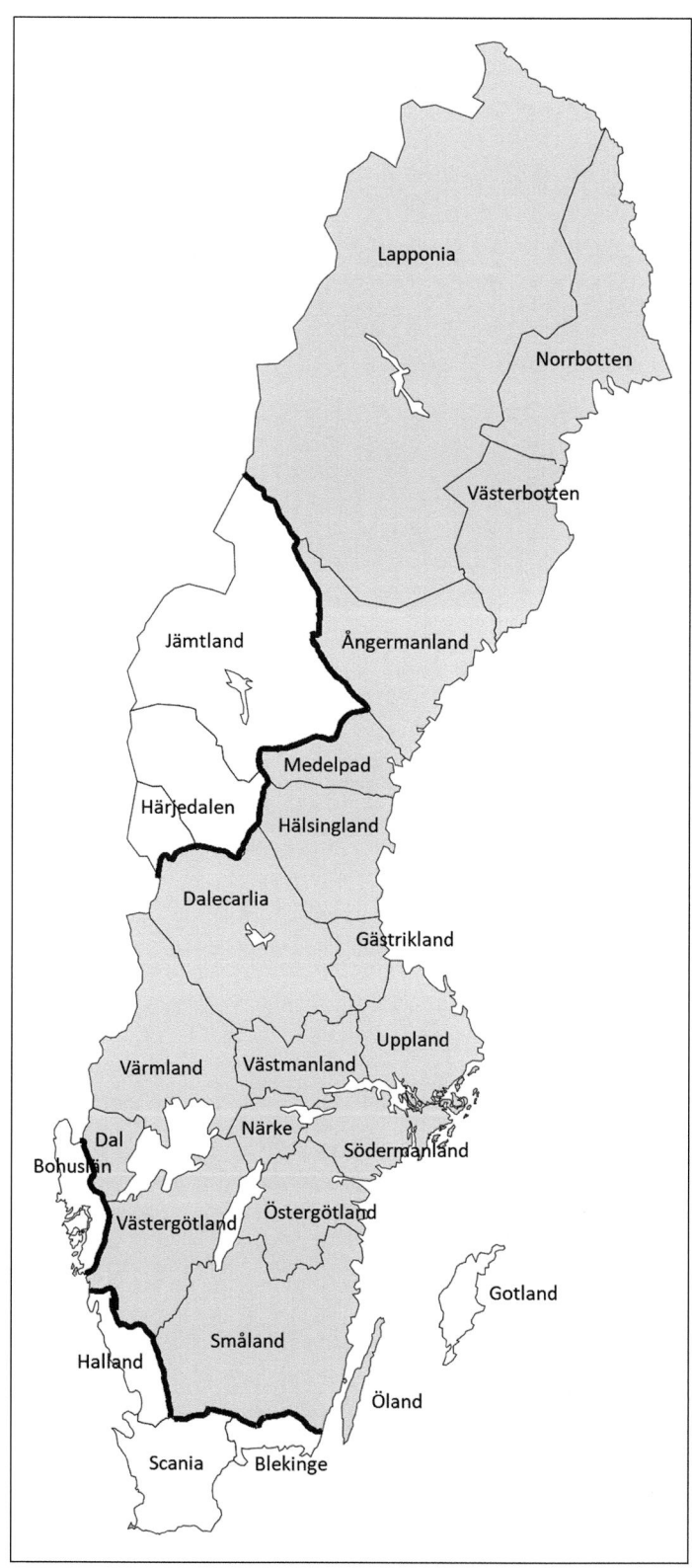

1
The Origin of the Kalmar War

Despite the traditional antagonism between Denmark and Sweden, the primary cause of the Kalmar War was mercantile rivalry over the maritime trade. Both Denmark and Sweden had territories that were separated by sea, including the important Danish possession of Norway and the Swedish possession of Finland, in addition to numerous islands and, for Sweden, the overseas territory of Estonia on the other side of the Baltic Sea.[1] Both thus faced the very real need to maintain a naval power that could safeguard the supply lines between their different territories and possessions. But this naval power also made the two kingdoms a threat to one another and to their respective trade interests.

A particularly persistent problem between the Danish and Swedish kingdoms was the Sound Toll. Whoever controlled the Danish Strait, or 'Sound', also controlled the means to raise customs revenue there. These revenues accrued not to the Kingdom of Denmark but to the King personally, for whom it was a key source of income. Sweden was exempt from the Sound Toll in a reciprocal free trade agreement dating from the Treaty of Stettin (1570), which ended the Nordic Seven Years' War. Initially, this had mattered little to the Danish Crown since most of Sweden's limited foreign trade went through the southern Baltic ports and accordingly did not enter the strait. However, from around 1600, Sweden began to export growing volumes of iron, copper, and essentials for shipbuilding such as tar, pitch, hemp, flax, and especially timber through the strait to Dutch and English ports. King Christian gradually perceived the loss of revenue as because of the Swedish exemption. The Sound Toll was not the only mercantile dispute, though. King Christian reasoned that the Treaty of Stettin gave Denmark the right to free trade with Muscovy through Narva, which had become Swedish through the 1595 Treaty of Teusina. King Charles did not share the Danish interpretation of Narva's

---

1   Sweden and Finland constituted the same country. Its provinces and peoples had the same rights and obligations. Hence, any reference to Swedish soldiers, nobles, and so on can be assumed to also include those from Finland, unless stated otherwise. Estonia, too, was part of the Swedish kingdom, although with separate rights and obligations. Soldiers from these territories were all national troops.

status since he hoped to eventually control the Muscovy trade himself. In short, both sides wanted to retain the toll exemption for themselves but deny it to the other. King Christian also complained over the Swedish blockade of and imposition of customs duties on the trade through Riga, which related to the ongoing war between Sweden and the Commonwealth but harmed Danish mercantile interests. The blockade also impacted negatively on the revenues from the Sound Toll, King Christian argued, since it reduced the total volume of trade in the Baltic region.

Meanwhile, the Danish Crown by tradition regarded the northern seas from Norway to Greenland as its sovereign possessions. International law for the right of sovereignty over open sea recognised that the waters in gulfs and bays of a country belonged to that country. It had previously been believed that Norway and Greenland were connected by a northern landmass, which would have made the Arctic seas one immense bay. Yet international law also stipulated that a country that held the territory on both sides of a sea could claim the sea, as well, as a sovereign possession. Old Norse colonisation of the Faeroes, Orkney, Shetland, Iceland, and Greenland proved the point, especially since the Crown of Norway still possessed these territories (or claimed so in the case of Orkney and Shetland). In legal terms, this was 'dominion of the North Sea' (*dominium maris Septentrionalis*), which, in the same manner as the 'dominion of the Baltic Sea' (*dominium maris Baltici*) in the Baltic, made the northern waters a 'closed sea' (*mare clausum*) under Danish sovereignty. Seafarers of other countries could voyage there but only if they paid Danish tolls.

Claiming sovereignty in the Arctic was one thing, upholding it another. To accomplish the latter, the Danish Crown established the fort Vardøhus in northern Lapponia in 1523. At first of minor importance, the fort gained in relevance when, in 1553, the English merchant-venturer Richard Chancellor rounded the North Cape and reached the Northern Dvina, thereby opening a northern route by way of Arkhangelsk for trade by the Muscovy Company, established in 1555. The English for a while resisted the imposition of Danish tolls on the trade but, in 1583, agreed to pay an annual fee and customs duty at Vardøhus. France and Hamburg followed suit. In 1586, Danish King Frederick II formally claimed the whole of Lapponia, as Arctic Scandinavia was then called.

The Danish claims of sovereignty also included the potential Northeast Passage and the alleged Northwest Passage to the Indies that European merchants eagerly sought. To uphold these claims, in 1579 and 1581, King Frederick II sent unsuccessful expeditions to recontact Greenland, with which communications had been lost for a century. Yet other expeditions were sent in 1605, 1606, and 1607, this time with orders to formally claim Greenland as Danish sovereign territory.[2]

---

2   In 1619, the endeavour culminated in Jens Munk's attempt to find the Northwest Passage, which ended in the loss of all but two crewmen. The follow-up expedition planned for 1621 was abandoned because of a shortage of volunteers.

Under these legal and mercantile conditions, it particularly irked King Christian that King Charles, soon after he, in 1599, seized the Swedish throne from his Polish rival within the House of Vasa, put forth territorial claims of his own in Lapponia. The background of the Swedish claims was that Denmark and Norway had not been alone in expanding their territories in the Arctic North. Farther to the east, both Sweden and Muscovy over the same time period gradually expanded their respective influence towards the north, levying taxes on both settled and nomadic populations there. Sometimes, to enforce taxation, tax collectors had to follow nomadic groups into territories claimed by the neighbouring states. The Treaty of Teusina of 1595 enabled Sweden to assume previous Muscovite rights of taxation in the region. This implied Swedish sovereignty. Although Danish arbitrators in 1603, against King Christian's will, acknowledged the Swedish rights of taxation in Lapponia (both sides had agreed to refer the issue to impartial arbitration), the new Swedish rights conflicted with traditional Danish claims of sovereignty over these vast and sparsely populated territories. In 1607, King Charles added the formula 'King of Lapps in Northern lands' to his titles based on the Swedish claim. The Danes suspected, rightly, that Sweden wanted to establish a naval presence in the Arctic North (although for practical reasons, we will see that this plan never materialised).

The Treaty of Teusina also confirmed Swedish rule in Estonia and, as we have seen, awarded Sweden the port of Narva, until then the only Muscovite port in the Baltic. If Sweden also could gain control of Archangelsk, the Swedish Crown would achieve a monopoly over the maritime trade with Muscovy. A major cause of the previous Nordic Seven Years' War had been Sweden's demand that Denmark and Lübeck cease their trade with Muscovy through Narva.

In 1599, King Christian personally led a naval expedition to Vardøhus as a show of force in the Arctic. He commanded the expedition incognito, under the name 'Captain Christian Frederiksen'. He also needed to display his maritime strength in the waters near England and the Dutch Republic. In 1606, the King commanded a more lavish voyage under his own name as a state visit to England, during which he showed off his fleet.

Yet Sweden did not back down. In 1607, King Charles established the new town of Gothenburg on the island of Hisingen opposite Elfsborg Castle as a centre for the Swedish North Sea trade. Gothenburg and Elfsborg ('River Castle'), on opposite sides of the River Göta Älv Estuary, were then the only Swedish ports with easy access to the North Sea and thereby sea lines of communication with the rest of western Europe. Access was available through the Skagerrak Strait, the section of the North Sea between the Jutland peninsula of Denmark, the south-east coast of Norway, and the west coast of Sweden. Another important shipping route traversed the Kattegat, a continuation of the Skagerrak Strait bounded by the Jutland peninsula in the west, the Danish islands in the south, and the west coast of Sweden and Danish Halland and Scania in the east, which connected the North Sea with the Baltic Sea by way of the Danish Strait.

The territory surrounding the River Göta Älv Estuary functioned as a wedge between Denmark and Norway. In 1608, King Charles granted the burghers of the new town the right to trade and fish north of the Titisfjord Estuary in northern Norway, which marked the southern boundary of the disputed Arctic territories. In response, King Christian claimed that the new town and its burghers' activities infringed upon Danish trading and fishing rights. More importantly, the establishment of the town resulted in a reduction in the Sound Toll paid to the Danish Crown. Suddenly, part of the maritime trade with Sweden was diverted from the Danish Straits to the Gothenburg–Elfsborg region. Moreover, King Charles allowed Dutch merchants to re-register in Gothenburg so that they sailed under the Swedish flag through the Sound, thereby avoiding the Sound Toll. The Swedish King also continued his attempts to prevent others from trading with Muscovy through Riga, Mitau, and Libau on the eastern Baltic coast.

The River Göta Älv constituted one of the great waterways that – together with Lakes Mälaren, Vänern, and Vättern and their lesser tributaries, the Baltic Sea, Gulf of Bothnia, and Gulf of Finland – linked territories that in prehistoric times already displayed common cultural characteristics and by the Viking Age had coalesced into the Swedish kingdom.[3] Because of its waterways, Sweden customarily looked east instead of west when expansion and military campaigns were contemplated. The outlet into the sea of the River Göta Älv did not become Swedish territory until the mid thirteenth century. Before then, the western, downstream extent of the river formed the traditional border between Denmark and Norway. Henceforth, however, the River Göta Älv grew increasingly important as Sweden's sole link to the west.

The River Göta Älv also saw the first two settlements in the region that, in the eleventh century, developed into towns. One was Kungahälla on a western tributary. The other was Lödöse, located on a small river island on the Swedish side of the river some 50 km upriver of the estuary. Lödöse became the first Swedish town on the River Göta Älv. Soon, the Norwegian Crown built a castle, strategically located in a position from which it could strangle Lödöse's overseas trade. Over time, it grew into the powerful Bohus Castle, which also gave its name to the province of Bohuslän.[4]

3　The River Göta Älv was commonly known as 'Elfr' (The River) in Old Norse and 'Albis' in Latin, from an old Germanic word for river from which also derives the name of the River Elbe in northern Germany. Those who wanted to be more specific used the name 'Gautelfr' (Latin: Gothelba), which translates to 'Gothic Elbe'.

4　The name of the castle and province derived from the small island of Bagaholm, on which the castle was erected on a 40m-high rock. First known as 'Bagha Hus' (Baga Castle), the name was soon shortened to 'Baahus' and 'Bohus', which gave its name to the province of Bohuslän (Bohus County).

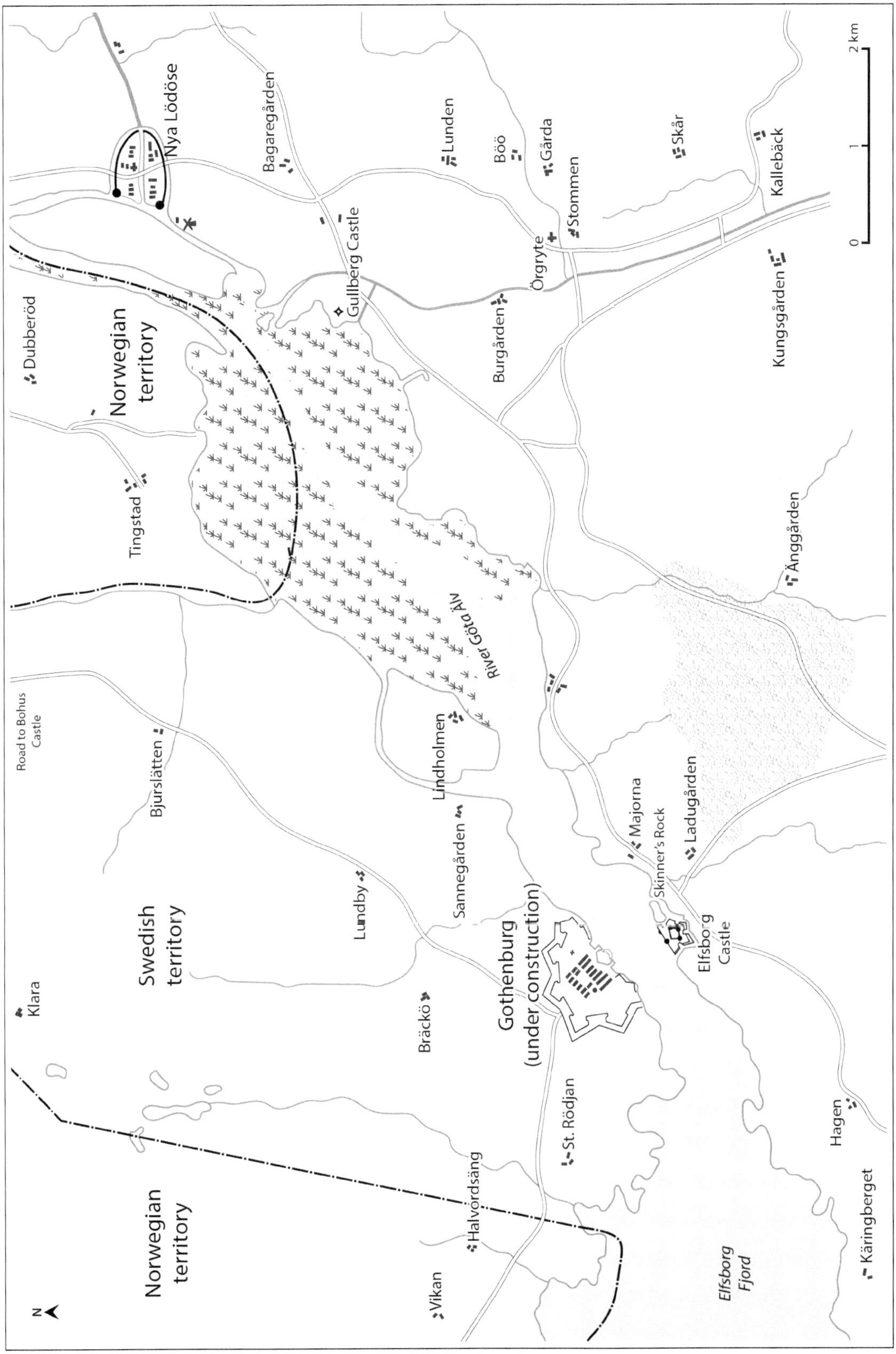

THE ORIGIN OF THE KALMAR WAR

Map 3. River Göta Älv Estuary

THE KALMAR WAR

THE ORIGIN OF THE KALMAR WAR

The Danish Sound, as seen from the south, with Kronborg Castle and Helsingør in the foreground and inset. Top: Scanian coast, with the towns of Helsingborg, Landskrona, and Malmö, here called 'Elbogen'. The island of Hven is positioned incorrectly since, in reality, it was located farther to the east. (*Freti Danici* or *Sundt Acuratiss Delineatio*; first published in *Civitates orbis terrarum* in 1588 from a drawing by Hans Kneiper forwarded to Georg Braun and Franz Hogenberg by Henrik Rantzau)

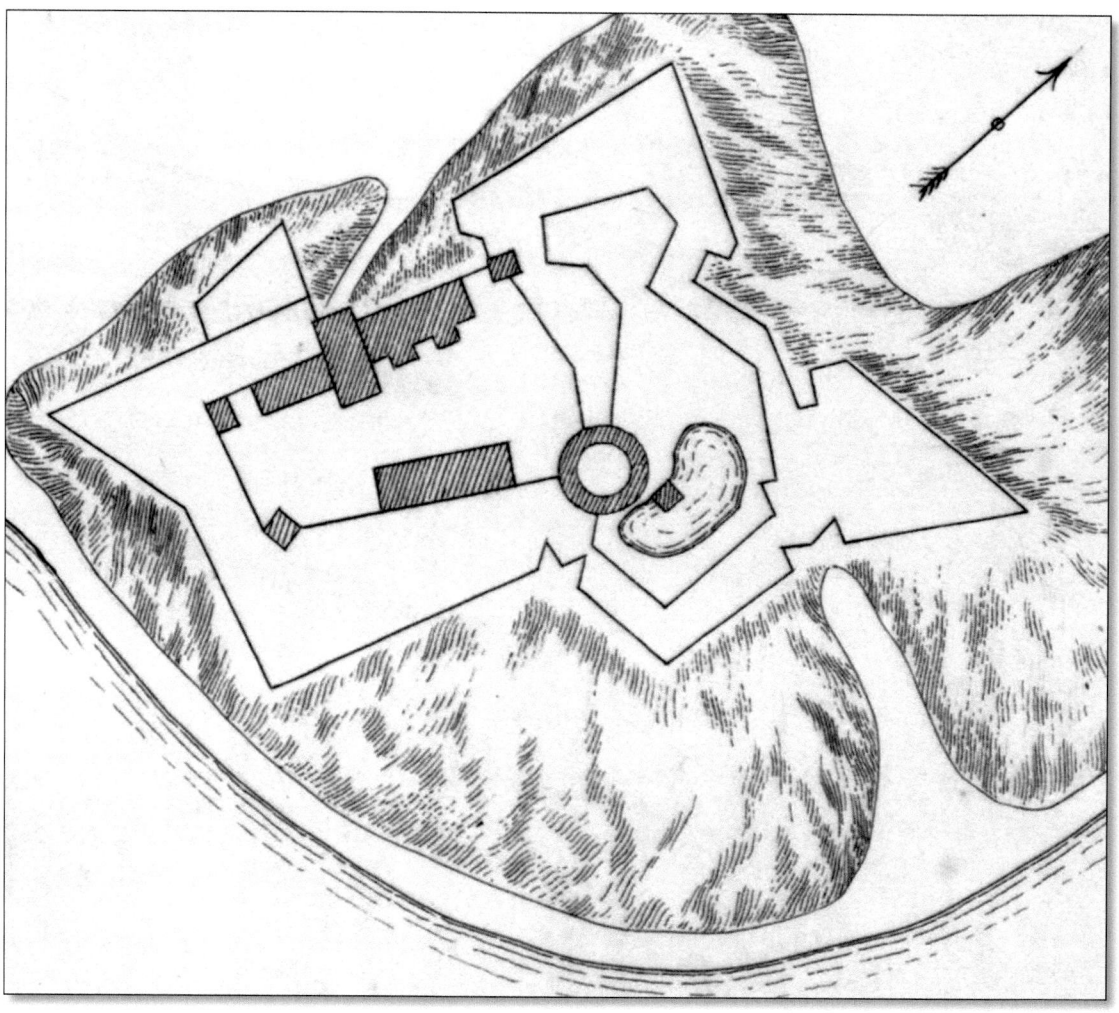

Above: Bohus Castle, *c.* 1600. The bastion system was first projected in 1566 by the Flemish architect Hans Hendrik van Paesschen. (Swedish Military Archives)

Facing page, top: Bohus Castle, *c.* 1990. The outer bastions (the trace of which is recognisable from the plan of the castle, illustrated above) – further upgraded in the years 1593–1604 by another Flemish architect, Hans van Steenwinckel – were as up to date as could be at the time of the Kalmar War. However, the obsolete medieval inner wall remained, and three round towers and an arsenal (the ruins of which appear in this photograph) were only built in the period 1648–1656. (Photo: Jan Norrman, Swedish National Heritage Board)

Facing page, bottom: Bohus Castle, *c.* 1965. The massive renaissance bastions, built to fit the shape of the rock, still dominate the island. (Photo: Pål-Nils Nilsson, Swedish National Heritage Board)

THE ORIGIN OF THE KALMAR WAR

Sigismund, King of Poland and Grand Duke of Lithuania, *c.* 1624. (Paul Soutman; photo: Medström)

As a result, Swedish merchants established a more secure town downstream of Bohus Castle. By then, the fourteenth-century Elfsborg Castle, farther downriver and on the south bank of the River Göta Älv, as well as the small contemporary castles at Gullberg and Lindholmen, on opposite sides farther inside the estuary, secured land and sea access.[5] The new town became known as Nya ('New') Lödöse. The original Lödöse remained but lost most of its former importance and henceforth was known as Gamla ('Old') Lödöse.[6] Nya Lödöse soon became Sweden's largest mercantile town after the capital, Stockholm. In 1607, King Charles IX founded the new town of Gothenburg, on the north bank opposite Elfsborg Castle, to promote further trade with the western maritime powers, primarily the Dutch Republic. In fact, the town, under a Dutch mayor, Abraham Cabeliau (1571–1645), was deliberately established to function as a Dutch-speaking mercantile centre, with town administration and judicial court proceedings conducted in the Dutch language and following Dutch standards. Even the common language spoken in town was Dutch, not Swedish.

This was important because, despite the vast Dutch trading network, which encompassed both the Far East and the Americas, the Baltic Sea trade was the primary source of income to Dutch merchants and hence Dutch wealth. In the seventeenth century, they referred to the Baltic Sea trade as the 'mother trade' (*moedernegotie*), which shows its relative importance in comparison with, for instance, the more spectacular and hence more memorable East India trade for spices and silk. In addition to the raw materials for shipbuilding already mentioned, imports from the Baltic included Polish corn, which was needed to satisfy local demand for grain in much of north-western Europe. The Far Eastern imports were luxury goods; the Baltic imports consisted of essentials that the Dutch Republic could not survive without.

Meanwhile, Swedish tax collectors continued to levy taxes on the sparse population throughout Lapponia. In 1609, King Christian responded by ordering his officials (*lensmænd*, more on which later) in Norway to attack the Swedish tax collectors and their men, chasing them back to Sweden or killing them. The King knew that Sweden had one serious weakness: the

---

5   Gullberg was generally known to the Danes as 'Guldborg' (Gold Castle).

6   Old and New Lödöse were generally known to the Danes as, respectively, 'Gammellöse' and 'Nylöse'.

ongoing war for dynastic reasons with the Polish–Lithuanian Commonwealth. Poland's King Sigismund still laid claim to the Swedish throne. Sigismund was King Charles's nephew and, moreover, represented the senior line of the Swedish royal House of Vasa. Sigismund could indeed be said to have had a better claim to the throne than both his uncle, King Charles, who ostensibly had deposed his nephew because of the young man's Catholic beliefs, and his cousin Gustavus Adolphus, who was next in line. Formally, Charles referred to the provisions of the 1560 last will of King Gustavus I, his father, which stipulated that any of his children who left the Lutheran religion would lose his inheritance. Charles then successfully fought for power over Sweden and took control of Finland, both of which he ruled sternly, while Sigismund had to be satisfied with the wealthier but more loosely organised Commonwealth.[7] Commonwealth military power was real. Only six years previously, in 1605, a Swedish army had been thoroughly defeated by Commonwealth hussars at Kircholm (modern-day Salaspils), near Riga.

Jacob De la Gardie, 1606. (Photo: Medström)

As if the war with the Commonwealth had not been enough, early in 1611, war also broke out between Sweden and Muscovy, with which Sweden shared a common border in the north-east. In Muscovy, this was the Time of Troubles, the difficult period of Russian history following the death of Fyodor Ivanovich in 1598, the last tsar of the Rurik Dynasty. During this time, Muscovy suffered from uprisings, usurpers, anarchy, famine, and in 1610 the suppression of a revolt in Moscow by an invited Swedish intervention army under Jacob De la Gardie. The Polish–Lithuanian Commonwealth was the common enemy of both Sweden and Muscovy, but De la Gardie could not prevent the occupation of Moscow by the Commonwealth later in the same year. In desperation, Muscovite representatives offered the crown to several Polish and Swedish princes, including Gustavus Adolphus.[8]

---

7   When Gustavus Adolphus finally inherited the throne, no more than a short-term armistice had recently been negotiated between Sweden and the Commonwealth. Fortunately for Sweden, Gustavus Adolphus's representatives managed to extend the ceasefire agreement several times, ultimately until September 1616. O. S. Rydberg and C. Hallendorff (eds), *Sverges Traktater med främmande magter* (Stockholm: P. A. Norstedt & Söner, 1903), vol. 5, part 1, p.227.

8   Michael Fredholm von Essen, *Sweden's War in Muscovy, 1609–1617: The Relief of Moscow and Conquest of Novgorod* (Forthcoming: Helion & Company, 2023).

2

Tactical Doctrines

By the early seventeenth century, Western military organisation, armament, and tactics typically followed one of two models: the Spanish or the Dutch. The older model was the Spanish, which from the outset was characterised by its use of solid squares of pikemen supported by flanking detachments of arquebusiers and musketeers. Such a unit was formed in what was known as a Spanish square (*cuadro*), each with an establishment strength of 3,000 men (often significantly less in reality).[1] Abroad, the formation also became known as a *tercio*, named for an administrative unit for raising troops akin to a regiment. The Spanish model, in its original form, provided a strong offensive capability and was good for all-round defence should a flank be turned. However, the formation was slow and clumsy with regard to battlefield mobility. Moreover, since the formation's arquebusiers and musketeers were deployed on the flanks, its firepower could not be concentrated in one direction. The ratio of officers and under-officers to common soldiers was fairly low, which reduced manoeuvrability further.

In contrast, the Dutch model – introduced in the years between 1590 and 1610 by Maurice of Nassau (1567–1625), eventually Prince of Orange, and his cousins William Louis (1560–1620) and John of Nassau (1561–1623) – relied on much smaller tactical units (i.e. battalions), each of which officially (but not in practice) consisted of 550 men in imitation of the ancient Roman cohort. On the field of battle, the battalions would form up in a linear formation, typically 10 but frequently only six ranks deep, each with pikes in the centre and musketeers on each side of them. Two or more battalions would form a regiment. The army as a whole would form up in two to three lines. The Dutch model was designed to exploit firepower to the fullest extent since it allowed all musketeers to fire. This was accomplished by rotation of ranks, an evolution known as the countermarch, with each rank firing a simultaneous salvo. William Louis of Nassau in 1594 read an account of the drill practiced by the ancient Roman army. He then suggested the countermarch in a letter to his cousin Maurice. Soon enough, it became

---

1   Sancho de Londoño, *El discurso sobre la forma de reduzir la disciplina militar, a meyor y antiguo estado* (Brussels: Rutger Velpius, 1589), p.14.

TACTICAL DOCTRINES

Ship's cannon. The cannons of Swedish warships were not provided with wedges under the breech to adjust elevation and range. Instead, there would be a simple bar across the back of the gun carriage that was set for point-blank elevation. (Vasa Museum, Stockholm; author's photo)

a key feature of the Dutch model, which primarily used the rotation of ranks of musketeers defensively. Having fired, each rank retired to reload while the next rank took its place.

The battalion was easier to manoeuvre on the battlefield than the Spanish square. In addition, its proportion of officers and under-officers was larger. The model thus offered greater mobility, defined as rapidity of movement and ease of manoeuvre, although it was far more vulnerable to flank and rear attack.

However, the linear formation lacked the offensive capability of the old Spanish formation. The Dutch model focused on mobility and firepower rather than shock. Moreover, neither the Spanish nor the Dutch model provided a significant role to artillery and cavalry. Artillery was typically dispersed along the front of the line of battle. Artillery could be moved only slowly, or not at all, so it may change hands if overrun by the enemy and, if not spiked (i.e. made inoperable), be turned against its former owners. If the fortune of battle then turned, the artillery might change hands several times in the same battle. Cavalry typically employed caracole tactics.[2] This meant that the cavalrymen would advance in deep formation, at less than a gallop. As each rank came into

---

2   A term meaning 'snail' (Spanish: *caracol*), translated into German as *Schnecke* and into French as *limaçon* (ultimately from the Latin '*limax*', snail). Previously, before the introduction of the countermarch, the tactics were also used by infantry. Hans Delbrück, *History of the Art of War, Volume IV: The Dawn of Modern Warfare* (Lincoln: University of Nebraska Press, 1990), p.123. On the caracole, see Wendelin Schildknecht, *Harmonia in fortalitiis construendis, defendendis & oppugnandis* (Stettin: Johann Valentin Rheten, 1652), vol. 3, pp.168–69; Johann Jacobi von Wallhausen, *Kriegskunst zu Pferdt* (Frankfurt-am-Main: Johann Theodor de Bry, 1616), p.65 (describes its execution without using the name); Theodor Jakobsson, *Lantmilitär beväpning och beklädnad under äldre Vasatiden och Gustav II Adolfs tid* (Stockholm: Generalstaben, 1938; published separately and as suppl. vol. 2 in Generalstaben, *Sveriges krig 1611–1632*), pp.149–51.

THE KALMAR WAR

Chain shot and scissor shot. (Vasa Museum, Stockholm; author's photo)

range, the men would discharge their carbines or pistols, then wheel to the left (most common since the horseman was firing with the right hand), retire to the back of the formation to reload, and in due time repeat the manoeuvre. The whole unit might move slowly forwards as each rank fired or slowly retreat to keep its distance to an advancing enemy. It has been argued that the caracole was less significant for its practical use than for the drill itself, which integrated the horsemen in a tactical body governed by discipline, not by each man's individual fighting skill.[3] The cavalrymen were armed and sometimes armoured for melee, and the intention usually seems to have been to follow the caracole with a charge, in effect using the caracole to soften up the enemy. Nonetheless, infantry arquebusiers and musketeers enjoyed a much greater range and more reliable fire than the wheellock pistols of most cavalry, so the cavalry usually kept a respectful distance.

Both artillery and cavalry were accordingly relegated to what, in effect, was a support role. Cavalry held higher status due to its origin in noble service (the retinue of nobles, more on which later). Yet, in both the Spanish and Dutch models, the infantry, the proverbial queen of battle (although this term had not yet come into common use), was regarded as the chief means of winning the field. Besides, warfare came to focus more on outmanoeuvring the enemy in an extended campaign than on defeating him in a major battle. Campaigns, for this reason, also tended to focus on fortified positions since to deny the enemy an important stronghold was a means of wearing him down. Moreover, during the siege, there was finally an opportunity to fully utilise one's artillery.

Both the Danish and Swedish Crowns had noted the advantages of the Dutch model of war and begun work to adapt to the new organisational and tactical doctrines. However, neither side had progressed very far. Besides, military units in Scandinavia were often understrength and not quite able to live up to the theoretical doctrines. Neither Spanish squares nor Dutch battalions were used in Scandinavia during the Kalmar War.

At sea, tactics had changed, too. When the modern Danish and Swedish navies emerged in the early sixteenth century, both developed swiftly because of the struggle between the two countries over hegemony in the Baltic region. The Nordic Seven Years' War between Sweden on the one side and Denmark with its possession Norway, Lübeck, and the united Kingdom of Poland and the Grand Duchy of Lithuania on the other was the first modern war at sea in Europe between fleets of sailing ships armed with cannon. Tactics developed

---

3   Delbrück, *Dawn of Modern Warfare*, p.124.

that included engaging the enemy with cannon from a distance instead of boarding to fight it out. During this war, the Danish and Swedish navies grew to be the then largest sailing fleets in Europe, both becoming equal in size to the English around 1565 and each surpassing the English in numbers by 1570.[4]

Yet the tactics actually implemented at sea did not always reach the ideal of engaging with long-distance artillery fire. In the early seventeenth century, naval tactics still emphasised boarding and hand-to-hand combat, which indeed was often regarded as the preferred means of attacking the enemy and winning a sea battle. While the navy had master gunners, modern tactics could not be implemented without experienced sailing crews with the skills to manoeuvre the warships in a long-distance gunnery battle – such crews were not always available. There were few means to aim the individual cannons, so the entire warship had to be moved to allow its cannons the opportunity to fire. Even under the best of circumstances, not all cannons could bear on the same target. First, only the artillery on one side of the vessel could concentrate fire on one given target. However, the construction of seventeenth-century ships meant that it was impossible to bring even all guns on this side to bear. The stern and bow guns could only fire in their respective directions, so it was only possible to concentrate the guns in the middle of the ship – the broadside – on the same target. Besides, the curving shape of the ship meant that even guns positioned near the stern and bow might be unable to bear on an enemy directly to the side.

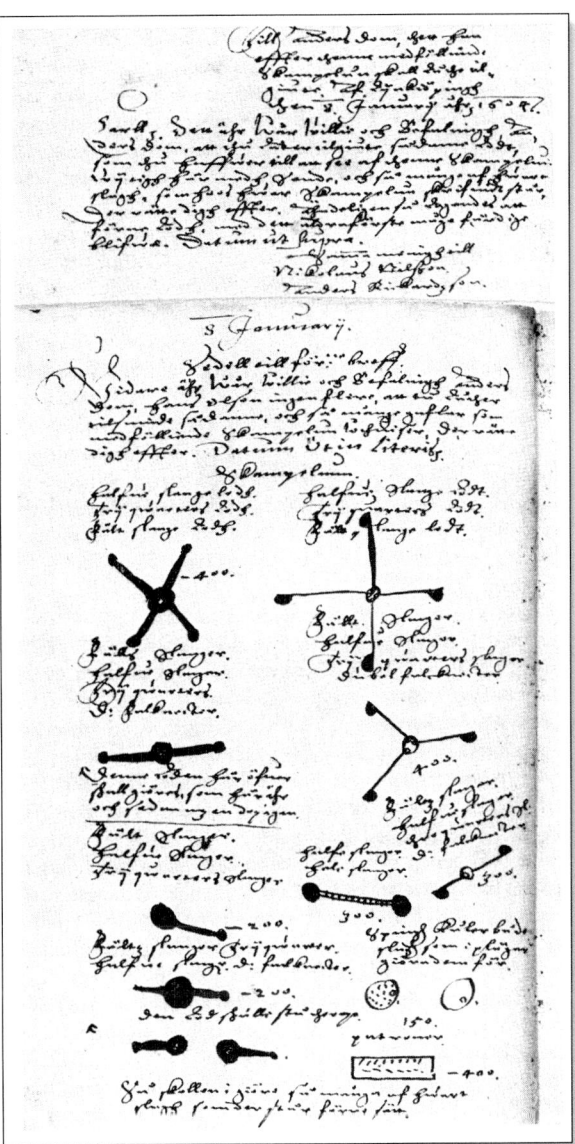

Swedish production order of various types of chain shot, sent to manufacturers on 8 January 1604. (Swedish National Archives)

In addition to round shot, which was the most common type of shot, navies also employed chain shot, which was designed to damage the rigging and tear holes in sails, both of which reduced the enemy ship's ability to manoeuvre. Other, less common types of shot included spike shot and scissor shot, which were believed, probably in error, to cause more damage in close quarters. Ships also did not carry large supplies of ammunition. The Swedish navy generally allocated 30 shots per cannon to its warships, along with the appropriate volume of gunpowder.

---

4   On the early modern Danish and Swedish navies, see Jan Glete, 'Naval Power and Control of the Sea in the Baltic in the Sixteenth Century', in J. B. Hattendorf and R. W. Unger (eds), *War at Sea in the Middle Ages and Renaissance* (Woodbridge: Boydell Press, 2003), pp.221–25, 227–28, 230, 232.

3

The Danish Military Establishment

Manpower

By the early seventeenth century, Denmark was both more populous and wealthier than Sweden. Unfortunately, few population details from this period are known, and most recent studies only cover the territory of modern Denmark, not the Kingdom's greater extent at the time of the Kalmar War. Nonetheless, we can estimate that Denmark had a population of about 1,500,000 people. About one-third of the population lived on the Danish islands, another one-third in the Scanias, and the rest in the Duchies, which constituted half of the Kingdom.

However, Denmark's permanent military establishment was small, bordering on nonexistent. When the country was at peace, Denmark did not really have any organised army. Nor was there any real military establishment, beyond a few garrisons and the occasional field unit.

Nobility

The Danish nobility was not numerous. In 1600, there were 1,847 nobles, 568 of whom were males of the 15–50 age group that was most amenable for military service.[1] Unlike in Sweden and most other European countries, there was little real distinction between the upper and lower ranks of nobility. Because of the lack of influx of new blood, the number of nobles tended to shrink over time. On the other hand, this meant that land and wealth remained in comparatively few hands, for which reason most Danish nobles were wealthy in comparison to their Swedish counterparts. Many Danish nobles had no need to enter the service of the state to gain economic and social advancement. Despite their Danish identity, in the sixteenth century, they had already transformed themselves into members of a pan-European

---

1 Gunner Lind, *Hæren og magten i Danmark 1614–1662* (Odense: Odense Universitetsforlag, 1994), p.131. Lind based the figure on comprehensive biographical data collected for Svend Aage Hansen, *Adelsvældens grundlag*. 1964. Copenhagen University, PhD, p.233.

nobility, which sent their sons to study at the great universities on the Continent. Most had extensive estates, which enabled an easy life. The Schleswig-Holstein nobility was separate from the Danish equivalent, but the two groups merged easily and had much in common.

Cavalrymen

The nobility still provided some armed and equipped cavalrymen who fought as cuirassiers in the retinue of nobles, based on the nobility's traditional military duty to serve on horseback. Most other cavalry were enlisted. Cavalry in Scandinavia still operated in company-sized tactical units known as banners.

Infantrymen

Most infantry in the Danish military establishment were enlisted on the Continent. There were few conscripts. The German-speaking Duchies were fully exempt from conscription, although men still might be levied in times of need. Conscripts primarily served in the infantry. Conscript duty was very unpopular, and many deserted or caused trouble in various ways.

From 1609 onwards, groups of Scanian levies were conscripted to the fortresses for a month's exercise, and they also received new weapons. It seems likely that a few levies from Zealand were conscripted as well. The idea was that, instead of calling up untrained levies only when they were needed, the conscripts would be trained in the Dutch model of war, serve for a while, and then return into agricultural production until their military services were needed. When the war began, an estimated 1,000 Scanians had been trained so.[2] Most or all were then conscripted into the King's Regiment (more on which later). Although no longer regarded as levies, and henceforth available for the field army, the experiment seems not to have been very successful. These men seem to have provided the bulk of the 1,000 Danish conscripts in the army about whom King Christian, after the first attack on Kalmar in 1611, complained that they were 'worse than beasts'.[3]

Other conscripts were raised to serve as garrisons in Christianopel (a company of foot of 300 men), Varberg (at least 50 men), and Halmstad (possibly 300). On Zealand, 325 levies were called up to renovate existing fortifications, and yet more to protect the coastline.[4]

---

2   Lind, *Hæren*, p.35.

3   Carl F. Bricka, Julius A. Fridericia, and Johanne C. E. Skovgaard (eds), *Kong Christian den Fjerdes egenhændige Breve* (Copenhagen: Selskabet for Udgivelse af Kilder til dansk Historie, 1887–1947), vol. 1, p.59.

4   Axel Larsen [Liljefalk], *Kalmarkrigen. Et Bidrag til de nordiske Rigers Krigshistorie* (Copenhagen: G. E. C. Gad, 1889), p.13; J. W. Gordon Norrie, *Kalmarkrigen 1611–1612* (Copenhagen: Sixtus, 1978), p.9.

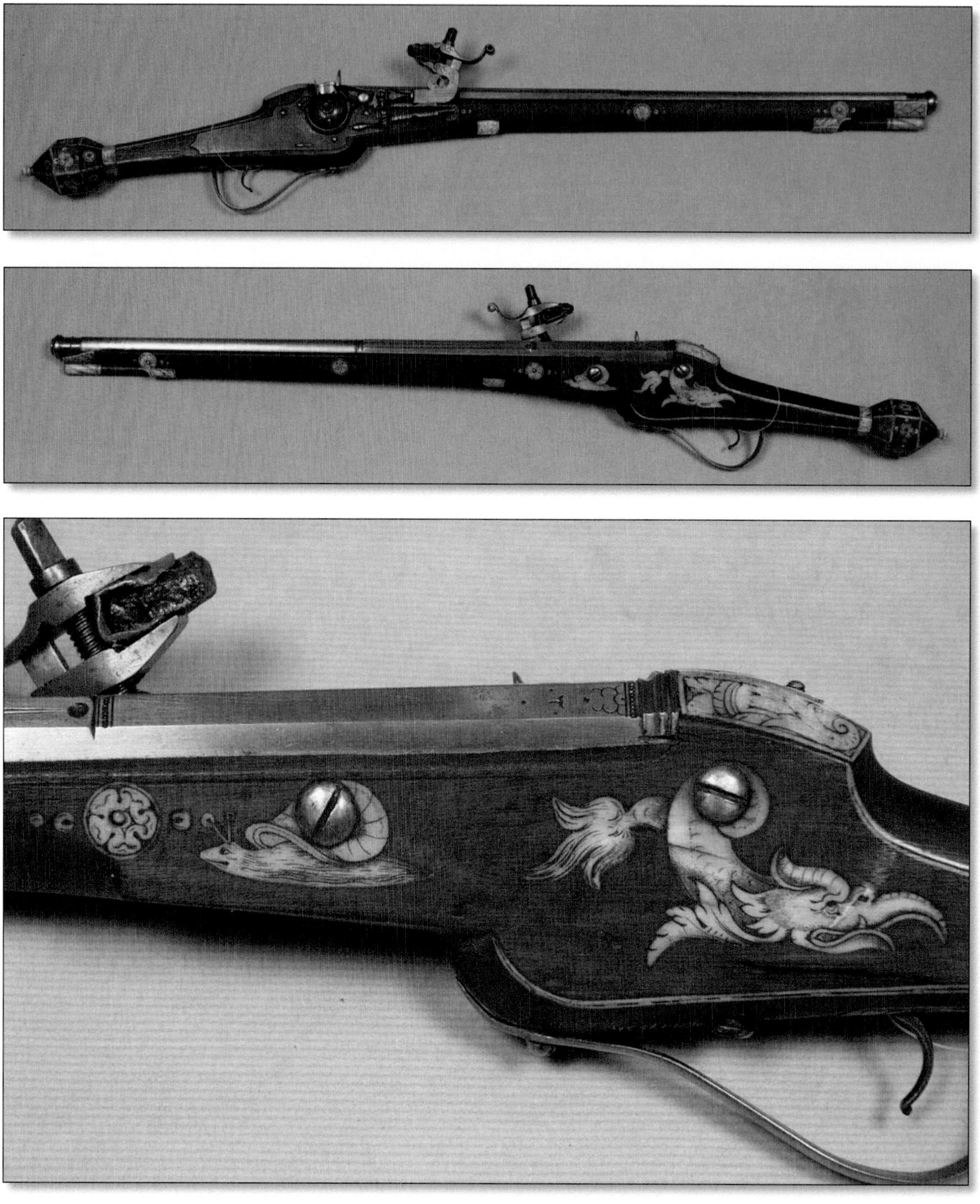

THE KALMAR WAR

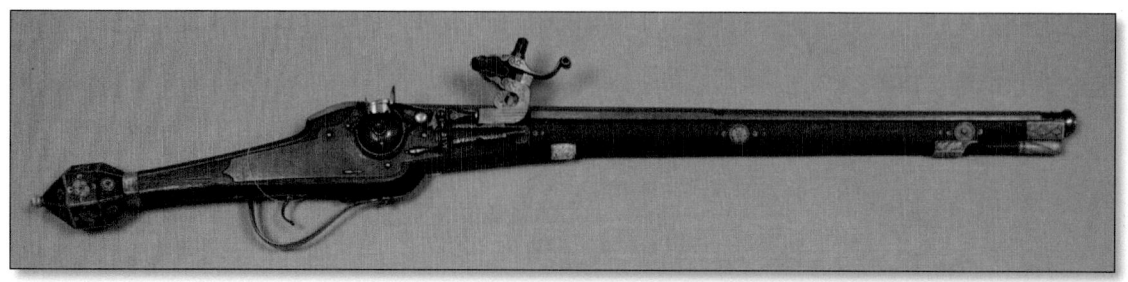

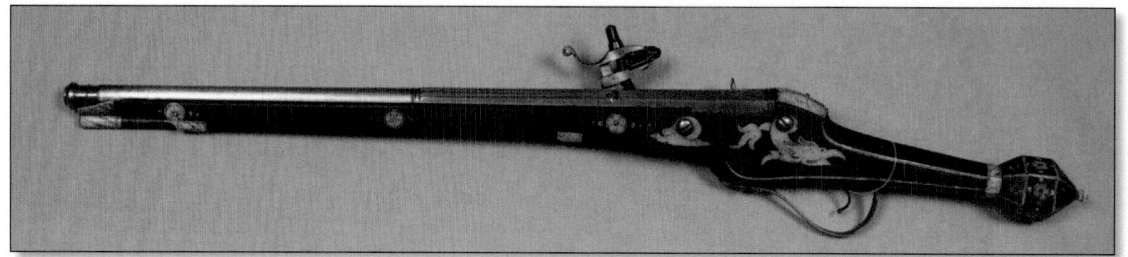

Danish wheellock pistol, one of a pair dated to 1608. Weight 1.88 kg, barrel length 54 cm, total length 78.5 cm. Calibre 12 mm. (Army Museum, Stockholm, AM.040663; formerly of Gustav von Essen's collection, split up in 1898)

Artillerymen

There was no formal unit organisation in the artillery. Instead, artillerymen served in forts and citadels as needed. By tradition and for eminently practical reasons, all artillery personnel were enlisted among semi-civilian professionals. All were specialists: officers (up to the rank of captain) or under-officers. Infantrymen detached from their units provided the necessary additional muscle.

In Copenhagen, all artillerymen worked under the supervision of the Arsenal. While the most skilled gunners customarily served at sea, artillerymen were sent to the army or navy as needed, without distinguishing between the two services.

Levies and Burgher Militias

For home defence, the Danish military establishment used levies who served on foot. They were at least at times collectively known as *landeværn* (territorial defence). Levies were raised through a quota that peasants and burghers had to fill. The mechanisms for raising levies varied between the King's domains. Levied troops had to pay for their own weapons and supplies. Training was poor or nonexistent. On the other hand, they were only required to serve at home. Levied troops were usually used to man castles or fortresses. The levies would serve for a time, commonly but not invariably for a month, then be replaced by other levies from the same area. The system was used in Scania, Zealand, and Fyn. Burghers were levied, too, but most men sent from towns were probably vagrants and other undesirables put into the ranks instead of solid burghers. In 1599, it was decided that the Zealand burghers should muster twice a year.[5]

In addition, Danish kings still claimed the right, in times of need, to raise a general levy (Danish: *almindeligt opbud*) of peasants and burghers. Both castles and villages were generally well supplied with weapons. Moreover, peasants often carried sidearms, if not on their person, then at least in their cart when travelling.

The terms of service generally depended on old traditions. Some men so raised had to serve in the field for extended periods, being effectively conscripts for the duration of the conflict. Most had to supply themselves for a certain period of time, generally a few weeks or months, after which they expected to be replaced by others of their kind. Others consisted of every available male. Generally, the obligation to serve in the levy in a certain community was relative to the numbers conscripted. The fewer conscripts, the higher the demand for levies. The Crown only assumed the responsibility to feed and supply levies after many months.

Most units of levies were commanded by the local *lensmand*. This was a small group of royal officials each responsible for a local administrative area known as a *len* (domain or fief). Such a man, known as a *lensmand* (pl. *lensmænd*), combined military and civilian functions. By royal decree, although one imposed on the King by the nobility through his accession

---

5   Lind, *Hæren*, p.35; Larsen, *Kalmarkrigen*, p.13.

THE KALMAR WAR

Left: Pikeman. (Jacob de Gheyn II, *Wapenhandelinghe van Roers, Musquetten ende Spiessen*)

Above: Musketeer. (Jacob de Gheyn II, *Wapenhandelinghe van Roers, Musquetten ende Spiessen* (Amsterdam: Robert de Baudous, 1608))

charter, all *lensmænd* had to be native nobles of Denmark, Norway, or Schleswig-Holstein. Foreigners were not allowed to serve in this prestigious position. A few did, but they were generally naturalised Danes, often tied by marriage to the traditional Danish nobility.

On at least Zealand and Fyn, the local nobility organised, commanded, and even armed the levy. On Fyn, the nobility selected one 'general' and two 'lieutenants' among themselves to command the levy. These men hired experienced professional captains and lieutenants as commanding officers and appointed under-officers selected from the levied peasants. When they were satisfied with the men's training, they discharged the professionals to save money and appointed suitable peasants in their stead. The nobility also tended to apportion the burden of service primarily on those peasants who did not serve on their own estates. By all accounts, the local nobility fully controlled the levy.

In times of war, the Danish Crown retained the option to raise additional, temporary units. This was decided by the Crown on a case-by-case basis and was apparently primarily implemented in the German-speaking Duchies, which otherwise were exempt from conscription into national units. This was referred to as a 'take-out' (German: *Ausschuss*). In Schleswig-Holstein, the Duke of Holstein-Gottorp attempted to make the population pay a special tax to fund a few permanently hired captains to lead the *Ausschuss*.

The mediocre performance of most levies, coupled with the difficulties that border guard service entailed for the hard-pressed Scanian levies who lost crops and income during the prolonged Kalmar War, convinced King Christian that perhaps another method to raise men for border defence was preferable. On 18 April 1612, he ordered the levying of a special border defence tax among the peasants, which would be used to hire enlisted soldiers to protect the borders.[6] In addition to the tax, the peasants in Göinge, Villand, Lister, and Bräkne districts also had to supply the soldiers with food and beer. The result was four border units of enlisted soldiers. The units merged into one in September the same year.[7]

Yet there was another task for which levies were required. The Danish Crown regularly raised peasants for dedicated labour units. Known as 'bastion diggers' (Danish: *skansegravere*), they were paid only three-quarters of the usual soldier's pay, but in return seem not to have been intended for combat duties. The noncombatant labour units seem to have formed part of the artillery. So was, for instance, the artillery officer Caspar von Miltnitz (Mildeniz) in 1611 authorised to raise a company of 400 soldiers for the King's Regiment and another 400 Zealand peasants for a labour unit.[8]

---

6   Finn Askgaard, *Christian IV: 'Rigets væbnede Arm'* (Copenhagen: Tøjhusmuseet, 1988), p.34.
7   Kim Hazelius, *De kallades snapphanar: Friskyttar, rövare & bondeuppbåd* (Bjärnum: Bokpro, 2006), p.45.
8   Knut Olav Alhaug, *Angrepet på Kalmar 1611. Militæradministrative forhold under Kalmarkrigens oppløp og innledende fase*. 2018. University of Bergen, Master Thesis, p.43.

Chain of Command

The Danish system of chain of command was, even for its time, uniquely opaque. In times of peace, the King personally fulfilled the role of senior military commander. There were no other corresponding senior officers. Denmark had no appointed commander of the army nor any regional military organisation. In a European context, the Danish military hierarchy remained very small and undeveloped. In a strictly military sense, there was no intermediate peacetime position between that of the King and the few captains of such companies of the army that existed in garrisons or were available for mobilisation. In times of peace, the chain of command began with the King, who directly commanded each captain in person. For practical purposes, the only officer who then might function as a go-between the King and his captains would be the local *lensmand*, who, as noted, combined military and civilian functions.

This setup might seem odd because Denmark actually had a senior military officer formally known as the Grand Marshal of the Realm (Danish: *Rigsmarsk*). However, this officer was selected by the Council of the Realm (*Rigsraadet*) and was accordingly regarded more as the spokesman for or representative of the Danish nobility than the representative of the King. There is nothing to suggest that the Grand Marshal in the early seventeenth century served as any kind of overall military commander. Nor had the holder of this office done so in the past. In the first half of the sixteenth century, he had merely been the wartime commander of the retinue of nobles. Yet he had exercised this command only in war and enjoyed no particular link to the units of the retinue of nobles in times of peace. Moreover, the Grand Marshal had not served even in this function during the previous Nordic Seven Years' War. Nor did the office of the Grand Marshal exercise meaningful command during the Kalmar War. If the Grand Marshal served as a senior commander of some stature in war, it was only due to the authority of the temporary warrant that the King might give him in a personal, not official, capacity. Odd as it may sound, we must therefore conclude that the office of Grand Marshal played no dedicated role in the military hierarchy either in war or peace.[9]

Moreover, the position of Grand Marshal was often vacant. While Steen Maltesen Sehested served as Grand Marshal at the outbreak of war, Denmark had no Grand Marshal in the period from late 1611 to 1616. Earlier, there had been a similar post, the Territorial Marshal (German: *Landmarschalk*), in Schleswig-Holstein. However, this post had, except for the infrequent ceremonial occasion, remained vacant ever since 1545, so he played even less of a military role than the Grand Marshal.

The same conclusion can perhaps be drawn about the Grand Admiral of the Realm (*Rigsadmiral*). When the post fell vacant in 1610, King Christian appointed one of his firm supporters, Mogens Ulfeldt, as Grand Admiral of the Realm. Ulfeldt had accompanied the King both to the North Cape in 1599 and England in 1606. Ulfeldt commanded a fleet during the war, but,

---

9   Lind, *Hæren*, p.284.

like his counterpart, Sehested, he did so on the authority of a temporary warrant that the King had given him in a personal capacity.

The senior member of the Council of the Realm, the Steward of the Realm (Danish: *Rigshofmester*), found himself in a similar position. When the holder of this office died of old age in 1601, King Christian did not bother to appoint a replacement until in 1632.

Modern historians often attribute King Christian's unwillingness to appoint senior military officers to the supposed rivalry between the King and the Council of the Realm. Certainly, the Council regarded its own role as that of guarantor of the state, the interests of the nobility, and the status quo, while the King was eager to expand his personal power. Whether the Council also opposed the King's attempts to expand his, and accordingly Denmark's, power and influence abroad is somewhat less easily proven from the available sources. Yet there was a conflict of interest between the King and Council. The wealthiest nobles owned estates in the fertile and prosperous farmlands of Jutland and Scania, from which their wealth and power derived. While they were not necessarily averse to war, they did not want one to be fought in Jutland and Scania, which would devastate their estates.

Perhaps a more relevant explanation to King Christian's appointment policies is that the King did not wish to share political or military control with other senior officers of the state. King Christian was characterised by an extreme distrust of delegation. Possibly, he worried that awarding any single individual too much power of command might turn this officer into a rival. On numerous occasions, the King's refusal to delegate authority resulted in lost opportunities. Over time, he created a system that could not cope effectively in his absence. Whether he realised this, or merely accepted it as a reasonable trade-off, is unknown.

King Christian's unwillingness to appoint senior commanders was not merely a peacetime convention. While the King would enlist colonels with regiments of foreign soldiers for war, he did not automatically appoint any senior level of command just because war broke out. Instead, he would then give warrants of command to trusted leaders as needed. During the Kalmar War, because of the geographical distances involved, he issued warrants of command to the leaders of any army that he did not command in person: the Norwegian army in the province of Bohuslän, the western army that set out from Halland, and the eastern army that set out from Blekinge. The Danish Articles of War allowed for the option of appointing two types of senior commanders between the King and his colonels. One was the colonel general and lieutenant (Danish: *generaløverste og lieutenant*), who served as the King's lieutenant or deputy when he was temporarily away from the army. The other was the field marshal (*feltmarskall*), who exercised individual command in another theatre of war.[10] The practice had already been tried during the Nordic Seven Years' War, when the colonel general was called 'field colonel' (*feltoberst*) or 'field colonel and captain general' (*feltoberst og generalkaptajn*). The term 'field colonel' was, by then, used in Sweden as

---

10   Christian IV's Articles of War of 1611, preamble.

well and essentially meant 'general'. Yet King Christian never appointed any colonel general during the Kalmar War. He did not need to since he personally led the main army for most of the war. The other two armies were commanded by field marshals (Steen Maltesen Sehested and Gert von Rantzau), which signified the independence of their commands. However, both received their respective warrants at the last possible moment and only then because the King *had* to appoint a commander.

In times of peace, lower-level commanders had no formal ranks. Most were regarded as captains. Three infantry officers were occasionally referred to as an 'artillery master colonel' (Danish: *øverste artillerimester*). Duke George of Brunswick-Lüneburg was once referred to as a 'major general' (German: *Generalwachtmeister*; Danish: *generalvagtmester*). Gert von Rantzau, too, was later said to have been a major general before the King made him a field marshal. The title appears to have been real because it was used in royal orders. Yet it seems never to have been presented as a formal title accompanied by a warrant. Nor was it ever more than an ad hoc title used only for as long as it was convenient.

Even these informal ranks were only seldom used. Instead, King Christian appointed a large number of men styled as commissars (Danish: *kommissær*, pl. *kommissærer*). Representatives of the royal power, their task was to handle musters, the requisition of supplies, distribution of funds, arrangement of quarters, and so on. However, not all commissars were equal in rank. Some were no more than administrators, for instance, those accounting commissars (*zahlkommissærer*) who handled the distribution of funds. Superior in power were those specifically called 'war commissars' (*krigskommissærer*) or even, at least in later periods, 'war commissar generals' (*generalkrigskommissærer*) who carried significantly greater responsibilities and commensurate status. They were members of the Council of the Realm, most were *lensmænd* before the war, and they generally retained this rank in addition to that of commissar. A war commissar might receive command of an entire army or corps, sometimes together with a field marshal, sometimes on his own. In addition, the war commissar had the customary duties and privileges of a commissar when it came to mustering men and requisitioning supplies. If a war commissar and a field marshal served together, the division of authority between them was opaque. The warrants provided to field marshals not only stipulated that they must request the advice of the commissar before making decisions, but they also stipulated that the commissar, like any other officer, was obliged to obey the field marshal. The key difference between the two posts was probably that a field marshal did receive a formal royal warrant while commissars seem to have been appointed as needed and through significantly more informal means. Field marshal was a rank, commissar a position. Both were appointed by royal command. On the other hand, the commissar received verbal instructions directly from the King, which meant that he effectively spoke for the King. This gave the commissar a wide latitude. In contrast, a field marshal had to follow his written instructions – which might not offer the same freedom of manoeuvre. However, the less formal appointment of a commissar meant that the King easily could dismiss or disavow him. The deliberate lack of clarity with regard to the position of commissar seems to have been introduced by King Christian. During the previous Nordic Seven Years' War, the position of commissar was a formal appointment and constituted a regular part of the hierarchy.

When the King was present, he was in full and sole command and responsible for operational as well as any other decisions. But how was he to handle command when the King was absent? To avoid sharing political and military control with any single individual, King Christian insisted on maintaining rule by committee when military orders were issued. As a result, the army was ruled by committee in the form of a council of war consisting of all officers and officials present. This was a Danish peculiarity that reached its final shape during the reign of King Christian and was linked to his appointment of commissars instead of generals. Although the Danish army had previously known of rule by committee in the form of the council of war, including during the Seven Years' War, the kings back then appointed commanding officers who, although expected to consult a council of war, at least held formal command. Under King Christian, however, the chain of command was deliberately blurred. Henceforth, committee rule became the norm, in which each participant had an essentially equal vote. This rule applied even when participating officers lacked military experience. Henceforth, committee rule would become the standard type of command in the Danish army and, over time, produce some spectacular failures.

The Danish army was quite unique in emphasising collective command to the extent it did. Why would King Christian adopt such an unusual and detrimental practice? He must have realised that the practice of collective command hampered and slowed down decision making. Possibly, the King introduced the custom as a means to secure the integration of army and state.[11] If so, this might be understandable in light of the number of enlisted foreigners that he depended on whenever military assets were needed. After all, war commissars were selected from the men of the Council of the Realm, which was dominated by the Danish nobility. On this issue, the King enjoyed the support of the Council of the Realm, which was anxious to preserve the influence of the Danish nobility over that of foreign military entrepreneurs. Since foreign officers generally were far more experienced than Danish ones, it was easier to retain a degree of native influence under conditions of rule by committee. The King and Council presumably agreed that it was better to appoint senior Danish nobles to positions where they at least to some extent could control the enlisted, foreign officers and their unruly men. However, since so few Danish nobles had any relevant military experience, they could hardly be appointed officers and so were instead appointed commissars. In effect, the King and Council chose to appoint commissars instead of generals. And since most commissars were militarily inexperienced, perhaps they argued that committee rule would decrease the risk for truly fatal mistakes.

---

11   Lind, *Hæren*, p.288, certainly suggests this explanation, although his explicit comparison with other contemporary states is unconvincing. For sure, most contemporary European states appointed nobles to the highest commands regardless of their military experience or lack thereof but not as a means to introduce command by committee.

However, King Christian's motive for introducing the custom may well have been another. Rule by committee reduced the individual power of officers and officials. Possibly, the King introduced the custom not to secure Danish power over enlisted foreigners but rather to thwart the attempts of the Danish nobility to perpetuate its own influence over royal power through the Council of the Realm. It seems certain that King Christian aimed to make sure that he personally remained at the undisputed apex of the command structure. Why else would he deliberately avoid both appointing officers to senior rank and, unlike his father in the Nordic Seven Years' War, inviting famous generals to bring their enlisted men to his army?[12]

It was only in the final phase of the war, during Gert von Rantzau's and Jørgen Lunge's various campaigns in Sweden, that one could actually speak of a commanding officer. Presumably, this was the result of a growing understanding that appointing experienced officers to command positions was a more efficient way of leading an army than rule by committee. Besides, professionals such as Rantzau and Lunge were native nobles who did not threaten the prerogative of royal rule.

Military Organisation

Danish military establishment and military organisation remained essentially unchanged since the sixteenth century. Like then, the core of the Danish army was the retinue of nobles, a handful of fully armoured cavalry, financed and raised by the nobility in exchange for their status as exempt from taxation. Since the retinue of nobles was weak in numbers, the Crown hired Danish and foreign mercenaries, both foot and horse, according to need and financial resources, to complement the small native cavalry force. In the previous century, German *Landsknechts* had been particularly popular. By the early seventeenth century, German enlisted units remained the military of choice of Danish kings.

There was little consistency in unit organisation and numbers. In times of peace, the number of military officers on duty was very small, consisting of less than 10 men in the entire country. They could be described as professionals of two types. There were up to two captains in charge of the largest fortress garrisons. In addition, there were up to four artillery specialists or engineers who handled technical matters in these and other important fortresses. None of these men was in command of the fortress itself; this was the task of a *lensmand*, the aforementioned royal official who combined civilian and military functions. The Crown dispersed the handful of professionals among garrisons as needed. To this little band might be added the occasional professional captain who was hired to train peasant levies for a short while or at least until locals could do the job reasonably well. This was the arrangement in Holstein and perhaps elsewhere, too.

---

12 Lind, *Hæren*, pp.288–89.

A slightly larger group of officers was those referred to as 'of the House' (German: *von Haus aus*). These were officers who received 'waiting pay' (German: *Wartegeld*; Danish: *vartgæld* or *pension*). In return, they did not serve but were supposed to be available and ready for mobilisation. When needed, their task was to enlist men. Usually, this group consisted of a colonel, who was expected to enlist a regiment of foot, a couple of captains, who were each expected to raise a company of foot, and a couple of cavalry captains, who were each expected to raise a banner of cavalry, which was a company-sized unit. When these officers were called up, they would receive enlistment money to raise the expected number of men. At other times, they could remain at home, serve in other positions (e.g. at court, in the navy, or, if Danes, in charge of a castle or fortress as a *lensmand*), or even go into foreign service as soldiers (but not in the service of enemies of the Crown).[13] Officers 'of the House', whether in field or garrison units, swore an oath of loyalty to the King, not the Country.

The men 'of the House' typically served for many years in a military capacity, so they can be said to have constituted the core of a standing army or at least of a permanent military establishment. There was no standing army as such, if one is defined as consisting of regularly trained units of career professionals living in barracks. Whether the men 'of the House' were actually experienced in warfare mostly depended on the individual. The bulk of military officers who received waiting pay were of foreign origin, generally German, English, or Scottish. Most were nobles or at least represented themselves as nobles.

Most artillery officers were non-nobles, usually burghers, for whom the technical expertise both made the profession prestigious and set it apart from that of other officers.

When mobilisation was ordered, the *lensmand* received increased military duties. He handled mobilisation in the local area that he was responsible for. He might receive a garrison to command in his castle or fortress, or he would join the retinue of nobles as a captain.

Mobilisation also meant that the number of military officers rapidly rose, increasing from the handful on duty during peace to up to a hundredfold more.

The Danish army consisted of a few small permanent units at the Royal Court and as garrisons of royal castles and fortresses. The latter ranged from obsolete medieval castles to modern, well-fortified designs such as the large Kronborg and Varberg fortresses and the smaller fortresses at Christianopel and Krempe. Castle garrisons were very small, altogether less than 500 men dispersed among eight to 10 strongholds. It was only the company-sized garrison of Kronborg that could even be called a 'military unit'. It usually consisted of a few hundred men under a captain. However, it nonetheless remained too small to actually defend the large fortress in the case of an attack without receiving additional reinforcements. We can assume that all strongholds were manned by a few trained artillerymen and skeleton units only, to which others would be attached only after mobilisation. There was also a garrison in the Copenhagen Armoury (Danish: *Tøjhuset*), which comprised

---

13 Lind, *Hæren*, p.128.

a company of 200 to 400 artillerymen, although they were regarded more as part of the navy than the army. The Armoury was well stocked with weapons and military equipment, in these years, commonly having 10,000 to 20,000 firearms, several thousand sets of armour, and 500 to 1,000 cannons.[14]

When units were actually raised, primarily through enlistment, a regiment of foot had a nominal establishment strength of 3,000 men. This ambition was seldom achieved. Besides, there were not yet any permanent regiments. The first were only established after the Kalmar War, in 1614–1615.

A company of foot (Danish: *fænnika* or *fennik*, presumably from the German term '*Fähnlein*', 'little flag', which also appeared in Danish as '*fenlin*') was expected to count 300 men. A company of foot was commanded by a captain (German: *Hauptmann*; Danish: *hopmand*, pl. *hopmænd*). A cavalry banner (Danish: *fane*) commonly consisted of 200 to 400 men.[15] A cavalry banner was commanded by a captain (German: *Rittmeister*; Danish: *ritmester*). However, as can be expected with the emphasis on temporary unit structures, real numbers varied considerably in both infantry and cavalry units.

The structure of fundamentally everything in the Danish military establishment – including garrisons, permanent units, recruitment, funding, military disposition, and tactics – remained traditional. While not yet obsolete, many officers of the Crown realised that it was only a matter of time until the system would have to adapt. The Court recognised the Dutch model as advantageous, but, so far, very few aspects of it had entered Danish military organisation and thinking.

The Royal Court

The Danish Royal Court was in effect a small, self-contained military organisation, whose attending nobles (Danish: *hofjunker*, pl. *hofjunkere*) served mounted in a cavalry unit known as the 'Court Banner' (*hoffanen*). The Court Banner was commanded by the Marshal of the Court (*hofmarskall*), the administrative official in charge of the royal household and the court's financial affairs. However, the unit was small. Generally, the Court Banner included some 20 attending nobles, each of whom was accompanied by three to five serving men (*svende*). As implied by its name, the Court Banner was of company strength only.

The Court also included the men of the Drabant Guard (*drabanter*) and royal serving men (*enspændere*). They were enlisted as infantry and cavalry, respectively. By the end of the war in 1614, there were some 50 Drabant Guards and a handful of royal serving men. The latter name derived from the name of those serving cavalrymen who followed a nobleman in the old medieval 'lance' armoured cavalry organisation. They served as guards and messengers in times of peace. At war, they followed the King on horseback in a role corresponding to the serving men of the court nobles.[16]

---

14 Lind, *Hæren*, p.28.
15 Lind, *Hæren*, p.128.
16 Lind, *Hæren*, p.30.

THE DANISH MILITARY ESTABLISHMENT

Danish soldiers playing cards, as depicted in one of the 26 tapestries celebrating events during the Kalmar War that King Christian ordered for display in Frederiksborg Castle in 1616. The series was delivered from 1619 to 1621, but all tapestries were destroyed in the castle fire of 1859. Fortunately, some of them were copied by the diligent Frederik Christian Lund, who had a special interest in historical military dress, one year before the fire destroyed the originals. (F. C. Lund, after Karel van Mander II)

Retinue of Nobles

After the Royal Court, the King's most important source of fighting men was the retinue of nobles. Based on a traditional military duty, the retinue was known by an old name that can be translated as 'military service' but originally signified 'knight service', that is, service on horseback (Danish: *rostjeneste*). This was a force that was only raised in times of war. Mobilisation orders were directed at the nobility as a whole, not individual captains of the retinue of nobles. By tradition, its members owed their service to King and Country, not solely the Crown. Until just before the Kalmar War, the retinue of nobles remained solely a device for raising cavalrymen for war. They were never called up for training purposes. The organisation encompassed some 1,200 armoured cavalrymen in the Kingdom of Denmark and about 600 in the Duchies.[17]

---

17 Lind, *Hæren*, pp.30–31.

However, the retinue of nobles was reformed in 1609, when it was divided into fixed units according to a geographical organisation consisting of seven banners: three in Jutland (the Aarhus, Aalborg, and Ribe Banners) and one each in Fyn, Zealand, Scania, and Halland. Each banner had three officers personally appointed by King Christian: a captain, a lieutenant, and an ensign. The King also designated a few, typically young nobles whom he expected to serve. As for the rest, the nobles were free to send a cavalryman in their stead. As a result, no unit ever had more than 18 nobles on active service (e.g., the Aarhus Banner only had 13). The rest were hired men. Since available numbers in any case were too small to form banners of 200 men each (the avowed establishment strength), the Crown almost certainly enlisted men to fill up the numbers. Nonetheless, full establishment strength was never reached.[18] The novelty in the reform was that this division of the retinue of nobles into units with dedicated officers, appointed by royal command, took place when the country was already at peace and was intended as a permanent organisation. Henceforth, unlike before, orders from the King were directed at the captains, not the nobility as a whole. Although an identical organisation had been used during previous wars, the units were always disbanded when the war ended.

However, even after the introduction of this reform, military preparedness remained low. Musters and training took place only seldom and were very brief. In 1604, Eske Brock (1560–1625), a member of the Council of the Realm, wrote in his diary:

> On 24 November in the morning, at 6 o'clock, they blew the trumpets thrice, and there … His Royal Majesty met us … And we were all mustered, first the Council [of the Realm], then the *lensmænd*, and then the other nobles, and when the muster was concluded … we were first deployed in order of march, five men strong, and then in order of battle, 30 men strong, and then … thanked on behalf of His Majesty [after which] the entire nobility was invited, including wives and maidens … and celebrated until 3 in the morning.[19]

Apparently, the training session consisted of no more than forming up in order of march and in order of battle. Arguably, the ensuing banquet constituted the main activity of the event. Moreover, even though the

---

18 In 1609, the total number for the seven banners reached 1,120 men, to which the Court Banner of some 150 men could be added to produce a grand total of 1,270 horse. Details were as follows: Aarhus 172, Aalborg 185, Ribe 170, Fyn 149, Scania 119, Halland 117, and Zealand 208 men. Emil Madsen, 'Om Rytteriet i de danske Hære i det 16de Aarhundrede', *Dansk Historisk Tidskrift*, 7:1 (1897–1899), p.433; Larsen, *Kalmarkrigen*, p.8. The diligent Askgaard, *Christian IV*, pp.32–33, corrects the Fyn figure to 149 1/2 and the Zealand figure to 218, which would produce a total of 1,130 men. However, when war broke out, only about 1,050 horse joined the field army, and this number included the men of the Court Banner. Generalstaben, *Sveriges krig 1611–1632* (Stockholm: Generalstaben, 1936), vol. 1: *Danska och ryska krigen*, p.133.

19 L. Moltke (ed.), 'Rigsraad Eske Brocks Dagbøger for 1604, 1609, 1619 og 1622', *Danske Samlinger*, 2:2 (1872–1873), pp.270–71.

organisation was regarded as permanent, special orders of mobilisation nonetheless had to be sent out to activate the units.

Yet the retinue of nobles remained an elite unit of sorts. Its members were sufficiently wealthy to arm themselves well, many had received individual training in combat, and, since the nobles all knew each other and the serving men from numerous social occasions, the unit was characterised by a certain esprit de corps even though it seldom mobilised or trained together.

In times of peace and for service at home, the retinue of nobles was funded and its members paid by the nobility. If units of the retinue of nobles were sent to fight abroad, they were supposed to be funded and paid by the Crown based on the same terms as enlisted units.

By the early seventeenth century, functioning retinues of nobles only remained in Scandinavia. In Germany, this old institution was by then seldom used and, even if it existed, usually was regarded as part of the general levy.

Dutch-Model Infantry

As noted, there was considerable interest in the Dutch model in Scandinavia. The possibly most famous work from the Dutch tradition, Jacob de Gheyn II's 1607 *Wapenhandelinghe van Roers, Musquetten ende Spiessen* (known in English as *The Exercise of Arms for Calivers, Muskets, and Pikes*), was translated into Danish and published for the Danish market in the same year.[20] As its title implies, it describes the use of arquebuses, muskets, and pikes. By then, King Christian wanted to raise companies of foot of conscripted Danes formed up according to the Dutch model. However, the result was meagre: only six independent companies of foot were raised.[21] No more men were available.

Immediately before the outbreak of war, King Christian ordered the raising of 1,000 men divided into three conscripted companies: one from Zealand, one from Copenhagen and parts of Scania, and the third from Scania. We do not know, but can assume, that some or all of these men were raised from the small number of conscripts already trained from 1609 onwards. The men were formed into companies of the King's Regiment of Foot (Danish: *Kongens Regiment*), which henceforth also included the Royal Guard company of some 300 guardsmen and 40 guard musketeers (*livskytter*) from Frederiksborg Castle.[22] The regiment was organised according to the Dutch model. To make up the numbers (and perhaps instil some professionalism), more enlisted companies were quickly added, bringing the regiment's strength up to 12 companies.

Enlisted Units

From the fifteenth century onwards, the Danish Crown habitually contracted enlisted units abroad, mostly on the Continent, whenever there was a risk of war. Examples include King Christian's confrontation with Hamburg in 1604,

---

20 Jacob de Geyn [Gheyn] II, *Waabenhandling Om Rør, Musketter oc Spedser* (The Hague: Publisher unknown, 1607).
21 Lind, *Hæren*, p.32.
22 Larsen, *Kalmarkrigen*, pp.72–73.

THE KALMAR WAR

Above: Musketeer. (Jacob de Gheyn II, *Wapenhandelinghe van Roers, Musquetten ende Spiessen*)

Below: Pikeman. (Gheyn II, *Wapenhandelinghe van Roers, Musquetten ende Spiessen*)

when enlisted units mustered in Holstein, and in the Duchy of Brunswick-Lüneburg in 1605, when the Danish Crown supported Duke Henry Julius, Prince of Brunswick-Wolfenbüttel, against the Hanseatic town of Brunswick, which refused to recognise his overlordship. The Kalmar War was no exception. Except for the Court Banner, the seven banners of the retinue of nobles, and the three conscripted companies of the King's Regiment, the entire field army in Denmark consisted of units enlisted abroad.

For this reason, Denmark relied to a considerable extent not only on officers but also on common soldiers enlisted in Germany. The overwhelming share of the infantry in the Danish army was of German origin. The Duchies were treaty bound to provide 150 cavalry from the retinue of nobles; however, the Estates preferred to have the Dukes enlist these men and were even willing to contribute twice the cost so as to avoid serving themselves. Ultimately, a cavalry banner under Duke Philip of Glücksburg joined the King's army as representatives of the Duchies – not raised by treaty but as an enlisted unit commissioned by the Danish Crown.[23]

It took time to muster the enlisted units, not least because most were enlisted in Germany and had to be shipped to the theatre of operations. During the Kalmar War, the Danish Crown authorised patents to enlist a total of some 33,000 men (30,000 foot and 3,000 horse). The enlistment was quite successful, eventually reaching 26,000 foot and 3,000 horse. However, not all served at the same time. Available forces generally counted from 15,000 to 20,000 men.[24]

Some enlisted cavalry were used to reinforce the retinue of nobles. Otherwise, the enlisted formed up in their own units, as foot regiments and cavalry companies, under the military entrepreneurs who formed them. The military entrepreneurs were a heterogeneous lot. At the top end was Gert von Rantzau, one of the wealthiest men of Holstein and a subject of the King. Rantzau was not only an entrepreneur; he had also been in Dutch service and knew modern warfare. He raised eight units of which at least four received a commanding officer from the Schleswig and Holstein nobility, which made Schleswig and Holstein nobles well represented in the Danish army. Like Rantzau, they were subjects of the King. Because of Rantzau, about half the commanders of enlisted units were men with existing links to the Crown even before they were hired. One could argue that without Rantzau's wealth and entrepreneurial ability, hardly any units of the enlisted army would have been commanded by royal subjects.

Rantzau also hired commanders who belonged to the native Danish nobility. However, most of the Danish nobles whom he appointed officers seem to have had little or no military experience prior to the war. Other officers, mostly of German origin, were far less wealthy, but they were professional soldiers. Quite a few already received waiting pay from the Crown in return for their readiness to enlist a unit when needed. This means

---

23   Alhaug, *Angrepet på Kalmar*, p.37, citing Danish National Archives (*Rigsarkivet*), Tyske Kancelli, Slesvig-holsten-lauenburgske Kancelli, Militære bestallinger og reverser m.v. (1610 - 1659).

24   Lind, *Hæren*, p.32.

that they, too, had existing links to the Crown. Such men can be described as salaried officers or the King's personal clients.[25]

Two German princes, Duke George of Brunswick-Lüneburg and Duke Ernest Louis of Saxe-Lauenburg, promised to raise the major contingent of enlisted units. Reports from Swedish observers on the Continent suggest that they and other military entrepreneurs successfully raised up to 7,000 men there. However, many of the enlisted Germans refused to serve when they were told that their destination was overseas, in Sweden. Instead, they went into the service of Duke Christian of Brunswick-Lüneburg, George's elder brother, who needed men for a local dispute.[26] Dukes George and Ernest Louis did eventually join King Christian but with very few men. King Christian had hoped to enlist some 15,000 men before the outbreak of war, but he failed to reach this figure.[27] Perhaps this was fortunate for the Danish population: whenever the King's enlisted units marched through the country towards the north, they plundered and abused the population so badly that King Christian received constant complaints.[28]

Because officers were more expensive to hire than men, most enlisted companies for financial reasons were relatively strong: 300, 250, and 200 men, respectively. As a result, the ratio of officers to men was small. Each regiment consisted of usually 10, but occasionally as few as five, companies. The patents to enlist a company specified that, following Continental practices, a third of the men should be pikemen.[29]

Weapons, Equipment, and Uniforms

Officers and Under-Officers

Officers provided their own arms and armour. In battle, each officer would typically be armed with two wheellock pistols and a rapier.

An under-officer, too, was armed with rapier and perhaps pistols. Those serving in the infantry would mostly carry halberds. The Drabant Guards carried gilded halberds to make a splendid show.[30] The partisan does not seem to have become a Danish service weapon until later in the century.[31] Under-officers probably wore helmets as well as gorgets as a symbol of rank,

---

25 Lind, *Hæren*, p.138.
26 Larsen, *Kalmarkrigen*, p.74, n.2.
27 Norrie, *Kalmarkrigen*, p.9.
28 Larsen, *Kalmarkrigen*, p.167.
29 G. B. C:son Barkman, *Gustaf II Adolfs regementsorganisation vid det inhemska infanteriet: En studie över organisationens tillkomst och huvuddragen av dess utveckling mot bakgrunden av kontinental organisation* (Stockholm: Meddelanden från Generalstabens krigshistoriska avdelning, 1931), p.40.
30 Henry Roberts, *The Most Royall and Honourable Entertainement, of the Famous and Renowmed King, Christiern the Fourth, King of Denmarke, &c ...* (London: William Barley, 1606), p.23.
31 The partisan was, however, known in Denmark under the terms '*bassan*' (1563) and '*tisan*' (1583). Emil Madsen, 'Om Fodfolket i de danske Hære i det 16de Aarhundrede', *Dansk Historisk Tidskrift*, 7:1 (1897–1899), p.213.

as depicted in the tapestries celebrating events during the Kalmar War that King Christian, in 1616, ordered from the well-known artist Karel van Mander II (*c.* 1579–1623) for display in Frederiksborg Castle. Some might have also worn a cuirass, with tassets to protect the upper thighs if serving in a pike unit.

Musketeers

Since most musketeers in the Danish army were enlisted on the Continent, it seems fair to assume that most were armed with matchlock muskets that were used with fork rests. We know little about the calibres in common use, but it seems likely that the Dutch 10-bore matchlock musket, drilled for a ball weighing one-tenth of a pound (which corresponds to a nominal calibre of 19.7 mm), was coming into use even though it was not yet very common. This seems to be the type of musket illustrated in Karel van Mander II's tapestries for Frederiksborg Castle.

The inventories in the Copenhagen Armoury present a complex picture of Danish firearms. By 1609, the Armoury had a variety of weapons and locks. Snaplocks, wheellocks, and matchlocks were all used with either arquebuses or muskets.

Table 1. Handguns in the Copenhagen Arsenal, 1 May 1609[32]

Type of Firearm	No.
Matchlock muskets	2,598
Wheellock muskets	109
Snaplock muskets	16
Matchlock arquebuses (*Lange Rør*)	6,852
Wheellock arquebuses	1,445
Snaplock arquebuses	6,043
Wheellock carbines or more likely short arquebuses (*Stakkede Rør*)[33]	99
Wheellock bandolier arquebuses	68
Wheellock pistols	71
Total	17,301

The arquebus was of smaller calibre than the Dutch musket. Calibres ranged widely, but 12 bore (that is, drilled for a ball weighing one-twelfth of a pound, which corresponds to a nominal calibre of 18.5 mm) or thereabouts was common. However, much heavier calibres existed as well, including those drilled for balls weighing one-sixth or one-seventh of a pound. For the

---

32 Otto Blom, *Kristian Den Fjerdes Artilleri, Hans Tøihuse og Vaabenforraad* (Copenhagen: C. C. Lose, 1877), pp.53, 63.

33 The firearms referred to as '*Stakkede Rør*' have been interpreted as pistols by some, primarily because they were sometimes carried in holsters. Be that as it may, the weapon type seems to have grown obsolete during the Kalmar War. Blom, *Kristian Den Fjerdes Artilleri*, p.87.

heavier muskets, some Danish musketeers used gorgets made of leather to ease the recoil of the weapon.[34]

Danish musketeers generally did not wear other armour, although they still wore helmets. Some of those who carried the lighter arquebus may still have worn armour as well, even though this practice was disappearing rapidly. The armourer Zakarias in Helsingør delivered cuirasses and helmets manufactured for infantry arquebusiers to the Copenhagen Armoury as late as 1603. Arquebusiers and musketeers continued to use helmets at least until about 1620.[35]

The wheellock was not considered optimal for infantry use since it was prone to malfunction. In fact, in 1611–1612, the Danish Armoury ordered 5,000 Dutch muskets with fork rests, each of which was supposed to carry two locks, one matchlock and one wheellock, each with its own cock. From at least 1613 onwards, a small number of rifled muskets were used in the Danish army.[36]

As sidearms, some conscripted Danish musketeers were issued cutlasses (Danish: *kortelasser*, from French: *coutelas* or Italian: *coltellaccio*, 'knife').[37] This sidearm may have been similar to the *tessak* used in Norway (more on which later). Some were straight, while others were slightly curved. These weapons were essentially cutting swords.

Pikemen

Those infantrymen who did not carry muskets were mostly armed with pikes. Each pikeman carried a rapier as a sidearm. By tradition, a pikeman was valued higher than an arquebusier. However, at the time of the Kalmar War, they no longer received higher pay.[38] Garrison units did not employ pikes but might have used half-pikes. Pikemen were expected to wear a full set of armour consisting of a helmet, breastplate, backplate, gorget, and tassets to protect the upper thighs. During the Kalmar War, some Danish pikemen appear to have begun to wear breastplates without backplates. The breastplate was then supported by two leather straps that were crossed over and attached to the soldier's back.[39]

Continental practices encouraged a pike regulation length of nine cubits (5.35 m), so this was probably the standard length of pikes employed by Continental soldiers in Danish service. However, based on a surviving specimen of a slightly younger date, Danish pikes may have been only 4.55 m long, with about 3.5 cm-thick shafts made of ash or pine wood. The rhomboid or flat, rounded pikehead was around 19 cm long.[40] Pike shafts

---

34 Jakobsson, *Lantmilitär beväpning och beklädnad*, pp.137–38.
35 Blom, *Kristian Den Fjerdes Artilleri*, pp.327, 333.
36 Jakobsson, *Lantmilitär beväpning och beklädnad*, p.137.
37 Blom, *Kristian Den Fjerdes Artilleri*, pp.84–85, 311–12, 318.
38 Madsen, 'Om Fodfolket', pp.180–81.
39 Blom, *Kristian Den Fjerdes Artilleri*, pp.334–35.
40 Blom, *Kristian Den Fjerdes Artilleri*, p.319. Scandinavian readers need to remember that Blom employed the 1835 Danish foot for measurements (1 ft = 0.3138535 m).

were imported from Norway in the sixteenth century, but, by the time of the Kalmar War, it seems that production had shifted to manufacturers in Germany. Pike shafts may, for this reason, have been painted black since this seems to have been a common practice in Germany.

When the Danish army moved into the heavily forested Swedish heartland, King Christian and his commanders realised that pikes were less useful than musketeers. The King accordingly ordered more musketeers since, in the frustrated words of Breide Rantzau, in the forests 'one cannot do anything with the long pikes'.[41]

Enlisted pikemen generally carried rapiers. Conscripted Danish pikemen were issued cutlasses (*kortelasser*) as sidearms, just like conscripted Danish musketeers.[42]

Cuirassiers

It was primarily the retinue of nobles who fought as cuirassiers in the Danish army. Danish cuirassiers were fully armoured until perhaps as late as 1650.

Danish cuirassiers looked and functioned much the same as those on the Continent. A cuirassier was armed with a pair of wheellock pistols and a rapier. He wore a visored close helmet or burgonet, a gorget for the neck, three-quarter armour that covered the entire upper body and both arms as well as the front half of the legs down to and including the knee, gauntlets, a culet (a piece of plate armour consisting of small, horizontal lames that protected the small of the back and the buttocks), and high riding boots.[43] Cuirassier armour was generally blackened and always shot proof.[44] Until about 1620, the breastplate was commonly of the peascod-belly or goose-belly type, which then fell out of fashion. Germany led the way, where the influential military theorist Johann Jacobi von Wallhausen, in his *Kriegskunst zu Fuß* in 1615, argued that the style was 'more suited to pregnant women than to soldiers'.[45] The weight of the cuirassier armour (between 20–30 kg) demanded the use of large horses. This was not a problem for the Danish nobility since such breeds were easily available in both Jutland and northern Germany.

It seems fairly certain that a noble cuirassier was also expected to bring at least one serving cavalryman (Danish: *svend*) into the unit. The serving man's horse might be smaller, and he customarily was only supplied with a helmet (possibly a cheaper type), a gorget with possibly added spaulder-

---

41　Breide Rantzau to Chancellor Christian Friis, 31 May 1611, cited in Gustaf Petri, *Kungl. Första livgrenadjärregementets historia 1: Östgötafänikorna till och med år 1618* (Stockholm: P. A. Norstedt & Söner, 1926), p.383.

42　Blom, *Kristian Den Fjerdes Artilleri*, pp.311–12.

43　Madsen, 'Om Rytteriet', p.454, citing an armament order dated 10 February 1611.

44　Madsen, 'Om Rytteriet', p.450. Danish cavalry armed with firearms were instructed to wear blackened armour from at least 1552. Other Danish cavalry were then instructed to wear polished armour as before. The introduction of blackened armour coincided with the introduction of cavalry firearms.

45　Josef Alm, *Blanka vapen och skyddsvapen från och med 1500-talet till våra dagar* (Stockholm: Rediviva, 1975), pp.242, 251.

Facing page: Cuirassier on horseback. (Wallhausen, Kriegskunst zu Pferdt)

style shoulder and upper-arm protection, a 'common' or 'simple' (*gemene* or *slette*) breast- and backplate that might or not be shot proof, and often but not invariably gauntlets. In 1609–1610, the price in Denmark for a set of cuirassier armour was 25 *Reichsthalers*. In comparison, a shot-proof set of 'common' armour for a serving cavalryman was 10 *Reichsthalers*, while a non-shot-proof ('simple') one cost only eight.[46] Similar to their masters, each serving cavalryman was armed with a rapier and a pair of wheellock pistols. Little is known of how the serving cavalrymen formed up in battle, but we can assume that they provided the rear ranks in a cuirassier unit.

Harquebusiers

In addition to cuirassiers, the Danish Crown employed enlisted harquebusiers. Although details are seldom available, it seems that most enlisted German cavalry were harquebusiers. Contemporary Danish sources describe cavalry units sometimes as banners and sometimes as companies, apparently not making a distinction between either the old and new organisational forms or their primary armament. Perhaps this is unsurprising: both types of cavalry employed similar tactics. Each harquebusier carried an arquebus or carbine as primary armament, one or two wheellock pistols, and a rapier or, for some Danish cavalry, a sidearm referred to as a 'cavalry cutlass' (Danish: *rytterkortelass*), which was presumably a shorter, cheaper weapon.[47] Danish harquebusiers were supposed to wear a helmet as well as a breast- and backplate.[48] Some Danish harquebusiers apparently wore helmets and breast- and backplates until as late as 1650.

The cavalry arquebus usually came with a wheellock, although a few snaplocks or snaphance locks were in service as well. A snaplock employed a firestone, often a flintstone, to strike fire, so the mechanism foreshadowed the later flintlock. The cavalry arquebus was hung from a swivel attached to a bandolier across the left shoulder. It could be fired without unhooking from the bandolier. By the time of the Kalmar War, the bandolier arquebus was commonly around 1.2 m long and had a calibre of around 16.8 mm (16 bore). On the left side of the gunlock, a fairly large leather flap was screwed in place that could be folded over the gunlock to protect it. On his right side, the harquebusier carried a special leather strap from his belt with a powder horn, priming flask, ammunition pouch, and wheellock spanner.[49]

Strictly speaking, the harquebusiers were already in the process of replacing the arquebus with the larger-calibre carbine. Carbines were certainly known in Copenhagen in 1600, when 100 such weapons were exported to Sweden.[50] Yet the arquebus remained the more common cavalry weapon.

---

46 Jakobsson, *Lantmilitär beväpning och beklädnad*, pp.155–56.
47 Blom, *Kristian Den Fjerdes Artilleri*, pp.310, 312.
48 Christian IV's Articles of War of 1611, Cavalry Regulations (*Rytter-Ret*), Article 54.
49 Josef Alm, *Eldhandvapen 1: Från deras tidigaste förekomst till slaglåsets allmänna införande* (Stockholm: Rediviva, 1976), pp.196–97.
50 Jakobsson, *Lantmilitär beväpning och beklädnad*, p.9.

THE DANISH MILITARY ESTABLISHMENT

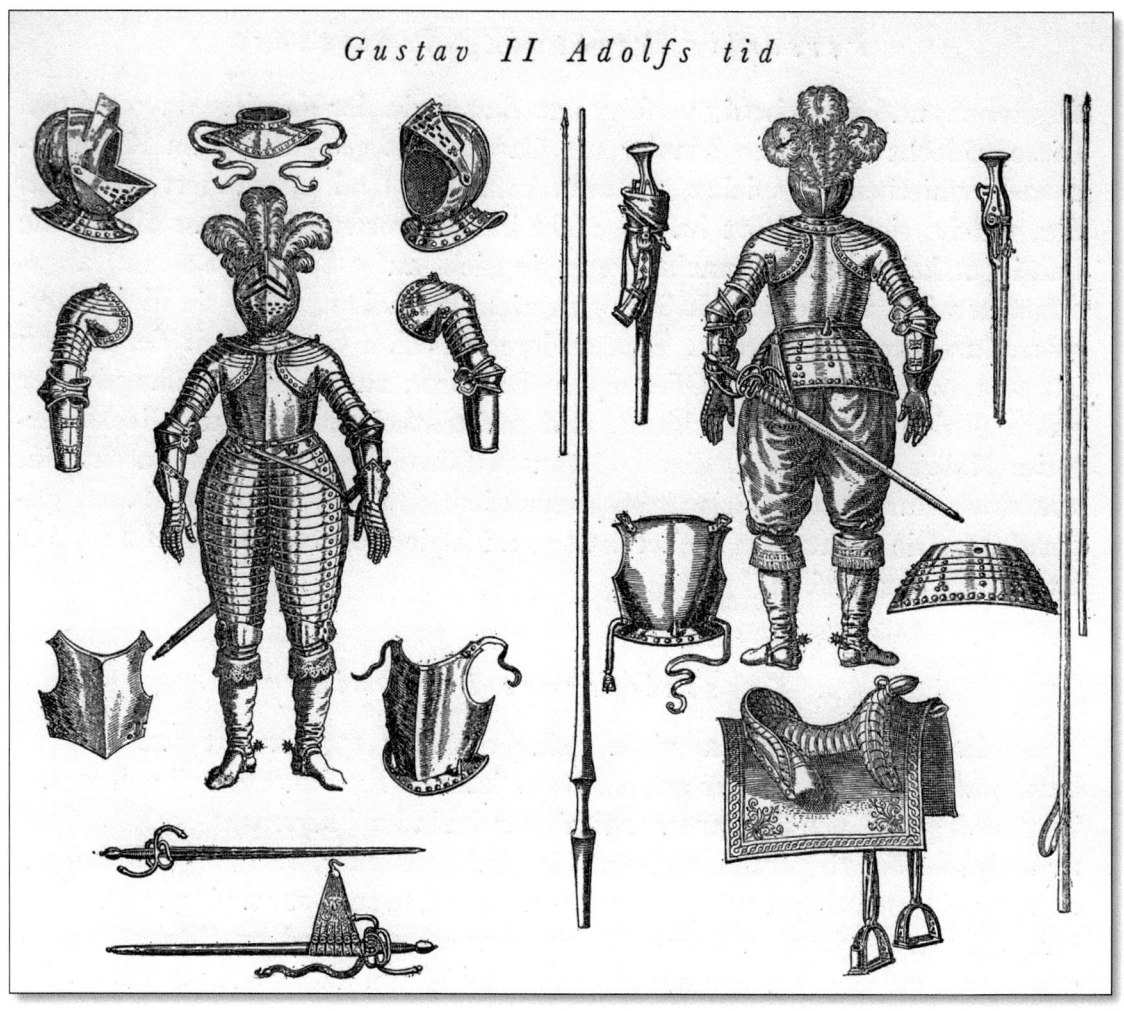

Above: Cuirassier armour. (Wallhausen, *Kriegskunst zu Pferdt*)

Facing page:
Full set of blackened, Danish, shot-proof cuirassier armour, 1620–1650 (Army Museum, Stockholm)

Blackened, Danish cuirassier's visored helmet, 1620–1650 (Army Museum, Stockholm)

THE DANISH MILITARY ESTABLISHMENT

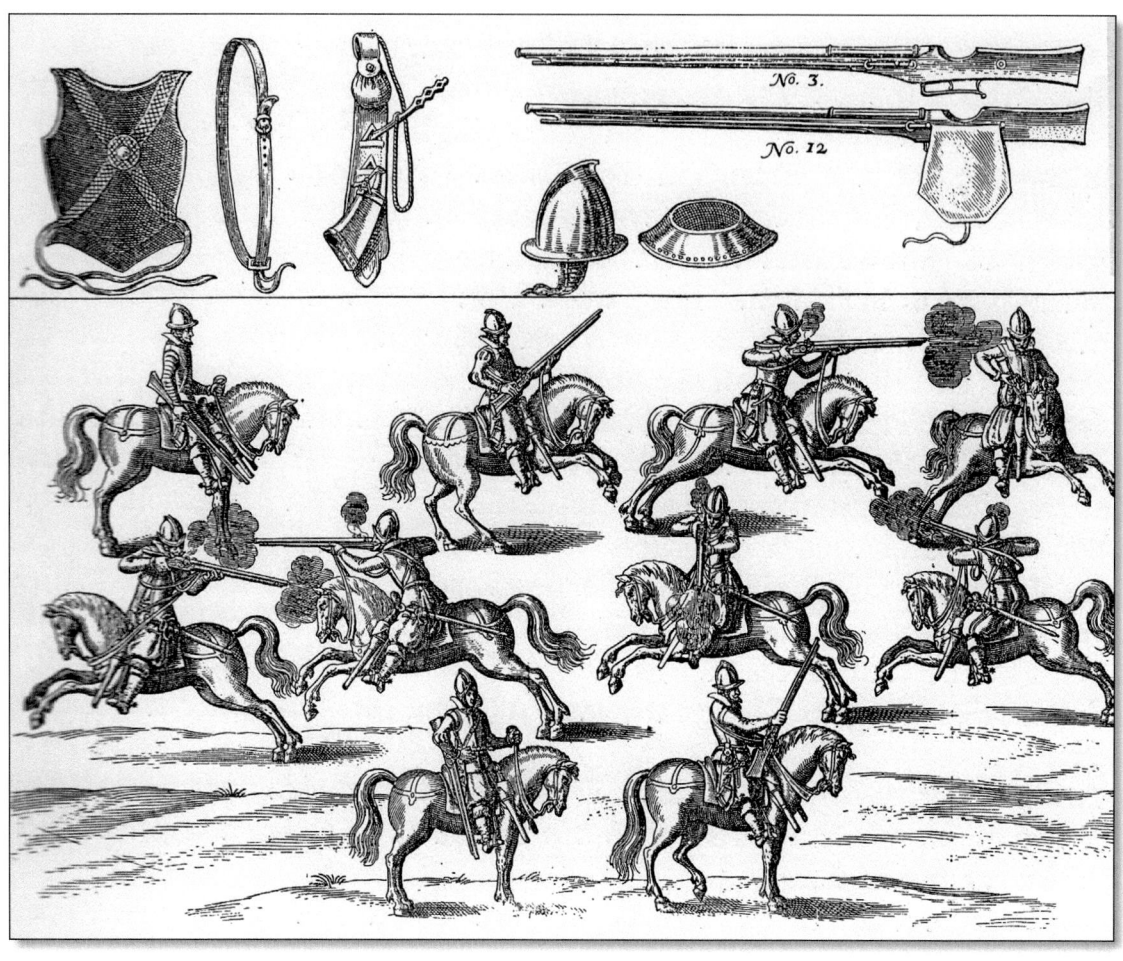

Above: Harquebusier weapons and equipment: breastplate, bandolier with arquebus hook, leather strap with ammunition pouch, wheellock spanner, gunpowder flasks, arquebuses, one with lock cover, helmet, and gorget. (Wallhausen, *Kriegskunst zu Pferdt*)

Facing page: Dragoon with equipment. (Wallhausen, *Kriegskunst zu Pferdt*)

THE DANISH MILITARY ESTABLISHMENT

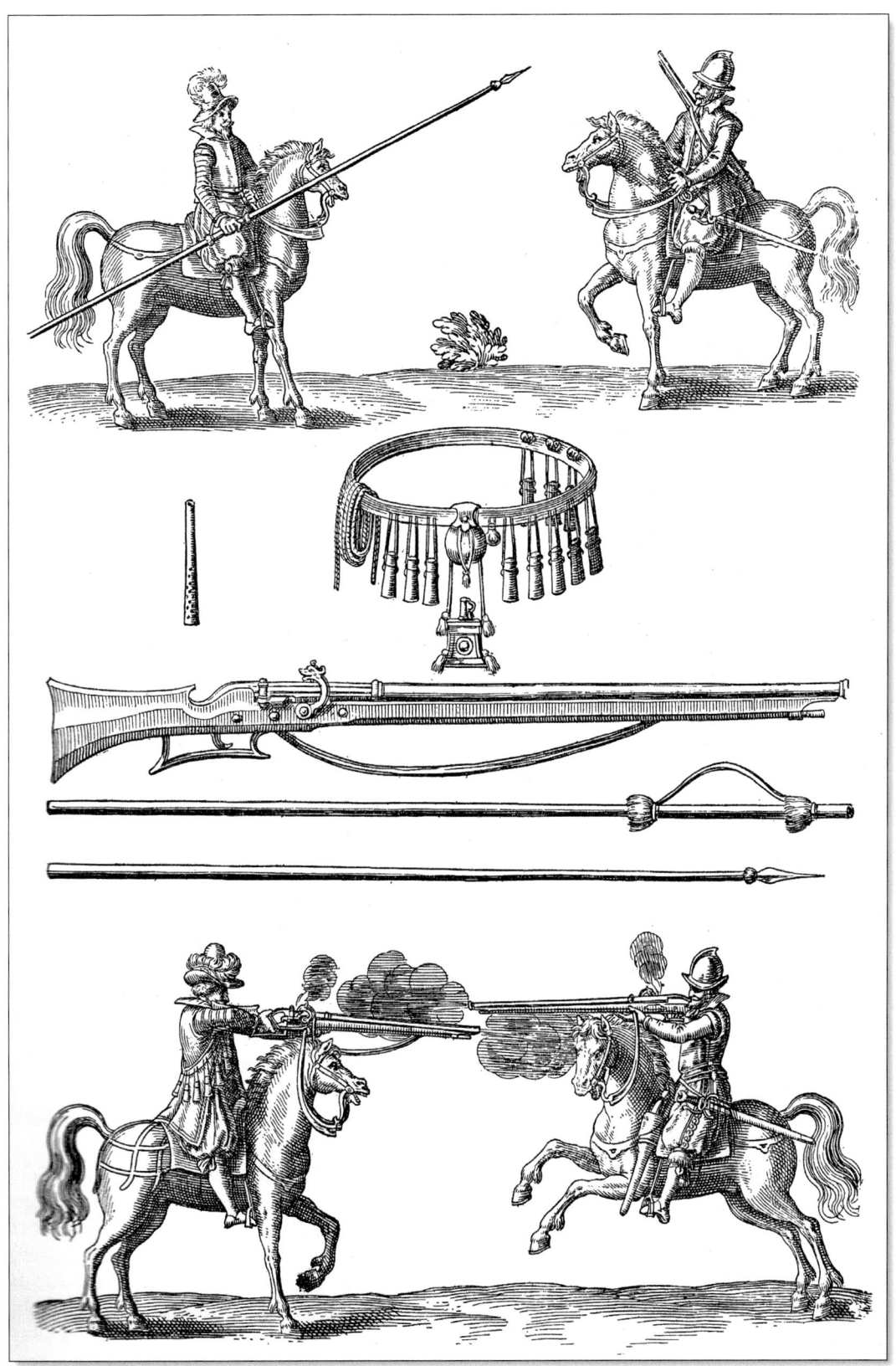

Dragoons

Among other enlisted units, the Danish Crown hired dragoons. These were mounted musketeers who moved on horseback but fought on foot. Each also carried a rapier. They typically wore shoes, not riding boots, and no spurs. We know of two dragoon units in Danish service during the Kalmar War. Both were enlisted in France by French officers.

Artillerymen

Denmark had adopted the Spanish–Dutch artillery system, which quickly was turning into the common standard for central and north European artillery. The Spanish–Dutch system matured in 1609, when General of Artillery in the Spanish Netherlands Charles Bonaventure de Longueval (1571–1621), Count of Bucquoy, together with the artillery professionals Cristóbal Lechuga (d. 1621) and Diego Ufano (fl. 1609–1612) simplified and reduced the large number of previous artillery calibres into a comprehensive system of only four standard calibres. Ufano explained the need for reform: '… the diversity and great confusion among the old cannons caused a lot of effort and labour in obtaining the appropriate cannon balls. Nowadays we have but a single range of artillery, all based on the full cannon and its fractions drawn to the eighth, so the appropriate munitions are easy to obtain and handle'.[51] Within a year, an anonymous French translator was so enthusiastic about the innovation that he expanded upon Ufano's declaration of intent: '… all the necessary munitions are very easy to find. It is truly remarkable to be content with these four calibres'.[52]

The Spanish–Dutch system used the same terminology as the obsolete sixteenth-century German system, from which it had emerged, but for different calibres. First, as in the past, the new system divided the artillery into two basic classes: the short-barrelled, short-range siege artillery (German: *Mauerbrecher*, 'battering ram') and the long-barrelled, long-range field artillery (German: *Schlange*, 'snake'; better known as 'culverins' in other languages, ultimately from the Latin *coluber*, 'snake', and *colubrinus*, 'serpent-like'). The long-barrelled culverins were henceforth indeed regarded as the primary class of artillery since they were more versatile, higher-velocity weapons of longer range. While both classes of artillery were also used as shipboard cannons, the long-barrelled ones seem to have been preferred in this role.

---

51 Diego Ufano, *Tratado de la artilleria y uso della, platicado por el capitan Diego Ufano en las guerras de Flandes* (Brussels: Juan Momarte, 1613), p.38. Ufano's work is generally believed to have first appeared in 1612. Incidentally, Ufano seems to have been the first European artillery specialist to identify the origin of cannons and gunpowder in China.

52 Diego Ufano, *Artillerie, ou vraye instruction de l'arttillerie et de ses appurtenances* (Rouen: Jean Berthelin, 1628), pp.14–15. The first French edition was published in 1614 by Johann Theodor de Bry, who simultaneously had the book translated and published in German.

Table 2. The Spanish–Dutch artillery system

Artillery Type	English Name	German Name	French Name	Spanish Name	Munition (Calibre)[53]
Field (Culverin)	Full or whole culverin	*Volle* or *Ganze Feldschlange*	*couleurine commune*	*culebrina comun*	24
	Demi-culverin	*Halbe Feldschlange*	*demie couleurine*	*media culebrina*	12
	Quarter culverin	*Quartierschlange* or *Viertelschlange*	*quart de couleurine*	*quarto de culebrina*	6
	Falcon	*Falkon, Falkaune,* or *Achtelschlange*	*faulcon* or *faulconneau*	*falcon*	3
Siege	Full or whole cannon	*Volle* or *Ganze Kartaune*	*canon commun*	*cañon comun*	48
	Demi-cannon	*Halbkartaune*	*demie canon*	*medio cañon*	24
	Quarter cannon	*Quartierkartaune* or *Viertelkartaune*	*quart du canon*	*quarto de cañon*	12
	Eighth cannon	*Achtelkartaune*	*huictiesme du canon*	*octavo de cañon*	6

Each class of artillery was then divided into four standard calibres. The system used the 48-pounder as baseline for siege artillery and the 24-pounder as baseline for field artillery (see Table 2). In addition to the 48-pounder, the Spanish–Dutch artillery system made allowance for the continued use of the old *Doppelkartaune* or *cañon double*, a 96-pounder that was very difficult to move.[54] However, professionals soon noticed that even the 48-pounder was too heavy for easy operation. They also discovered that the 24-pounder was not only lighter, easier to move, and took up less space than the 48-pounder, but it also consumed less gunpowder and had a higher rate of fire yet produced almost the same effect against a masonry wall. Henceforth, the 24-pounder became the standard siege cannon, a position it would retain until the end of the nineteenth century when the 24-pounder was finally superseded by modern rifled artillery.

Although the Spanish–Dutch artillery system quickly became the common standard among professionals, different master artillerymen occasionally used inconsistent terminology. A quarter culverin might, for instance, be called a 'pelican', and the falcon (more properly, the eighth culverin) inspired the name 'falconet' for yet smaller-calibre, long-barrelled guns. Moreover, cannons for practical reasons often fired significantly lighter

---

53 Determined according to the base weight in pounds of iron of the appropriate cannon ball.
54 Interestingly, the German term '*Kartaune*' derives from from the Italian '*quartana bombarda*' (i.e. a quarter cannon). Now, it was the turn of the *Kartaune* to be subdivided into increasingly smaller fractions. Armies were rapidly exchanging the huge siege cannons of the past for more efficient light-weight models.

loads than their official rating would suggest.[55] Nonetheless, it is obvious from contemporary orders and reports that the north European armies fully embraced the Spanish–Dutch artillery system.

The Danish artillery park was extensive but still constituted of a large variety of types and calibres. In 1602, the Copenhagen bronze cannon inventory even included a huge 96-pounder (Danish: *dobbelt kartov*). There were six 48-pounders (*hele kartover*), twenty-one 36-pounders (*trekvarter kartover*), fourteen 24-pounders (*halve kartover*), some 12-pounders (*kvarter kartover*), and a large variety of older cannons. Many more cannons were of iron, including no less than fifty-seven 24-pounders.[56] The iron cannons were intended as siege artillery or for shipboard use and were generally regarded as inferior. Iron cannons were much cheaper than bronze cannons. However, they were also heavier since iron is weaker than bronze and an iron cannon accordingly needs a thicker barrel. Moreover, if suffering from manufacturing flaws, iron cannons might burst without warning. Bronze cannons might burst, too, but if so, would usually show a revealing swell first.

The long-barrelled culverins were generally lighter. They might be used during sieges or on ships, but some were included in the field artillery. Of those cast of bronze, the Copenhagen Arsenal included a dozen 24-pounders (Danish: *hele slange*, *nothslange*, or *hele feltslange*, 'field snake'), an equal number of 18-pounders (*trekvarter slanger*), as many as sixty-five 12-pounders (*halve slanger*), and three 6-pounders (*kvarter slanger*). Again, many more long-barrelled cannons were made of iron. Most were certainly intended for shipboard use rather than siege or field artillery. However, the Arsenal also included 33 smaller-calibre, long-barrelled cannons known as falcons (*falkonner*) or sakers (*sagere*) and, of even smaller calibre, 48 falconets (*falkonetter*).[57] Danish falcons often seem to have been two-pounders or thereabouts, while most falconets may have been one-pounders. Among the smallest pieces of ordnance were the long-barrelled serpentines or serpentinels (*skerpentiner*), which had calibres of around 30–40 mm and essentially functioned as heavy-duty sniper guns (a comparison to the modern-day anti-tank gun might be appropriate). In 1602, the Copenhagen Arsenal had eight of them.[58]

Finally, there were mortars and petards, which were used for siege operations. In the years from 1604 to 1607, the Danish Crown acquired several iron mortars rated at respectively 60 and 30 pounds. The former

---

55 This, together with differences imposed by the quality of gunpowder, made some contemporary descriptions of artillery fire so unlike the manuals by Ufano and others that misunderstandings frequently arose among later scholars regarding the respective calibre–weight ratios of the two classes of cannons.

56 Blom, *Kristian Den Fjerdes Artilleri*, pp.146–47; Jakobsson, *Lantmilitär beväpning och beklädnad*, pp.68–69.

57 The falcons and sakers may or not have been identical, but the terms share the same origin. The term 'saker' derives from the Arabic '*saqr*' (falcon). Some suggest that the Danish falconet was heavier than the falcon. Blom, *Kristian Den Fjerdes Artilleri*, pp.169–71. Yet this seems unlikely.

58 Jakobsson, *Lantmilitär beväpning och beklädnad*, pp.68–69.

THE DANISH MILITARY ESTABLISHMENT

mostly weighted 655 kg, the latter 204 kg. Petards are known to have been frequently used during assaults on fortified positions during the Kalmar War, for instance, that on Gullberg Castle in 1612. They ranged from a weight of 61 to 200 pounds (21 to 68 kg).[59] Most small-calibre cannons were intended for shipboard use. There was also a field artillery, consisting of lesser pieces. However, it lacked mobility, which often precluded it from being put to efficient use. A particular Danish problem with artillery was that the country lacked the raw materials to produce bronze. As a result, the Danish artillery consisted of far more iron than bronze cannons.

In addition to other weapons, hand grenades were in common use, especially during sieges. These were handled by artillerymen. Since artillerymen also served as sappers, they carried a variety of tools such as pickaxes, spades, shovels, and axes. In 1608, the Copenhagen Arsenal included a total of 8,400 spades and even more shovels. On the battlefield, artillerymen also spread caltrops. In the year 1607–1608, the Copenhagen Arsenal purchased as many as 53,000 caltrops.[60] Artillerymen were armed with muskets and rapiers for personal protection and as a means to protect their cannons.

Petard attached to a gate, with its constituent parts on the floor below. (Christoph Dambach, *Büchsenmeisterey*, 1605)

Naval Personnel

Denmark manufactured both cannons and sidearms for its navy. As noted, most naval cannons were inferior-quality iron guns. Naval sidearms included some kind of naval sword (Danish: *entresverd*, 'boarding sword'), although neither depiction nor specimen seems to have survived into the present. Possibly, they were akin to the rapiers used by the infantry or, indeed, the short cutlasses that also existed. In addition, Denmark manufactured broad longswords for naval use that either had no point or only a blunt one. These so-called 'command swords' were given to admirals and ship captains. This was a sixteenth-century custom that the navy still retained.

Uniforms

We have only limited information on uniforms for the Danish army at the time. During King Christian's visit of state to England in 1606, an observer described the officers and men of his court as uniformed in rich garments:

> His Pages, and garde of his person, in Blew Veluet laide with Siluer Lace, for their best sute, and one sute for to exchange of other silke: whitish coloured Hattes, with bands embrodered: most of them, either white or blew stockins: his

---

59 Jakobsson, *Lantmilitär beväpning och beklädnad*, pp.306–07.
60 Jakobsson, *Lantmilitär beväpning och beklädnad*, p.312.

Trumpetors in white Satten Dublets, Blew Veluet hose trimd with silke and siluer lace, watched cloakes guarded with sundry colours, & white Hattes with Blew silke and golde bands embrodered: his common garde of Souldiers, with Muskets furnished, very riche: white Fustian dublets, watched hoase with white and Blew Lace, loose Casackes large and faire, like our foot-mens coates, with white and Blew lace, Hattes with bands suted like: and all his common souldiers, in casacks and hoase of watched colour: the maister and his mates, Gunners and chiefe officers, being very riche in their apparell, his Trunckes and other prouision for carriage, couered with redde Veluet, trimmed with blew Silke and Golde lace: his Sumpter clothes and couerings to couer his lading, of redde Veluet, with blew silke, and gold lace, all made after the English fashion.[61]

A supplementary description of the Danish trumpeters from the same visit of state reports on them, too: 'Then follow the Denmarke Kinges Trumpeters, beeing aleuen in all, decently attyred after our English fashion, in Cloackes of Watched, guarded with blacke and striped white; Blew Veluet Hose, and white Satten Doublets trimmed with Siluer Lace; White Hattes, with Bandes imbrodered with Gold.'[62]

While we cannot know how typical these garments were, the descriptions allow us to recreate the uniforms of the Danish guard units and their officers. The Drabant Guards wore garments made of blue velvet with silver lace, white hats with embroidered bands in probably blue and gold, and white or blue stockings. The trumpeters seem to have worn the same uniform but with satin doublets trimmed with silver lace and nonuniform cloaks trimmed in black and white or gold, presumably to distinguish them from other soldiers. Musketeers (of the Royal Guard, we may presume) wore white doublets of durable cloth woven from cotton, breeches and casacks trimmed with white and blue lace, and presumably white hats again with embroidered bands in probably blue and gold.[63] Officers wore garments of red velvet, trimmed with blue and gold lace.

When the retinue of nobles was reorganised in 1609, the three newly established Jutland banners became known by their respective colours. The Aarhus Banner was called the 'White Banner', the Aalborg Banner was named the 'Red Banner', and the Ribe Banner henceforth was called the 'Yellow Banner'.[64] Did these colours derive from their cornets, uniforms, or both? In 1611, Danish cuirassiers were ordered to wear 'cuirassier coats' in the same colours as their standard, instead of the customary field signs (more on

---

61 Roberts, *Most Royall and Honourable Entertainement*, pp.4–5.
62 Roberts, *Most Royall and Honourable Entertainement*, pp.20–21.
63 The casack was an outer upper garment that was popular with soldiers. The garment, as used in northern Europe, was probably of Eastern, possibly Hungarian, origin. However, by this time, the word 'casack' may have meant no more than a military-style coat, possibly of tunic form, with short sleeves or shoulder pieces and open at the sides (i.e. a tabard-like coat). Such cloaks had a long history as working garments and should not be confused with the elaborate dress emblazoned on the front and back that was used by heralds.
64 Larsen, *Kalmarkrigen*, p.8.

which later).⁶⁵ The obvious conclusion is that at least these three banners of the retinue of nobles wore uniforms, and that their names mirrored both the colour of their cornet and their uniform. Contemporary illustrations show that cuirassier coats were used also in the Dutch Republic.

The later seventeenth-century historian Johan Widekindi may give some further information. Widekindi described how units under Breide Rantzau in May 1612 included Marquard von Pentz's first unit of 300 cavalry dressed in white coats under two 'blind' (i.e. white) cornets, Pentz's second unit dressed in red coats (250 men), yet another unit in yellow coats (230 men), and a specifically Danish unit in blue coats (300 men).⁶⁶ Pentz's units were enlisted. It is plausible that a colonel of an enlisted unit would purchase cloth for all his men at the same time, which would produce a uniform colour of the type described. What speaks in favour of the veracity of Widekindi's description is that he mainly relied on original sources, some of which have since been lost. We also know that contemporary sources made similar references, among them a comment about Tessen von Parsow's 'white-coats' at the 1611 siege of Kalmar, almost certainly a reference to a company (*fähnlein*) within his infantry regiment.⁶⁷ Moreover, the new Danish national units raised in 1618, after the Kalmar War, received casacks in unit colours.⁶⁸ There is thus little doubt that some Danish units wore garments of uniform colour.

More certain is the use of field signs to distinguish between friend and foe. In 1611, in his Articles of War, King Christian prescribed the use of red and yellow bands as a field sign for his soldiers. Ominously, the Article continues, 'Should anybody be found without it, he will be regarded as an enemy.'⁶⁹ We know from later data that red and yellow bands then were used as field signs for soldiers from the Kingdom (i.e. Jutland, the Danish islands, and the Scanias) and Schleswig, while soldiers from Holstein instead wore red and white bands. Possibly, this usage reflected an older tradition that also existed at the time of the Kalmar War.

---

65 Madsen, 'Om Rytteriet', p.454.

66 Johan Widekindi, *Then fordom Stormächtigste, Högborne Furstes och Herres Herr Gustaff Adolphs den Andres och Stores Sweriges, Götes och Wändes etc. konungs Historia, och Lefwernes Beskrifning, Then Första Deel* (Stockholm: Niclas Wankijf, 1691), p.90. Widekindi spells the name 'Pentz' as 'Bensen', a common spelling at the time.

67 Anon. [Ernst Werckman], 'Journal über alles des Jenige, so sich in dem so genannten Calmarschen Krieg zugetragen', in H. Rørdam (ed.), *Monumenta Historiæ Danicæ. Historiske kildeskrifter og bearbejdelser af dansk historie, især fra det 16. Aarhundrede* (Copenhagen: G. E. C. Gad, 1887), pp.697–98.

68 Jakobsson, *Lantmilitär beväpning och beklädnad*, p.393.

69 Christian IV's Articles of War of 1611, Article 71. Strictly speaking, the article only mentions the requirement to wear the field sign. The use of red and yellow bands, the colours of the House of Oldenburg, derived from King Frederick II's Articles of War of 1563, and there is good reason to believe that the same colours remained in use under King Christian since they were also used later. Madsen, 'Om Fodfolket', p.214.

THE KALMAR WAR

Cuirassier in a cuirassier coat, as seen from the side, rear and front. This style of buttoned casack was of Eastern origin. (Jacob de Gheyn II, *Die Reitschule oder Übungen der Kavallerie* (Amsterdam: C. J. Visscher, 1599–1600))

THE DANISH MILITARY ESTABLISHMENT

Banners

Early seventeenth-century infantry colours remained at three to four metres in breadth and length. Each was carried in a short hand grip, less than about 30 cm in length. Cavalry units carried standards of a type known as a cornet. The cornet was usually about 50–55 cm in breadth and 50–70 cm in length and edged with a fringe of thread. Based on surviving specimen, a cornet pole was shaped like a fluted lance and usually painted. Since all dragoon units were enlisted, we can assume that dragoon guidons had swallowtails in the Continental style. As far is known, they commonly were about one metre in breadth and 1.4–1.8 m in length.

Danish national infantry colours, as well as possibly cavalry cornets, apparently invariably included the red and white Danish flag in canton. This practice may not have extended to the enlisted, foreign units.

A list from 1607 mentions seven newly delivered infantry colours. All carried animal motifs, respectively described as 'a lion on a blue field, a swan on an orange field, a tiger on a pale yellow field, an ostrich on a green field, a horse on a red field, a salmon on a yellow field, and a stag on a white field'.[70]

Regimental Music

The music played an important role in maintaining order since it could be used for signalling on the field of battle and elsewhere. The music, no doubt, was also intended to reinforce the men's morale both in battle and on the march. By tradition, trumpeters were also used as envoys, for instance, when discussing conditions of surrender.

Colours and standards, as well as musical instruments, were regarded as important trophies, so they were eagerly captured in battle. It was deemed a disgrace to lose a standard since a captured standard was a sure sign of defeat. However, the loss of standards and musical instruments also made it difficult to gather and reorganise the survivors since standards and music were important means of leading a military unit.

Danish cavalry units included trumpeters, while the infantry included drummers and pipers. Only drums were stored in the arsenals, so we can assume that trumpets and pipes were, if not individually owned, at least used by dedicated individuals.[71]

---

70 Blom, *Kristian Den Fjerdes Artilleri*, pp.325–26.
71 Blom, *Kristian Den Fjerdes Artilleri*, p.326.

THE DANISH MILITARY ESTABLISHMENT

Dutch cavalry trumpeter in partial armour and cuirassier coat. Cavalry trumpeters in Danish service would have dressed in a similar manner, especially since many were Dutchmen. (Jacob de Gheyn II, *Die Reitschule oder Übungen der Kavallerie*)

The Armament Industry

Denmark hardly had an armament industry at the outbreak of war. Small quantities of firearms were manufactured at Kronborg in the years 1600–1603 and 1610, but these were clearly insufficient to support the army's needs. Most firearms, primarily muskets, were accordingly imported, typically from manufacturers in Hamburg, Schmalkalden, Bremen, Emden, The Hague, and Amsterdam.[72]

The situation was similar with artillery. In the sixteenth century, Denmark had only one state foundry capable of manufacturing cannons. It was located in Copenhagen. The failure to provide sufficient cannons during the Nordic Seven Years' War had showed that production capacity was insufficient, so, in 1586, the foundry was expanded and moved into a former monastery seized from the Catholic Church. The foundry cast bronze cannons, but neither Denmark nor Norway had indigenous copper ore deposits, so most bronze

---

72 Jakobsson, *Lantmilitär beväpning och beklädnad*, pp.159–60.

derived from recycled supplies from primarily church bells but also obsolete cannons and even cooking implements.

During the Nordic Seven Years' War, the Danish Crown also began importing large numbers of cast iron cannons from England. Despite the known inferiority of cast iron cannons as compared to those of bronze, the Danish Crown continued to import cast iron cannons. Between 1566 and 1579, Denmark imported over 500 such cannons. King Christian accordingly inherited a large artillery park in 1597, consisting of 171 bronze cannons, 306 cast iron cannons, and 359 older and smaller wrought iron cannons. Most were intended for shipboard use.[73]

In 1599 or 1600, King Christian established a new cannon foundry at Helsingør. To safeguard the availability of raw materials, he ordered additional confiscations of church bells in 1601 and an export ban on copper goods in 1603. In 1602 or early 1603, he ordered one hundred 16-pounder bronze cannons to be cast by the two foundries according to the same specifications in an attempt to introduce a degree of standardisation. Notably, the attempt to introduce standardisation nonetheless departed from what was growing into the aforementioned Spanish–Dutch cannon classification system. The order, effectuated by two master foundrymen Borchard Quelkmeyer in Copenhagen and Hans Wolfenfelder in Helsingør, took four years to complete. Quelkmeyer completed his order in 1605, while Wolfenfelder only did so in 1608, presumably because of the smaller capacity of this recently established foundry. The cannons were named 'Old Kings' (Danish: *gamle Konger*) since each was named after and carried the picture of one of Denmark's past historic or mythical kings. The average weight of the Old Kings was 834 kg, and each fired 4.8 kg shots. These cannons were the most advanced guns produced in Denmark at the time. As soon as this order was completed, King Christian ordered the casting of at least 42 considerably more light-weight bronze cannons of the same calibre and length. These cannons, known as 'Triangles' (*Triangler*), had an average weight of 527 kg but employed shot of the same weight as Old Kings did, 4.8 kg. The gunpowder charge was significantly smaller, however, which would have affected range and hitting power.[74] The term 'Triangles' was then commonplace for light-weight cannons that could only take a reduced charge. The early attempt at standardisation was soon forgotten, however, and henceforth King Christian ordered large numbers of cannons of all calibres, sizes, and weights. While the King was eager for carrying out tests of the various types of cannons and willing to experiment, the overall impression is that of a man who wanted to impose his perceived need for control in the production process yet lacked the in-depth knowledge of artillery systems needed to introduce a standardised system.

Gunpowder was mostly manufactured within the country. The Crown owned one gunpowder factory at Lyngby, near Copenhagen. A major gunpowder factory under private ownership was established in Flensburg,

---

73 Martin Bellamy, *Christian IV and His Navy: A Political and Administrative History of the Danish Navy 1596–1648* (Leiden: Brill, 2006), p.130.

74 Jakobsson, *Lantmilitär beväpning och beklädnad*, p.301.

on Jutland, in 1599. Small-scale gunpowder production facilities existed in most towns. By the time of the Kalmar War, Danish gunpowder seems to have been of high quality. In 1611, soldiers were ordered to load only a third of the amount of gunpowder previously used since the new supplies were more powerful and otherwise might cause the barrel to burst.

In 1610, the King moved the Copenhagen foundry into new and bigger buildings. He hired foreign master foundrymen, primarily from Germany. Those wrought iron cannons that were clearly obsolete were scrapped. Altogether, King Christian had more than 200 bronze cannons cast in the decade that led up to the Kalmar War. From 1605 onwards, he resumed the import of cast iron cannons from England, with one contractor alone supplying at least 150. Since iron cannons lacked the ornaments on bronze cannons, they lacked names (along the line of the Old Kings) and were instead referred to according to calibre. By 1610, the Danish Crown had 437 bronze cannons, 811 cast iron cannons, and 166 wrought iron cannons in its inventory. More than two-thirds of the cannons were guns of the largest calibre (up from one-third in 1597).[75] King Christian was well prepared for the planned war with Sweden.

Castles and Fortresses

As noted, in times of peace, the only active units within the Danish military establishment were those that garrisoned important castles and fortresses. In 1611, the Danish Crown had garrisons and field units on Zealand (at Kronborg and Copenhagen), in Holstein along the southern border (at Krempe), in Halland (at Halmstad), and on the islands of Bornholm, Gotland, and Ösel. In Norway, the strongest fortress was Bohus Castle in Bohuslän province, the primary Norwegian bulwark against Swedish intrusions. Other Norwegian fortresses (more on which later) were both weaker and less exposed. Originally a medieval castle, King Christian had, in the years 1593–1604, modernised and refurbished Bohus Castle into a strong and magnificent renaissance fortress with modern bastions, magnificent gables, and strong towers.[76] In Halland, the main castle was in Halmstad, the fortifications of which were modernised by the Flemish architect Hans van Steenwinckel from 1598 onwards. There were also castles in Varberg, repaired and modernised by Steenwinckel from 1588 onwards, and Laholm, on which a major, not yet concluded, modernisation project had begun in 1610. The Scanian side of the Sound was defended by strong but old-style fortresses in Helsingborg, Landskrona, and Malmö. There were no substantial fortifications in eastern Scania and Blekinge before King Christian, in 1599, built Christianopel with bastions in the modern manner, a project again led by the hard-working Steenwinckel.

---

75 Jakobsson, *Lantmilitär beväpning och beklädnad*, p.301; Bellamy, *Christian IV and His Navy*, pp.130–31.

76 In its long history, Bohus Castle was under siege at least 14 times (12 times by Swedes, twice by Norwegians and Danes) but never fell to enemy action. Built in 1308, it was last attacked in 1676 and 1678 by the Danes during the Scanian War.

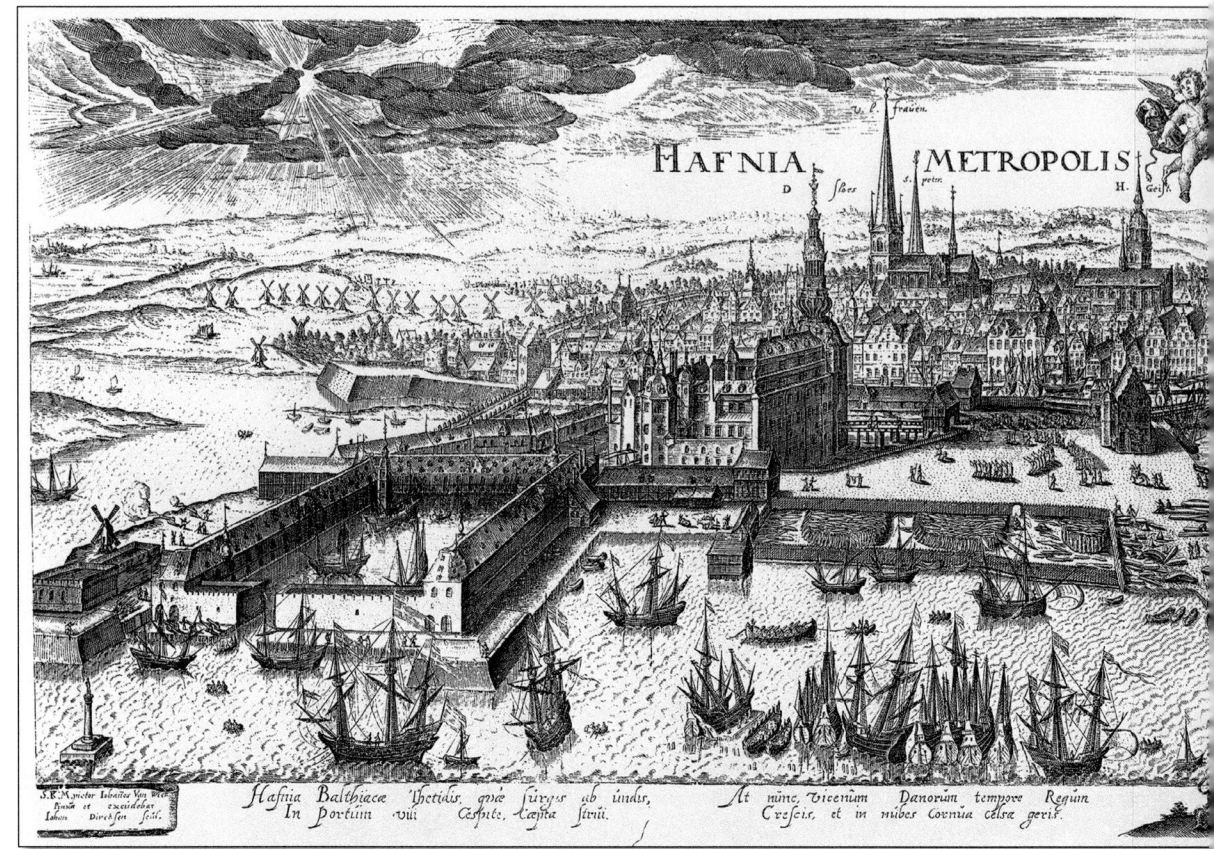

The Navy

Warship Strength

Denmark and Norway had separate armies, but the navy was a common undertaking. The navy had developed further than the army and already had a more permanent structure. While German officers dominated King Christian's army, his navy was mostly crewed and officered by Danes and Norwegians, with a significant share of Dutchmen. This ensured that the navy was abreast with technical and tactical developments in naval warfare as it was practiced on the Continent. A key reason for the navy's fundamentally native composition was the reliance on conscription. The practical need of everybody aboard the ship communicating in the same language may have been a factor, too.

As noted, King Christian regarded the navy as his personal possession and one that he could use to further his own influence at home and abroad. The Council recognised the need for a strong navy but regarded it as an instrument of the state and was less eager to employ it as a tool of foreign expansion.

The construction of warships was, at first, primarily handled by foreign shipwrights. This enabled King Christian to acquire professional skills from abroad while still maintaining political and centralised control by avoiding the need to involve the Danish nobility. Until the 1590s, the Danish Crown

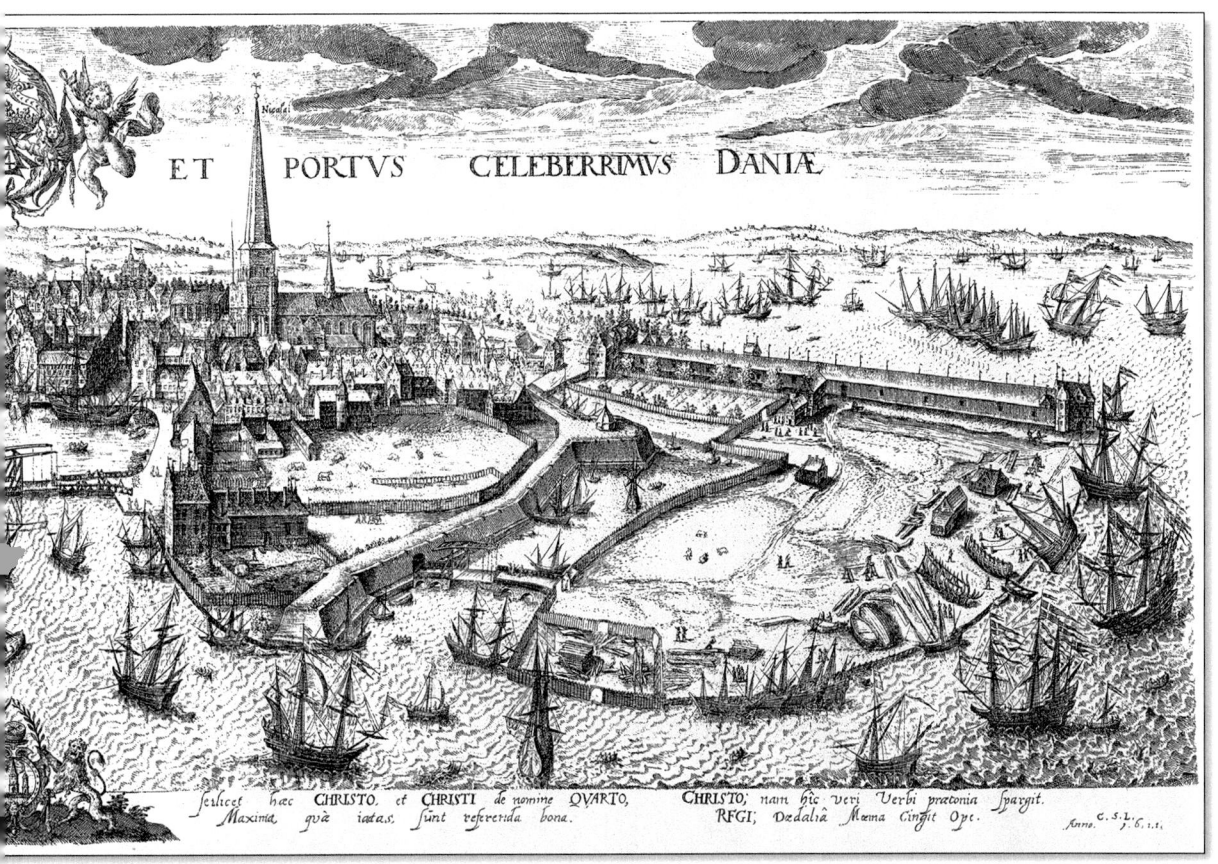

Copenhagen, as seen from Amager Island. Left: the enclosed Armoury. Right: the naval dockyard of Bremerholm, immediately east of the city wall. (Hafnia Metropolis, engraving by Jan Dircksen van Campen, after a painting by Johan Classzen van Wijck, 1611; Royal Library, Copenhagen)

primarily hired English shipwrights, but then relations deteriorated because of disputes concerning trading and fishing rights. From his ascension to the throne in 1596, King Christian instead began to hire Scottish shipwrights – the first Robert Peterson, who received a contract to build an originally 44-gun warship to be called the *Victor* on Crown land at Haderslev in southern Jutland. King Christian liked the ship and frequently used it. In the following year, Peterson was followed, and ultimately surpassed, by David Balfour, who in 1597 was awarded a contract to first build a 24-oar galley in Copenhagen and then a 30-oar galley in the province of Blekinge. In 1599, the Crown contracted Balfour to build a 54-gun warship to be called the *Argo*, the first of several conventional warships that he built for King Christian. Balfour was then taken on as a state employee. Within a few years, Balfour built yet another large warship but this time as a fully independent contractor at Flensburg. Soon, he also built warships in Norway and Holstein. During the Kalmar War, yet another Scottish shipwright, Daniel Sinclair, went into business as a private contractor in Denmark. Both Sinclair and Balfour were employed at the naval shipyard at Bremerholm, in Copenhagen, after the war.[77]

---

77 Bellamy, *Christian IV and His Navy*, pp.104–09.

In addition to skilled workers, the Danish Crown regularly sent convicts and prisoners of war (POWs) clapped in iron to work at the shipyard. The practice had begun in 1566 when orders were issued to round up as many vagrants, gypsies, beggars, thieves, and other undesirables as possible for use as forced shipyard labour. Henceforth, numerous convicted prisoners had to serve at Bremerholm, including those sentenced to death who had their sentences commuted to a life of hard labour there. When there were enough prisoners, some were also sent to carry out hard labour at Frederiksborg Castle, the Crown gardens, and the Arsenal. The naval shipyard was under the command of the admiral in charge of the dockyards, often referred to as the 'Port Admiral' (Danish: *Holmens amiral*). The Port Admiral was also responsible for the recruitment and examination of seamen and naval officers. When there was no Grand Admiral of the Realm, the Port Admiral was the senior naval officer in the fleet, and many spent long periods at sea, commanding the fleet. In 1610, the King appointed Godske Lindenow as Port Admiral. He very soon had to neglect his shipyard duties to take command at sea, and this situation continued until his death in 1612. In 1613, Steen Villumsen Rosenvinge was appointed the new Port Admiral.

The Scottish shipwrights were too few for King Christian's needs, so, from 1613 onwards, he encouraged private entrepreneurs from the Dutch Republic to establish shipyards on Crown lands in Schleswig and Holstein. The first seems to have been the Dutch private entrepreneur and shipwright Peter Michelsen.

At first, contracts for shipbuilding were fairly vague, with no specific dimensions or proportions beyond the statement that the new ship was to be built in a similar manner to a named, already existing ship. As a young prince, Christian had learnt shipbuilding from a professional shipwright during the construction of a small, three-masted ship. While it is now impossible to ascertain the depth of King Christian's knowledge of ship design, he was certainly sufficiently competent to understand ship plans and models. We know that his shipwrights used ship plans both on paper and in the form of three-dimensional wooden models. By 1610, some models were very large, requiring the use of numerous workmen and considerable volumes of materials for construction, in effect being a fully functioning scale model of the proposed design. King Christian personally reviewed the submitted designs from his shipwrights for approval and clearly understood what to look for. From 1613 onwards, when he first contracted a ship from Peter Michelsen, King Christian made sure to enter his requirements into the contract. The King specified essentially everything from keel length to the breadth and width of the transom, as well as the arrangement of decks, masts, rudder, gun ports, and even cabins. The King was apparently mostly influenced by English patterns, surely because of the long period of English and Scottish shipwrights, but, from the time of the Kalmar War, he approved designs that also display Dutch influences.[78]

---

78   Bellamy, *Christian IV and His Navy*, pp.100–101, 103, 118.

Unsurprisingly for a man as extroverted as King Christian, he was particularly interested in prestige ships of the largest type. He inherited the *Fortuna*, perhaps built in the early 1590s and reportedly of 1,400 tonnes, from his father, King Frederick II. However, the ship had poor sailing characteristics and spent most of her time in Copenhagen as a floating gun barge. Instead, he built the *Tre kroner* ('Three Crowns'), a large warship of 2,100 tonnes completed in 1604. Its name derived from the three crowns of Denmark, Norway, and Sweden, all of which had once constituted the Kalmar Union. It seems possible that King Christian named the warship thus in response to Swedish Duke Charles's (soon-to-be King Charles) 1599 warship of the same name.[79] King Christian brought the warship along on his voyage to England in 1606, where an observer noted that the *Tre kroner* was:

> a most huge ship … so adorned with rich gold and very excellent workemanship, as many thousands vpon report thereof, of purpose haue gone to Grauesend, where shee doth ryde, to view her. Besides, the beautie and riches of this great ship, she is appointed with most huge ordinance, men and victualls, fit for so Kingly a presence. The rest likewise accordingly complete, all riche in Ordinance, men and munition.[80]

Unfortunately, the *Tre kroner* had no better sailing characteristics than the *Fortuna*, so she, too, spent most of her time on display in Copenhagen. She participated in the Kalmar War but seems not to have engaged in combat.

In the mid sixteenth century, the Danish Crown introduced galleys into the navy. These were primarily used for the protection of coastal shipping against piracy. Galleys were based in several harbours, particularly in Norway. The galleys were either small versions of the Mediterranean galleass or square-rigged warships that could be powered either by sail or oar. Some may have been sailing ships with auxiliary oars. They had up to three masts and a gun deck above the oarsmen, equipped with several small-calibre transverse mounted cannons. Most Danish galleys were from 25–30 m long, had 30 to 50 oars, and could sail in squadron with regular sailing ships.[81] However, only one plan of an oared vessel has survived into the present, and it shows a Mediterranean-style galley section.[82] When on active duty, there is reason to believe that soldiers manned the oars. However, there is also some evidence that, at times, convicts from the Copenhagen naval shipyards were commandeered as rowers.[83]

---

79 Bellamy, *Christian IV and His Navy*, p.140.
80 Roberts, *Most Royall and Honourable Entertainement*, pp.3–4.
81 Thomas Hauge, 'Galeier i den dansk-norske marine', *Norsk Tidskrift for Sjøvesen*, 69 (1954), pp.351–58.
82 Bellamy, *Christian IV and His Navy*, p.143, citing *Rigsarkivet*, Søetatens Kort og Tegning Samling, Des. E.3.
83 Bellamy, *Christian IV and His Navy*, p.143.

THE KALMAR WAR

Danish warship, traditionally believed to represent the *Tre Kroner* during King Christian's visit of state to England in 1606. However, there is no evidence for this identification, and historians nowadays tend to regard the print as depicting a generic Danish warship. Be that as it may, it is certain that the print shows all the splendours expected by King Christian in one of his major warships. (Engraving by Jan Dircksen van Campen, after a drawing by Christian Møller; Royal Library, Copenhagen)

Interestingly, there was another, smaller class of galley called a 'rowing yacht' (Danish: *roersiacht*). At least some of them were reportedly 'built in the Norwegian manner'.[84] In the early seventeenth century, it was difficult to find a Norwegian shipwright who had the skills to build carvel ships, so this possibly meant that they were clinker-built in the old Viking tradition. Each rowing yacht carried around six small guns and 12 oars.

A yet smaller vessel was the skerry boat or gun boat, which constituted the Norwegian coastal navy (more on which later).

---

84 Warship deployment list, 6 December 1635, Bricka, Fridericia, and Skovgaard (eds), *Kong Christian den Fjerdes egenhændige Breve*, vol. 3, pp.451–52.

There seems to have been two types of indigenous cargo ships. One was a small, open-decked, clinker-built vessel that could carry a load of around 40 tons. Apparently deriving from the old Viking tradition, it might have been referred to with one of the generic names for 'ship' (Danish: *skude*; Swedish: *skuta*). Another cargo ship was the kray – a small, carvel-built, square-rigged merchantman with two or three masts and a cargo capacity of up to around 60 tons. This type was known in the Baltic as a *kraier* or, in Danish and Swedish, *krejer* or *krejare*.

Based on available records, dockyard accounts in particular, the number of warships in King Christian's fleet seems to have declined slightly from around 1600. While the number of large warships, never very great to begin with, dropped from three at the start of King Christian's reign to only one in 1603, this reflects the withdrawal from service of the older, obsolete warships. Moreover, the apparent overall decline is probably the result of the absence of preserved accounts rather than a real reduction. Very few dockyard accounts from the period 1600–1620 have survived in Danish archives. Even if there was a decline, it did not last long. Already before the Kalmar War, the number of warships available to the Danish navy again increased.

Table 3. Number of warships and galleys in the Danish navy[85]

Year	100–500	501–1,000	1,001–1,500	1,501–2,000	2,001–2,500	Total	Galleys[86]
1595	14	6	2	–	1	23	3
1600	11	7	1	–	1	20	5
1605	13	5	1	–	1	20	–
1610	23	7	1	–	1	32	–
1615	20	9	2	–	1	32	–
1620	21	8	3	–	1	33	–

Naval Officers and Sailors

By the time of the Kalmar War, there was no real separation of Denmark's armed forces on land and on water. The navy had not yet fully separated from the army. A group of officers were known as captains 'on land and at sea' (Danish: *til lands og til vands*). Most of their service took place at sea, and they were also known as 'ship's captains'. However, during mobilisation, some of them also had to serve as commanders of the levies raised to protect the borders. This certainly happened in 1603–1604. A small number also served on land during the Kalmar War, but, from this time onwards, those who did received commissions as army officers.

---

85 Warship numbers are divided into size groups of metric tons. Jan Glete, *Navies and Nations: Warships, Navies and State Building in Europe and America, 1500–1860* (Stockholm: Almqvist & Wiksell International, 1993), vol. 1, p.596; Bellamy, *Christian IV and His Navy*, pp.275–77.

86 The figures for galleys include only those identified with names. There were many more, probably dozens, but archive documents lack details.

The navy commonly employed about 600 permanent sailors. These were supplemented with a specified number of conscripts, provided by local officials, who had to serve for a fixed term, apparently five years in most cases (a term of five years was certainly stipulated in 1616). A sufficient number of men was apparently mostly found. In times of war, large numbers of men were conscripted into the navy, but the term regulations may have been largely ignored.[87] Cases are known, at least from later in the century, when foreign sailors who merely happened to be in Copenhagen were pressed into service.

In winter, the number of sailors was reduced to about 60 percent of the total as a cost-saving measure. Gunners were retained throughout the year, being merely returned to the Arsenal for service there during the winter months.

The total number of sailors who served at any given time during the Kalmar War is uncertain. It is likely that the total consisted of some 3,000 to 4,000 men, these figures known from later periods of war or crisis. The number is unlikely to have been lower than that of 1620, when 1,378 officers and men served in the navy.[88]

The best sailors were not the conscripts but those recruited, or pressed into service, from merchant ships. They already knew the tasks that had to be carried out. In addition, they were more resistant to the many diseases that commonly decimated naval crews since they already had encountered, and survived, some of them.

Except the Grand Admiral of the Realm and the Port Admiral, there was no permanent rank of admiral in the Danish navy. A captain who was placed in command of a squadron still retained the rank of captain and served as such on his own ship. If the King or the Grand Admiral commanded a fleet, he was accompanied by a flag captain (Danish: *flagkaptajn*), who served as captain on the flagship.

The captain was assisted by, at most, two commissioned lieutenants. A captain might, or not, have previous naval experience and was just as likely to receive orders to serve in the army. In fact, well into the 1620s, naval captains were still customarily appointed as 'captain on land and at sea' (Danish: *kaptajn til lands og til vands*), a vestige of the remaining lack of formal separation between the two services of army and navy.[89] Lieutenants might command smaller ships. However, unlike that of a captain, a lieutenant's commission seems to have been specific to the navy, appointing him 'ship's lieutenant' (*løjtnant til skibs*).[90]

In times of war, each warship was usually manned by soldiers. This contingent was commanded by a 'captain of soldiers' (*kaptajn over soldaterne*).

---

87 Bellamy, *Christian IV and His Navy*, pp.230–33.

88 Bellamy, *Christian IV and His Navy*, p.233.

89 Christian IV's Articles of War of 1611, preamble; Commission for Jens Vognsen, 23 February 1625. *Kancelliets Brevbøger vedrørende Danmarks indre Forhold, 1624–1626* (Copenhagen: Rigsarkivet, 1925), p.336.

90 At least, this was the form used a generation later. Commission for Frants van Steenwinckel, 10 April 1631. *Kancelliets Brevbøger vedrørende Danmarks indre Forhold, 1630–1632* (Copenhagen: Rigsarkivet, 1932), p.448.

He was commonly assisted by a 'lieutenant on land' (*løjtnant til lands*). If there was no army captain on board, the lieutenant might be promoted to lieutenant captain (Danish: *kaptajnløjtnant*; German: *Kapitainleutnant*), a title of Continental origin.

The senior non-commissioned officer (NCO) aboard was the ship's master (*skipper*), who was a professional mariner. Unlike the officers, he would stay with the ship throughout the winter since he was in charge of maintenance and preparations for the next sailing season. On a small ship or transport, the ship's master would be in sole command since no officer would serve on board. On a large ship, the ship's master was assisted by a master's mate (*underskipper*). Another important non-commissioned post was that of boatswain (*højbådsmand*), who supervised the common sailors (*bådsmænd*). There would then be a pilot (*styrmand*) who was responsible for navigation. A pilot had to supply his own navigational instruments. The sailing crew was divided into two watches, each of which included a leading sailor (*skibmand*) to assist the officer, usually a lieutenant, in command of the watch. A watch was subdivided into two quarters, each directed by a quartermaster (*kvartermester*). The sailing crew took turns on duty, with each watch spending four hours on duty at a time. The crew also included specialists of various kinds, including the cook, a carpenter (*tømmermand*) or sometimes several, and a drummer, trumpeter, piper, or shawm player for signalling. The master gunner (*arkelimester*) supervised the gunners (*bøsseskytter*) who directed the soldiers who were assigned to handle the shipboard artillery. A large ship would have a chaplain. Most ships would carry a barber surgeon.[91]

Following Continental practices, we have seen that King Christian issued Articles of War, in both Danish and German, that governed discipline within the army. Likewise, ship's articles were prepared to govern naval discipline and legislation. As far as is known, written ship's articles were first prepared in the early sixteenth century. They were issued to every warship before she set out. Most were similar, although they were not standardised and published until 1625, well after the Kalmar War.[92]

---

91 Bellamy, *Christian IV and His Navy*, pp.220–27, with additions from other materials.

92 This was earlier than in Sweden, where Gustavus Adolphus's Articles of War of 1621, although written for the army, were enforced for those serving on ships, too. Although a concept for a naval version of the articles was prepared in 1628, it was not really implemented until 1644, when special legislation for the Swedish navy was finally adopted. Skibsartikler, 8 May 1625, in V. A. Secher, *Corpus Constitutionum Daniæ: Forordninger, recesser og andre Kongelige Breve, 1558–1660* (Copenhagen: Gad, 1897), vol. 4, pp.256–87.

4

The Norwegian Military Establishment

Manpower and Armament Industry

Norway had a smaller population than Denmark. Although few population details from this period are known, and most recent studies only cover the territory of modern Norway, we can estimate Norway's population in the early seventeenth century as somewhere between 450,000 and 500,000, this figure including the population of the subsequently lost province of Bohuslän. Norway enjoyed high population growth and had done so for more than half a century. Because of this high population growth and the difficulties of subsistence farming caused by the climate, Norway functioned as a source of manpower for the Danish army and navy comparable to the role that we will see that Finland played for the Swedish army.

The permanent Norwegian military establishment was correspondingly small. In 1611, garrisons and field units in Norway were only based at Oslo, Bergen, and Bohus Castle.[1]

Generally, the Norwegian military establishment resembled both its Danish and Swedish counterparts in character. For instance, Norway made significantly more use of levies than Denmark, and, like in neighbouring Sweden, Norwegian levies were frequently used for offensive action in addition to border defence. In this, the Norwegian military was more similar to that of Sweden. Levies generally served on foot. On the other hand, most conventional military units based in Norway were sent from Denmark and accordingly followed Danish practices. The Norwegian and Danish nobility were highly integrated, too. We have already seen that the navy was a common undertaking between Denmark and Norway. For these reasons, such military practices that were the same in Norway and Denmark will not be repeated in this chapter.

At the outbreak of war, King Christian expected Norway to raise an army of 6,000 men at Akershus Castle, near Oslo, under Governor General Enevold Kruse (1554–1621); 2,150 men at Trondheim under Steen Bille

---

[1] In 1624, King Christian renamed Oslo as 'Christiania' in honour of himself.

(1565–1629), the local *lensmand*; and 2,000 men in Bohuslän under Steen Laxmand (d. 1615), *lensmand* and commandant of Bohus Castle. The King also expected the Norwegian nobility to raise one or two banners of cavalry.[2] In hindsight, the figures appear ridiculously optimistic and, as Steen Bille responded, corresponded to a quarter of the male population (he attached the tax records to prove his point).[3] There was neither sufficient artillery nor gunpowder and shot. Yet King Christian apparently had high hopes that Norwegian invasion armies could be dispatched into Sweden from both Trondheim in the north and Bohus Castle in the south.

Norway did not yet have any modern armament industry. Akershus had the capacity to cast a few cannons, but output was limited. In 1610, King Christian contracted a German master foundryman, Paul Smelter, to establish ironworks at Bærum, near Oslo. Norway had iron ore reserves, so the plan was to produce iron cannons. However, the ironworks at Bærum seem not to have been completed until 1624. As a result, production never reached more than a few cannons per year, which was far from sufficient for Norwegian needs.[4]

Incidentally, the transformation of the defences of the old-style Bohus Castle (after its first modernisation project in 1567, led by the Flemish architect Hans Hendrik van Paesschen, who introduced the bastion system at Akershus Castle) was, from 1593 onwards, led by the same Hans van Steenwinckel who led most other such projects in King Christian's realms.

Chain of Command

Norway was ruled by a governor general appointed by the King. Once, Norway had its own government, the Council of the Realm, headed by the Lord High Chancellor of Norway (*Norge riges kansler*). However, in 1536, Copenhagen instituted direct rule by abolishing the Norwegian Council of the Realm. While Copenhagen retained the position of Lord High Chancellor of Norway, this office often stayed vacant for long periods. Henceforth, Copenhagen ruled Norway through an official known only as the Governor General of Norway (*Statholder i Norge*). Moreover, the Governor General usually doubled as *lensmand* of Akershus Castle, and his responsibilities and most of his authority were limited to this domain. As in Denmark, there were hardly any senior military commanders in times of peace and hence no real chain of command.

---

2   King Christian to Enevold Kruse, Steen Bille, and Steen Laxmand, 3 March, 4 March, 5 March 1611, *Norske Rigs-Registranter* (Christiania: Det norske historiske kildeskrift-fond, 1870), vol. 4, pp.408–12; Generalstaben, *Sveriges krig 1611–1632*, vol. 1, p.135. The Norwegian equivalent of the Danish *lensmand* was the *lensmann*. In modern Norwegian historiography, the term '*lensmann*', ultimately of Danish origin, is often replaced with '*lensherre*' to avoid confusion with a lower-ranking native Norwegian functionary, the (*bonde-*)*lensmann*, who essentially served as an intermediary between the *lensmann* and the peasants of his domain.

3   Steen Bille to Christian Friis, 28 March 1611. Christian C. A. Lange (ed.), *Norske Samlinger* (Christiania: Feilberg & Landmark, 1860), vol. 2, pp.42–45.

4   Jakobsson, *Lantmilitär beväpning och beklädnad*, p.307; Bellamy, *Christian IV and His Navy*, p.131.

THE KALMAR WAR

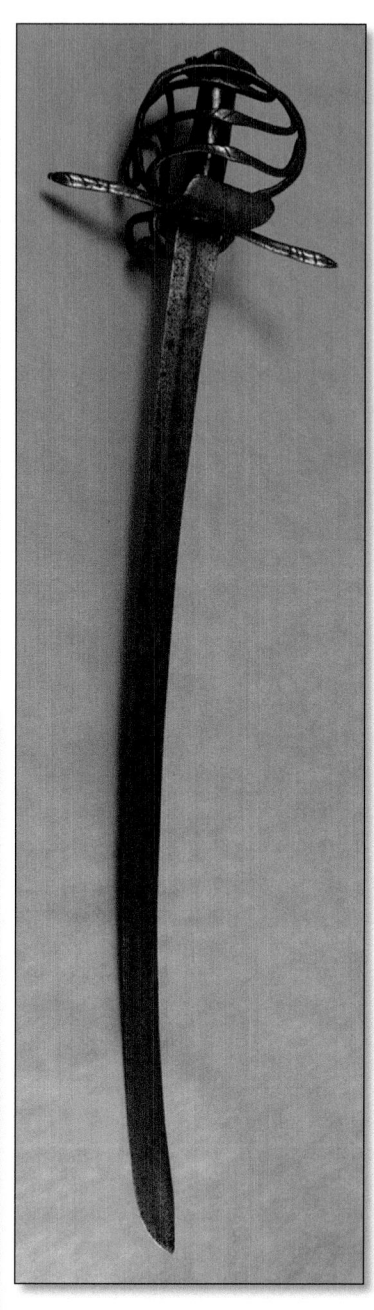

Late sixteenth-century *tessak* purchased for Norwegian levies, formerly of the Gösta Benckert collection. (Army Museum, Stockholm, AM.091090)

THE NORWEGIAN MILITARY ESTABLISHMENT

Above: Halberds and other weapons alleged to have been used by seventeenth-century Norwegian peasant levies (Nineteenth-century drawing)

Left and top left: Late sixteenth-century *tessak*. (Author's collection)

Military Organisation

Norway had a retinue of nobles that encompassed some 300 men. However, in the early 1600s, they never served as a combined cavalry unit. Instead, individual nobles served on horseback together with the peasant levies or else functioned as mounted scouts or messengers.[5] Any other units deployed in the country came from Denmark. There was no fixed establishment strength.

At the beginning of the war, there were, as noted, plans to form a Norwegian army of conscripts. While quite a few men were successfully called up, we do not know how many. The Norwegian military establishment made extensive use of levied peasants (Norwegian: *landeværn*, 'territorial defence'). Levies were raised through a quota that the peasants had to fill. They had to attend annual musters, which were very unpopular. Levied troops would not be trained, and they would have to pay for their own weapons and supplies. This meant that weapons were not uniform. In the Bergen region, for instance, the men preferred guns with matchlocks, while those in the Trondheim region relied on snaplocks. Levied troops were usually used to man defensive positions along the external borders, in effect operating as a border guard. The levied peasants would serve for a time and then be replaced by other levies from the same area. Occasionally, a professional captain was hired to train peasant levies.

In 1604, King Christian had regulated levy procedures and mandatory weapons and equipment for Norwegian peasants. Each owner of a full farmstead had to have a long arquebus with gunpowder and shot, a *tessak* (cutting sword), and an axe. Poorer peasants could dispense with the *tessak* or the axe but had to nonetheless own a long arquebus. Those with least land, or those who were employed by another peasant, needed only an iron-reinforced 'halberd' (presumably a poleaxe) and an axe. A farmstead worker should have a hunting spear and a *tessak*, or a spear and an axe if very poor. Any peasant who occupied an abandoned (i.e. ruined) farmstead only needed to arm himself after a period of three years and then with a halberd and a *tessak*.[6]

To assist the Norwegian peasants in acquiring acceptable weapons, King Christian purchased large quantities of arquebuses and sidearms, which the Crown then sold to the peasants at cost. From 1607 to 1610, a merchant in Bergen named Gregorius Kettvig delivered large amounts of weapons, including 6,366 cutlasses (*kortelasser*), 1,000 cavalry cutlasses (*ryttarkortelasser*), and much else besides.[7] Although we can assume that a cavalry cutlass was longer than a regular cutlass, it seems certain that all these weapons were of the type also known as *tessak*.

The *tessak* (from German: *Tisacke*, *Dusack*, *Dussägge*, or Czech: *tesák* – the origin of the name is disputed) was a new weapon in Norway, but it was

---

5 Larsen, *Kalmarkrigen*, p.8.
6 *Norske Rigs-Registranter*, vol. 4, p.72; Larsen, *Kalmarkrigen*, p.16; Alhaug, *Angrepet på Kalmar*, p.71.
7 Blom, *Kristian Den Fjerdes Artilleri*, p.310; Alm, *Blanka vapen*, p.30; Heribert Seitz, *Svärdet och värjan som armévapen* (Stockholm: Kungl. Armémuseum, 1955), pp.34–38, 92–94.

already considered obsolete on the Continent.[8] The Danish Crown acquired them as surplus weapons. The *tessak* was a cutting sword, occasionally curved but mostly straight and, unlike the Eastern sabre, always with a western hilt of the basket or clam-shell type. Blade length varied from about 55–83 cm, with a total length of up to 96 cm. Blade width usually ranged from three to five centimetres. Cavalry weapons were longer, with a blade length of about 101 cm and a total length of about 115 cm, but were otherwise similar.

The Coastal Navy

During the Nordic Seven Years' War, the King of Denmark and Norway had revived the traditional duty of Norwegian coastal regions to raise warships and crews. Several coastal towns were ordered to raise armed merchantmen. However, these auxiliaries had performed badly in the war, so the policy was effectively abandoned afterwards.[9] Although Denmark and Norway had separate armies, they shared the navy, which the Crown expected to primarily operate in Danish waters. Since Norway accordingly could not expect to receive much naval support in case of war, the Norwegians set up a distinct coastal navy, crewed by peasants from the coastal districts. The duty to build vessels was regulated in 1604, together with regulations on the raising of levies.[10] The coastal navy was raised upon orders of the King when faced with war. The coastal navy consisted of small vessels known as skerry boats (Norwegian: *skjærbåter*; Danish: *skærbåder*) or gun boats (Norwegian: *skyttebåter*; Danish: *skyttebåder*). Up to 15m in length, these vessels were open rowing boats that might carry a mast or two, although the chief means of propulsion was up to 20 oars. Each carried a crew of up to 60 men. A large skerry boat was typically armed with four falconets and, sometimes, a larger cannon in the bow.

The coastal navy also included galleys. We have only limited information on them. Galleys, at least those built in Denmark, carried three masts, the first two of which were square rigged and the third latin rigged. The Norwegian galleys were primarily or exclusively square rigged. Norwegian galleys are believed to have been decked vessels with 30 to 40 oars.[11]

For geographical reasons, the coastal navy did not play a major role in the Kalmar War.

---

8   The weapon was commonplace in southern Germany, Austria, and the western Balkans in the late fifteenth and sixteenth centuries and remained in use among peasants and brawny Viennese journeymen into the eighteenth century. Many believe that the term derives from the Old German '*sax*' (a single-edged short sword).

9   The policy was only reintroduced through an ordinance of 1630 whereby each Norwegian *len* was obligated to build a number of armed merchantmen (*defensionskibe*), the guns of which the traders, in times of peace, used to protect themselves from piracy. In times of war, the Crown could requisition the armed merchantmen as auxiliaries to the navy.

10 Larsen, *Kalmarkrigen*, p.20.

11 Hauge, 'Galeier', pp.351–71.

5

The Swedish Military Establishment

Manpower

By the early seventeenth century, Sweden had a small population, an underdeveloped and poorly monetised economy, and an agricultural base that suffered from a short growing season. The population constituted no more than an estimated 1,350,000: some 850,000 in Sweden, 350,000 in Finland, and 150,000 in Estonia. The military establishment was correspondingly small. While mobilisation potential was higher, the total Swedish military establishment rarely reached an actual strength exceeding 15,000 men, and expeditionary forces were usually no larger than 3,500 to 7,000 men.[1] The national army was thus no larger than it had been under King Gustavus I.[2] In 1600, King Charles asked parliament to agree to a permanent military organisation based on horse and foot not only raised in provincial regiments but also funded by the provinces. Parliament turned down the proposal to fund a standing army but agreed to the proposed provincial regimental organisation of horse and foot in peacetime since this corresponded to already existing practices.[3]

By tradition, most Swedish troops were raised in the Swedish and Finnish heartland. In 1612, about 85 percent of the soldiers came from Sweden and Finland.[4] In comparison, Estonia provided only a few men, and they were primarily enlisted. Sweden and Finland constituted the same country, with equal rights and obligations, and records typically do not specify ethnic or linguistic background. When troops were identified as deriving specifically from Sweden or Finland, this only meant that they were raised there, not

---

1. Michael Fredholm von Essen, *The Lion from the North: The Swedish Army during the Thirty Years War* (Warwick: Helion & Company, 2020), vol. 1, p.96.
2. Generalstaben, *Sveriges krig 1611–1632*, vol. 1, p.67.
3. Generalstaben, *Sveriges krig 1611–1632*, vol. 1, p.85.
4. Lars Ericson and Fred Sandstedt, *Fanornas folk: Den svenska arméns soldater under 1600-talets första hälft* (Stockholm: Armémuseum, 1982), pp.9–10.

that they were Swedish or Finnish speakers. The coastal areas of Finland were primarily Swedish speaking, and there were Finnish settlements in Sweden. From 1570 onwards, the number of Finnish troops in the army grew dramatically until Finns were disproportionally represented. While in 1570 there had been only two Finnish infantry companies as compared to 31 Swedish, in 1601, there were 25 Finnish, 68 Swedish, and two Estonian companies. By 1618, after the Kalmar War and the simultaneous wars in Muscovy, there were 23 Finnish and 36 Swedish companies. In 1601, there were 18 cavalry banners (Swedish: *fana*) in Sweden (including the retinue of nobles and Court Banner), as compared to the eight in Finland (including the retinue of nobles).[5] In 1604, it was decided to maintain 15 provincial cavalry banners in Sweden and 10 in Finland.[6]

Estonia was exempt from conscription. However, a locally enlisted infantry company (Swedish: *fänika*) garrisoned Reval. Another was raised to garrison Narva. The Estonian nobility provided a banner of the retinue of nobles.

The reasons for this significant growth in the share of Finnish troops were two. First was geography: the sixteenth-century wars against Muscovy had been fought on Finland's border, which naturally focused military attention to the eastern half of the country. Second was poverty: Finland was significantly poorer than the Swedish heartland, which meant that military service was regarded as no worse, and possibly better, than subsistence farming. The prospects of subsistence farming were uncertain, at best, where farmlands were scarce and the population growing. Over time, the poor farmlands probably constitute the chief explanation for why Finland supplied troops at a level far above its relative share of the total population.

Enlisted units, whether cavalry or infantry, were by tradition primarily raised in Germany and Scotland. Dutchmen were enlisted from 1592 onwards.

The outbreak of the Kalmar War took place at a moment when Sweden was militarily weak. The Swedish expeditionary army in Muscovy had, in June 1610, been destroyed at Klushino, and another Swedish army mutinied at Ivangorod later in the same year.[7] Remaining units on the eastern front (they were many since Sweden had to safeguard Estonia from the Commonwealth and Finland from Muscovite incursions) had to remain in position. King Charles could not leave the eastern border undefended only because of hostilities along the long Danish and Norwegian borders. Having to maintain vigilance on three fronts at the same time – the eastern, southern, and western – left Sweden unable to concentrate available forces against any single enemy. Finnish and Estonian units were needed on the eastern front.

---

5   Generalstaben, *Sveriges krig 1611–1632*, vol. 1, pp.86, 574–79. See also Rainer Fagerlund, 'De finska fänikorna under äldre Vasatid: Forskningsläge och problem', *Turun historiallinen arkisto*, 38 (1982), p.99.

6   Generalstaben, *Sveriges krig 1611–1632*, vol. 1, p.89.

7   Generalstaben, *Sveriges krig 1611–1632*, vol. 1, pp.336–41; Fredholm von Essen, *Sweden's War in Muscovy*.

THE KALMAR WAR

Nobles (but not necessarily their serving men) of the Swedish retinue of nobles were armed as cuirassiers. (Jacob de Gheyn II, *Die Reitschule oder Übungen der Kavallerie*)

Because of the ongoing operations on the eastern front, which to a large extent were carried out by units raised in Finland and Estonia, the Swedish army fought in the Kalmar War primarily with units raised in Sweden itself. During the winter of 1610/1611, available military forces in Sweden only consisted of one cavalry banner and four infantry companies of enlisted soldiers, three life banners (including two ducal) of cavalry, two or three banners of the retinue of nobles, 13 provincial cavalry banners, and 41 conscripted infantry companies. Most were understrength. The cavalry banners (altogether an estimated 2,640 horse) had an average strength of 139 men each, while the conscripted companies (altogether 7,102 men) had an average strength of only 173 men each.[8]

In December 1610, parliament in Örebro agreed to a major conscription effort, with a conscription rate of one in 10 for all peasants and burghers. This, incidentally, doubled the quota for the nobility, whose peasants previously had only had a quota of one in 20. The conscription effort returned most companies to establishment strength. At the outbreak of war in 1611, the 41 companies of foot consisted of a total of 16,905 men. The Crown expected

---

8 Generalstaben, *Sveriges krig 1611–1632*, vol. 1, pp.95–96, 145, 147–48.

these figures to rise further, through additional mobilisation, to 60 companies and a total of 19,338 men.[9]

It is possible that the army reached a total strength of between 4,000 and 4,500 horse and some 19,000 foot.[10] However, real results were not quite as satisfactory as those reported. Some men never showed up for service, others deserted, and shortages of weapons meant that not all could serve in field units even if they reported for duty. An examination of the 30 infantry companies that provided the bulk of the field army in the Kalmar War has shown that, out of 12,259 technically available men, only 7,020 actually served in the field.[11] Of these men, many were newly raised and insufficiently trained. The share of armoured pikemen was significantly lower than what the Crown desired because of a lack of training as well as a lack of equipment. Moreover, Sweden lacked the resources to mobilise much more cavalry than was already available. We will see that especially the retinue of nobles never showed up in the numbers expected of them.

Nobility

The Swedish and Finnish nobility were small but constituted the traditional core of the army and provided the bulk of the officer corps. By tradition, war was their primary purpose, and many, among the Finnish nobility in particular, benefited from military service. The early seventeenth century saw the transformation of the Finnish nobility from what could be referred to as a group of illiterate, medieval-style strongmen into members of a pan-European nobility, which like the Danish nobles sent its sons to study at the great universities on the Continent. The Swedish nobility had experienced the same change, although like the Danes in the previous century. The nobility's collective wealth increased rapidly, too, particularly with regard to tax-free land grants.

However, many nobles remained individually poor, and, from the second half of the sixteenth century, state service became an important path of both economic and social advancement for them. While military service no doubt provided opportunities to most, service as administrators and what might be called 'civil servants' provided rewards, too. During the seventeenth century, salaries formed an important and increasing share of the income of most nobles, with only the highest born as an exception to the rule.

However, the almost uninterrupted wars of the previous century had, by the time of the Kalmar War, produced a situation in which a significant share of the officer corps was not of noble but instead common origin. In addition, it was understood that the mobilisation of real aptitude included the ennoblement of talented commoners, who then had to rely chiefly on state salaries to support themselves. For them, military service was a career, not a social obligation. By 1610, commoners and newly created nobles constituted 14 percent of all cavalry captains and, more significantly, 68 percent of all

---

9   Generalstaben, *Sveriges krig 1611–1632*, vol. 1, p.95.

10   Generalstaben, *Sveriges krig 1611–1632*, vol. 1, pp.149–51.

11   Generalstaben, *Sveriges krig 1611–1632*, vol. 1, pp.96, 580–81.

infantry captains. The corresponding figure for colonels and generals was 11 percent.[12]

Cavalrymen

Until the reign of Gustavus Adolphus, early modern Swedish kings (with the single exception of Erik XIV) regarded the cavalry as the primary combat arm. Unlike the infantry, which was conscripted or levied, the Swedish cavalry was raised on a voluntary basis in exchange for noble status, land, and freedom from taxation. There was good reason for this: most campaigns were fought on the border with Muscovy or the Polish–Lithuanian Commonwealth in the east and Denmark in the south. While the Danish–Swedish borderlands were characterised by difficult terrain that brought its own particular tactical problems, the Scanian plains were excellent for cavalry operations. Meanwhile, cavalry retained a key role in warfare in the east. Cavalry in Scandinavia still operated in company-sized tactical units known as banners.

Like in Denmark, the nobility still provided some armed and equipped cavalrymen who fought as cuirassiers in the retinue of nobles. This duty was generally understood to have begun around the age of 17.[13] Although a noble was expected to serve in person, many hired a cavalryman to attend in his stead. The retinue of nobles was held the senior cavalry regiment in the army but usually only served at home in defence of the country. The obligation to serve in foreign campaigns changed over time. Under King Erik XIV, the retinue of nobles had been obliged to serve abroad but at their own expense for only three months per year, after which the Crown had to cover costs. Under King John III, the retinue of nobles only had to serve abroad for up to two weeks per year. Under Gustavus Adolphus, the retinue of nobles was required to serve at their own expense for up to two months per year when away from home.[14] The retinue of nobles constituted three companies in Sweden, one in Finland, and one in Estonia.

Since the Kalmar War was fought at home, these restrictions did not affect the duty to serve. However, in the eyes of Gustavus Adolphus, the retinue of nobles was a disappointment. In comparison to Denmark, they were also very few. When called up for war in 1612, no more than 30 men showed up for service out of the entire retinue of nobles, which technically should have consisted of at least some 300 men in Sweden alone. Moreover, most were merely hired cavalrymen even though the nobles themselves were obliged to serve. Gustavus Adolphus reportedly described the resulting unit as a 'loose bunch of useless men'. Another eyewitness noted that no more than eight actual nobles served for the entire campaign.[15]

---

12 Gunnar Artéus, *Till militärstatens förhistoria: Krig, professionalisering och social förändring under Vasasönernas regering* (Stockholm: Probus, 1986), pp.47, 50.

13 Henning Hamilton, *Afhandling om krigsmaktens och krigskonstens tillstånd i Sverige, under Konung Gustaf II Adolfs regering* (Stockholm: Kongl. Vitterhets Historie och Antiquitets Academiens Handlingar 17, 1846), p.175.

14 Hamilton, *Afhandling*, p.173, citing a decision dated 10 January 1612.

15 Hamilton, *Afhandling*, pp.179–80.

Due to the small size of the retinue of nobles, additional cavalry units had to be raised. Since it was difficult for the Crown to raise enough cash to pay for its troops, Swedish kings customarily employed land grants as a money-saving measure. Already in the 1540s, King Gustavus I attempted to raise both horse and foot by hiring volunteers, each of whom would serve in exchange for a tax-exempt farmstead. For common soldiers, the farmstead typically consisted of a small cottage and some land to cultivate. Ultimately, the reform failed for the infantry. However, for the cavalry, the traditional concept of military service in exchange for tax-exempt farmsteads remained. In 1603, King Charles instructed that every cavalryman be provided a farmstead to provide for his upkeep and place of residence in times of peace. It also became possible for an individual to contract to provide a cavalryman with equipment in exchange for a farmstead exempt from taxation to defray the costs. Since the basis of the income was land revenues, this type of cavalry became known as territorial cavalry (Swedish: *landsryttare, landssåtare*). Some instead served as enlisted cavalry (*besoldningsryttare*). They received pay and board, usually in a royal castle but occasionally in a farmstead, which was then compensated through tax exemption. In reality, there was little difference between these two types of cavalry. They were also generally equipped and armed alike. Certain groups of specialists, too, who could afford to raise cavalrymen, went together to form cavalry units in exchange for exemption from some types of taxation as well as conscription. These included the game wardens in 1611 and a group of mining professionals in 1612.[16]

Already before the Kalmar War, the ongoing wars in the Polish–Lithuanian Commonwealth had shown that the Swedish cavalry as it was then armed, equipped, and trained – as harquebusiers – could not withstand the fearsome Polish winged hussars. Most urgent was the reintroduction of armour, that is, cuirassiers of the Continental type. As a result of the disastrous defeat at Kircholm, King Charles announced in 1606 that anybody who could supply himself with a helmet, breast- and backplate, vambraces, rerebraces, and cuisses of plate (i.e. full armour), a warhorse, saddle, and the appropriate weapons to serve as a cavalryman would, in effect, become a noble and enjoy a number of privileges including the right to carry a special coat of arms that depicted an armed hand in silver on a blue and yellow field. It was not hereditary nobility; the Crown could, if it wished, decline the services, which effectively removed the exemption from taxation. This programme, which was called 'shield-knight service' (*skölderusttjänst*), resulted in some additional cuirassiers, but state poverty was too severe for the initiative to have a major impact. King Charles hoped to raise nine cavalry banners of such volunteers, but those who volunteered were too few to form banners of their own, so they had to be incorporated into existing banners.[17] Besides, the announcement came several decades too late. Public attitude to what constituted noble rank

---

16 Hamilton, *Afhandling*, pp.184, 187–88.
17 Hamilton, *Afhandling*, pp.144, n.275, 173, n.299; Alm, *Blanka vapen*, p.244; Generalstaben, *Sveriges krig 1611–1632*, vol. 1, p.93.

was changing, and nobility was already being seen more as a matter of birth than a function within the army.

Infantrymen

In 1600, parliament in Linköping ruled that every province should raise a certain number of soldiers and that the Crown should provide all soldiers, including infantrymen, with a farmstead. In 1604, parliament in Norrköping again confirmed the principle that all soldiers, including infantrymen, be provided a farmstead. Through these decisions, King Charles again extended the practice to the infantry. As a result, the officers of the national army were provided, as part of their salary, with tax-exempt Crown land to farm (i.e. farmsteads subsequently known as 'military homesteads', *militiehemman*) of a size appropriate to the rank held. Alternatively, the officer received the appropriate rent corresponding to the tax owed while the farmstead remained in private hands. In 1611, King Charles ordered that officers and under-officers would continue to be paid according to this system. Moreover, he also ordered that those common soldiers of the national army who did not yet have any tax-exempt land should be provided a small farm. Gustavus Adolphus issued the corresponding instruction in 1614.[18] The decision to establish a national army in part paid for with land grants was taken since such an army was cheaper to raise and maintain and because it enabled a degree of domestic control.

The principle of tax-exempt land grants as payment for military service laid the foundation for the organisation ultimately known as the *indelningsverk*, from a word perhaps best translated as the 'allotment authority'. The *indelningsverk* provided for the existence of cavalry units (and, in principle although not yet in practice, infantry units as well) through the permanent allotment (*indelning*, 'division') of sources of revenue for their needs.

However, the land grant system did not yet produce enough common soldiers for service on foot and as sailors. For this, the foundation had to be the old national army. Since King Gustavus I had already found that the once semi-voluntary character of the national army was clearly insufficient to produce enough men, the only answer remained conscription (*utskrivning*).

Conscription was the arbitrary raising of men from a population, in most cases from peasants on Crown land. Although resented, the concept still had a certain legitimacy since, in Sweden, the peasant estate enjoyed parliamentary representation. Based on a decision by parliament in Västerås in 1544, parliament had to grant all acts of conscription. The conscripted soldiers had to be armed, trained, and provisioned by the Crown. On the other hand, they could be used anywhere, overseas or at home, as well as indefinitely. Many peasants regarded conscription as a death sentence, which ultimately it often was, and numerous conscripts attempted to desert, especially before they were shipped overseas.

---

18   Hamilton, *Afhandling*, pp.143–45, 147–50.

Artillerymen

The Swedish artillery emerged as a service arm in the sixteenth century under German master artillerymen who previously had served under Emperor Charles V. For this reason, the Swedish artillery adopted Continental artillery traditions. One of them was the artillery's first right to the church bells in every captured town. This was a practice that went back to the need for bronze to cast cannons. Sweden had abundant copper deposits, yet the Swedish artillery retained this tradition at least until the 1660s.[19] Like in Denmark, artillery personnel were enlisted among semi-civilian professionals. Most artillerymen were enlisted within the Swedish kingdom, so the artillery arm in many ways remained national in composition. Both Swedish and Finnish artillerymen were moved to Stockholm for training. In war, infantrymen were temporarily detached as labour to assist as needed.[20] Artillery personnel were generally detached to remote garrisons throughout the kingdom. Some were also included in the field army when it mobilised.

Engineers and sappers, too, belonged to the artillery. The first professional engineers seem to have been enlisted in the Dutch Republic in 1610, and this source of manpower henceforth remained important for the development of a Swedish engineering arm. In the field, the supply train also fell under the command of the artillery, including replacement arms supplies that were brought along by the field army.[21]

Levies and Burgher Militias

Neither conscription nor enlistment provided sufficient manpower for an extended war. If so, the Crown could still levy troops among the peasants. This was done through a quota that the peasants had to fill. Levied troops served on foot, received no training, and had to pay for their own weapons and supplies. On the other hand, they were only required to serve at home. Levied troops were usually used to man defensive redoubts along the external borders, in effect functioning as a border guard. The levied peasants would serve for a time and then be replaced by other levies from the same area. The Crown directed that former soldiers should be selected as leaders of the levies.

In times of need, the Crown also had the right to raise a general levy. A general levy consisted of all men able to bear arms and usually was called out to defend an external border. The levied troops had to arm and supply themselves. Their use was accordingly restricted, for practical reasons, to certain geographical areas and short durations of time. Levies could also be called out in the form of burgher militias, which would have to take some responsibility for defending their towns when under siege.

Most towns were very small, and burghers might be counted in dozens, not hundreds. As a result, there was fundamentally little difference between

---

19 Michael Fredholm von Essen, *Charles X's Wars. Volume 1 – Armies of the Swedish Deluge, 1655–1660* (Warwick: Helion & Company, 2021), p.80.
20 Jonas Hedberg (ed.), *Kungl. Artilleriet: Yngre vasatiden* (Stockholm: Militärhistoriska Förlaget, 1985), p.25.
21 Hedberg (ed.), *Kungl. Artilleriet: Yngre vasatiden*, pp.46, 304.

most burgher militias and peasant levies. However, in the largest towns, there was a degree of voluntary service in the burgher militias, and those burghers who served in them could usually be expected to afford the necessary military armament.

In times of war, yet another option was to raise additional, temporary troops from those areas that otherwise were exempt from conscription. This was decided by the Crown on a case-by-case basis and granted by parliament. This was referred to as a 'take-out' (*utskott*). The troops raised in this manner were armed, trained, and supplied by the Crown yet only needed to serve in the nearest theatre of war within the country and only for as long as the present war lasted. They could accordingly not be sent overseas. They were, in effect, temporary troops intended to be disbanded when the war ended.

The Crown in times of need also might negotiate additional cavalry from any individual or group in society who could afford to raise cavalrymen, such as the nobility, the civil service, the priesthood, and so on. Although the Crown then did not have to provide for men, horses, and weapons, such troops, similar to the temporary troops of a take-out, only needed to serve within the country and only for as long as the present war lasted.

Chain of Command

The King naturally stood at the apex of the chain of command. Like the situation in Denmark and Norway, the military hierarchy remained underdeveloped. However, unlike these two countries, the Swedish military establishment had developed with the times and was arguably more modern than those of its two neighbours. The Council of the Realm (Swedish: *Riksrådet*) carried out the functions of a national government. Its leading members were the five great officers of state. First among them was the Lord High Justiciar (*Riksdrots*), who took precedence. The second and third were, respectively, the Grand Marshal of the Realm (*Riksmarsk*), who was in command of home defence and the army, and the Grand Admiral of the Realm (*Riksamiral*), who commanded the navy.[22] These officers were followed in precedence by the Lord High Chancellor (*Rikskansler*) and the Lord High Treasurer (*Riksskattmästare*).

The Grand Marshal and the Grand Admiral controlled the military establishment: the units of the army and navy. At the time of the wars covered in this volume, first Magnus Brahe (1564–1633) and then, from 1612, Axel Ryning (1552–1620) served as Marshal of the Realm. Until this advancement, Ryning instead served as Grand Admiral of the Realm, a position in which Göran Gyllenstierna (1575–1618) succeeded him. In 1612, Brahe was engaged in the defences of the province of Småland while Gyllenstierna

---

22 The position of Grand Admiral of the Realm was instituted in 1571 with the appointment of Claes Fleming (*c.* 1535–1597), whom the future King Charles incidentally regarded as an enemy.

commanded the main fleet, but their primary activities were administrative, not military.[23]

The King could, and did, appoint provincial commanders as needed. By tradition, an army commander was called 'field colonel' (Swedish: *fältöverste*) or 'colonel general' (*generalöverste*), terms that essentially meant 'general'. Such a man only commanded the provincial field army. Any garrisons within his area of operations remained under the command of their respective commandants. This, at times, caused difficulties in the chain of command, which only the King could override by issuing direct orders to the commandants. The reason for this anomaly was probably that, in times of peace, the governors at Kalmar and Elfsborg Castles were in formal command of all the soldiers in Småland and Västergötland, respectively. Since these provinces were particularly exposed in times of war, it was natural, then, to appoint field colonels in command of provincial field units. Yet the governors at these important castles remained in place and naturally retained an influential position vis-à-vis their respective garrisons.

The situation was different when a commander was appointed to exercise individual command in a theatre of war in which the King was not present or likely to be present. Such a commander might be appointed field colonel general (*generalfältöverste*). The only officer who received the full title and mandate was Pontus De la Gardie, who in 1581 received authority to command both land and naval units on the eastern front against Muscovy. An earlier title for this office was that of commanding general (*fältherre*). While the title remained in use and would reappear, in the early 1600s, the officer who served in this position was instead known as a lieutenant general (*generallöjtnant*), which meant that he served as the King's lieutenant or deputy. Soon, however, the title of field marshal (*fältmarskalk*) appeared for an officer in this position. Previously, this title had indicated a commander of cavalry, roughly equivalent to a colonel in status. Although the term 'field marshal' sometimes appears in texts produced during the first two decades of the seventeenth century, the rank was not really formalised until later, during the Thirty Years' War, when it gradually superseded the other two.

Military Organisation

The Swedish army had adopted the Spanish model of warfare during the reign of King Erik XIV (r. 1560–1568), who simultaneously was at war with both Denmark and what then was the united Kingdom of Poland and Grand Duchy of Lithuania. King Erik realised the necessity of modernising the military establishment by introducing armoured pikemen organised according to the Spanish model. Yet he was dissatisfied with the large formations of the Spanish model and saw the need to add tactical flexibility. Widely read in

---

23 After the Kalmar War, Gustavus Adolphus and Lord High Chancellor Axel Oxenstierna began the process of establishing properly authorised government departments, including a department of war, to which the King, in the late 1610s, would delegate his authority.

classical literature, King Erik accordingly added elements taken from ancient Roman military manuals to the prevalent model. By doing so, he preceded the military reforms of Maurice of Nassau and his cousins by at least 30 years.

King Erik established a standard company of foot consisting of 525 men, divided in five quarters. Twelve companies would form a regiment of 6,000 men. He also aimed for standardised equipment. Pikemen were expected to wear half armour, that is, a helmet, gorget, cuirass, vambraces, and rerebraces. Under-officers and officers wore tassets as well. Arquebusiers might wear helmets but, as far as is known, no other armour. King Erik also standardised the cavalry banner as 300 men, again divided into five quarters. King Erik wanted his heavy cavalry to wear three-quarter armour and carry two pistols each. The remaining cavalry would serve as harquebusiers. Both types of cavalry units were to form up in near-square formations 15 ranks deep and employ the caracole tactics common on the Continent.

However, King Erik's brother and successor, John, who deposed Erik, cancelled the reforms and instead focused on unarmoured arquebusiers both as foot and horse. King John also reduced the infantry company to about 300 men. Later historians have explained this with the need to appease King Erik's soldiers, who disliked wearing heavy armour and carrying the unwieldy and heavy pike.[24] A better explanation is probably Sweden's state poverty. In 1574, King John reduced his pikemen's pay, effectively putting them on a parity basis with arquebusiers, even though their workload was heavier and risks greater. Under such conditions, it was hardly surprising that the men preferred to serve as arquebusiers. Later historians have also suggested that the fresh emphasis on arquebusiers was the result of a new doctrine that focused on defending Sweden's forested areas, for which unarmoured arquebusiers were more suitable.[25] However, a more compelling reason is the change of focus in theatre of operations. Having wrapped up the war with Denmark, King John's only real adversary was Muscovy, and he may have, correctly, perceived unarmoured arquebusiers as more efficient for fighting Muscovite cavalry, which by then primarily consisted of mounted archers.[26] King John's field commander on the eastern front, Gustav Banér (1547–1600), who had learnt his trade in military service on the Continent, disagreed but to no avail.[27]

24　Petri, *Kungl. Första livgrenadjärregementets historia*, pp.201–02.

25　Bertil C:son Barkman, *Kungl. Svea livgardes historia: 1560-1611* (Stockholm: Stiftelsen för Svea livgardes historia, 1939), vol. 2, pp.201–02.

26　This explanation was never explored by nineteenth-century and later Swedish historians, who almost universally entertained the notion that Muscovite armies were so inferior in quality that there was no need for either tactical or technical sophistication to defeat them. See, for example, Petri, *Kungl. Första livgrenadjärregementets historia*, p.206; Barkman, *Kungl. Svea livgardes historia*, vol. 2, p.204. In reality, the Swedes were hard-pressed in Estonia and eastern Finland for years before they could go on the offensive, and a sustainable peace was only accomplished in 1617 under Gustavus Adolphus, which would seem to disprove this facile assumption.

27　In 1572, Banér requested 4,000 pikeheads and 6,000 pike shafts. Petri, *Kungl. Första livgrenadjärregementets historia*, p.209.

Nonetheless, late in the reign of King John, production of pikes and cuirasses resumed.[28] King John's brother and eventual successor, Charles, ordered the reintroduction of pikemen and halberdiers among the infantry and shot-proof cuirasses among the harquebusiers, in addition to, in Livonia, mobile defences such as swinefeathers, the use of wagon forts for protection, and, upon the initiative of the Dutch expert John of Nassau, a hundred carts with affixed pikes (Swedish: *spetskärror*) that might provide a modicum of protection against armoured cavalry such as those fielded by the Polish–Lithuanian Commonwealth.[29] Of these various measures, the most long lasting was the swinefeather (elsewhere also known as the Swedish feather). This was a short pike with a total length of approximately 1.8–2m, including the 30 cm-long head. Under the right circumstances, the swinefeather formed an efficient protection against cavalry. A unit of arquebusiers or musketeers with swinefeathers firmly planted in the ground in front of them would give the appearance of a wall of spear points. Moreover, with the addition of logs to link them together, several swinefeathers could be arranged into a *cheval-de-frise*, an anti-cavalry obstacle that was positioned in front of the infantry ranks to provide protection against a cavalry charge.

Sweden was fortunate in having in the army a number of experienced soldiers who had fought in the long period of wars preceding the Kalmar War. Already by the late sixteenth century, the majority of native officers in the Swedish army (i.e. captains, lieutenants, ensigns, and indeed sergeants) were already highly professionalised in everything but theoretical education. First, they were experienced in the military position they held. By 1590, 77 percent of native infantry captains and 62 percent of cavalry captains had served in their present rank for three years or more. In addition, most or all would have served in junior ranks for some time before being promoted to captain. Furthermore, 35 percent of all infantry captains and 31 percent of all cavalry captains had, in fact, served for 11 years or more, and most of this time had been spent at war. This fortunate situation endured. By 1610, 63 percent of native infantry captains and 71 percent of cavalry captains had served in their present rank for three years or more. By then, 29 percent of all infantry captains and eight percent of all cavalry captains had served for 11 years or more.[30] The latter figure can be explained: by this time, a far higher share of cavalry officers (48 percent of the total) were of foreign origin. The number of foreign infantry officers had risen as well, but not as dramatically, to 27 percent. The foreign officers had, of course, not served for as long in the Swedish army, but they had often gained considerable experience elsewhere.[31]

---

28 Barkman, *Kungl. Svea livgardes historia*, vol. 2, p.207.
29 Jakobsson, *Lantmilitär beväpning och beklädnad*, pp.14, 20. See also Carl Carlsson Gyllenhjelm, 'Egenhändiga anteckningar af Carl Carlsson Gyllenhjelm rörande tiden 1597–1601', *Historiska Handlingar*, 20 (1905), pp.258–395; John of Nassau, 'Grefve Johans av Nassau relation angående kriget i Livland 1601–1602', *Historiska Handlingar*, 20 (1905), pp.396–438.
30 Artéus, *Till militärstatens förhistoria*, p.36.
31 Artéus, *Till militärstatens förhistoria*, pp.47, 50.

There was accordingly no need to build an army from scratch. A professional core already existed.

What was the origin of the foreign officers? Most were Germans, either from the Continent or the eastern side of the Baltic. Indeed, it is often difficult to distinguish in the records between Baltic Germans from Livonia or Estonia who were Swedish citizens and those who technically were foreign nationals. The second-largest group consisted of the Scots, English, and Irish. This group was followed in numbers by a mixed group of Frenchmen, Walloons, Swiss, Italians, and Spaniards, and a slightly smaller group comprising men of Dutch, Frisian, or Flemish origin. Men of other backgrounds served, too, including some Poles, Muscovites, Hungarians, and the occasional Dane or Norwegian.[32] It is obvious that Lutheran faith was not a prerequisite for service in the Swedish army despite its insistence on *attending* Lutheran sermons. It is also obvious that the Swedish army sought different types of military expertise in different foreign regions. By 1610, 67 percent of foreign cavalry captains were of German or Baltic German origin; 17 percent were Scots, English, or Irish; 16 percent had a French, Walloon, Swiss, Italian, or Spanish background; and only the occasional individual was of Commonwealth, Muscovite, or Hungarian origin. In comparison, by 1610, 56 percent of foreign infantry captains were of German or Baltic German origin; 32 percent were Scots, English, or Irish; six percent were Dutch, Frisian, or Flemish; five percent had a French, Walloon, Swiss, Italian, or Spanish background; and, again, only the occasional individual was of Commonwealth, Muscovite, or Hungarian origin.

It is thus clear that officers of Scots, English, or Irish origin were more likely to serve in the infantry. Those of Dutch, Frisian, or Flemish origin only served in the infantry (or, coincidentally, in the navy, which hosted many officers of Dutch origin). In contrast, officers of French, Walloon, Swiss, Italian, or Spanish origin were far more likely to serve in the cavalry.[33] There was a reason for enlisting so many foreign officers for the cavalry. As noted, with Sweden's native cavalry force still based on the nobility, the available manpower was insufficient. A new source of cavalry officers was required, and, for this, foreign nationals were enlisted.

Unit Organisation

The existing Swedish army was obsolete and insufficient regarding both organisation and armament. By the turn of the century, regiments in the Swedish army were temporary in nature, usually enlisted abroad, and had no standard establishment strength. The Swedish national military establishment was not organised in multiple-level formations nor in higher formations. There was no military administrative organisation. Each company or banner was independently raised and, in times of peace, independent and directly subordinated the king.[34] The only unit level that

---

32 Artéus, *Till militärstatens förhistoria*, p.87.
33 Artéus, *Till militärstatens förhistoria*, p.89.
34 Barkman, *Gustaf II Adolfs regementsorganisation*, p.71.

THE SWEDISH MILITARY ESTABLISHMENT

existed was that of the banner and company. It accordingly constituted the only administrative and tactical unit, with the two roles combined into one. There was no permanent regimental organisation, nor did the Dutch-style battalion yet exist in Sweden. An army was raised by combining a number of banners and companies. Although companies of foot would generally be deployed collectively in a line of battle, the line was no more than a practical solution for battlefield use. It did not signify any kind of permanent identity or higher formation.

The Crown had made some recent attempts to reform the cavalry. The old 300-strong cavalry banner was, in 1603, reorganised as a company and reduced to a strength of 120 horse (cavalry units counted their strength in horses, not men).[35] However, in 1611, some cavalry companies were again increased to a strength of 200 or 300.[36] Whether this was the practical result of the outbreak of war, which always necessitated the need for extra men, or because the new company was regarded as too weak remains unclear. In any case, some banners never reached establishment strength.

There was no standard establishment strength for national companies of foot. Yet, since the late sixteenth century, there was an understanding that a company of foot should consist of some 300 men, even though many were significantly smaller. By the time of the Kalmar War, a company of foot raised in Sweden generally had a strength of between 200 and 300 men.[37] In one perhaps ideal case, the company consisted of 191 common soldiers, 68 *doppelsöldner* (corporals or similar who presumably served as pikemen – common pikemen no longer received higher pay), four drummers, four pipers, 30 trainee officers (*adelsburst*, *adelsburs*, or *adelsbuss*, who presumably served as pikemen), and about three officers. The trainees were often, but not invariably, young nobles who served as volunteers without pay. There is some uncertainty regarding their service conditions. According to the regulations of Kings John and Charles, young nobles not yet of age to serve on horseback had to still serve but as common soldiers.[38] However, the term seems to derive from the Dutch term *adelburst*, which signified a naval midshipman or cadet. If so, this group of soldiers may have served as volunteers (similar to the *adventurers* or *voluntaries* in England, *soldati di fortuna* in Italy, *soldats de fortune* in France, and *aventureros* in Spain, all of whom were generally youths of gentle or noble birth) who were still regarded as in training for later promotion to officer rank. In the distant past, under King Erik, pikemen had received higher pay. From 1574 onwards, however, we have seen that pikemen and arquebusiers received the same pay.[39]

---

35 John of Nassau already attempted to reduce the cavalry banner from the traditional 300 to 100 in 1601, but the reform was never fully implemented, and establishment strength, such as it was, soon reverted to 300 in 1602.
36 Hamilton, *Afhandling*, p.210.
37 Barkman, *Gustaf II Adolfs regementsorganisation*, pp.81, 207.
38 Hamilton, *Afhandling*, p.128.
39 Barkman, *Kungl. Svea livgardes historia*, vol. 2, pp.700–05.

Nor was there any standard establishment strength for enlisted foreign units. At the time, the foreign regiments in Swedish service did not adhere to any particular type of organisation. The decisive factor seems to have been the availability of men and opportunity to enlist them. These regiments generally included from five to eight companies of 150 to 200 men each. Occasionally, a regiment had more companies, which generally was the result of the amalgamation of two previous regiments.[40]

King Charles frequently experimented with different organisational forms and different types of armaments. However, over time, he grew to favour the enlistment of professional soldiers abroad instead of training national units. In 1609, the Swedish army included no less than 10,000 soldiers enlisted abroad.[41] Most served on the eastern front, which meant that they did not take part in the Kalmar War.

In addition to national and enlisted units, in times of war or imminent threat of war, certain groups of professionals joined to form temporary cavalry units in exchange for exemption from some types of taxation as well as conscription into the infantry. These included the game wardens, who formed such a temporary cavalry unit in 1611. We know nothing about this unit beyond its existence. It may have been no more than a harquebusier cavalry company raised among the men who served the game wardens, who, after all, constituted a category of civilian officials. We will see that at least one game warden, Mickel Jönsson of Tenhult, raised men to repulse a Danish attack. Or, which seems to have been the case 20 years later, they were mounted 'shooters and game wardens' who fought on foot as dragoons or more likely *jägers*. Being few in number yet skilled huntsmen, they may have been used for reconnaissance or duties relating to the small war or counterinsurgency.[42]

Another specialty that set the Swedish army apart from Continental armies was the employment of ski troops. Ski troops were used both for reconnaissance and surprise flank attacks. Every year, Finnish ski troops were sent to Livonia, and ski troops were frequently used in the campaigns against the Polish–Lithuanian Commonwealth and Muscovy.

Guard Units

Already, King Gustavus I founded the Court Banner (Swedish: *Hovfanan*) as an enlisted elite armoured cavalry unit. Its members received higher pay than the retinue of nobles (who, moreover, were only paid under certain conditions). In 1575, King John incorporated the retinue of nobles into the Court Banner, which in 1576 consisted of 156 men. The incorporation of the old retinue of nobles probably reduced the combat readiness of the Court Banner. Perhaps for this reason, King John's son and successor, Sigismund, during his rule in Sweden in 1591, established yet another guard cavalry unit, the Vanguard Banner (Swedish: *Kännefanan*; Finnish: *Päälippue*), under the command of

---

40   Barkman, *Gustaf II Adolfs regementsorganisation*, p.79.
41   Generalstaben, *Sveriges krig 1611–1632*, vol. 1, p.92.
42   Fredholm von Essen, *Lion from the North*, vol. 1, p.182.

THE SWEDISH MILITARY ESTABLISHMENT

Claes Hermansson Fleming. The Vanguard Banner was ranked higher than the Court Banner.[43] However, the unit was soon disbanded in 1593.

Having gained the throne, King Charles constituted a new permanent cavalry unit, henceforth known as the King's Life Banner (*Kungl. Majestäts Livfana* or *Konungens Livfana*) or, with the more modern terminology that came into use in the seventeenth century, the King's Life Company of Horse. This was an enlisted cavalry company that, although technically a guard unit, in reality functioned as a permanent fighting unit.

There were two additional life banners in Sweden: the two ducal life banners or life companies of Dukes Gustavus Adolphus and John, respectively. Yet another was being formed under Duke Charles Philip, who was still a minor.

When Gustavus Adolphus inherited the army from his late father, he immediately merged his life company of horse into the King's Life Company of Horse. Since this was an enlisted cavalry company that functioned as a fighting unit, the company was no permanent structure and did not continuously follow the King. For instance, in 1613, the King's Life Company of Horse, under Herman Wrangel, deployed with the field army to Muscovy and in 1614 was present at Novgorod.[44]

The, by tradition and for reasons of combat readiness, most prestigious regiment of the Swedish army was the King's personal Life Guard of Foot. It was always enlisted. Being the military unit closest to the King, the Life Guard frequently changed designation, leadership, organisation, and, to some extent, armament. This was particularly the case at times of royal succession when the new sovereign found it particularly important to retain a loyal guard unit.

The Life Guard, too, originated with King Gustavus I. In time, his small, personal infantry guard grew into a company-sized unit, known as the Drabant Guard (*Drabantkåren*). This unit continuously followed the King. In addition, there was a second, and generally larger, infantry unit at the King's disposal. This was the Household Company (*Gårdsfänikan*), which guarded the royal palace. In 1600, King Charles redesignated the Household Company as the 'Stockholm Company' and turned his Drabant Guard into a regular infantry company known as the 'Drabant Company' (*Drabantfänikan*). He used both this and the Stockholm Company as regular combat units. However, in 1608, he reassigned the Stockholm Company in status to that of a provincial company in Uppland.[45] Between 1600 and 1605, King Charles also employed a third guard unit, the Arquebusier Company (Swedish: *Hakeskyttefänikan*).

---

43 Sebastian Jägerhorn, *Hårdast bland de hårda: En kavalleriofficer i fält* (Stockholm: Medström, 2018), pp.25, 233, n.67. The term 'kännefana' (kennefana), with the apparent synonym 'rännefana' (rendefana), was known since the Nordic Seven Years' War, when both Danes and Swedes used it with the meaning of 'vanguard' (Danish/Swedish: *Fortrav/Förtrav, Forvagt/Förvakt*).

44 Bertil C:son Barkman and Sven Lundkvist, *Kungl. Svea livgardes historia: 1611–1632* (Stockholm: Stiftelsen för Svea livgardes historia, 1963), vol. 3, part 1, pp.180, 215.

45 Barkman, *Kungl. Svea livgardes historia*, vol. 2, pp.351–52, 417, 421–22, 425, 428–29, 434, 437.

THE KALMAR WAR

The Drabant Guard of Duke John of Östergötland, at some point between 1598 and 1619 (probably earlier rather than later). One guardsman has drawn his swept-hilt rapier, while the other carries a halberd decorated with tassels, which was customary among Drabant Guards. Interestingly, the halberd corresponds to the old Swedish style, which may be explained by the fact that this is the provincial Ducal Drabant Guard, not the Royal Drabant Guard.
(Vadstena Castle; photo: Adam Ingesson)

THE SWEDISH MILITARY ESTABLISHMENT

When Gustavus Adolphus ascended to the throne in the middle of the Kalmar War, he inherited the Drabant Company from his late father. Retaining this unit as an independent life guard company, in 1613, Gustavus Adolphus ordered Colonel Reinhold Taube to enlist a whole infantry regiment for the King's personal use. Taube had commanded regiments in Swedish service since the campaign in Muscovy in 1609–1610, after which he fought in the Kalmar War. Primarily raised from Germans and Scots in Swedish service, the new regiment became known as the King's Regiment (formally, *Hans Kungliga Majestäts regemente*). It consisted of four companies, each with a planned strength of 300 men. In reality, the total strength reached only 915 men. Taube and the King's Regiment fought in Muscovy in 1613, where Taube fell in battle. Because of the death of Taube, and the unit's considerable losses, Gustavus Adolphus had the remnants of the King's Regiment reconstituted. In practical terms, this became a mostly new enlisted regiment but with the same name. It served with the King at the siege of Pskov in 1615, after which it was disbanded in 1616.[46]

Weapons, Equipment, and Uniforms

Officers and Under-Officers

As elsewhere in the region, officers provided their own arms and armour. In battle, each officer would be armed with two wheellock pistols and a rapier. A handful of officers may have instead carried a sabre, a sidearm that acquired a certain level of popularity during the years when the late King John maintained good relations with the Commonwealth. However, by the time of King Charles, the use of sabres was mostly discontinued.

An under-officer, too, was armed with rapier and perhaps pistols. Unlike officers, under-officers in the Swedish army received their arms from the Crown. At the time of the Kalmar War, infantry under-officers typically carried halberds. In the sixteenth century, the Swedish halberd essentially was a short poleaxe fitted with a spearhead. The cutting edge was convex in the manner of an axe, and the weapon was primarily used as a cutting weapon. However, in the 1570s, a more elaborate style of halberd with a concave cutting edge and a longer pole was introduced from Germany. This halberd was primarily used as a stabbing weapon in the Continental manner. The German halberd was used by Drabant Guards and likely under-officers in other infantry units as well. The 'Drabant-style halberd', as it was called, appears to have been larger and heavier, as well as longer. Some halberds were apparently called 'double halberds', so they are believed to have had two cutting edges.[47]

Partisans were known in Sweden but were issued to under-officers instead of halberds only in 1590 and then again from some point between 1616 and

---

46 Barkman and Lundkvist, *Kungl. Svea livgardes historia*, vol. 3, part 1, pp.180–81, 211–16, 230–32, 243–44.

47 Barkman, *Kungl. Svea livgardes historia*, vol. 2, pp.606–17.

THE KALMAR WAR

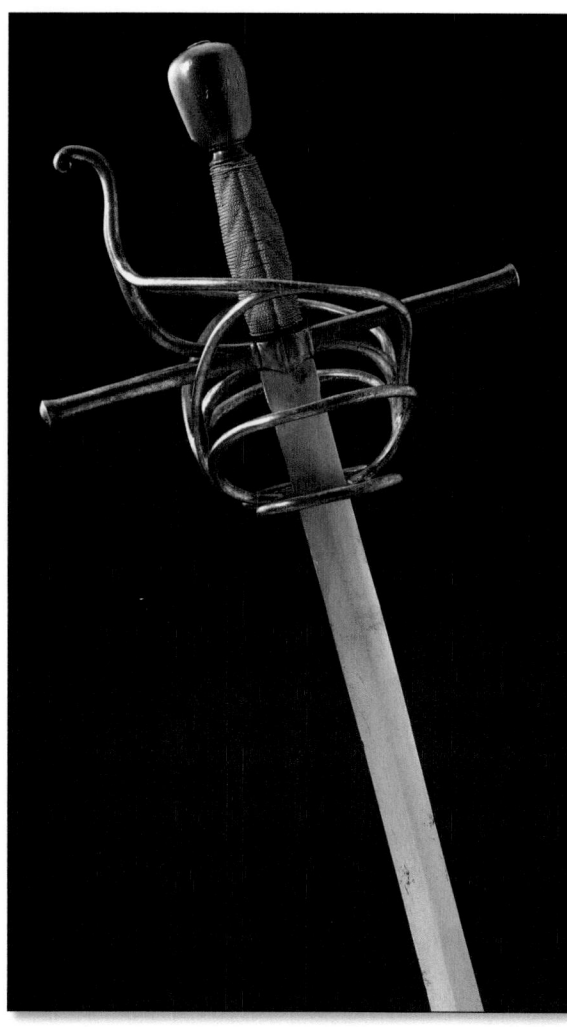

Rapier hilt dated to c. 1600, made either in the Swedish arms factory at Arboga or in Germany. Swept hilt of gilded steel with the grip bound in gilded brass wire, attached to a later blade. Owned by King Charles, who employed it in tournaments. Total weight 1.59 kg, blade length 93.6 cm, width 27 mm, total length 112.4 cm. (Royal Armoury, Stockholm)

1622 (an exact year cannot be determined since records for these years seem to be missing).[48] In 1608, the Stockholm Armoury distributed 1,441 regular halberds, 207 Drabant-style halberds, and four partisans.[49]

From 1600 onwards, the captain and lieutenant of the Drabant Guard each carried a highly decorated gilded partisan with tassels. All other men of the Drabant Guard carried halberds, which, from King Charles's coronation in 1607 onwards, were gilded in the manner of the late King Erik's time.

Under-officers probably wore helmets and gorgets as a symbol of rank, at least judging from examples a decade later.[50] Some might also have worn a cuirass, with tassets to protect the upper thighs if serving in a pike unit.

In 1609, King Charles ordered the arms factory in Arboga to resume production of round shields (Swedish: *rudass*, *rundass*, or *rundel*; on the Continent known as *rondache*). His reasons for this decision are unclear. It is possible that some infantry officers, perhaps the company captains, each carried a round shield. While such shields were distributed in small numbers (apparently one per company), we do not know how they were used. Although originally intended for use on the battlefield by *rodeleros*, or sword-and-buckler men, in the Spanish and Dutch manner, in the Swedish army since the reign of King John, they were far more frequently used in siege warfare.[51] The use of soldiers armed with round shields in the life guard of Maurice of Nassau may have influenced Swedish practices.[52] In 1610, Arboga delivered full sword-and-buckler gear for 162 men and 288 additional shields to the Crown.[53]

---

48 Barkman, *Kungl. Svea livgardes historia*, vol. 2, p.635; Jakobsson, *Lantmilitär beväpning och beklädnad*, p.90.

49 Jonas Hedberg (ed.), *Kungl. Artilleriet: Medeltid och äldre vasatid* (Stockholm: Militärhistoriska Förlaget, 1975), p.475, Appendix 11.

50 Evident from the 1626 painting of the Norrland Territorial Regiment by Nicolas de la Fage, Karlberg Palace.

51 Hamilton, *Afhandling*, p.119; Jakobsson, *Lantmilitär beväpning och beklädnad*, p.115; Barkman, *Kungl. Svea livgardes historia*, vol. 2, p.212.

52 Eduard Wagner, *European Weapons & Warfare 1618–1648* (London: Octopus Books, 1979), p.104.

53 Barkman, *Kungl. Svea livgardes historia*, vol. 2, pp.622–23.

THE SWEDISH MILITARY ESTABLISHMENT

Left: King Charles's rapier. A German blade made by Clemens Horn, Solingen, c. 1595–1600. The swept hilt of silver made at the turn of the century by Johan Pedersson, Stockholm. Weight: 1.5 kg. Blade length: 92.7 cm. Width: 38 mm. Total length: 114.4 cm. (Royal Armoury, Stockholm)

Right: Swedish halberdier with a halberd of the traditional poleaxe style, 1560s. (Drawn by King Erik XIV while in captivity)

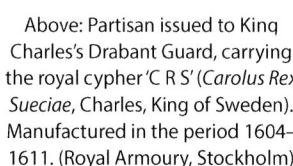

Above: Partisan issued to King Charles's Drabant Guard, carrying the royal cypher 'C R S' (*Carolus Rex Sueciae*, Charles, King of Sweden). Manufactured in the period 1604–1611. (Royal Armoury, Stockholm)

THE KALMAR WAR

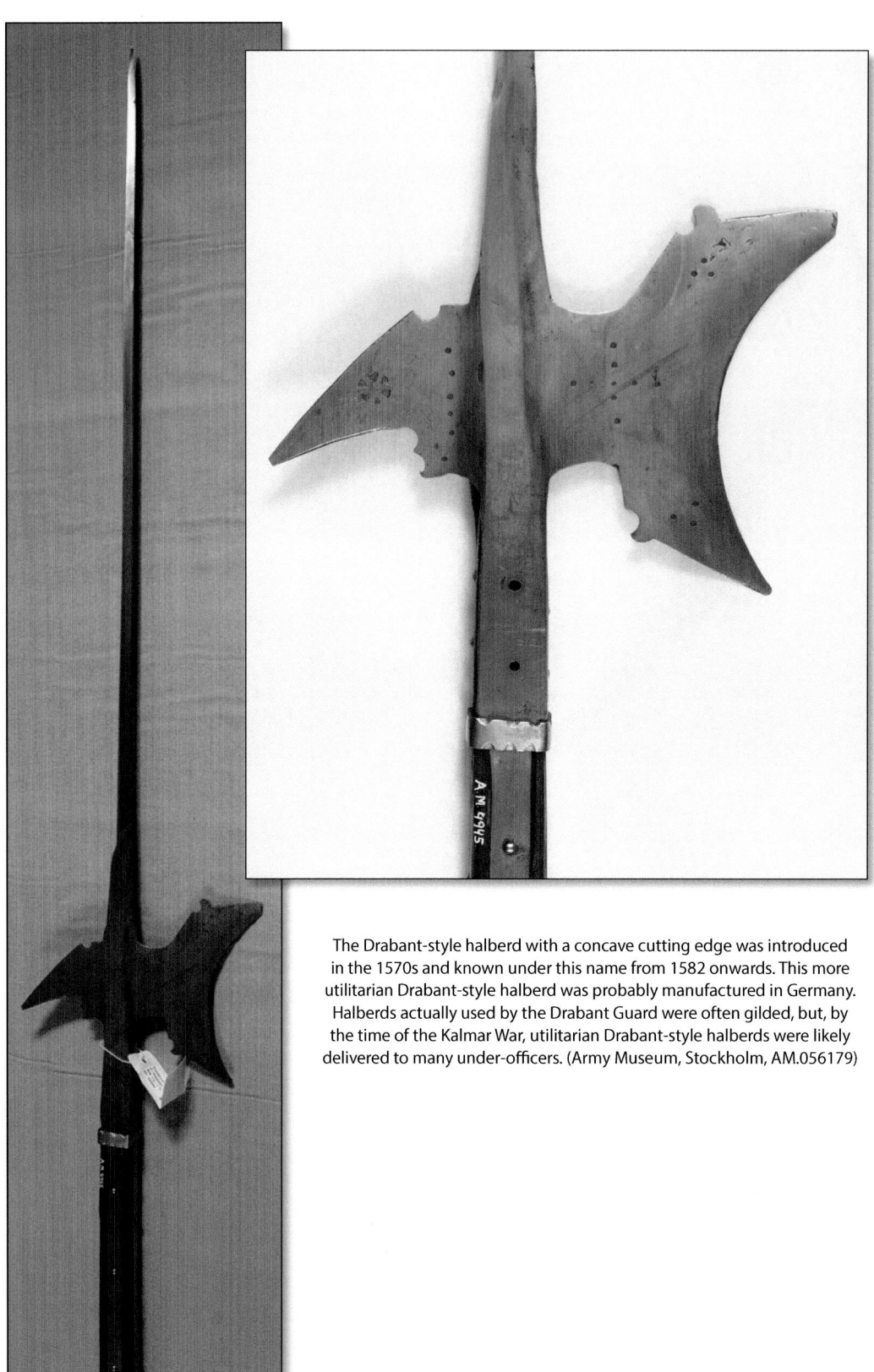

The Drabant-style halberd with a concave cutting edge was introduced in the 1570s and known under this name from 1582 onwards. This more utilitarian Drabant-style halberd was probably manufactured in Germany. Halberds actually used by the Drabant Guard were often gilded, but, by the time of the Kalmar War, utilitarian Drabant-style halberds were likely delivered to many under-officers. (Army Museum, Stockholm, AM.056179)

THE SWEDISH MILITARY ESTABLISHMENT

Soldier armed with a round shield. A Swedish infantry captain was probably armed in this manner. (Adam van Breen, *De Nassausche Wapen-Handelinge, van Schilt, Spies, Rappier, ende Targe* (The Hague: Aert Meuris, 1618))

THE KALMAR WAR

Below: Early seventeenth-century *tessak* with a clam shell hilt. War booty popularly known as 'Zisca's sword'. Blade length 78 cm. total length 90 cm, width 5 cm. (Skokloster Castle; photo: Göran Schmidt)

Above: Late sixteenth-century *tessak*. (Royal Armoury, Stockholm; photo: Samuel Uhrdin, Livrustkammaren/SHM)

Arquebusiers and Musketeers

At the beginning of the Kalmar War, most Swedish infantry were unarmoured arquebusiers. In Sweden, the infantry arquebus (Swedish: *hake* or *rör*) was, apparently, quite long since they were known as 'long guns' (*långbössor*). The typical caliber tended to increase over time, from 30 bore (i.e. drilled for a bore size equivalent to a ball weighing one-thirtieth of a pound or, expressed differently, equivalent to 30 balls per pound of lead, which corresponded to a nominal calibre of 13.9 mm) in the early 1590s to mostly 16 bore (16 balls per pound of lead, with a nominal calibre of 16.8 mm) at the time of the Kalmar War.[54] This weapon frequently came with a snaplock or snaphance lock, which, as noted, employed a firestone to strike fire. The firestone was often a flintstone, so the mechanism foreshadowed the later flintlock. The arquebus was not used with a fork rest.

The province of Småland was known for its production of fine-calibre rifled hunting guns, which were sometimes used in war. We do not know if the men who carried them were dedicated snipers or simply had to rely on local stocks.[55]

The significantly heavier and more powerful Dutch 10-bore matchlock musket (10 balls per pound of lead, corresponding to a nominal calibre of 19.7 mm) was known in Sweden. It was possibly first introduced from the Dutch Republic in 1592, when 65 muskets were procured (even though the Dutch government preauthorised the sale of 200).[56] These guns were used with a fork rest. In 1608, the Stockholm Armoury distributed 1,875 matchlock muskets, as compared to 1,108 snaplock ones. Yet, in the same year, the Armoury also distributed 671 snaplock arquebuses, 536 arquebuses of other types, and 50 carbines.[57] Clearly, no uniformity for firearms had yet developed in the army. Gustavus Adolphus soon learnt to prefer the heavy and sturdy 10-bore matchlock musket, which was also cheaper to manufacture and maintain. When, after the Kalmar War, he modernised the armament of the Swedish army, he ordered the replacement of the arquebus with the matchlock musket.[58] Perhaps it was the inferior performance of the Swedish arquebus that convinced young Gustavus Adolphus of the need to rearm.

At first, matchlock muskets were imported from the Continent, where this weapon already was in common use. The matchlock was an old design and not the most advanced type of gun lock. It was not the lock but the calibre of the old arquebus that was obsolete. Swedish gunsmiths were experienced in manufacturing both wheellock and snaplock (snaphance) guns, which relied on gun locks that were more advanced than the imported matchlocks.[59] Some have even suggested that the snaplock was invented in Sweden, which

---

54 Alm, *Eldhandvapen 1*, pp.151, 197.
55 Alm, *Eldhandvapen 1*, p.151.
56 Alm, *Eldhandvapen 1*, p.152; Generalstaben, *Sveriges krig 1611–1632*, vol. 1, p.76, n.2.
57 Hedberg (ed.), *Kungl. Artilleriet: Medeltid och äldre vasatid*, p.475, Appendix 11.
58 Fredholm von Essen, *Lion from the North*, vol. 1, pp.155–65.
59 The wheellock was known as '*Züntschloss*' in seventeenth-century German. Another common term was '*Feuerschloss*' (firelock), which, however, might be used for any gunlock. The corresponding Swedish terms were then '*sintlås*' and '*fyrlås*'. The modern German term for wheellock is '*Radschloss*'.

Musketeer, 1611. The jacket has several short tails and shoulder straps divided into tongues. Sleeves and breeches are fairly wide. The hat is decorated with tall plumes. The collar is flat and semi-wide. King Charles's funeral armour, made in Stockholm in 1611. (Strängnäs Cathedral)

is unknown but possible.[60] A wheellock works by spinning a spring-loaded steel wheel against a piece of pyrite to generate sparks, while in a snaplock, a spring-loaded cock strikes a flintstone onto hardened steel (known as the frizzen) to generate a shower of sparks. In either case, the sparks ignite the gunpowder in the priming pan. In comparison, a matchlock is a simple mechanism that merely lowers a burning slow match, held in a clamp at the end of a small, curved lever (known as a serpentine), into the priming pan to ignite the gunpowder.

In 1612, new muskets from the Continent arrived, which were then used to arm the infantry from Dalecarlia and Västmanland. The rest of the infantry was instructed to use snaphance weapons, which must have meant either their old 16-bore arquebuses or newly made 12-bore muskets, with a nominal calibre of 18.5 mm. In 1613, the Stockholm arsenal received not only 2,094 matchlock muskets but also 1,419 snaphance muskets. In some regiments, the old 16-bore arquebus remained in service into the 1620s.[61]

Even though Gustavus Adolphus set out to rearm his troops with muskets after the war, rearmament took time. Snaphance weapons continued to be manufactured for many years, although, when made for military use, they were henceforth more often 12-bore muskets.

During the Kalmar War, arquebusiers and musketeers generally did not wear armour. As a sidearm, they carried rapiers or possibly the occasional remaining sabre. Instructions from 1601 for service sidearms describe rapiers as broad at the hilt (for strength) and narrow at the point (for thrusting). Sabres should be straight and suitable for thrusting, that is, less curved than those employed in the Commonwealth, from which the weapon type hailed. A sabre should have quillons and a bar to protect the hand, which made it look more like a rapier and less like a sabre. The instructions suggest that the two weapon types were converging in Sweden.[62] Some Swedes also carried the *tessak* (Swedish: *tasshake*) or the cutlass (Swedish: *kortlass*, from French: *coutelas* or Italian: *coltellaccio*, 'knife').[63] By the time of King Charles, all these terms seem to have been used more or less interchangeably.

---

60 Josef Alm, *Arméns eldhandvapen förr och nu* (Stockholm: Kungl. Armémuseum, 1953), p.36.
61 Alm, *Eldhandvapen 1*, pp.160, 163.
62 Alm, *Blanka vapen*, p.29.
63 Alm, *Blanka vapen*, p.30; Seitz, *Svärdet och värjan*, pp.34–38, 92–94.

THE SWEDISH MILITARY ESTABLISHMENT

Pikemen and Halberdiers

As in Denmark, most infantrymen who did not carry muskets were armed with pikes. The pike (early seventeenth-century Swedish: *spets*, 'point') was an important offensive and defensive weapon that also safeguarded the infantry from enemy cavalry. On the Continent and until recently also in Sweden, a pikeman traditionally was valued higher than an arquebusier. However, the task of carrying a pike and the associated armour had been unpopular with the men ever since their pay was reduced to that of an arquebusier.

First John of Nassau, and then King Charles himself at the disastrous defeat at Kircholm, realised that the Swedish army needed more armoured pikemen. As mentioned, Sweden also needed armoured cuirassiers, so the same means were taken to raise both. In 1606 the Crown announced the aforementioned programme known as 'shield-knight service' (*skölderusttjänst*), which meant that anybody who could supply himself with the required armour and a warhorse would, in effect, become a noble and enjoy a number of privileges (but not, as we have seen, hereditary nobility). Although this programme was primarily introduced to raise cuirassiers, those who had the means to acquire a helmet, breast- and backplate, and pike and who were willing to serve on foot as pikemen were eligible too. King Charles hoped to raise 13 companies of such pikemen. However, the programme was a failure and produced few volunteers. Ultimately two companies of pikemen were raised, one in Småland and one in Västergötland, and remained in service when the Kalmar War broke out. The programme was not extended to Finland, which lacked suitable men of means, and moreover, needed immediate replacements for those men who had been lost at Kircholm.[64]

It seems that the failure of the shield-knight programme made King Charles rethink his options. From the defeat at Kircholm until the beginning of the Kalmar War (i.e. from 1606 to 1611), the Crown issued so many halberds relative to the number of pikes to the infantry that it seems possible that King Charles wanted to create units of halberdiers instead of pikemen. He possibly regarded the halberd, with its increasingly long spearhead, as a more versatile thrusting weapon than the longer pike.[65] If so, the plan failed. We hear nothing of units of halberdiers, even though individuals armed with this weapon may have fought in the war. Moreover, as soon as Gustavus Adolphus succeeded his father, he made a strong effort to increase the number of pikemen. In 1612, he appointed a special pike manufacturer who was ordered to make 'as many pikes as were needed or he could manage'.[66] In 1613, he ordered every peasant in Stockholm and Uppsala Counties to deliver two to three pike shafts. Similar instructions followed elsewhere and in later years. Ash wood was recommended, but pine was acceptable, the instruction clarified. In 1613, the pikes were required to be 10 cubits (5.94 m) long. Because of the ongoing wars on the eastern front against the Commonwealth and Muscovy, Swedish officers generally held that pikes had to be longer than the long lances

Halberd of the Swedish army type, found during excavations at King Charles's Ryssby camp and almost certainly used by a Swedish soldier in the Kalmar War. Believed to have been made in Sweden in the late sixteenth century. Only the metal part survives. Present length: 71.5 cm. Present width: 23 cm. (Kalmar Museum)

---

64 Generalstaben, *Sveriges krig 1611–1632*, vol. 1, pp.93–95.
65 Barkman, *Kungl. Svea livgardes historia*, vol. 2, pp.616–17.
66 Petri, *Kungl. Första livgrenadjärregementets historia*, pp.413–14.

employed by Polish hussars for infantry successfully to withstand a Polish cavalry charge. However, in 1616, the regulation length was decreased to nine cubits (5.35 m), which, as we have seen, corresponded to Continental practices and henceforth remained the standard Swedish pike length. Based on surviving seventeenth-century pikes in the Royal Armoury, Stockholm, and Skokloster Castle, the pikehead was made of hard steel, about 10–14 cm in length (longer if the socket was included), and four-sided in shape. The pike shaft had a nonuniform diameter that ranged from about 3–3.75 cm and was, from the head downwards, strengthened by two iron reinforcements 50–70 cm in length.[67] The section used as a hand grip – sometimes designated with two rings, one at each side – was often square or grooved to facilitate a safe grip or covered in cloth. Pike shafts were preferably of ash or maple wood, although, as noted, pine and eventually aspen were acceptable, too.[68] The pike shafts may have been painted black, especially later in the century since this seems to have been a common practice in Germany and, based on the surviving pikes, apparently in Sweden. There is, unfortunately, no way of knowing whether surviving, black-painted pike shafts were so painted when first issued or only later.

The pike was exclusively a battlefield weapon. Most garrison regiments only carried arquebuses. In fact, when a pike-armed unit was deployed to garrison a town or fortress, standard practice was to supply the pikemen with arquebuses instead of pikes. The commandant would be ordered to store the pikes until the unit again was ordered into the field.[69] Likewise, for obvious reasons, pikes were not used when troops were sent out to forage or for the small war. Pikemen deployed for shipboard duty were also rearmed, this time with guns with snaphance locks.[70]

Pikemen were expected to wear a full set of armour consisting of both a breast- and backplate, gorget, and tassets to protect the upper thighs. A pikeman would also wear a helmet, commonly of the cabasset type (in Scandinavia, often referred to as a 'pear helmet' because of its pear-, some say almond-, shaped top with a small point). Inside the helmet, the soldier wore padding made of flax or, for those officers who could afford it, cotton.[71] Some Swedish pikemen possibly wore helmets of the morion type. After the war, in 1615–1616, King Christian purchased 119 sets of captured Swedish infantry armour from the military entrepreneur Jørgen Lunge, including helmets of a type in Danish referred to as a 'moulun'.[72]

---

67 Alm, *Blanka vapen*, pp.140–41.
68 Hamilton, *Afhandling*, p.122. The common practice among modern-day reenactors to employ factory-made pike shafts of uniform diameter from point to butt does not correspond to early modern practices and, moreover, makes the pike wobbly when in operation.
69 There is no reason to believe that the practice then was a new one. Alm, *Blanka vapen*, p.142, citing a letter dated 28 July 1630 to Lars Kagg, the commandant in Anklam.
70 Alm, *Eldhandvapen 1*, p.161.
71 Alm, *Blanka vapen*, p.253, citing Johann Jacobi von Wallhausen, *Kriegskunst zu Fuß* (Leeuwarden: Claude Fontaine, 1630).
72 Blom, *Kristian Den Fjerdes Artilleri*, p.336.

THE SWEDISH MILITARY ESTABLISHMENT

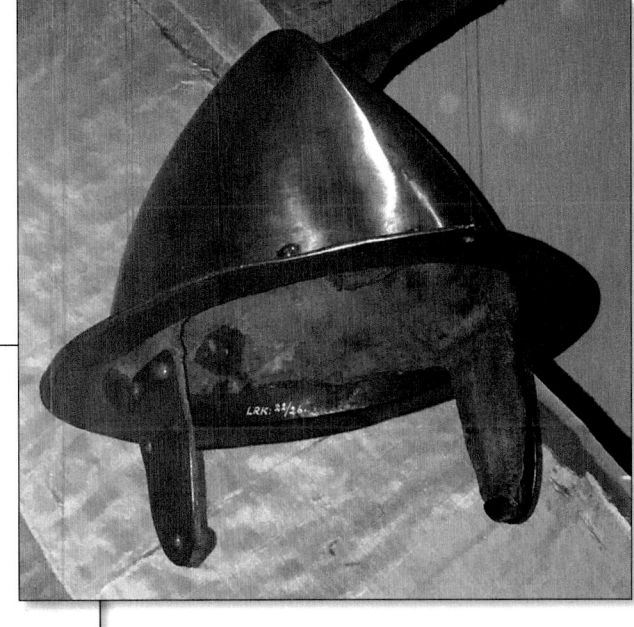

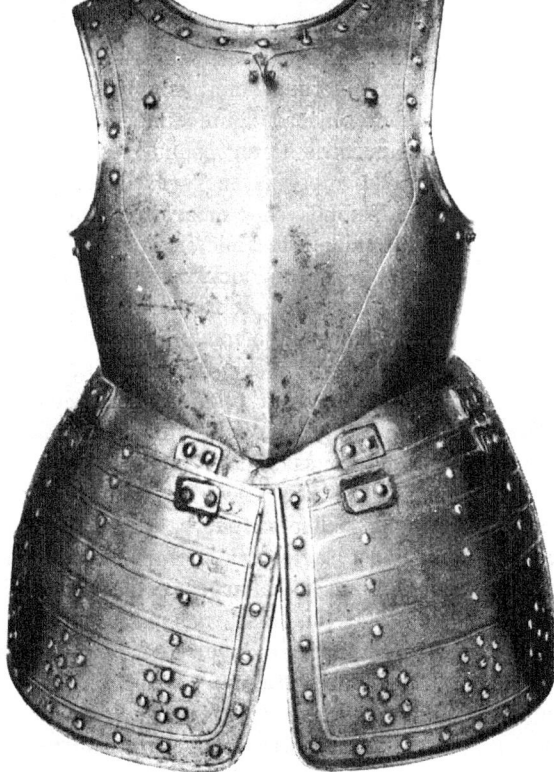

Above: Infantry helmet, 1600–1630.
(Army Museum, Stockholm)

Left: Pikeman armour, 1600–1630.
(Royal Armoury, Stockholm)

Each pikeman carried a rapier as a sidearm. Pikemen in some regiments might be armed with an axe instead of rapier. For instance, in late 1611, an order was issued to supply some soldiers with axes instead of rapiers.[73] Whether this was the result of a shortage of rapiers, perhaps the most likely explanation, or an expected need for fortification tools remains unknown.

Harquebusiers

At the beginning of the seventeenth century, most Swedish cavalry, whether of provincial or enlisted origin, served as unarmoured harquebusiers. Unfortunately for the historian, the available narrative sources hardly ever distinguish between cuirassiers and harquebusiers, all of whom routinely are described only as cavalry. The armament was certainly similar. Each harquebusier carried a fine-calibre arquebus or carbine as primary armament, a rapier, and one or two wheellock pistols. Some may have worn a helmet, gorget, breastplate, and occasionally even a backplate and armour for the upper arms. The full set of harquebusier armour (Swedish: *skyttetyg*) was probably only worn by a minority.[74]

The cavalry arquebus usually came with a wheellock, although a few snaphances were used as well. As noted, the Continental manner of employing the cavalry arquebus at this time involved hanging it from a swivel attached to a bandolier across the left shoulder so that it could be fired without unhooking from the bandolier. For this reason, in Sweden, the weapon was referred to as a 'bandolier arquebus' (*bantlärhake*). Swedish harquebusiers were identical to those enlisted in the Danish army. Following Continental style, the bandolier arquebus was commonly around 1.2 m long and had a calibre of 16 bore (16.8 mm). On the left side of the gunlock, a fairly large leather flap was screwed in place, which could be folded over the gunlock to protect it. On his right side, the harquebusier carried a special leather strap from his belt with a powder horn, priming flask, ammunition pouch, and wheellock spanner.[75]

At this time, the Swedish harquebusiers were already in the process of replacing the arquebus with the carbine. As far as is known, carbines were first introduced to Sweden in 1600, when 100 such weapons were ordered from Copenhagen. They were to have a barrel length of about 0.7 m.[76] Based on later examples, the total length was probably similar to the arquebus or possibly slightly shorter. A carbine – like the musket, which was also introduced around this time – had a larger calibre than the obsolete arquebus. However, the wheellock remained in common use among horsemen.

The practice of firing the gun without unhooking from the bandolier was discontinued with the introduction of carbines. Instead, the carbine was carried in a saddle holster. Likewise, the harquebusier's belt strap for equipment was discarded in most cases, too. Instead, the men would carry a

---

73 Hamilton, *Afhandling*, p.121.

74 Jakobsson, *Lantmilitär beväpning och beklädnad*, p.116.

75 Alm, *Eldhandvapen 1*, pp.196–97.

76 Jakobsson, *Lantmilitär beväpning och beklädnad*, p.9.

powder horn, priming flask, ammunition pouch, and wheellock spanner on the outside of the saddle holster.⁷⁷

Cuirassiers

First instituted in (probably) 1280, when members of the nobility agreed to raise a force of armoured cavalry from their retainers when called to arms, the oldest unit in the Swedish army was that of the noble cavalry. This traditional military duty was known by an old name that can be translated as 'military service' but originally signified 'knight service', that is, service on horseback (Swedish: *rosstjänst, russtjänst, rusttjänst*). From 1571 onwards, it was known as the retinue of nobles (*riddarskapets russtiänst*, later *adelsfanan*). The retinue of nobles served as cuirassiers but was numerically small, consisting only of a few hundred men. Swedish cuirassiers looked much the same as those on the Continent and in Denmark.⁷⁸

Cuirassiers were few in the Swedish army since the armour was costly and out of reach even for many nobles and since the weight of the armour demanded the use of larger horses than Sweden could easily breed at home. According to regulations from 1621, which reflected older practices, each cuirassier should bring a good and strong horse of 14 hands (140 cm). He should also bring a second cavalryman on a horse of 13 hands, armed with a helmet, breast- and backplate, rapier, and a pair of wheellock pistols. A third horse and baggage servant should be brought as well but for the supply train.⁷⁹ Although these regulations were issued after the Kalmar War, it is likely that the Crown held similar expectations before then.

A cuirassier was armed with a pair of wheellock pistols and a rapier. Pistols made in Sweden in the first years of the seventeenth century occasionally came with snaphance locks instead of wheellocks. However, wheellocks soon became standard equipment.⁸⁰ Early in the century, pistols were long, up to around 75 cm in length, with calibre varying widely around 57 or 58 bore

Full set of shot-proof cuirassier armour, 1620–1630. Blackened and lined with soft leather. Those used during the Kalmar War were identical in most cases. (Skokloster Castle)

---

77 Alm, *Eldhandvapen 1*, pp.121, 154, 196, 213 and *Arméns eldhandvapen*, pp.121–22.
78 The retinue of nobles was last raised in 1743 and remained as an organisation until 1901.
79 Hamilton, *Afhandling*, pp.201–02; Jakobsson, *Lantmilitär beväpning och beklädnad*, p.118.
80 Alm, *Eldhandvapen 1*, pp.154, 202, 213 and *Arméns eldhandvapen*, pp.118, 121–22.

THE KALMAR WAR

Gorget for cuirassier armour, originally blackened, first half of the seventeenth century. (Skokloster Castle)

(about 11 mm).[81] Later, the calibre increased to 18 bore (around 16.2 mm), which over time became the standard Swedish pistol calibre.[82]

A cuirassier wore a visored close helmet or burgonet, a gorget for the neck, three-quarter armour that covered the entire upper body and both arms as well as the front half of the legs down to and including the knee, and high riding boots. A full set of Swedish cuirassier armour (Swedish: *drabbtyg*) weighed around 25 kg and was generally blackened. Until about 1620, the breastplate commonly was of the peascod-belly or goose-belly type, which then fell out of fashion. As noted, this had already happened in Germany, where Wallhausen, in 1615, argued that the style was 'more suited to pregnant women than to soldiers'.[83]

Dragoons

We have seen that dragoons were mounted musketeers who moved on horseback but fought on foot. Sweden began to use dragoons early. There were dragoons in the Swedish army already in 1580, and at least one English dragoon company, under Captain Robert Halswell (or Haulswell), a dragoon and petardier, was enlisted for service in Sweden in 1611.

Dragoons used the same muskets as other infantry. Each also carried a rapier. Some may have been equipped with axes as well. Dragoons wore helmets but no breastplates. They wore shoes, not riding boots, and were not issued spurs.

Artillerymen

Like Denmark, Sweden had adopted the Spanish–Dutch system of classifying artillery. The types and calibres of cannons were the same as those used in Denmark. The siege artillery included 96-pounders (Swedish: *dubbelkartoger*), 48-pounders (*helkartoger*), 36-pounders (*trekvartskartoger*), 24-pounders (*halvkartoger*), and 12-pounders (*kvartskartoger* or *kvarterstycken*).

In addition, the Swedish artillery included long-barrelled cannons of the culverin class: 24-pounders (*helslangor, notslangor*, or *fältslangor*, 'field snakes'), 18-pounders (*trekvartsslangor*), 12-pounders (*halvslangor*), and six-pounders (*kvartsslangor*). Yet smaller-calibre, long-barrelled cannons were known as falcons (*falkoner*) and, of even smaller calibre, falconets (*falkonetter*).[84]

---

81 Alm, *Eldhandvapen 1*, p.200.
82 Jakobsson, *Lantmilitär beväpning och beklädnad*, p.116, n.3.
83 Alm, *Blanka vapen*, pp.242, 251.
84 Jakobsson, *Lantmilitär beväpning och beklädnad*, pp.165–68.

THE SWEDISH MILITARY ESTABLISHMENT

The total number of cannons was large, but the cannons were distributed throughout the country's castles in Sweden, Finland, and Estonia. In 1600, the Stockholm Armoury alone contained an artillery park consisting of two 96-pounders (more on which later), five 48-pounders, four 36-pounders, and ten 24-pounders. The number of culverins was far larger, including fifty-one 24-pounders, thirty-five 18-pounders (of which 18 of bronze), one hundred four 12-pounders (of which 79 of bronze), and large numbers of cannons of smaller calibre.[85]

It was understood that common calibres were beneficial for logistics and generally made the army more efficient. However, this was not yet reflected in the existing artillery parks. When the Danes took the castles of Kalmar and Gullberg, they found cannons of several different calibres, including 12-pounders, 10-pounders, and three-pounders.[86] In 1582, two remarkably large, long-barrelled 96-pounders (*fyrdubbla notslangor*) were cast in Stockholm. Having a weight of 10,200 kg each, the two cannons were named '*Makalös*' (peerless).[87] The poor road conditions in Sweden meant that siege artillery often could not be moved at all, except by river boat or ship. Even the field artillery, established in 1541 and kept up to date since then, lacked mobility, which often precluded its efficient use.

Sweden also had abundant copper deposits, so the production of bronze cannons was never a problem. Even so, quite a few iron cannons were in the inventory, too.

Petards were first introduced in Sweden from France in 1592. Cast of bronze or iron, petard sizes varied from 20–70 kg.[88] They were first used in 1599, in a failed attack on Elfsborg Castle on behalf of King Sigismund. From 1602 onwards, the Swedish army used petards in Livonia.[89] As a countermeasure, King Charles ordered two or three fences to be erected in front of important gates to deny hostile petardiers access. The Swedes apparently first encountered this countermeasure in Muscovy, where it was developed to counter Swedish petardiers.[90]

Mines were manufactured to destroy the walls of enemy fortresses. The Stockholm Armoury contained huge mines of gunpowder weights corresponding to 270, 1,303, and 1,480 pounds (112, 541, and 614 kg, respectively).[91]

Although nowadays little known, Sweden employed pyrochemical munitions of various types. Rockets for battlefield illumination and incendiary uses were already in common use. This was a field in constant development, and the numbers and types of pyrotechnics in Sweden grew rapidly from 1540 onwards. A Firework Corps, separate from the Ordnance

---

85 Hedberg (ed.), *Kungl. Artilleriet: Medeltid och äldre vasatid*, p.470, Appendix 7.
86 Jakobsson, *Lantmilitär beväpning och beklädnad*, p.65, n.3.
87 Hedberg (ed.), *Kungl. Artilleriet: Medeltid och äldre vasatid*, p.196.
88 Hedberg (ed.), *Kungl. Artilleriet: Medeltid och äldre vasatid*, pp.196, 203.
89 Barkman, *Kungl. Svea livgardes historia*, vol. 2, p.406.
90 Hedberg (ed.), *Kungl. Artilleriet: Medeltid och äldre vasatid*, p.203.
91 Hedberg (ed.), *Kungl. Artilleriet: Medeltid och äldre vasatid*, p.227.

THE KALMAR WAR

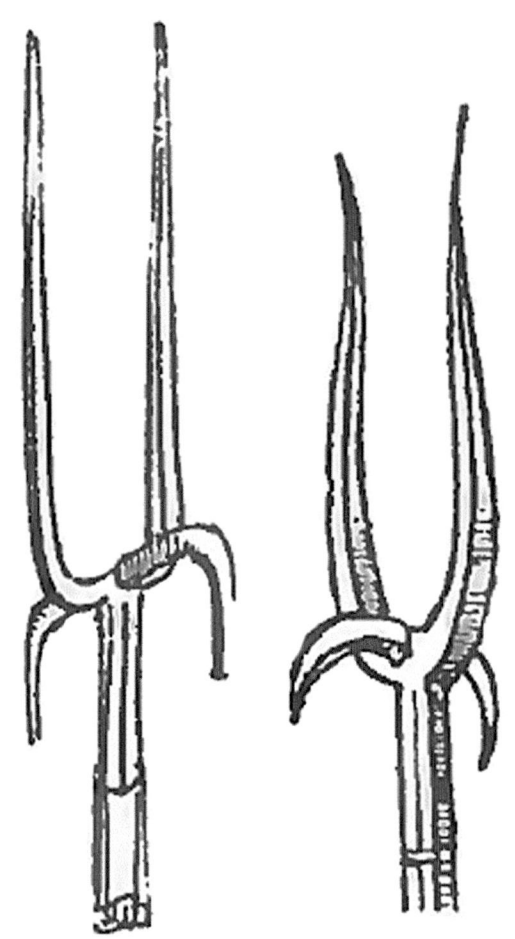

Above, right: Italian military fork employed at Geneva, 1612. Left: Italian or Swiss military fork from roughly the same period. Swedish military forks are generally believed to have been of a similar type. (August Demmin, 1893)

Corps, was established in 1570.[92] Pyrotechnical munitions remained in use in the seventeenth century, when mortars of various types, capable of launching pyrotechnics, were added to the weapons package. On occasion, the artillery also fired toxic fuming balls (Swedish: *dunstkulor*) – smoke-filled cannon balls that emitted a toxic fume – an early form of chemical warfare.

Since artillerymen also served as sappers, they carried a variety of tools such as pickaxes, spades, shovels, and axes. Attempts were made to introduce combination tools that also served as weapons. In 1600, the Crown ordered 6,000 military forks (German: *Sturmgabel*; Swedish: *stormgaffel*), a weapon type commonly employed for the destruction of gabions and fascines when storming enemy field fortifications.[93] Being essentially a civilian tool with some added offensive capability, the shape of military forks varied considerably. Most seem to have had hooks on the back to enable the pulling down of fascines and, possibly, enemies. However, the military fork is often confused with the *roncone* (also known as *runca*), which existed in great numbers on the Continent and by this time seems to have been more common than the outwardly somewhat similar partisan.[94] The *roncone* was characterised by its tines, which were widened out to form cutting blades, while the central prong often was extended into a spike or spearhead. Since the Swedish Crown ordered such a large number of military forks at a time when soon-to-be King Charles experimented with halberds as surrogate pikes, there is some doubt about which weapon type he had in mind and exactly what the Swedish military fork looked like.

Artillerymen also handled most aspects of field engineering. The Swedish artillery train for this reason also carried 12 or 13 pontoons or boats, each about 4.5 m by 2 m in size, for the construction of temporary bridges, together with all other necessary materials.[95]

As in the Danish army, Swedish artillerymen were armed with muskets and rapiers for personal protection and to protect their cannons.[96] They generally dressed similar to the infantry.

---

92 Hedberg (ed.), *Kungl. Artilleriet: Medeltid och äldre vasatid*, p.241.
93 Barkman, *Kungl. Svea livgardes historia*, vol. 2, pp.617–18.
94 To confuse matters further, there was also a presumably Corsican variant known as *korseke*.
95 Hedberg (ed.), *Kungl. Artilleriet: Medeltid och äldre vasatid*, p.231.
96 Hedberg (ed.), *Kungl. Artilleriet: Yngre vasatiden*, p.80.

THE SWEDISH MILITARY ESTABLISHMENT

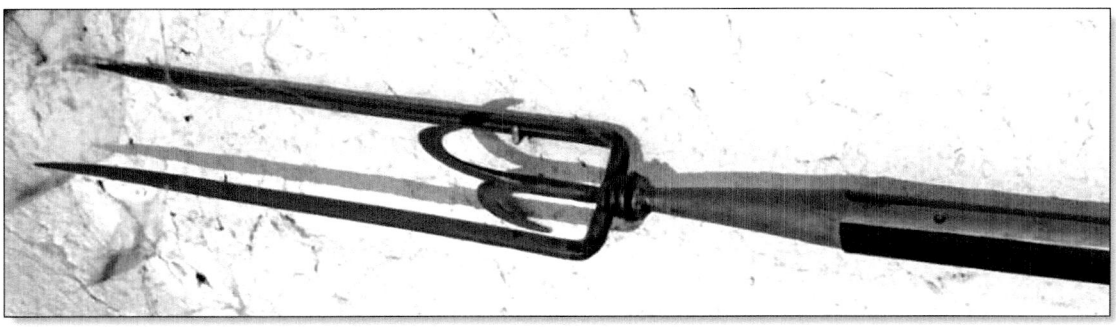

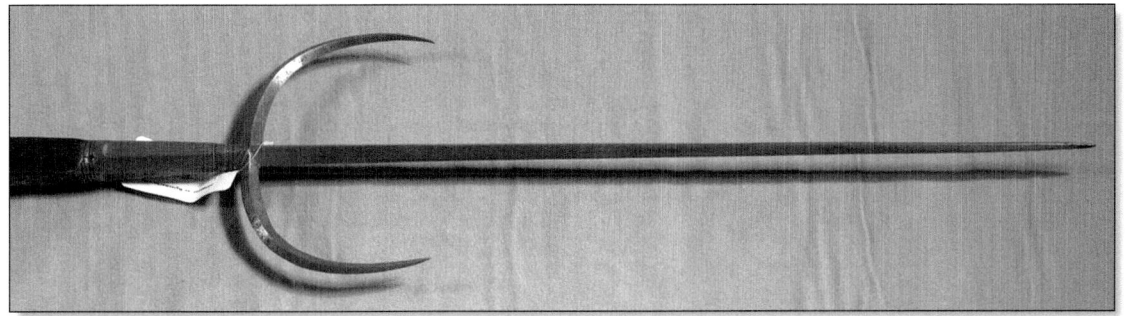

Top: Military fork of Continental type. (Author's collection)

Bottom: *Roncone* of uncertain date and provenience, from a Swedish collection. Essentially a civilian hay fork with an extended prong functioning as spike or spearhead, the *roncone* just as easily functioned as a partisan or half-pike. (Army Museum, Stockholm, AM.049495)

Naval Personnel

Sweden manufactured both cannons and sidearms for its navy. Among them was a kind of naval sword (Swedish: *äntersvärd*, 'boarding sword'), although, as in Denmark, neither depiction nor specimen seems to have survived into the present. Some naval swords were broad longswords that either had no point or only a blunt one, of a type that had been manufactured since 1554 in the arms factory in Arboga. Some of these were so-called 'command swords' given to admirals and ship captains following sixteenth-century customs. Others may have been more similar to the rapiers used by the infantry or, indeed, the sabre-like cutlasses that also existed in small numbers. The navy often received army surplus rapiers. In addition to swords, the navy employed a variety of spears, half-pikes, and pikes. Naval pikes were to be 10 cubits long in 1613, but, in 1616, naval regulations prescribed a pike length of nine cubits. In other words, navy and army regulations for pikes were identical. Half-pikes were to be five cubits in length, again the same as in the army. Sailors also employed axes, both as tools and weapons. As for firearms, the navy employed arquebuses, muskets, blunderbusses, and pistols. The navy knew that matchlocks were a fire hazard and accordingly preferred snaphance locks. Pistols intended for the navy, so-called 'boarding pistols' (*änterpistoler*), usually had snaphance locks and were occasionally carried several at a time, hanging from bandoliers.[97] Finally, the navy employed hand grenades and a large variety of incendiaries.[98]

---

97 Josef Alm, 'Flottans handvapen', in *Sjöhistorisk Årsbok 1953-54* (Stockholm: Föreningen Sveriges Sjöfartsmuseum i Stockholm, 1954), pp.72, 76–83, 85–87.

98 Alm, 'Flottans handvapen', p.91. See also Michael Fredholm von Essen, 'On the Trail of Rocketry: The Enigma of Scandinavian Naval Pyrotechnics in the Sixteenth to Eighteenth Century',

The navy did not employ uniforms, but they commonly received plain woollen grey cloth for their garments. Grey cloth was distributed to naval personnel in at least 1615, 1617, 1621, and 1624.[99] Woollen cloth preserves heat even when wet, which was an obvious advantage in the navy.

Uniforms

Although national uniforms were not worn at the time of the Kalmar War, units often presented a uniform appearance since most Swedish soldiers received cloth for uniforms. Since cloth of the same type and colour (plain woollens were rarely issued except to the navy) were distributed at the same time, this meant that the men of a given unit commonly shared the same style and colour – at least until clothes wore out and individuals had to replace them wherever garments were found. However, details usually remain elusive. Some information gleaned from archival records shows units and colour combinations that still may have been current at the time of the Kalmar War.

Even so, later records show that cloth was sometimes issued every year or every second year and that the colour of the new cloth was typically different from the previous distribution. In short, the units would indeed often present a uniform appearance, but there were no fixed or even customary colours for particular units (occasionally, the only exception being guard units dressed up for festive occasions in the colours of the ruler's house). So much is clear that Swedish and Finnish infantry often wore blue garments, but this was presumably because of common availability rather than choice.

[See Table 4, **Known Swedish unit uniform colours, 1609–1610**, end of chapter]

Banners

By the turn of the seventeenth century, Swedish infantry colours and cavalry standards are believed to have mostly retained the characteristics of the previous century in that they consisted of only two colours and were geometrically divided into squares, rhombi, lines, and similar patterns. Such banners may have remained in use at the time of the Kalmar War. Yet, by then, the Swedish army had adopted similar styles in military banners and colours as those already predominant on the Continent. Colours and banners were painted with royal cyphers and devices in the form of texts or

---

Arquebusier, 30:6 (2008), pp.24–39, 'On the Trail of Rocketry 2: Early Eighteenth-Century Gas Warfare and Other Norwegian Innovations in Naval Pyrotechnics', *Arquebusier*, 32:1 (2010), pp.2–5, and 'Early Eighteenth Century Naval Chemical Warfare in Scandinavia: A Study in the Introduction of New Weapon Technologies in Early Modern Navies', *Baltic Security and Defence Review*, 13:1 (2011), pp.122–51.

99   Lars-Eric Höglund, *Från Karl Knutsson till Kristina: Svenska fälttecken och beklädnad från senmedeltid till trettioåriga kriget* (Karlstad: Acedia Press, 2012), p.99.

THE SWEDISH MILITARY ESTABLISHMENT

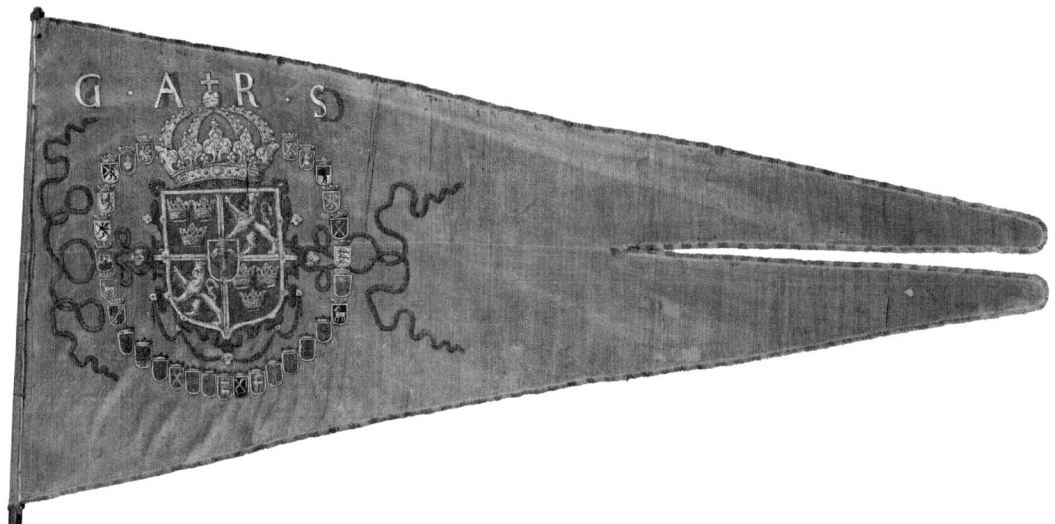

The Swedish national banner was not carried in the field but used for ceremonies. Painted by the craftsman Holger Hansson on blue silk, the national banner was employed at the coronations of both King Charles (in 1607), for whom it was made, and Gustavus Adolphus (in 1617), for whom the cypher 'G A R S' (*Gustavus Adolphus Rex Sueciae*, Gustavus Adolphus, King of Sweden) was added. Breadth 1.75 m, length 3.82 m. (Royal Armoury, Stockholm)

emblems in the Continental tradition. King Charles used the device 'C R S' (*Carolus Rex Sueciae*, Charles, King of Sweden), while his son and successor, Gustavus Adolphus, adopted the cypher 'G A R S' (*Gustavus Adolphus Rex Sueciae*, Gustavus Adolphus, King of Sweden) upon succession.

Until about 1620, colours were three to four metres in breadth and length. Hand grips were still short, less than about 30 cm in length. The hand grip might be covered with green wax, with the grip itself covered in cloth. Cavalry units carried standards of a type known as a cornet. The cornet was usually about 50–55 cm in breadth and 50–70 cm in length and edged with a fringe of thread. Based on surviving specimen in the Trophy Collection, Stockholm, a cornet pole was shaped like a fluted lance and usually painted. Since all dragoon units were enlisted, we can assume that dragoon guidons had swallowtails in the Continental style. As far as is known, they commonly were about one metre in breadth and from 1.4–1.8m in length.[100]

Almost the only reasonably comprehensive early seventeenth-century information we have on Swedish colours and banners derives from the epic poem *Carolomachia*, which was written by Laurentius Bojerus, a Swedish Jesuit, to celebrate the Commonwealth victory at Kircholm in 1605.[101] The poem's descriptions are sufficiently detailed to allow the identification of each banner with a particular provincial unit – as long as we accept the premise that Swedish cavalry units already flew banners with the coat of arms of their respective province. This conclusion indeed seems likely since the provincial coats of arms already played an important heraldic role and they certainly appeared on banners later in the century. Regardless, we should bear in mind that Bojerus's descriptions do not constitute conclusive evidence. In

---

100 Richard Brzezinski, *The Army of Gustavus Adolphus (2): Cavalry* (London: Osprey Publishing, 1993), pp.39, 41.

101 Laurentius Bojerus, *Carolomachiae liber* (Vilnius: Jesuit Academy, 1606), vol. 3. Bojerus (1563–1619) was a Swedish Jesuit who mostly wrote poems on religious topics. *Carolomachia* is his best-known work. Bojerus published his poems under various pseudonyms.

the absence of actual surviving banners, the possibility remains that the poet intended his banner descriptions as allegoric, not literal, descriptions.

In no case does Bojerus mention the colour of the field of the provincial banners. If more than one unit was raised in a province, we can assume that each carried a banner with the same provincial coat of arms but on fields of different colour.

Based on Bojerus, King Charles's Life Banner of Horse flew a snow-white cornet with the three golden crowns of Sweden. Apparently, the colour white already signified the status of a life company.[102]

The Uppland cavalry flew a cornet with the royal orb and cross (Latin: *globus cruciger*, 'cross-bearing orb'). In the Empire and Sweden, it was somewhat irreverently known as 'apple of the state' (German: *Reichsapfel*; Swedish: *riksäpple*).

The banner of the Småland cavalry flew a cornet with a standing lion carrying a crossbow.

The Östergötland cavalry flew a cornet with a fierce griffon.

The Västergötland cavalry's cornet displayed a proud lion on a bicolour field, which, based on later banners, can be assumed to have been black and yellow.

The Södermanland cavalry flew a cornet with a black griffon, which the poet described as terrible in countenance.

The Finland cavalry (later to be known as the Åbo and Björneborg regiment) cornet was decorated with a standing bear wielding a sword. According to Bojerus, the cornet also displayed a star, although two stars is more likely since this was included in the contemporary coat of arms.

The Nyland cavalry from Finland (later to be known as the Nyland and Tavastehus regiment) flew a cornet with a helmet crowned with two flags (presumably blue with a cross of yellow or white, that is, heraldic gold or silver).

Other information on colours and standards is limited. In 1607, the Drabant Guard of Foot fought under a yellow colour. In 1609, newly raised cavalry banners, including Lars Andersson's cavalry banner in Finland, received cornets of red damask. In 1610, Jacob De la Gardie's life banner of horse (of two companies) received cornets of unknown but likely white damask with silver embroideries, including four flames each, presumably one in each corner.[103]

---

102 The custom of white standards may have derived from the practice on the Continent to display, in the immediate vicinity of the commanding general, a small white flag (Berthold von der Becke, *Soldaten-Spiegel: Historische Anweisung welcher Gestalt ein Guarison oder Vestung nicht allein mit aller jhrer Notturfft vnnd Zugehörung wohl zu versorgen hohen vnd nidern Aemptern recht anzuordnen* (Frankfurt am Main: Johann Spieß und Johann Jacob Porschen, 1605), p.85, a book printed on behalf of King Christian). Possibly, the standard was known (in Dutch or German) as '*Kendefahne*' (recognition banner), a term that disseminated to Denmark (as '*Kendefane*'), where the expression was known since at least 1565, and Sweden (as '*Kännefana*'), also from 1565 onwards, which became the name of the aforementioned Vanguard Banner.

103 Höglund, *Från Karl Knutsson till Kristina*, p.44.

THE SWEDISH MILITARY ESTABLISHMENT

Cavalry cornet in cuirassier armour. Cornets in Swedish service, especially those in the retinue of nobles or any of the life banners, would have dressed in a similar manner. (Jacob de Gheyn II, *Die Reitschule oder Übungen der Kavallerie*)

In early 1612, the cavalry (possibly life banner) under Gustavus Adolphus flew a black cornet, which the Danes then captured together with several other cornets and colours in the area around Vittsjö.[104] A hand-drawn copy of one of Karel van Mander II's tapestries for Frederiksborg Castle, which depicts the second invasion of Öland later that year, shows two Swedish infantry colours of the early type. One features a St Andrew's Cross, while the other looks like a modern Swedish blue and yellow flag. Although the original colours of the tapestry are no longer known, the blue and yellow flag is known from the 1550s and is believed to have been older still.

Kettledrums and trumpets were accompanied by flags, too, of unknown colour but with silver embroideries.[105] As noted, colours and standards, as well as musical instruments, were regarded as important trophies, so they were eagerly captured in battle. It was deemed a disgrace to lose a standard since a captured standard was a sure sign of defeat. The loss of standards and musical instruments also made it difficult to gather and reorganise the survivors of a unit since standards and music were important means of leading a military unit. In the Swedish army, each company standard was carried in battle by the ensign, who in turn was protected by two men armed with long, straight, two-handed swords of the Continental *Zweihänder* style.[106] The custom reached Sweden with the *Landsknechts* in the early sixteenth century.[107] By the time of the Kalmar War, the sword-armed guard primarily played a ceremonial role, and Gustavus Adolphus abolished the custom early in his reign.

---

104 Anon., 'Journal', p.728.
105 Höglund, *Från Karl Knutsson till Kristina*, p.44.
106 Barkman, *Kungl. Svea livgardes historia*, vol. 2, p.633.
107 Seitz, *Svärdet och värjan*, p.46.

THE KALMAR WAR

King Charles's Life Banner of Horse

The Uppland Banner of Horse

This page and facing: Banners as described in the poem *Carolomachia* (see p.135). (Author's illustrations)

The Småland Banner of Horse

The Östergötland Banner of Horse

THE SWEDISH MILITARY ESTABLISHMENT

The Västergötland Banner of Horse

The Södermanland Banner of Horse

The Finland Banner of Horse

The Nyland Banner of Horse

THE KALMAR WAR

Soldier with a ceremonial two-handed sword, 1611. The jacket is buttoned all the way down and has protruding shoulder straps. The sleeves are slit, and the breeches fairly narrow. The linen collar has elongated tips. King Charles's funeral armour, made in Stockholm in 1611. (Strängnäs Cathedral)

THE SWEDISH MILITARY ESTABLISHMENT

Left: The command sword owned by Axel Oxenstierna next to two ceremonial, double-handed *Zweihänder* swords, dated to c. 1600, with parts of a suit of armour. Under Gustavus Adolphus, command swords were only used in the navy, while the use of ceremonial double-handed swords was discontinued. (Royal Armoury, Stockholm)

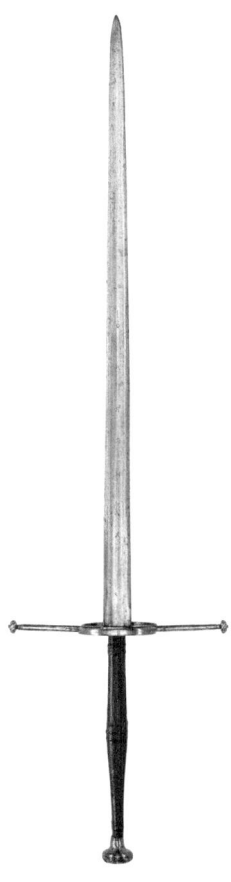

Above: The two-handed command sword owned by Axel Oxenstierna, dated to the end of the sixteenth century. Made in Germany, with the running wolf mark of Passau and Solingen swordsmiths inlaid in brass. Blade length 102.9 cm, width 51 mm, total length 142.2 cm. Weight: 2.7 kg. (Royal Armoury, Stockholm)

THE KALMAR WAR

Drummer.
(Jacob de Gheyn II)

Regimental Music

A Swedish infantry unit contained drummers and pipers, while cavalry units included trumpeters and kettledrummers (one kettledrum on each side of the horse). When possible, a cavalry trumpeter rode a piebald. Back in 1594, when the Drabant Guard participated in a parade on foot, they employed kettledrums hung on the back of a soldier and played by the man behind him.[108] This practice may have continued later as well. As noted, the music played an important role in maintaining order since it could be used for signalling on the field of battle and elsewhere. The music, no doubt, was also intended to reinforce the men's morale both in battle and on the march.

---

108 Göte Göransson, *Gustav II Adolf och hans folk* (Location unknown: Bra Böcker, 1994), p.217.

THE SWEDISH MILITARY ESTABLISHMENT

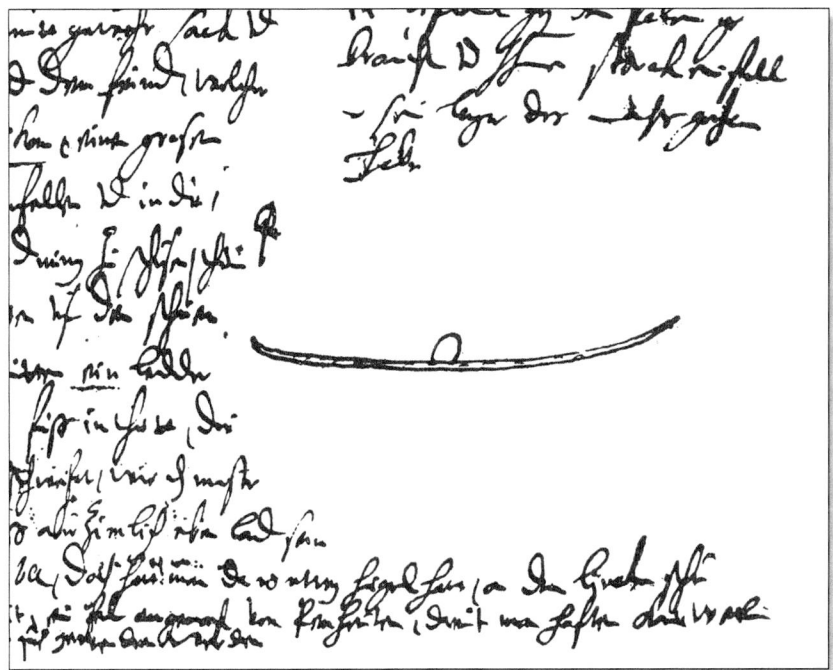

John of Nassau's description and drawing a Swedish ski. (Staatsarchiv Wiesbaden, Abt. 174 K 924, Altes Dillenburger Archiv fol. 123)

Skis

No description of the Swedish army would be complete without mentioning the use of skis when snow conditions permitted. When John of Nassau commanded the Swedish army in 1601–1602, the exotic skis made such an impression on him that he documented them in a drawing with accompanying text.[109] John of Nassau described the skis as eight feet long. Both the point and rear of the skis were turned up, and the left ski was lined with reindeer skin underneath so as to not slip backwards when moving uphill. Although John of Nassau did not mention them, other types of skis were used, too, each designed for a certain activity or type of snow cover. Skis had been used in previous wars, and most men from northern Sweden and Finland were experienced in their use. In the Arctic North, entire units regularly travelled on skis, accompanied by Lapp auxiliaries with reindeer for the carrying of provisions. In the previous century, Finnish ski troops had been armed with arquebuses, and, in the reign of Gustavus Adolphus, they likely carried either an arquebus or musket.[110]

---

109 For details, see John of Nassau, 'Grefve Johans av Nassau relation angående kriget i Livland 1601–1602', pp.396–438; Barkman, *Kungl. Svea livgardes historia*, vol. 2, pp.403–05.

110 Michael Fredholm von Essen, *Muscovy's Soldiers: The Emergence of the Russian Army 1462–1689* (Warwick: Helion & Company, 2018), p.59.

The Armament Industry

At the beginning of the seventeenth century, Sweden had only rudimentary arms production facilities. There was only one arms factory, in the town of Arboga. It belonged to the Crown. Some manufacture took place in the province of Hälsingland as well. Despite efforts to increase production there and elsewhere, Sweden still had to import handheld weapons.

But not artillery. Although tin had to be imported, primarily from England, Sweden had large copper reserves and thus had the capability to cast large numbers of bronze cannons. Foundries existed in several locations in Sweden – including Stockholm, Kalmar, and Nyköping – as well as in Reval in Estonia and Viborg in Finland. Gunpowder production facilities were available in the same locations or nearby. Sweden was self-sufficient in cannon and gunpowder production.

A persistent problem, however, was with the slow match, which was needed not only for artillery but also for matchlock muskets. Sweden never became self-sufficient in slow-match production.

Castles and Fortresses

The Italian Wars of the late fifteenth and early sixteenth centuries had shown that tall medieval towers and curtain walls were unable to withstand modern gunpowder artillery. Soon, the key element in fortification became the low, spacious, and solid artillery rampart that evaded or resisted enemy cannon fire and simultaneously functioned as a platform for defensive artillery. Even so, a fortress needed to have a moat and wall sufficiently formidable to deter enemy storming parties. In addition, the trace (i.e. ground plan) should be so arranged that it left no dead ground in which an enemy might take cover. The result of these developments was a system of polygonal and angled bastions, known as the *trace italienne* from its origins in Italy, that enabled interlocking fields of fire. The proponents of the new military architectural style rejected the old, generally circular designs of curtain walls and towers in favour of angular artillery bastions, which consisted of two outward-facing 'faces' and two sideway-facing 'flanks'. The long, straight faces enabled the defensive deployment of more cannons than in the old designs, while the flanks enabled the defender to direct efficient crossfire against any attacker who reached that far. Taken together, the bastion design opened clear fields of fire in all directions and removed the dead ground commonly found in front of circular medieval fortifications. The *trace italienne* and its subsequent developments radically changed the dynamics of siege warfare.

It took some time before the new bastion architecture reached Scandinavia. First followed a brief period of what may be termed 'reinforced old-style castles', built under the supervision of mostly German military architects. In Sweden, this included fresh work or upgrades on Gripsholm Castle in 1537, Kronoberg Castle in 1544, and Kalmar and Vadstena Castles in 1545. The earliest known example in Scandinavia of bastion architecture is generally assessed to be Uppsala Castle in central Sweden, built in the early 1550s

THE SWEDISH MILITARY ESTABLISHMENT

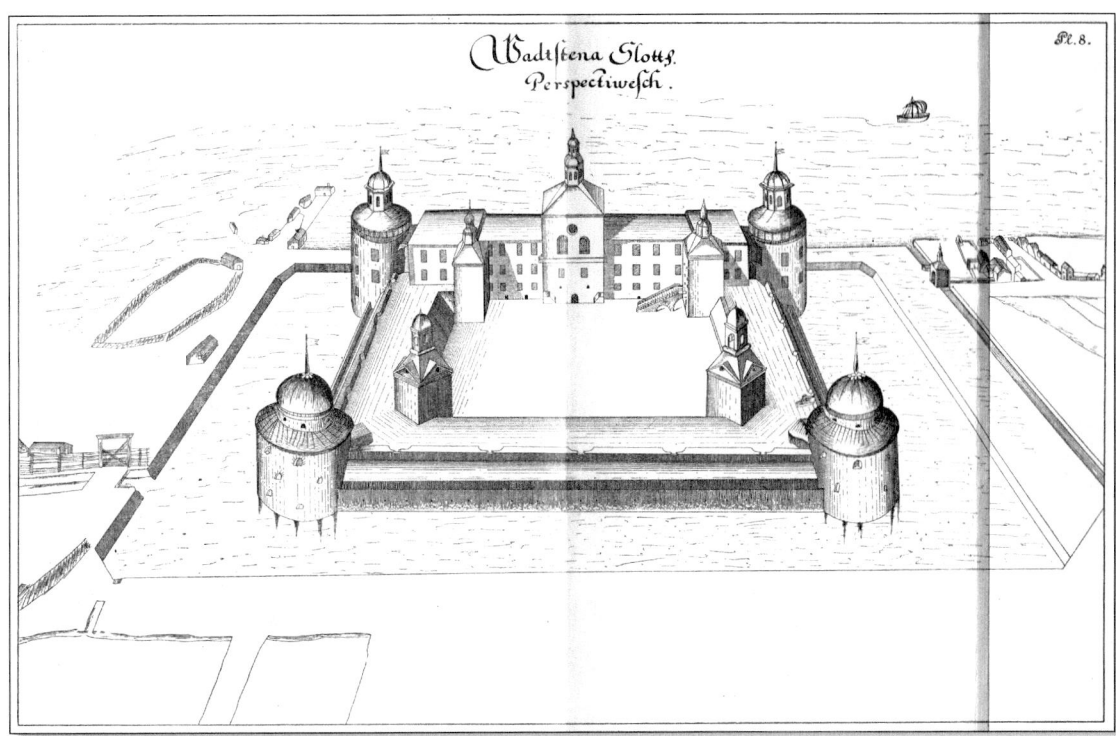

Vadstena Castle, 1587. When the Kalmar War broke out, Vadstena and most other Swedish strongholds remained reinforced old-style castles with round artillery towers as the primary improvement. Such artillery towers are omnipresent in Swedish castles built or upgraded under the Vasa kings and can almost be described as their trademark. The artillery towers remained when, and if, bastions were eventually added. Although a significant upgrade compared to the original ground plan, the artillery towers alone were a far cry from the modern bastion system. (Reconstruction, from contemporary plan, by Ludvig W:son Munthe, 1902)

under King Gustavus I. The bastions were possibly constructed under the supervision of the German artillery officer Heinrich von Cöllen (fl. 1533–1558) or, more likely, the architect Paul Schütz (d. 1576), another German. The Flemish architect Hans Hendrik van Paesschen (Hans Paaske; c. 1510–1582) projected bastions at Elfsborg Castle in 1559 or 1561. Paesschen did not get along with his Swedish employers, so, in 1564, he instead accepted employment by King Frederick II of Denmark, for whom he, in 1566, began the same kind of work on Bohus Castle and, in 1567, on Akershus Castle, both in Norway. The same Paesschen began the construction of bastions at Kronborg Castle in Denmark in 1574. By then, King John had brought into Sweden the versatile Pahr brothers, four military architects who henceforth upgraded and built new fortifications in the modern manner. The brothers were Johann (or Giovanni, also known as Hans) Baptista (fl. 1557–1586), Franz (Franciscus; fl. 1558–1580 or 1583 when he died), Christoph (fl. 1558–1579), and Dominicus (d. 1602/1603). Born in Austria, the family was possibly of distant Italian origin. The family may have derived from Milan or at least had learnt Milanese military architecture. In 1572, Johann and Dominicus began the construction of modern bastions at Kalmar Castle and Borgholm Castle on Öland (the work on Kalmar Castle was only concluded in the early 1600s). During 1574–1578, Johann also worked on Elfsborg Castle

145

and the nearby Gullberg Castle. Meanwhile, from 1573, Christoph led work on Nyköping and Eskilstuna Castles, while Franciscus made improvements to Uppsala and Stockholm Castles. In 1586, Johann was likely the architect who worked to upgrade Kexholm Castle on the eastern border.

Even so, it took time before the bastion system reached all strongholds at risk. Reinforced old-style castles continued to be built, including Jönköping Castle in 1593. This is surprising since this exposed stronghold formed an important part of Sweden's southern defences against Denmark. Likewise, Finland continued to be defended by four old-style castles: Åbo, Tavastehus, Olofsborg (Nyslott), and Viborg. To them was, in 1590, added a castle in Uleåborg. Although new, it was built in the old style. Improvements were also made on the important fortresses in Stockholm, Vaxholm, and Nyköping.

The Navy

Warship Strength

Being a country of far-flung settlements connected by waterways but few good roads, Sweden had always relied on ships for maintaining supply and communication links. The first modern navy had been established in 1522 by the future King Gustavus I, who, in this year, purchased 10 warships from Lübeck as one of several means to gain the throne (it remains unclear if the Lübeck merchants ever were paid). Since then, the navy had generally grown in size and strength, even though the reigns of Kings John and Sigismund had been characterised by a certain neglect of naval matters.

Table 5. Number of warships and galleys in the Swedish navy[111]

Year	100–500	501–1,000	1,001–1,500	1,501–2,000	2,001–2,500	Total	Galleys[112]
1595	12	4	-	1	-	17	15
1600	42	13	-	1	-	56	6
1605	52	16	-	-	-	68	3
1610	49	11	-	-	-	60	4
1615	25	5	-	-	-	30	3
1620	26	7	1	-	-	34	2

---

111 Warship numbers are divided into size groups of metric tons. Glete, *Navies and Nations*, vol. 1, p.607; Glete's revised figures as of August 2005.

112 As with the Danish navy, the figures for galleys are incomplete. There were many more, possibly dozens, but archive documents lack details for these years. In 1625, for instance, 24 galleys were used in an attack along the River Düna in Livonia, and, in 1626, the same number of galleys was used during the Swedish landing in Prussia. While the construction of galleys was halted after these operations, in 1632, the navy still had more than 20 galleys. Jan Glete, 'Vasatidens galärflottor', in H. Norman (ed.), *Skärgårdsflottan: Uppbyggnad, militär användning och förankring i det svenska samhället 1700-1824* (Lund: Historiska Media, 2000), pp.37–49.

Warships were built in several size groups. Smallest was the pinnace, a small, full-rigged ship of a type that later would develop into the frigate and accordingly could fulfil a number of roles for which the larger warships of a fleet were unsuitable.

Like in Denmark, the construction of warships was handled by private entrepreneurs. However, unlike the situation in Denmark, where shipyards were mostly centralised, Swedish shipbuilding, although under the supervision of the Crown, was contracted with yards all over the country, including in Lake Mälaren. While this meant that local labour and taxes paid in kind could be utilised, construction was slow, and the decentralisation probably made it difficult to learn from technical progress that took place elsewhere.

The navy yard Skeppsholmen ('ship island') was located in Stockholm, under the command of the admiral in charge of the dockyards, often referred to as the 'port admiral' (*holmamiral*).

A key task for the navy was to secure the sea lines of communication. The normal sailing season was from May through October. However, the needs of war tended to prolong the sailing season.

King Charles was interested in reinforcing his navy, so, at the outbreak of the Kalmar War in 1611, Sweden had a larger fleet than Denmark. However, while King Christian successfully mobilised the fleet, we will see that, despite available intelligence, King Charles stubbornly believed that the Danes would not attack. As a result, the Swedish fleet was not ordered to prepare for war, so many warships had to remain in port in 1611 because of a lack of supplies and preparations. It generally took half a year to equip a fleet for action. Sweden did not prepare for this contingency in time.

The Inshore Navy

In addition to blue-water warships, Sweden had an inshore navy, consisting of shallow-draught vessels. Most were square-rigged galleys and rowing boats of a type known as *lodja*, with a sprinkling of flat-bottomed river transports of a type known as *struts* (or *struss*). The name '*lodja*' was of Slavic origin, but it is unclear if it was only the name or also the type of river vessel that was adopted in the early seventeenth century. Either way, the *lodja* was an open rowing boat that also might carry a mast or two. It was sufficiently large to take soldiers and the occasional five- or three-pounder cannon. In 1607, the Swedish Crown ordered the construction of 60 vessels of the *lodja* type, each with 12 pairs of oars and able to carry 100 or 160 men and supplies for two months. Even so, the Crown ordered, the weight should not impede the crew from dragging the vessel a considerable distance overland, for instance, from one river to another in the style of the old Viking longship. Smaller vessels of the type were built, too, with a crew of only 40 men and from six to eight pairs of oars.[113]

---

113 King Charles to Henrik Tönnesson, 25 November 1607, R A, Riksregistraturet. The number of crewmen is almost illegible. S. Artur Svensson (ed.), *Svenska flottans historia* (Malmö:

Above: The Swedish fleet at the siege of Riga, 1621. This contemporary drawing depicts all types of ships then in the Swedish navy, including warships, pinnaces, galleys, and the smaller vessels of the *lodja* and *struts* type. (Georg Schwengel)

Right, top: Swedish galley (left) in Stockholm from the late sixteenth century. The only depiction of a Swedish galley from this period, it carries a cannon in the bow, one mast, and a superstructure in the style of a cabin aft. Detail from a portrait of King John. (Author's collection)

Bottom: Muscovite *lodja* rowing vessels, 1590s. Swedish *lodja* vessels presumably looked similar. (Author's collection)

THE SWEDISH MILITARY ESTABLISHMENT

THE KALMAR WAR

A pinnace in the port of Wismar. Although this is the Commonwealth ship *King David*, Swedish pinnaces were identical. The crew has taken down the main yard and are bending (i.e. tying) on the mainsail. (Author's collection)

THE SWEDISH MILITARY ESTABLISHMENT

THE KALMAR WAR

A small sailing vessel of the *struts* type. The spritsail is mistakenly depicted above, not below, the bowsprit. (Crest of the Strusshielm family, House of Nobility, Stockholm)

Plate A

Swedish Cuirassier, Retinue of Nobles

(Illustration by Sergey Shamenkov © Helion & Company 2023)

See Colour Plate Commentaries for further information

Plate B

Swedish Dragoon, Robert Halswell's Company

(Illustration by Sergey Shamenkov © Helion & Company 2023)

See Colour Plate Commentaries for further information

Plate C

Swedish Guardsman, Drabant Guard

(Illustration by Sergey Shamenkov
© Helion & Company 2023)

*See Colour Plate Commentaries
for further information*

Plate D

Swedish Pikeman, Hans Mattsson's Dalecarlian Company

(Illustration by Sergey Shamenkov
© Helion & Company 2023)

*See Colour Plate Commentaries
for further information*

Plate E

Swedish Musketeer, Per Månsson's Västergötland Company

(Illustration by Sergey Shamenkov © Helion & Company 2023)

See Colour Plate Commentaries for further information

Plate F

Swedish Infantry Under-Officer, Östergötland Ducal Arquebusier Company

(Illustration by Sergey Shamenkov © Helion & Company 2023)

See Colour Plate Commentaries for further information

Plate G

**Swedish Artilleryman,
Ordnance Corps**

(Illustration by Sergey Shamenkov
© Helion & Company 2023)

*See Colour Plate Commentaries
for further information*

Plate H

Enlisted Scottish Musketeer, Alexander Ramsay's Company

(Illustration by Sergey Shamenkov
© Helion & Company 2023)

*See Colour Plate Commentaries
for further information*

Plate I

Danish Officer 'of the House'
(Illustration by Sergey Shamenkov
© Helion & Company 2023)
*See Colour Plate Commentaries
for further information*

Plate J

Danish Cuirassier, Scanian Banner, Retinue of Nobles

(Illustration by Sergey Shamenkov
© Helion & Company 2023)

*See Colour Plate Commentaries
for further information*

Plate K

Danish Serving Cavalryman, Scanian Banner

(Illustration by Sergey Shamenkov © Helion & Company 2023)

See Colour Plate Commentaries for further information

Plate L

Danish Harquebusier Cavalryman, Gert von Rantzau's Harquebusier Company

(Illustration by Sergey Shamenkov © Helion & Company 2023)

See Colour Plate Commentaries for further information

Plate M

Danish Pikeman, Holger Rosencrantz's Company of the King's Regiment of Foot

(Illustration by Sergey Shamenkov © Helion & Company 2023)

See Colour Plate Commentaries for further information

Plate N

Danish Arquebusier, Peder Hundemark's Company of the King's Regiment of Foot

(Illustration by Sergey Shamenkov
© Helion & Company 2023)

See Colour Plate Commentaries for further information

Plate O

Norwegian Arquebusier, Akershus Castle Garrison Company
(Illustration by Sergey Shamenkov
© Helion & Company 2023)
See Colour Plate Commentaries for further information

Plate P

Norwegian Levied Irregular
(Illustration by Sergey Shamenkov
© Helion & Company 2023)
*See Colour Plate Commentaries
for further information*

Plate Q

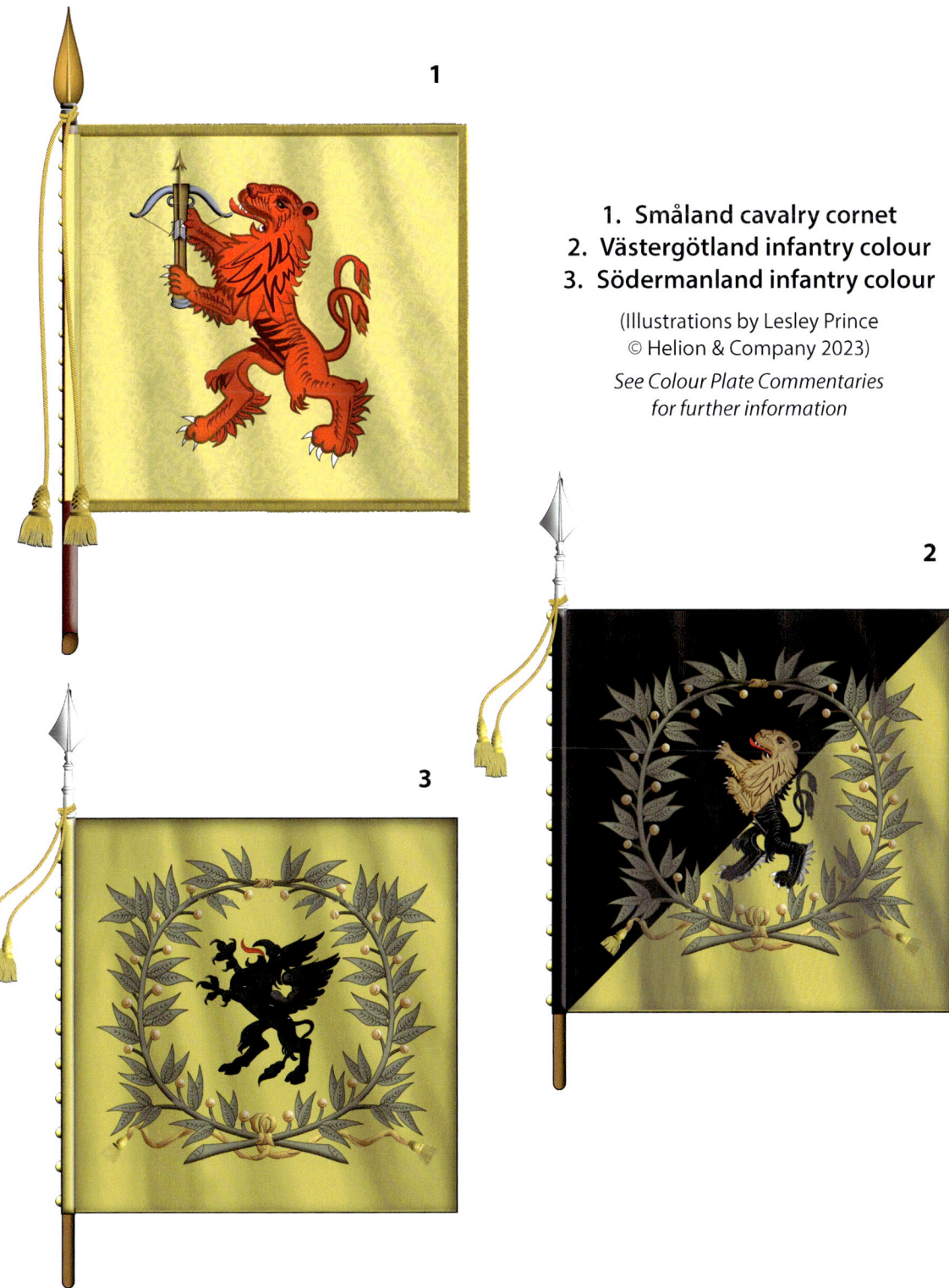

1. Småland cavalry cornet
2. Västergötland infantry colour
3. Södermanland infantry colour

(Illustrations by Lesley Prince
© Helion & Company 2023)

*See Colour Plate Commentaries
for further information*

Plate R

4

4. Finland infantry colour
5. Nyland cavalry cornet

(Illustrations by Lesley Prince
© Helion & Company 2023)

*See Colour Plate Commentaries
for further information*

5

Plate S

King Erik XIV's personal quarters, as restored in the 1860s
(Photo: Medström/Publisher Produktion)

Plate T

The *tempietto* ('small temple') in the inner courtyard, housing the castle's well
(Photo: Medström/Publisher Produktion)

Plate U

King John III's gate, which leads to the castle church
(Photo: Medström/Publisher Produktion)

Kalmar Castle

(Illustration © Medström/Publisher Produktion)
See photographs for further information

Kalmar Castle was built on an island close to Kalmar town, founded around 1200. The castle was extensively renovated and its defences modernised during the late 1540s, and again from the 1570s onwards. At the same time, the castle was refurbished as a spectacular renaissance palace. See also the overview of the castle on p.188.

The castle church, built in 1592 and used for church services ever since
(Photo: Medström/Publisher Produktion)

Plate Y

Above. Thick round artillery towers can almost be described as the trademark of the Vasa kings, and provided good protection for the castle artillery

Below. The gate to the inner courtyard, designed in beautiful Renaissance style, was the last of a series of gates built to increase castle security

(Both photos: Medström/Publisher Produktion)

Plate Z

Left: The original gate of the medieval castle, permanently closed under King Gustav I

Below: The entrance tunnel which connects the inner courtyards with the outer ramparts and artillery towers.

(Both photos: Medström/Publisher Produktion)

The *struts* (see illustration, facing page) was a flat-bottomed, one-masted boat that was commonly used for moving goods on rivers. Unlike the *lodja*, it was decked. It was very similar to the Dutch boyer (Dutch: *boeier*; Swedish: *bojort*), a small coaster, and there is some evidence that, in Sweden, the two terms were used interchangeably, for instance, the boyer *Oxen*, built in Stettin in 1641, which in 1656 was referred to as a '*gaffelstruts*'.[114] In the Swedish navy lists, the terms 'boyer' and '*struts*' seem to indicate the same type of vessel. Another type of transport was the pink (Swedish: *pinka*), a small, square-rigged, decked transport commonly with two masts and a high stern that could also be rowed. The pink closely conformed to the flute, the most common Dutch transport. The type seems to have been discontinued after 1615.[115]

The inshore navy existed because Sweden also had to maintain an amphibious capability, for which it, since about 1540, used galleys. The Swedish-built galleys were a new innovation that previously had not been used in Scandinavia. In those days, they were somewhat smaller than the typical Mediterranean galley, but, later in the century, larger galleys were built as well. By 1590, Sweden had the fourth-largest galley fleet in Europe, after Spain, the Ottoman Empire, and Venice. Their use could be defensive or offensive. It was not only the Baltic Sea that had to be secured, but Sweden also had to control estuaries, lakes, and important rivers on the border with Muscovy and in Livonia. During campaigns in Muscovy, Swedish forces often maintained an inland squadron on Lake Ladoga and, later, on Lake Peipus.

Incidentally, the apparently ubiquitous type of transport known as a praam (Swedish: *pråm*) might have been a development that grew out of the northern galley. The praam was a sailing vessel with up to three masts. Based on later sailing vessels known under this name, they could also be propelled by oars in calm weather. Over time, their naval use developed into that of a mobile gun battery. Ultimately, the term came to signify a barge, but, by the time of the Kalmar War, the praam remained a sailing vessel.

Naval Officers and Sailors

Like in Denmark, there was no real separation of Sweden's armed forces into an army and a navy. The King's officers served both on land and at sea, as did the King himself. The military personnel consisted of cavalry, infantry, artillerymen (gunners), and sailors, and it was only the cavalry units that, for obvious reasons, never were expected to serve at sea. Infantrymen and gunners, in particular, were often called out for shipboard service.

The navy remained fundamentally native Swedish in composition. As in the Danish navy, a key reason for this was the reliance on conscription. The practical need of everybody aboard the ship communicating in the same language may have been a factor, too.

Allhem, 1942), vol. 1, pp.76–77, reads 160; Generalstaben, *Sveriges krig 1611–1632* (Stockholm: Generalstaben, 1937), suppl. vol. 1: *Sveriges sjökrig 1611–1632*, p.30, reads 100.

114 Lars Bruzelius, 'Struss', *The Maritime History Virtual Archives*, <www.bruzelius.info/Nautica/Shipbuilding/Types/struss.html>, accessed 23 June 2023, citing AK reg. 14 March 1656.

115 Generalstaben, *Sveriges krig 1611–1632*, suppl. vol. 1, p.30.

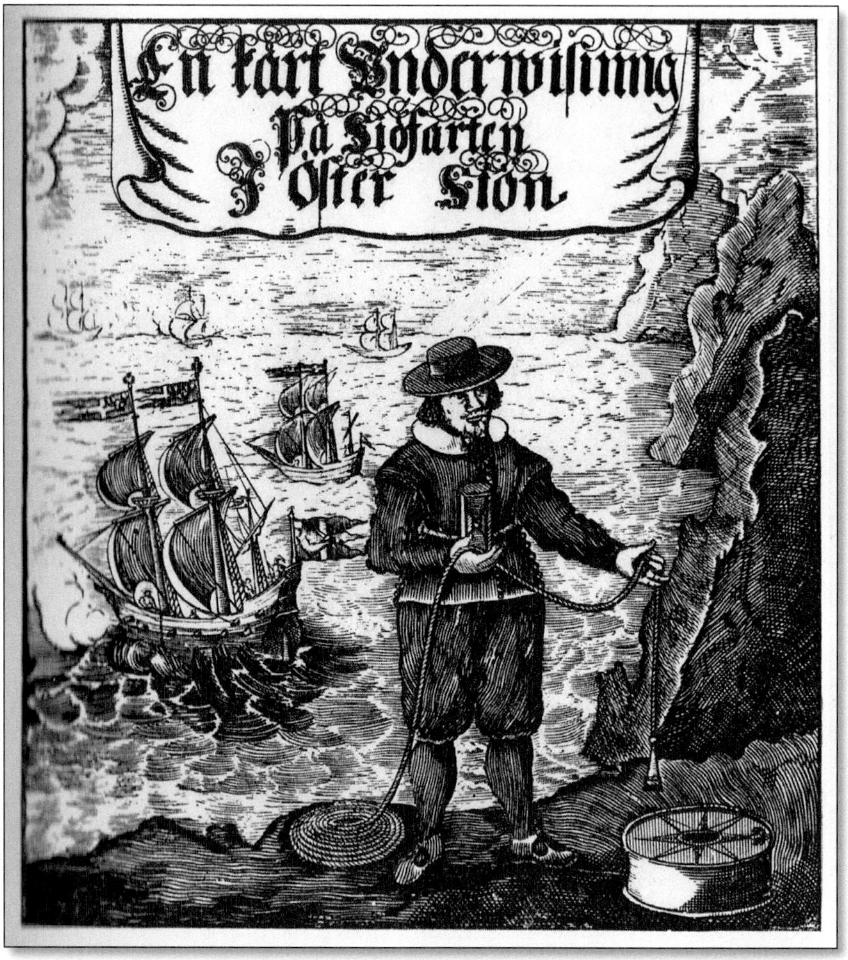
En kårt Vnderwisning
På Siöfarten
J Öster Siön

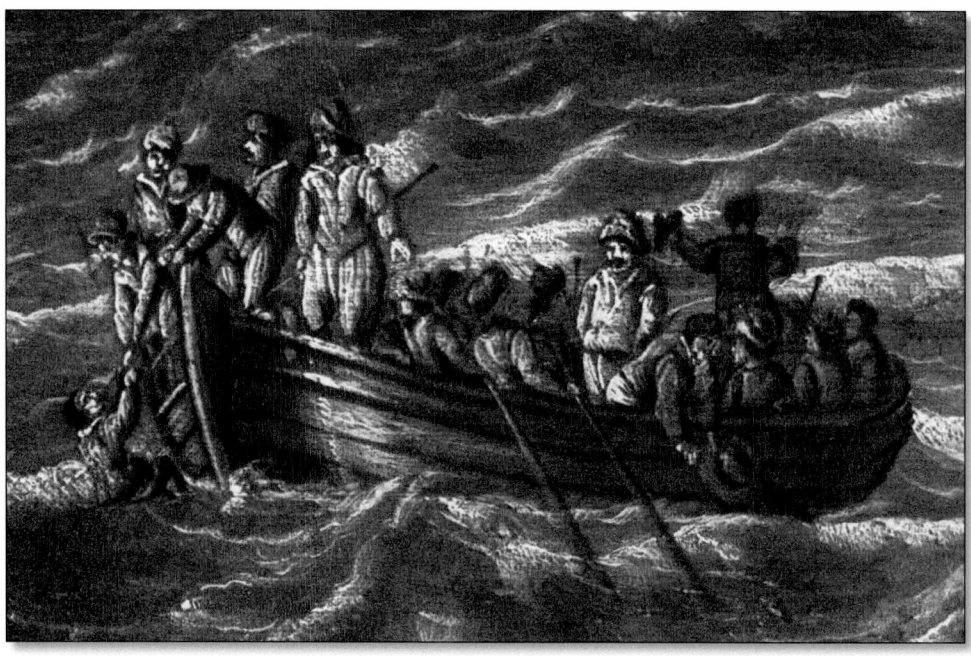

THE SWEDISH MILITARY ESTABLISHMENT

Top left: Swedish pilot, as depicted in the first Swedish naval instruction manual from 1644, written by Johan Månsson. Common sailors would not have been as well dressed as this pilot. (Johan Månsson)

Above: Ship's crew from a mid to late seventeenth-century votive ship, Kållered Church, Västergötland. From left to right: drummer, captain (armed with a broad longsword, possibly a command sword), pilot in jacket and breeches, trumpeter (instrument missing), and two crewmen. Most wear long coats to protect against the cold. (Author's collection)

Left: Swedish sailor, 1628. Clothes based on archaeological finds from the warship *Vasa*. (Vasa Museum, Stockholm; author's photo)

Far left: Swedish sailors at the Battle of Fehmarn, 1644. (Skokloster Castle)

Sweden had a modern navy, but the supply of personnel to the navy had been neglected. Since the Middle Ages, the tradition for some towns and coastal regions to provide men and ships if called to war and, at other times, pay a tax for the King's naval expenses had long since grown obsolete. It was still understood that certain groups with the required monetary resources, such as priests and burghers, would provide sailors when needed. However, it was unclear what should be done to retain the service and replenish the numbers of sailors. In 1610, the Crown ordered that those who hitherto had made sailors available would also have to provide for these sailors during the winter and replace any sailors who were lost. This system did not function very well and was abolished at the time of the peace of 1613, at the latest.[116]

Most of the navy's sailors were raised – conscripted – from the coastal population in the traditional manner. As a result, most were coastal fishermen rather than blue-water sailors, and their skills were insufficient to man modern warships. Sweden still relied on the tradition of raising men from the coasts to man its navy despite the inability of this obsolete system to supply experienced blue-water sailors.

Sweden had a geographical problem as well. The chief naval base and naval shipyard, Stockholm, was well protected within an extensive archipelago, but, with the prevailing winds, it was difficult to move the fleet out to sea. Moreover, Stockholm's harbour was blocked by ice until well into April each year. Finally, Stockholm was located far from the main theatre of operations, which caused communication and logistical problems both with regard to supplies and when repairs were needed.

In comparison, Denmark had the advantage of geography. Denmark's chief naval base, Copenhagen, was located on a main shipping lane, enjoyed the use of an almost continuously ice-free harbour, and, moreover, was located in the southern Baltic, which was the main theatre of operations in any war between Denmark and Sweden. Besides, Copenhagen usually enjoyed a westerly wind, which made it easy for the Danish fleet to leave port.

For these reasons, Danish naval crews were generally more experienced than Swedish ones. Their sailing season was longer, which meant that they had more time to get accustomed to their ships and tasks. Moreover, many of the Danish sailors, and an even larger share of those from Norway, had previously served on Dutch merchantmen or warships. The best sailors were those recruited from merchant ships since they already knew the tasks that had to be carried out and, moreover, were more resistant to the many diseases that commonly decimated naval crews. The Danish navy also employed many experienced foreign sailors, hired in Amsterdam and Hamburg. This, too, made their crews more skilled. The contrast with most Swedish sailors who, at best, had a background as inshore fishermen is striking. Sweden was far from the international centres of maritime commerce, and it was more difficult for the Swedish naval officers to find experienced crews than it was for their Danish counterparts, who had access to exactly this kind of men.

---

116 Urban Skenbäck, *Sjöfolk och knektar på Wasa* (Stockholm: Statens sjöhistoriska museet, 1983), pp.75–76.

A warship usually had only two or, at most, three commissioned officers: the captain and one or two lieutenants. Similar to the Danish navy, they might, or might not, have previous naval experience. As in the Danish navy, the senior NCO was the ship's master (Swedish: *överskeppare*), who was a professional mariner. Unlike the officers, he would stay with the ship throughout the winter since he was in charge of maintenance and preparations for the next sailing season. On a small ship, the ship's master would be in sole command since no officer would serve on board. The ship's master might be assisted by a master's mate (*underskeppare*). He was certainly assisted by a boatswain (*högbåtsman*), who supervised the common sailors (*båtsmän*) and was further responsible for damage control when in battle. The pilot (*styrman*) was responsible for navigation. A pilot had to supply his own navigational instruments. The ordinary sailing crew was divided into two watches, each of which included a leading sailor (*skeppman*) to assist the officer, usually a lieutenant, in command of the watch. A watch was subdivided into two quarters, each directed by a quartermaster (*kvartermästare*). The sailing crew took turns on duty, with each watch spending four hours on duty at a time. The crew also included specialists of various kinds, including the cook, a carpenter (*timmerman*) or sometimes several, and a drummer or trumpeter for signalling. The master gunner (*arklimästare*) supervised the gunners (*bysseskyttar*) who directed the soldiers who were assigned to handle the shipboard artillery. In times of war, each warship was commonly manned by a contingent of soldiers. A large ship would have a chaplain. By the time of the Kalmar War, only a large ship would have a barber surgeon.[117]

Sweden already had a tradition of employing privateers as a means to increase its naval strength. In 1612, Gustavus Adolphus authorised Dutch merchants, including the former mayor of the then destroyed Gothenburg, Abraham Cabeliau, to equip and run privateers on the west coast. The total number is uncertain, but Cabeliau alone had three privateers in operation there.

Tables

Table 4. **Known Swedish unit uniform colours, 1609–1610**[118]

Cavalry	
Unit (Location, Year)	Colours
Newly Raised Swedish Cavalry Banners (1609)	Officers: red, purple, sky blue, liver brown, or black Cavalrymen: red, blue, or black of inferior quality
Hans Boije's Cavalry Banner (Finland, 1609)	Red, blue, black, or brown

---

117 Frederick M. Hocker, *Vasa: A Swedish Warship* (Stockholm: Medström, 2011), pp.102–05.
118 Höglund, *Från Karl Knutsson till Kristina*, pp.43–44.

THE KALMAR WAR

Unit (Location, Year)	Colours
Lorentz Wagner's Cavalry Banner (Västergötland, 1609)	Brown, orange, red, liver brown, green, or fiole brown
Erik Bertilsson's Cavalry Banner (Finland, 1609)	Liver brown, blue, or green
Daniel Golowitz's (Golovachev's?) Cavalry Banner (1609)	Red, blue, or green
Tomas Olofsson's Cavalry Banner (Finland, 1609)	Red or blue
Hans von Lünden's Cavalry Banner (Germany, 1609)	Green, blue, or red
Lindved Claesson Hästesko's Cavalry Banner (Finland, 1609)	Green, red, or liver brown
Lars Andersson's Cavalry Banner (Finland, 1609)	Green, brown, or red
Carl Lake's Cavalry Banner (Västergötland, 1609)	Blue
Herman Dücker's Cavalry Banner (Germany, 1609)	Brown, red, orange, or green
Sten Carlsson's Cavalry Banner (Uppland, 1609)	Blue
Unidentified Cavalry Banner (1609)	Green or blue
Jacob De la Gardie's Life Banner (1610)	Ensign: red English cloth Corporals and Cavalrymen: blue or red

Drabant Guard	
Unit (Location, Year)	Colours
King Charles's Drabant Guard of Foot (1610)	Yellow and blue, with grey woollen casack and hat

Infantry	
Unit (Location, Year)	Colours
Jacob Balfour's Company (Scotland, 1609)	Red, blue, or liver brown
Thomas Kennedy's Company (Scotland, 1609)	Blue
Gustav Hansson's Company (1609)	Brown
Josef Jönsson's Company (Finland, 1609)	Blue
Mats Larsson's Company (Finland, 1609)	Blue
Nils Jönsson's Company (Dalecarlia, 1609)	Blue
Grels Jönsson's Company (Finland, 1609)	Blue
Peter Ogilvie's Company (Scotland, 1609)	Blue
Carl Hansson's Company (Dalecarlia, 1609)	Blue

6

The Outbreak of War

The Danish Campaign Plan

The Danish Council of the Realm authorised war against Sweden on 9 February 1611. By then, King Christian had already concluded most preparations for war. The King signed the declaration of war on Sweden on 4 April. A Danish herald, Claus Jacobsen de Vale, then brought the document to Sweden.

Although we know that King Christian had made detailed plans for the campaign against Sweden, the actual written plans have not been preserved into the present. The only surviving remnant of the campaign plan is King Christian's sharply formulated letter to Field Marshal Steen Maltesen Sehested on 12 June 1611, in which he rebukes the latter for marching against Elfsborg Castle instead of following the agreed-upon plan.[1]

Based on this letter and the actions taken then and during previous wars, it is possible to reconstruct the Danish campaign plan with a reasonable level of confidence. King Christian planned to follow a campaign plan previously developed for the Nordic Seven Years' War, that is, an offensive along the Baltic seaboard towards the Swedish core territories in the north.[2] It was easier to march along the coast because then the navy could provide logistical support, including the transportation of supplies. He would conquer the Swedish provinces one after another until he could move into the Swedish heartland and the capital of Stockholm. Meanwhile, the navy would blockade the Swedish coasts both in the Baltic and along the western shore, prevent the movement of supplies and reinforcements, and defeat the Swedish fleet whenever it showed up. Two Danish armies would assemble. The primary (but smallest) army would assemble at Christianopel, under King Christian, while the larger would gather at Halmstad, under Field Marshal Sehested. Halmstad was the traditional base area for operations against the Swedish

---

1 King Christian to Sehested, 12 June 1611. *Kancelliets Brevbøger vedrørende Danmarks indre Forhold, 1609–1615* (Copenhagen: Rigsarkivet, 1916), pp.385–86.
2 The plan was good but failed in the Nordic Seven Years' War because it depended on Denmark gaining naval supremacy.

THE KALMAR WAR

Nobles (but not necessarily their serving men) of the Danish retinue of nobles were armed as cuirassiers. (Jacob de Gheyn II, *Die Reitschule oder Übungen der Kavallerie*)

town of Jönköping since an old highway along the River Nissan, the Nissa Way (*Nissastigen*), ran between the two towns. King Christian probably planned to lead the smaller army against Kalmar, which he expected to conquer. Meanwhile, Sehested would lead the larger army towards Jönköping. Governor General Enevold Kruse would bring a Norwegian army across the River Göta Älv and to Lake Vänern. Another Norwegian army would advance from Trondheim into the provinces of Härjedalen och Jämtland, from which an offensive could be launched into the Swedish heartland. If King Charles attempted to relieve Kalmar, Sehested could attack him in the flank. If King Charles instead moved against Sehested, Sehested would tie him up until King Christian had taken Kalmar and thereby was in a position to move against the Swedish King.

This explains King Christian's angry outburst against Sehested on 12 June. Instead of moving north against Jönköping as agreed, Sehested had marched off towards the west, against Elfsborg Castle. This separated the two Danish armies and prevented them from supporting each other. Moreover, Sehested's action prevented the offensive north into the Swedish core territories envisaged in the campaign plan.

[See Table 6, **Danish Field Armies at the Outbreak of War, 1611**, end of chapter]

At sea, the main fleet (up to 21 warships), under Grand Admiral of the Realm Mogens Ulfeldt, would patrol the southern Baltic Sea and, if possible, engage the Swedish main fleet. The Skagerrak Squadron (seven warships), under Admiral Jørgen Daa, received orders to blockade Elfsborg Castle and the River Göta Älv Estuary on the Swedish west coast. Admiral Erik Urne's squadron (five warships) and Captain Peder Nielsen's so-named 'Kalmar Flotilla' (around 10 galleys and yachts) were ordered to blockade Kalmar and coordinate activities with the King's army.

[See Table 7, **Danish fleets and squadrons in spring 1611**, end of chapter]

King Christian's plan was aggressive, in fact, so aggressive that it disregarded the need to protect the country's borders. This was particularly true for Halland, where *Lensmand* Tage Krabbe (1553–1612) only had peasant levies for this purpose, supported by a single unit of cavalry: the Halland Banner of the retinue of nobles, which Krabbe commanded at Halmstad. The lack of men in Halland was either neglect or a calculated risk because it will be shown that Swedish Field Colonel Jesper Cruus, a veteran of the wars on the eastern front against the Commonwealth and Muscovy, stood at Elfsborg with 2,000 men. If the experienced Cruus moved against Halmstad and plundered Halland, he would cut Sehested's lines of communication and access to supplies.

Another problem was that King Christian, at the outset of the campaign, personally moved into Christianopel, in the distant east of the theatre of operations. A more central location, for instance at Sölvesborg, would have enabled him to exercise command to a higher extent than geography now allowed.

King Christian expected an easy victory. Swedish exiles who sought refuge in Denmark before the war got underway had led him to believe that the Småland peasants feared King Charles and that they would happily accept Danish rule if only King Christian led an army there and the Danish soldiers treated them decently. Similar to numerous other rulers, then and later, King Christian allowed himself to be deluded by what exiles with an agenda of their own told him.

Despite reports of Danish mobilisation and preparations for war, King Charles refused to believe that war would break out. Preoccupied with the situation on the eastern front against the Polish–Lithuanian Commonwealth and Muscovy, to which he, as late as in 1610, shipped massive reinforcements of both national and enlisted units, King Charles repeatedly dismissed reports on Danish military preparations as 'a bunch of lies'. Like numerous other rulers, then and later, King Charles allowed himself to overrule intelligence reports that did not conform to his prejudices.

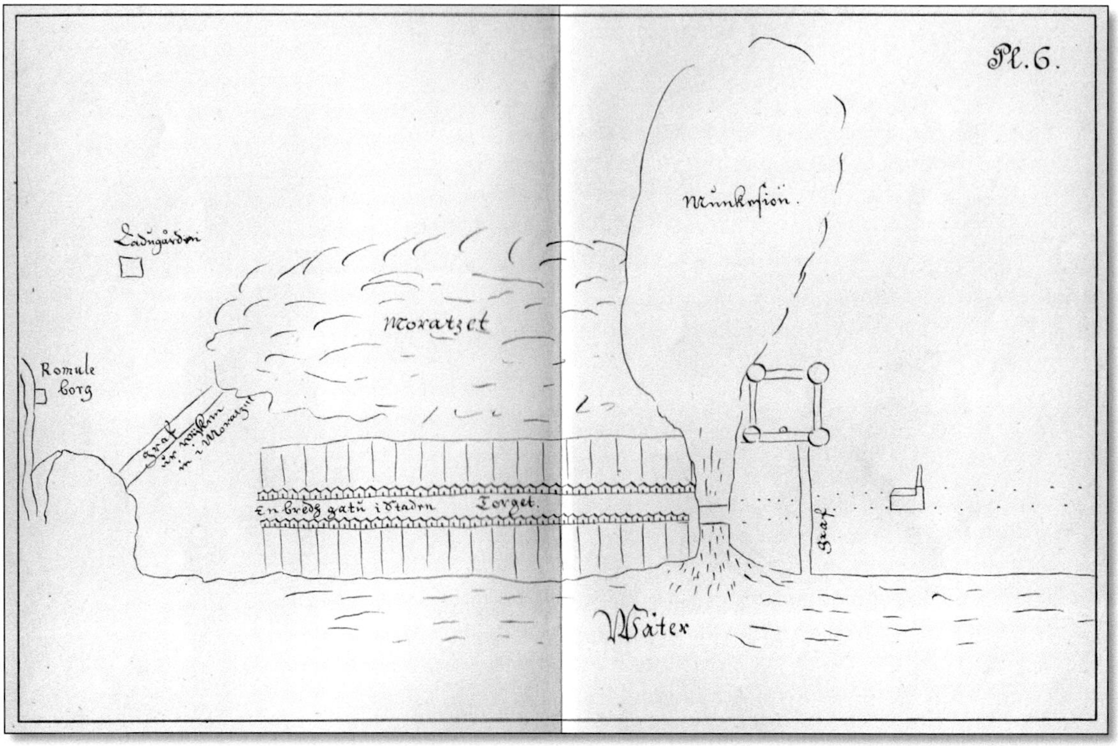
Pl. 6.
Moratzet
Romule
borg
Torget
Wäter

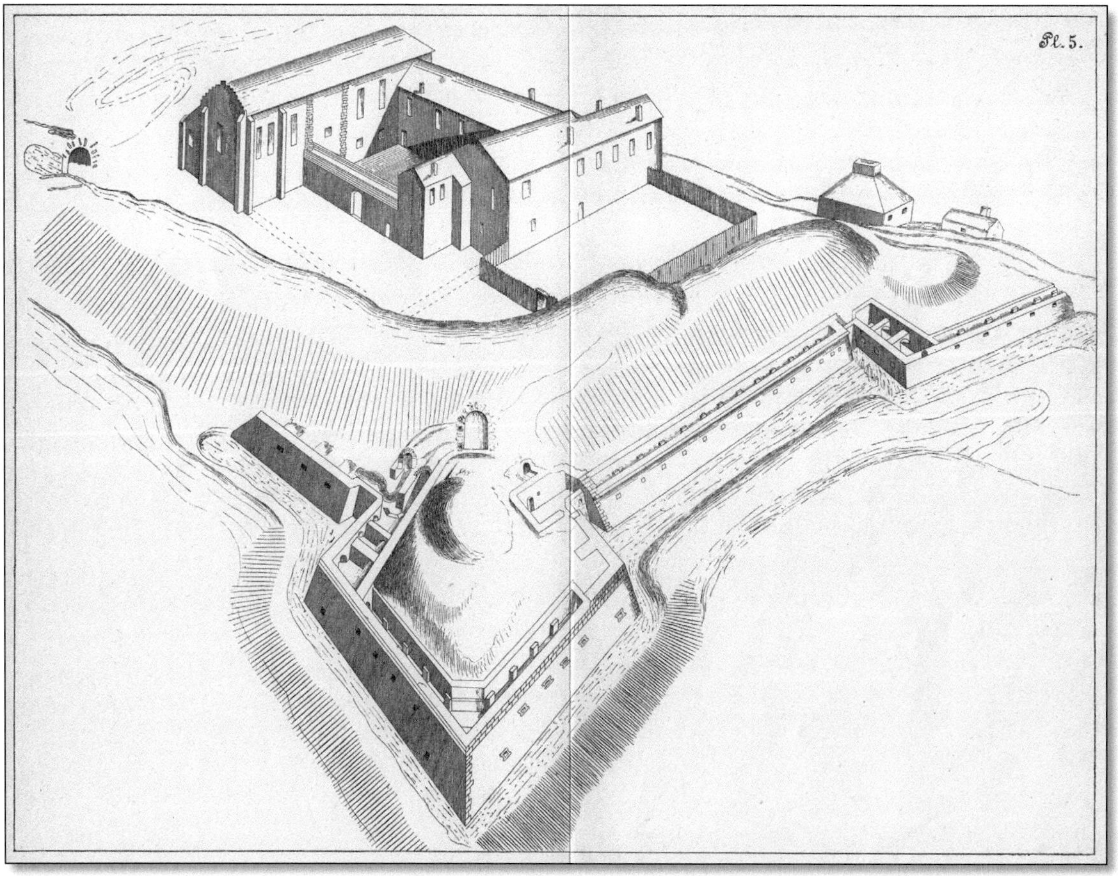
Pl. 5.

Facing page, top: Swedish military map of Jönköping, 1611. Jönköping was a small town, consisting of only one main street running parallel with the shore of Lake Vättern, north of the town but depicted in the bottom of the map. A bridge across the stream connecting Lake Vättern with the smaller Lake Munksjön (centre top) separated the town from the castle and church (both right, i.e. to the west). Otherwise, the town was only protected by a moat (left) and a section of rough ground (top). (Redrawn, from contemporary original, by Ludvig W:son Munthe, 1902)

Bottom: Jönköping Castle, 1605. Two bastions had been added, facing the inland (i.e. south), but work was far from completed. (Reconstruction, from contemporary plan, by Ludvig W:son Munthe, 1902)

The Swedish Deployment

When war broke out, the Swedes faced a distinct shortage of trained units. King Charles had dispatched fundamentally all enlisted foreign units in Sweden to the eastern front. Of foreign enlisted units, only one banner of horse and four companies of foot were available when the Danes attacked.[3] All military resources in Finland and Estonia were already engaged in the ongoing wars with Muscovy and the Commonwealth. As if this was not enough, most of the really experienced Swedish field commanders were on the eastern front. The war with Denmark would have to be fought with only those units and commanders who remained in Sweden itself.

King Charles was in Örebro, in part because he had recently concluded parliament there but primarily because Örebro, as well as Jönköping farther to the south, due to their central locations, by tradition served as the assembly points for the army when attacked from Denmark or Norway. Jönköping's convenient location at the southern end of Lake Vättern meant that an army assembled there was in position to move against a Danish invasion army aiming to march north regardless of whether they chose the route along the eastern or western shore of the lake. Yet, while Jönköping was a good assembly point, the town was not strongly fortified. Neither castle nor town was defended by modern bastions. Existing defences had been burned by the Danes in 1567, and work on a new castle had only begun in 1593 and then only in the old style with round towers. At the outbreak of war, two bastions had been added to the castle, but work was far from completed.

In December, King Charles had already appointed Jesper Matsson Cruus (1576 or 1577–1622) as field colonel in the province of Västergötland, seconded by Johan Göransson Rosenhane as colonel of cavalry and Ulf Bonde as colonel of infantry. Soon afterwards, in January, he appointed Christer Some (*c.* 1565–1618) as colonel general in Småland, seconded by Per Hammarskiöld as colonel of cavalry and Olof Hård as colonel of infantry.[4] Colonel General Some had distinguished himself in the wars in Livonia and Muscovy. In 1608, he had been described as a 'field marshal'. However, certain

---

3 Generalstaben, *Sveriges krig 1611–1632*, vol. 1, pp.145, 147–48.
4 The colonelcies of cavalry and infantry did not signify active command of regimental units, only formal administrative control. Generalstaben, *Sveriges krig 1611–1632*, vol. 1, p.158.

rumours about his person suggested a dark side. In 1601, Some carried out the extrajudicial execution of a number of Commonwealth POWs under unusually cruel circumstances, for which Carl Carlsson Gyllenhielm, King Charles's illegitimate son, had criticised him harshly. Then, Some himself fell into Commonwealth captivity yet was quickly released – some voices claimed that he later, in 1603, worked in collusion with Polish King Sigismund.

In Västergötland, there were major, modern fortresses in Elfsborg, Gullberg, and the new town of Gothenburg, which were all close to one another. However, the fortifications of Gothenburg were not completed, and the town was accordingly indefensible. Most burghers still lived in Gothenburg's immediate predecessor in the area, Nya Lödöse. They were now ordered to raise a wall around their town. King Charles ordered one infantry company to garrison Gullberg Castle, under the command of the commandant, Mårten Krakow (1538?–1616). The King ordered another infantry company to garrison Gothenburg, to which he also ordered what is described as 'four-and-a-half companies' as labour. Their task was presumably to work on the unfinished fortifications. Elfsborg Castle, under Nils Bengtsson Silfverbielke (fl. 1580–1640), was already garrisoned by an infantry company, and a second infantry company was sent there as reinforcements. Technically, the garrisons remained under the command of their respective commandants, not provincial commanders such as Cruus or Some. Not well informed about the King's garrison deployments in his area of operations, Cruus deployed yet another infantry company to Elfsborg, which, as a result, acquired a garrison of three companies of foot, in total some 500 men. Instead, Cruus ordered one of the companies in Gothenburg to join his field army. This gave Cruus an army consisting of three cavalry banners from Västergötland, in total 630 horses, and seven infantry companies from Västergötland, in total 1,439 men. By mid April, Cruus had assembled this army in the vicinity of Elfsborg.[5] King Charles expected the Danes to attack in this area since the new town of Gothenburg presented an immediate mercantile threat to Danish interests.

Table 8. Västergötland army under Jesper Matsson Cruus, May 1611[6]

Cavalry[7]		
Province	Banner	Strength
Västergötland	Colonel Johan Göransson Rosenhane	130
Västergötland	Tord Bengtsson	250?
Västergötland	Daniel Wagner	250?
	Total	630?

---

5 Generalstaben, *Sveriges krig 1611–1632*, vol. 1, p.166.
6 Generalstaben, *Sveriges krig 1611–1632*, vol. 1, p.166.
7 Bengtsson's and Wagner's banners together counted 600 horse. In addition, cavalry staff units might bring the total to 740. However, the number of horses also included horses in the supply train, for which reason the total number is an estimate. Most or all cavalry were harquebusiers.

Infantry[8]		
Province	Company	Strength
Västergötland	Lieutenant Colonel Per Månsson	320
Västergötland	Jon Ambjörnsson	140
Västergötland	Anders Jonsson	249
Västergötland	Nils Jonsson	304
Västergötland	Anders Månsson	138
Västergötland	Bengt Persson	124
Dal	Hans Andersson	164
	Total	1,439
	Grand Total	Approx. 2,070

To safeguard the border with Norway, half of the Dal and Värmland companies of foot were deployed there, under the command of their respective company lieutenants. This meant 200 men in Dal and 180 in Värmland.[9]

In Småland, there were major fortresses at Jönköping, Kalmar, and Borgholm on the island of Öland. Kalmar Castle was strongly fortified, and the wall around Kalmar town was almost completed, so orders were issued to finish the work quickly. In addition to garrisons, the province from the outset hosted three banners of horse and 14 companies of foot. However, the King had already ordered four companies of foot (under Jacob Jönsson Flensburg, Olof Ingelsson, Erik Kock, and Per Jönsson, respectively) to Kalmar to man the naval squadron there bound for Salis (modern-day Salacgrīva) in Livonia.[10] With war against Denmark imminent, the order was countermanded, and the naval squadron with its soldiers was ordered to remain in Kalmar for the time being. The four companies disembarked to garrison Kalmar.[11]

Although Colonel General Some was expected to defend the rest of Småland with the remaining units, King Charles ordered him to assemble his men at Jönköping. As a result, the border to Danish Scania remained undefended, and the way towards Kalmar lay open. Some accordingly ordered Hammarskiöld's Småland Banner to the border with Danish Blekinge as a first line of defence. He also deployed one infantry company at the border south of Jönköping. In the beginning of May, he was thus able to assemble two banners of horse and eight companies of foot in Jönköping. In total, his army then consisted of 1,451 foot and 365 horse.

When the first Danish warships appeared off Kalmar, the King ordered another three of Some's infantry companies (under Olof Svensson Hoffman,

---

8   Staff units can be added to these figures, which might bring the total to 1,467 men.
9   Generalstaben, *Sveriges krig 1611–1632*, vol. 1, p.167.
10 Erik Kock, presumably his company as well, was soon back in the field army. Per Jönsson returned to the field army, too, but as captain of a different company. Olof Ingelsson's company remained in the Kalmar garrison.
11 Generalstaben, *Sveriges krig 1611–1632*, vol. 1, p.167.

Sven Håkansson Krååk, and Nils Bryngelsson, respectively, the last with specific orders to move into Kalmar Castle) to reinforce the Kalmar garrison.[12]

[See Table 9, **The Småland Army under Christer Some, May 1611, and the Kalmar Garrison, July 1611**, end of chapter]

Always suspicious of treason, King Charles took special measures to safeguard the capital of Stockholm. He warned local officials to look out for traitors and deployed two provincial infantry companies to the capital, one from Hälsingland under Oluf Ingemarsson and one from Finland under Lars Eskildsson.[13]

King Charles planned to assemble his main army at Örebro (see Table 10). They would then march south to Jönköping since this would allow the King operational freedom regardless of where the Danes struck. Meanwhile, Duke John of Östergötland would deploy the Ducal Army at Jönköping. If the Danes marched against Jönköping, then the Swedes could meet them there. If they marched towards either Gothenburg or Kalmar, the King could attack them in the flank. Meanwhile, Cruus and Some remained free to carry out operations as needed. It was a good plan. However, Swedish mobilisation came too late, and the King's army did not reach the theatre in time to carry out these tasks.

[See Table 10, **Royal Main Army under King Charles at Örebro and Duke John's Östergötland Ducal Army, 2 June 1611**, end of chapter]

When combat operations began, the Swedish deployment of land forces in the south was as follows:

- Västergötland Army at Elfsborg (under Cruus): three banners of cavalry and eight companies of foot, in total about 630 horse and 1,439 foot
- Elfsborg Castle Garrison (under Nils Silfverbielke): three companies of foot, in total some 500 men
- Gullberg Castle Garrison (under Mårten Krakow): probably one company of foot, in total an estimated 300 men
- Småland Army at Jönköping (under Some): two banners of cavalry and eight companies of foot, in total 365 horse and 1,451 foot
- On the border with Blekinge: Hammarskiöld's Småland Banner of Horse, about 100 men
- Main Army at Örebro (under King Charles): five Swedish banners of cavalry and 12 Swedish (including Drabant Guard) and four English–Scottish companies of foot, in total 767 horse and 2,878 foot, as well as the field artillery
- Kalmar Castle Garrison (under Admiral Jacob Jacobsson Snakenborg Bååt): six companies of foot, in total 774 men

---

12   Generalstaben, *Sveriges krig 1611–1632*, vol. 1, p.168.
13   Larsen, *Kalmarkrigen*, p.88.

- Östergötland Ducal Army (under Duke John), ordered to Jönköping but (except for Mannerskiöld's company) not yet on the road because the Duke fell ill in mid May: three banners of cavalry and five companies of foot, in total an estimated 400 horse and 934 foot

In addition, King Charles contemplated, and apparently attempted, the carrying out of a strategic envelopment of Denmark. Enlisted units from the Dutch Republic, Scotland, or England could be shipped directly from their port of muster to the west coast of Jutland to open a second front there, which would force King Christian to divide his forces. King Christian realised the danger and ordered particular vigilance on the Jutland coast. Unfortunately for King Charles, who sent agents with patents to enlist soldiers, neither The Hague nor London was willing to condone Swedish recruitment at this time. King Charles also entertained ideas to enlist units in Germany for an overland offensive into Jutland from the south. The Danes captured a Swedish captain on route to Germany for this mission. He admitted that he acted upon orders from King Charles to this effect, so the Danes promptly had him executed.[14] Meanwhile, Heinrich von Falkenberg (1553–1629), a Swedish noble in Lübeck, worked to coordinate the enlistment of soldiers in Germany, as well as the provision of necessary supplies for Sweden from Lübeck merchants. Some results were achieved, but, with the Danish navy in command of the southern Baltic, it was difficult to ship men and supplies to Sweden.

The Swedish naval forces were strong, but, because of King Charles's reluctance to mobilise against the Danish threat, it took time before they were ready for action. When orders finally came, the King appointed Hans Claesson Bielkenstierna admiral and ordered him to assemble the main fleet at Älvsnabben, a natural harbour in the southern Stockholm Archipelago that functioned as the summer base for the Swedish navy. From there, he could easily set out to Kalmar if needed. In and near Stockholm, the sailing channels were comparatively narrow, so poor winds could delay a fleet for weeks. The summer base in the archipelago enabled increased flexibility in operations. Nonetheless, the King also ordered the squadrons engaged in shipping supplies to the eastern front and the blockade of Commonwealth ports there to retain their appointed tasks.

[See Table 11, **Swedish Fleets and Squadrons, Spring 1611**, end of chapter]

The Danes Open Hostilities

King Christian mobilised the fleet and ordered squadrons to be already stationed close to the Swedish southern ports before declaring war. This enabled him to cut Sweden's sea lines of communications and achieve a rapid

---

14 Larsen, *Kalmarkrigen*, pp.166–67.

and effective blockade of both Kalmar and Elfsborg, which immediately put the Swedes on the defensive.

King Christian had already sent a communiqué to Lübeck and all the Hanseatic centres of trade in the Baltic region, in which he directed them to desist from trading with Sweden for the duration of the war.[15] It was essentially an ultimatum: impose sanctions on Sweden and respect the Danish blockade or face the consequences.[16]

In early March, King Christian sent Admiral Jørgen Daa (d. 1619) with seven warships to blockade the exit of the River Göta Älv and Elfsborg Castle into the Skagerrak Strait and North Sea. Daa was not very successful, and, to the King's annoyance, which he expressed in several letters, Daa failed to prevent Swedish shipping from entering and exiting. Seeing what was underway, many Dutch merchants in Gothenburg abandoned the town.[17] In fact, Daa had a poor reputation, and, in the early stage of the war, he did little to ameliorate it.[18] In mid April, King Christian sent Port Admiral Godske Lindenow to take over the blockade and make it successful.

King Christian was determined to annex those Swedish territories that he could conquer. On 25 May, Admiral Lindenow demanded that the inhabitants of the Swedish islands off the River Göta Älv Estuary (specifically, the islands of Brännö, Asperö, Styrsö, Köpstadsö, Donsö, and Vrångö) swear loyalty to King Christian in the presence of the Admiral and his captains, thereby 'for all time' accepting Danish annexation. The islands were those over which Sweden had gained suzerainty in the thirteenth century.

Soon after Daa set out, King Christian sent Captain Gabriel Kruse with two ships, the *Markattan* and *Penitens*, to blockade Kalmar from the sea.[19] Later in March, King Christian sent another three warships, the *Rafael*, *Jupiter*, and *Sankt Michael*, under Admiral Erik Urne to reinforce the blockade. The King also ordered him, while on the way to Kalmar, to escort three merchantmen with a cargo of munitions to Christianopel. With Urne also arrived Captain Peder Nielsen with about 10 galleys and yachts to assist with inshore operations.[20]

---

15 Anon., 'Journal', pp.676–77.

16 Ingel Wadén, *Berättande källor till Calmarkrigets historia*. 1936. Lund University, PhD, p.196.

17 Most were stopped by Danish warships, although they were subsequently released. After the outbreak of war, the remaining Dutchmen skipped out, too. However, they accidentally ended up in Norway, where they were interned. Ultimately, King Christian ordered them released (except Abraham Cabeliau, the mayor of Gothenburg, who had to remain in custody), but he confiscated their ships and goods and had any of their belongings that remained in Gothenburg destroyed. In 1612, Cabeliau retaliated by investing in three privateers that carried out operations from the Dutch Republic against Danish vessels on the Swedish west coast. Larsen, *Kalmarkrigen*, p.118.

18 Granted, Admiral Daa's reputation was not quite as bad as that of his son, Admiral Herluf Daa, who, despite being widely known as a disreputable character involved in endless legal battles and corrupt practices, nonetheless enjoyed King Christian's trust.

19 Generalstaben, *Sveriges krig 1611–1632*, suppl. vol. 1, p.67.

20 Generalstaben, *Sveriges krig 1611–1632*, suppl. vol. 1, p.68.

THE OUTBREAK OF WAR

On 11 April, Grand Admiral of the Realm Mogens Ulfeldt received his orders. He was ordered to bring the main fleet to locate and defeat the Swedish fleet in the southern Baltic Sea. He set out on the *Argo*, together with the warships *Tre Kroner*, *Concordia*, *Gideon*, *Justitia*, *Trøst*, *Gabriel*, *Enhjørning*, and *Lindormen*. Yet more warships followed later.

On the Baltic Sea island of Gotland (held by Denmark at this time), the *lensmand* was ordered to make sure the levies were armed, coastal patrols maintained, and the fortifications around the town of Visby, as well as Visborg Castle, put in order. The *lensmand* received orders to send all old gunpowder to Copenhagen because fresh gunpowder was on its way. Any Swedes who lived on Gotland had to be ordered to swear fealty to the Danish Crown or be deported. The *lensmand* on the island of Bornholm received similar instructions.

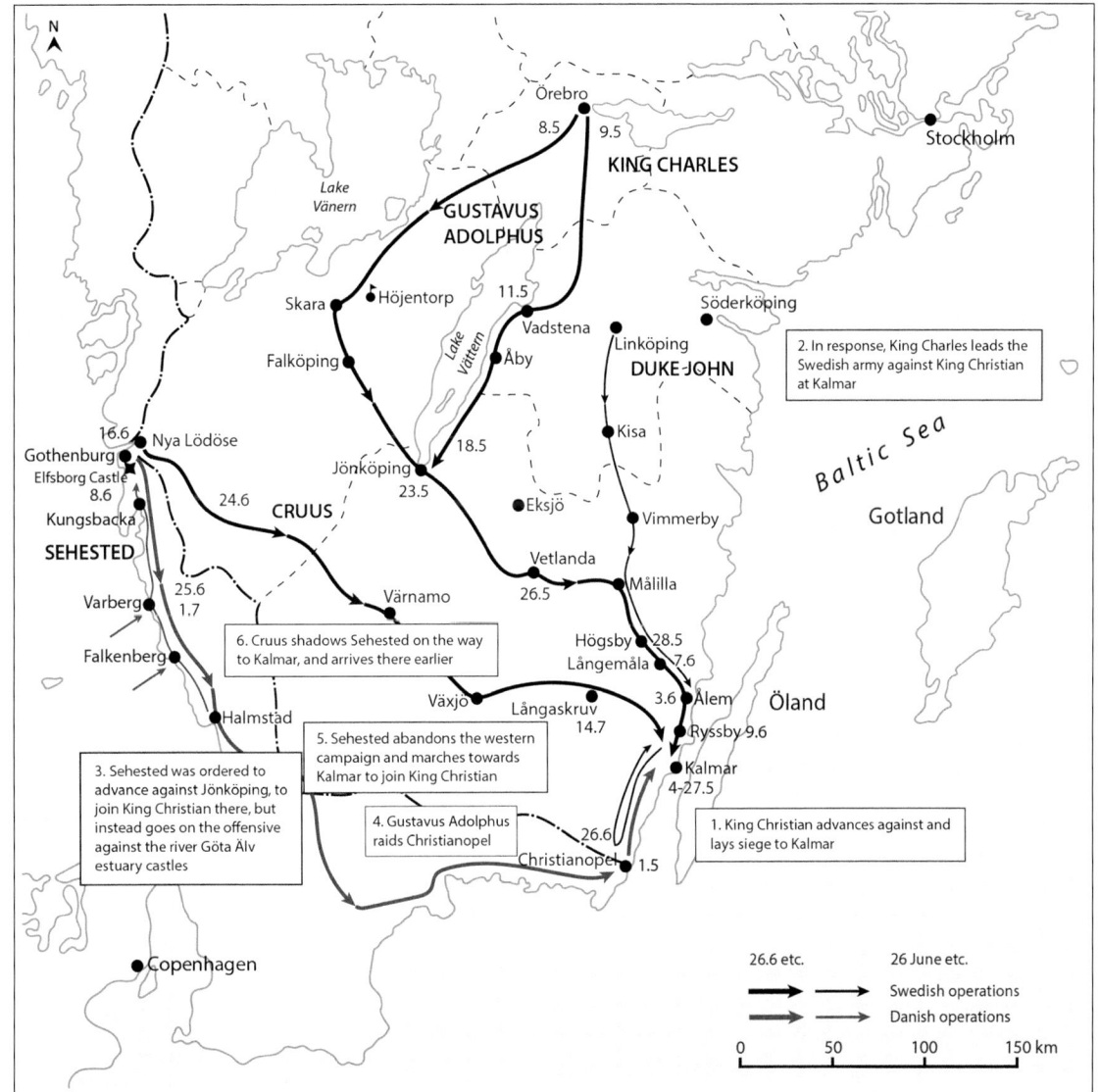

Map 4. Operations in 1611

THE KALMAR WAR

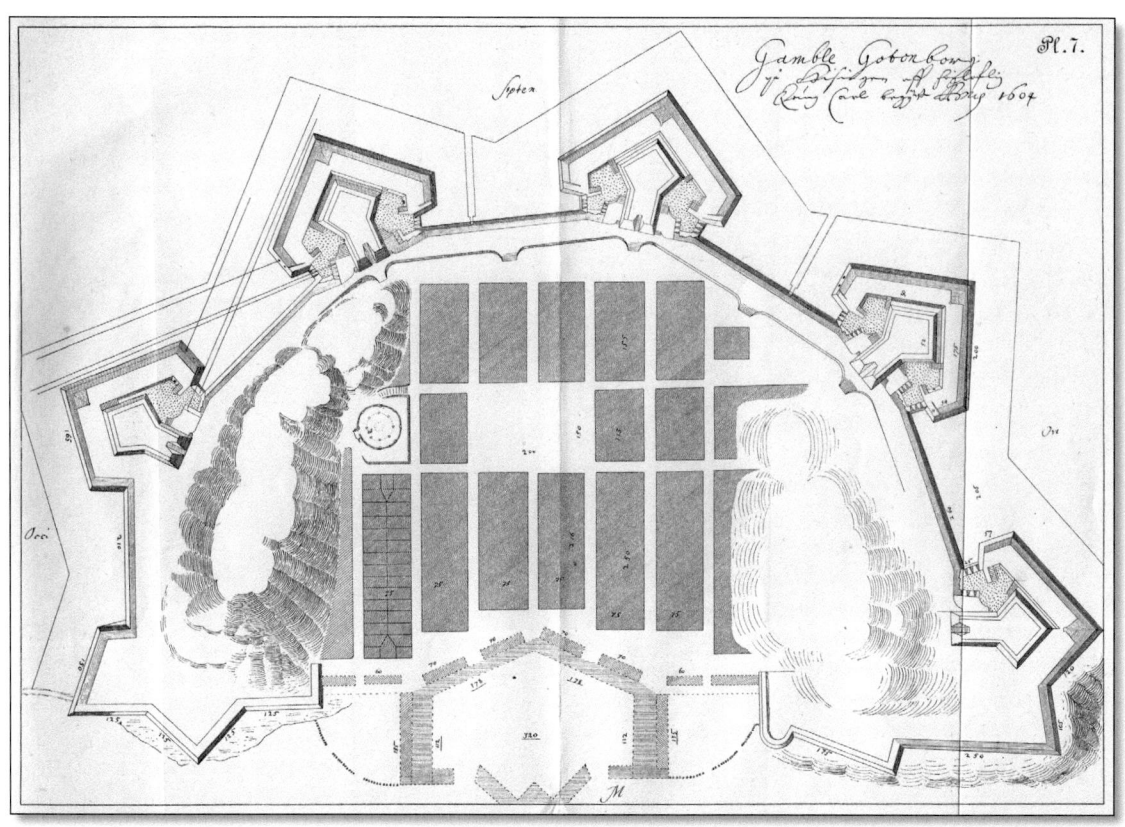

Swedish military map of the projected defences of Gothenburg, 1604. Most defences were planned to secure the town against Norwegian incursions from the inland. The port (below) was only lightly defended. In reality, work on the planned fortifications had not yet begun when the Kalmar War broke out. There was no way to defend the new town. (Redrawn, from contemporary original, by Ludvig W:son Munthe, 1902)

King Christian wanted the army units to be assembled in April so that the campaign could begin on 1 May. We have seen that Grand Marshal of the Realm and Field Marshal Steen Maltesen Sehested took command of the army at Halmstad. King Christian would personally take command of the army at Christianopel.

Several contingents of levies were called up to guard the borders: in Blekinge under Jens Sparre, *lensmand* in Christianopel; in Scania under Corfitz Rud, who also commanded the Fyn Banner, which soon was attached to the King's army; and in Halland under Tage Krabbe, who also commanded the Halland Banner. King Christian ordered that one-sixth of the peasants should be raised at once, with the rest to be prepared in case of need.

King Christian arrived in Christianopel on 24 April. The same day, he sent an order to Sehested, ordering him to await the German infantry and then advance to Jönköping with his entire army. To save time, he should only bring light artillery. If heavy artillery was needed to take Jönköping, he could send for it with the horses of the supply train and the field artillery. Sehested should bring the artillerymen from Halmstad, and they were to be commanded by Master Gunner (*arkelimester*) Hans Post from Kronborg. Peasants should be treated well so that they would accept Danish annexation.

The enlisted German units did not arrive as planned. King Christian had commandeered merchant ships to transport the soldiers. Embarked in Warnemünde, King Christian had ordered the men to be shipped to Halmstad, possibly because he wanted King Charles to believe that Gothenburg and the

River Göta Älv Estuary were the key Danish targets. However, the masters of the transports instead landed the enlisted soldiers on the Danish isles of Møn, Falster, and Zealand. There is reason to believe that they did so out of self-preservation because the enlisted units looted property and abused civilians wherever they went, including on the transports.[21]

Despite such difficulties, the Danish plans proceeded well – not so much the plans for Norway. The King's order to raise 6,000 men and move them to the Swedish border was unrealistic. First, Norway could not raise that many men. Second, there were no supplies for such an army. On 4 April, Governor General Enevold Kruse and the Norwegian commanders wrote to the King, asking him instead to send them 1,200 enlisted foreign foot. If the Swedes attacked, they wrote, then they would raise the general levy, which would produce 2,200 men at Idde and Marker (on the border with Swedish Västergötland and Värmland, respectively) and 3,555 at Solør (on the border with Swedish Dalecarlia). They also requested that the King send a fleet to protect the Norwegian coasts.[22]

The Norwegian requests made King Christian furious. On 28 April, he pointed out that the Norwegians should not make suggestions and demands and only follow orders and engage the Swedes.

When Kruse, months later, finally managed to raise some 2,500 men at Svinesund, the entire military system collapsed. Most new soldiers were untrained, and few were willing to fight. Many men deserted, while the rest drank themselves into a stupor and refused to follow orders. When officers and under-officers attempted to enforce discipline, the unruly soldiers simply threatened to shoot them. When attempts were made to prosecute the ringleaders, entire units showed up to rescue their comrades. Since officers and under-officers, too, were newly raised, most were too inexperienced to train the soldiers or, when need be, control them. Already in March, Steen Bille had warned that 'some 40 of the best burghers [of Trondheim] will be picked as officers, and they are all inexperienced people'.[23] Clearly, their lack of experience and authority precluded the installation of any discipline in the newly raised army.

On 14 July, the men were expected to swear loyalty to Governor General Kruse, but many refused, including the entire contingent from Tønsberg. Three days later, rumours emerged that the army would march out to invade Sweden. This resulted in further unrest, and, on 20 July, the entire contingents from Hadeland, Brunla, and Bratsberg deserted. By 22 July, 1,424 of the original 2,500 men had deserted – almost 60 percent of the total. Although 1,000 additional men arrived in camp in mid August, half of them deserted, too.[24]

Other bad news soon came from Sehested's army. In Halland, the Danish supply system collapsed almost at once. While the King's army could be

---

21 Larsen, *Kalmarkrigen*, p.167.
22 Larsen, *Kalmarkrigen*, p.80; Generalstaben, *Sveriges krig 1611–1632*, vol. 1, p.143. Norrie, *Kalmarkrigen*, p.17, reports Enevold's planned levy as 4,755 instead of 5,755 men, presumably a typing error.
23 Steen Bille to Christian Friis, 28 March 1611. Lange (ed.), *Norske Samlinger*, vol. 2, pp.42–45.
24 Alhaug, *Angrepet på Kalmar*, pp.72–73.

resupplied by sea, Sehested could not gather enough supplies to move overland towards Jönköping. He may have also feared exposing his Halland flank to Cruus's army at Elfsborg Castle.[25] He accordingly abandoned the carefully decided campaign plan and instead marched towards the River Göta Älv Estuary, where he expected to be able to receive supplies by sea.

Little then remained of King Christian's ambitious strategy. Governor General Enevold Kruse was unable to invade Sweden from Norway with any substantial force. Sehested, who commanded the largest of the two Danish armies, had abandoned the objective of taking Jönköping and instead proceeded towards Elfsborg. The German reinforcements had failed to arrive where the King wanted them. Only the King's army continued as planned. As a result, the Danish strategy of invading the Swedish core territories overland failed to materialise. Instead, the two Danish armies, out of contact with each other because of the long distances, operated only along the western and eastern coasts. The inland was left wide open for Swedish King Charles.

Tables

Table 6. Danish Field Armies at the Outbreak of War, 1611[26]

King Christian's Army (Kalmar Operation)			
Cavalry			
Unit	Commander	Coy	Strength
Court Banner	Ditlev Rantzau	1	150
Zealand Banner (retinue of nobles)	Peder Basse	½	104
Scanian Banner (retinue of nobles)	Anders Bille	1	132
Fyn Banner (retinue of nobles)	Corfitz Rud	1	129
The King's Life Banner (enlisted French and Dutch)	Joachim von Bülow	1	130
	Total	4½	645
Dragoons			
Unit	Commander	Coy	Strength
'Jean Dupuis' Company (enlisted French)	Jean Dupuis	1	124
	Total	1	124
Infantry			
Unit	Commander	Coy	Strength[27]
The King's Regiment	Life Company or Royal Guard: Lt. Thomas Nold	1	314*
	Copenhagen Men and Scanians: Peder Hundemark	1	308
	Zealanders: Caspar von Miltnitz (later Søren Bugge)	1	400*
	Scanians: Andrew Sinclair	1	314*

25 Generalstaben, *Sveriges krig 1611–1632*, vol. 1, pp.140, 144.

26 The table contains numerous estimates since few units ever reached their planned strength. Some units may have been omitted. Furthermore, a few units joined their assigned army only after the outbreak of war, among them Duke George of Brunswick-Lüneburg and Jean Dupuis, who arrived with their companies only after the fall of Kalmar. Generalstaben, *Sveriges krig 1611–1632*, vol. 1, pp.140, 225, 584–85; Alhaug, *Angrepet på Kalmar*, pp.37–52.

27 Asterisk indicates estimated strength.

THE OUTBREAK OF WAR

Gert von Rantzau's Regiment (enlisted Germans)	Lieutenant Colonel Blasius Belisarius	1	200*
	Paul Rantzau	1	200*
	Jacob Werkamp	1	225*
Godske von Ahlefeldt's Regiment (enlisted Germans)	Godske von Ahlefeldt	1	386*
	Henrik Ernst Brüning	1	217*
	Wilhelm von Friesendorff	1	190*
	Benedict Bernd von Hagen	1	234*
	Johan Kaufmann	1	240*
	Joachim Køller	1	202*
	Melchior Rantzau	1	203*
	Joachim Schultz	1	248*
Duke George of Brunswick-Lüneburg's Regiment (enlisted Germans)	Duke George	1	500*
	Magnus Kaas (?)	1	100*
	Tycho Lange (?)	1	100*
	Total	18	4,581*

Artillery			
Unit	Commander	Coy	Strength
Artillerymen			Unk.
Zealand Labour Company ('bastion diggers')			400
	Total		400*
	Grand Total		5,800*

Field Marshal Steen Maltesen Sehested's Halland Army (Elfsborg Operation)

Cavalry			
Unit	Commander	Coy	Strength
Aalborg Banner (retinue of nobles)	Ulrich Sandberg	1	150
Aarhus Banner (retinue of nobles)	Knud Brahe	1	164
Ribe Banner (retinue of nobles)	Albert Skeel	1	161
Zealand Banner (retinue of nobles)	Christer Hansen	½	100
Halland Banner (retinue of nobles)	Tage Krabbe	1	103
Duke Philip of Glücksburg's Harquebusier(?) Company (based on the retinue of nobles of the Duchies)	Duke Philip	1	200*
Duke Ernest Louis of Saxe-Lauenburg's Harquebusier Company (enlisted Germans)	Duke Ernest Louis	1	193
Gert von Rantzau's Life Company of Horse (possibly cuirassiers)	Gert von Rantzau	1	201
Gert von Rantzau's Harquebusier Company (enlisted Germans)	Gert von Rantzau	1	150
Marquard von Pentz's Harquebusier Company (enlisted Germans)	Marquard von Pentz	1	200*
Tessen von Parsow's Harquebusier Company (enlisted Germans)	Tessen von Parsow	1	196

173

THE KALMAR WAR

Jørgen Grubbe's Harquebusier Company (enlisted Germans)	Jørgen Grubbe	1	200*
	Total	11½	2,018

Infantry			
Unit	Commander	Coy	Strength
The King's Regiment	Enlisted Germans: Major Peter von Heinemark	1	314*
	Enlisted Dutchmen: Holger Rosencrantz	1	314*
	Enlisted Dutchmen: Christian Friis	1	260*
	Enlisted Dutchmen: Moritz Galde	1	314*
Gert von Rantzau's Regiment (enlisted Germans)	Gert von Rantzau	1	1,800*[28]
	Jørgen Baroldt	1	
	Heinrich von Dringelberg	1	
	Wollert Lützow	1	
	Jacob Sehested	1	
	Valentin Rosworm	1	
	Marquard von der Wick	1	
Tessen von Parsow's Regiment (enlisted Germans)	Unknown	1	307*
	Unknown	1	307*
	Unknown	1	307*
Jørgen Lunge's Company (enlisted Germans and Dutchmen)	Unknown	1	322
	Total	15	4,245*
	Grand Total		6,263*
	Combined Grand Total		12,000*

Table 7. Danish Fleets and Squadrons, Spring 1611[29]

Main Fleet (Total Strength: 21 warships)	
Commander	Grand Admiral of the Realm Mogens Ulfeldt
Base	Copenhagen
Ready for action	Late March (first squadron), mid April (second squadron), and mid June (third squadron)
Disbanded	Late September in most parts
First Squadron	
Commander	Erik Urne
Jupiter (16)	-
Sankt Michael ('St Michael', 20)	Envold Stygge
Raphael (18)	Erik Urne

---

28 The total estimated strength of Gert von Rantzau's regiment (enlisted Germans).

29 The captain of each vessel is, when known, given after the ship's name. When known, each ship's number of cannons in 1611 is given in parentheses, sometimes after a translation of the ship's name. Generalstaben, *Sveriges krig 1611–1632*, suppl. vol. 1, pp.278–79.

THE OUTBREAK OF WAR

Markatten ('Guenon', 16)	Gabriel Kruse
Penitens (14)	Gert Johansen Blok

Second Squadron

Commander	Herluf Daa
Tre Kroner ('Three Crowns', 64)	Hans Brun
Concordia (23)	John Cunningham (also known as Hans Köning or König)
Gideon (34)	Erik Høg
Sankt Anna ('St Anna', 36)	Herluf Daa
Argo (44) [Flagship]	-
Justitia (37)	Niels Rosencrantz
Trøst ('Consolation')	Holger Rosencrantz
Gabriel (22?)	Isaac Petersen
Enhjørning ('Unicorn', 18)	Jacob Clausen
Lindormen ('Serpent', 16)	Sten Willumsen

Third Squadron

Commander	Godske Lindenow
Victor (39)	Godske Lindenow (later Mads Bagge)
Krokodillen ('Crocodile', 24)	Mads Bagge (later Niels Rosencrantz)
Argorosa (38)	Jacob Beck
Josaphat (44)	-
Leoparden ('Leopard', 20)	-
Stjernen ('Star', 22)	Frans Brockenhuus

Skagerrak Squadron (Total strength: six warships and one pink)

Commander	Admiral Jørgen Daa
Base	Copenhagen
Ready for action	Mid March
Disbanded	Late December
Sorte Hund ('Black Dog', 12)	Peder Holst (later Jens Munk)
Røde Løve ('Red Lion', 6?)	Anders Nolk
Heringnæs (18)	Jørgen Daa
Turtelduen ('Turtledove')	Jens Munk (later Peter Jacobsen)
Forloren Søn ('Prodigal Son')	Johan Petersen Dalpil
Makrelen ('Mackerel', 6?)	Steffen Sørensen
Katten ('Cat', 4) [Pink]	Jørgen Holst

Kalmar Flotilla (Total Strength: approximately 10 yachts and galleys)

Commander	Captain Peder Nielsen
Base	Copenhagen
Ready for action	Late April
Disbanded	Not disbanded for winter

Table 9. Småland Army under Christer Some, May 1611, and the Kalmar Garrison, July 1611[30]

Småland Army

Cavalry

Province	Banner	Strength
Småland	Christer Some	125
Småland	Måns Persson Stierna	240
	Total	365

Infantry

Province	Company	Strength
Småland	Erland Andersson	185
Småland	Håkan Amundsson	150
Småland	Assar Arvidsson	296
Småland	Per Jönsson	88
Småland	Börje Clemetsson	300
Småland	Erik Kock	102
Småland	Sven Trulsson Spinke	100
Småland	Sven Svensson	230
	Total	1,451
	Grand Total	1,816

Kalmar Garrison

Commandant: Adm. Jacob Jacobsson Snakenborg Bååt, replaced by Colonel Per Hammarskiöld 14 July

Cavalry

Province	Banner	Strength
Småland	Per Hammarskiöld (later replaced by Per Nilsson 14 July)	106
	Total	106

Infantry

Province	Company	Strength
Drabant Guard of Foot (enlisted)	Lieutenant Jon Mårtensson	24
Småland	Nils Bryngelsson	132
Småland (Öland)	Lars Bryngelsson	190
Småland	Olof Svensson Hoffman	159
Småland	Sven Håkansson Krååk	131
Småland	Olof Ingelsson	162
	Total	798
	Grand Total	904

---

30 Kalmar town was also defended by a few hundred burgher militia. Most or all cavalry were harquebusiers. Generalstaben, *Sveriges krig 1611–1632*, vol. 1, pp.169–70, 176, 185.

THE OUTBREAK OF WAR

Table 10. The Royal Main Army under King Charles at Örebro and Duke John's Östergötland Ducal Army, 2 June 1611[31]

Royal Main Army[32]		
Cavalry		
Banner	Captain	Strength
The King's Life Banner		147
Ducal Life Banner	Gustavus Adolphus	130
Retinue of Nobles	Bengt Sparre	150
Uppland Banner	Sten Claesson Böllja	160
Charles Philip's Ducal Banner	Gödert Hane	180
	Total	767
Infantry		
Province	Company	Strength
Drabant Guard (enlisted)	Anders Larsson	127
Gästrikland	Per Hansson	327
Uppland	Nils Larsson	196
Västmanland	Hans Campbell	137
Västmanland	Olof Olsson	127
Mountain County (Bergslagen)	Christer von Linden	102
Dalecarlia	Hans Larsson	252
Dalecarlia	Hans Mattsson	245
Dalecarlia	Göran Olsson	216
Södermanland	Per Eriksson	227
Närke	Per Persson	261
Värmland	Sven Algotsson	189
	Total	2,406
Scotland (enlisted)	Bassart (Bassett, first name unknown)	110
Scotland (enlisted)	Alexander Crafoord (1577–1617)	130
England/Scotland (enlisted)	Ellingius (Elling, first name unknown)	112
Scotland (enlisted)	Gilbert Wauchope	120
	Total	472
	Total Infantry	2,878
	Grand Total	3,645[33]

---

31 The life banners and retinue of nobles were cuirassiers, and other cavalry mostly harquebusiers. Generalstaben, *Sveriges krig 1611–1632*, vol. 1, pp.171, 175–76; Petri, *Kungl. Första livgrenadjärregementets historia*, pp.370–71; Barkman, *Kungl. Svea livgardes historia*, vol. 2, p.425.

32 Unit strengths of the royal main army are based on roll calls after the long march to Kalmar. At the outset of the war, and before attrition set in, the total strength can be estimated as 900 horse and 3,000 foot, altogether 3,900 men.

33 Information on the field artillery and its strength is unknown and thus not included.

THE KALMAR WAR

Östergötland Ducal Army		
Cavalry		
Banner	Captain	Strength
Ducal Life Banner		
Östergötland Retinue of Nobles		200 (with Life Banner)
Östergötland Banner		200
	Total	400
Infantry		
Province	Company	Strength
Ducal Drabant Guard	Mats Göransson	22
Ducal Arquebusier Company	Mårten Hemmingsson	?
Östergötland	Per Esbjörnsson	312
Östergötland	Måns Töresson (?)	200
Östergötland	Ingolf Bengtsson (?)	200
Östergötland	Nils Assersson Mannerskiöld (en route to the King)	200?
	Total	934?
	Grand Total	1,334?
	Combined Grand Total	4,979?

Table 11. Swedish Fleets and Squadrons, Spring 1611[34]

Main Fleet (Total strength: 15 warships and one pinnace)	
Commander	Admiral Hans Bielkenstierna (at times Admiral Jacob Gottberg)
Bases	Nyköping (first squadron) and Stockholm (second and third squadrons)
Ready for action	Early June (first squadron), mid June (second squadron), and mid Aug (third squadron)
Disbanded	Early November in Stockholm
First Squadron (also known as the Nyköping Squadron)	
Commander	Captain Alexander Foratt
Draken ('Dragon', 16)	Joachim von Bergen
Leoparden ('Leopard', 16)	Casper Galle
Josua (10)	Alexander Foratt
Hollands Ängeln ('Dutch Angel', 16)	Anders Nilsson
Hollands Svanen ('Dutch Swan', 16)	Lars Bubb

---

34 The captain of each vessel is, when known, given after the ship's name. When known, each ship's number of cannons in 1611 is given in parentheses, sometimes after a translation of the ship's name. Because of transfers between fleets, some vessels are listed more than once. Generalstaben, *Sveriges krig 1611–1632*, suppl. vol. 1, pp.274–77.

THE OUTBREAK OF WAR

Second Squadron	
Commander	Admiral Jacob Gottberg
Tre Kronor ('Three Crowns', 32) [Flagship]	Hans Jönsson
Samson (24)	Per Andersson
Concordia (28)	Nils Bielkenstierna and Jöns Hansson
Röda Lejonet ('Red Lion', 16)	Jöns Eskilsson
Svarta Hunden ('Black Dog', 20)	Richard Clerck and Peter Fransson
Mjölkpigan ('Milkmaid', 18)	Johan Lackej

Third Squadron	
Commander	Admiral Richard Clerck
Mercurius (12)	Jacob Bülow
Justitia (16)	Göran Göransson
Nyckeln ('Key', 20)	Henrik Sönnensson
Meerman (14)	Hans Chrisman
Hälsinge Lejonet ('Hälsingland Lion', 8) [Pinnace]	Nils Mauritzson

Kalmar Squadron[1] (Total participating strength: 12 warships and one pink)	
Commander	Admiral Jacob Jacobsson Snakenborg Bååt (with Captain Christopher Olofsson in operational command)
Base	Kalmar
Ready for action	Early May
Disbanded	Scuttled in June by own crews
Salvator (10)	Christopher Olofsson
Rutenkrans (32)	-
Lejoninnan ('Lioness', 34)	-
Scepter (28)	Lars Bröms
Hannibal (22)	-
Orpheus (23)	Daniel Andersson
Spegeln ('Mirror', 18)	-
Obekant ('Unknown', 16)	-
Tigern ('Tiger', 10)	-
Jonas ('Jonah', 10)	Hans Kloppenberg
Sankt Per ('St Peter')	Hans Jönsson
Smålands Hjorten ('Småland Stag')	-
Lybska Ulven ('Lübeck Wolf') [Pink]	-

---

1 The *Orpheus* and probably the *Spegeln* and *Salvator* were later salvaged by the Swedes, while the Danes salvaged the *Sankt Per* and probably the *Jonas*, *Smålands Hjorten*, and *Lybska Ulven*.

THE KALMAR WAR

Ships of Kalmar Squadron not equipped in time to participate in the campaign	
Äpplet ('Apple')	-
Danziger Lejonet ('Danzig Lion')	-
Sankt Göran ('St George')	-
Kolmårdsbjörnen ('Charcoal-Forest Bear', named after Kolmården, one of Sweden's great forests)	-

Elfsborg Squadron (Total strength: seven warships)	
Commander	Until July, Captains Hans Persson and Lars Persson, afterwards Captain Jon Kock
Base	Elfsborg Castle
Ready for action	Early May
Disbanded	Not disbanded for winter
Hector (22)	Alexander Myr
Blå Ormen ('Blue Snake')	Mårten Livknekt
Franciskus	Anders Svensson
Krabban ('Crab')	Nils Stark
Lamprellen ('Lamprey')	Bengt Ragvaldsson
Erik Siggessons skepp ('Erik Siggesson's Ship')	Jon Kock
Skotska Lejonet ('Scottish Lion')	Bengt Trulsson

Little Fleet (Total strength: nine pinnaces, one galley, one praam, and one boyer)	
Commander	Captain Nils Engelsman (later Captain Erik Kyle)
Base	Stockholm
Ready for action	Mid July
Disbanded	Mid October
Lybska Salvator ('Lübeck Salvator', 10)	Gabriel Eriksson
Jägaren ('Huntsman', 10)	Erik Jacobsson
Kåter ('Lusty', 10)	Sven Lackej
Stå bi ('Stand Bye', 10)	Jacob Sack
Finken ('Finch', 8)	Hans Olofsson
Näktergalen ('Nightingale', 8)	Lars Torstensson
Pickala pinass (8)	Måns Eskilsson
Liljan ('Lily', 4)	Lars Bältare
Romulus (6)	Börje Olofsson
Laxen ('Salmon', 4)	Anders Larsson
Lilla bojorten ('Little Boyer')	Anders Jonsson
Förgyllda galejan ('Gilded Galley')	-

THE OUTBREAK OF WAR

Inshore Fleet[1] (Total strength: two yachts, four galleys, and 12 lodja-type vessels)	
Commander	Captain Isaac Behm (later Captain Anders Cordell)
Base	Stockholm
Ready for action	Early June
Disbanded	Late October
Vita jakten ('White Yacht') [Yacht]	Anders Cordell
Röda jakten ('Red Yacht') [Yacht]	Seved Mesen
Springvalen ('Dolphin Whale') [Galley]	Hans Persson
Stora Valen ('Great Whale') [Galley]	-
Rosengalejan ('Rose Galley') [Galley]	-
Lilla galejan ('Little Galley') [Galley]	-
Stören ('Sturgeon') [Lodja]	-
Braxen ('Bream') [Lodja]	Anders Eriksson
Gäddan ('Pike') [Lodja]	Lars Larsson
Gösen ('Pike-Perch') [Lodja]	Jon Tomasson
Helgeflundran ('Halibut') [Lodja]	Henrik Henriksson
Makrillen ('Mackerel') [Lodja]	Per Tomasson
Iden ('Ide') [Lodja]	Casper Galle
Rockan ('Stingray') [Lodja]	Johan Boreus
Sardinen ('Sardine') [Lodja]	Bertil Henriksson
Svärdfisken ('Swordfish') [Lodja]	Arvid Nilsson
Viborgslodjan ('Viborg Lodja') [Lodja]	Jacob Hansson
Kockbåten ('Cook Boat') [Lodja]	Eskil Mårtensson

Öland Squadron (Total strength: approximately 10 yachts of unknown names)	
Commander	Captain Lars Larsson
Base	Kalmar Strait
Ready for action	Early May
Lost	Late July

Livonian Squadron (Total strength: one warship, three pinnaces, and one boyer)	
Commander	Captain Lars Bubb
Base	Stockholm
Ready for action	Mid April
Disbanded	Late June (when the *Hollands Svanen* was ordered into the main fleet while the smaller vessels were mostly ordered into the little fleet)
Hollands Svanen ('Dutch Swan', 16)	Lars Bubb
Stå bi ('Stand Bye', 10)	Jacob Sack

---

1 The *Röda jakten*, all galleys, and seven *lodja*-type vessels (the *Stören, Gäddan, Makrillen, Iden, Sardinen, Svärdfisken,* and *Kockbåten*) were lost to Danish action in July. In late August, the inshore fleet instead received another eight *lodja*-type vessels, named in a curious mixture of imagination and lack thereof: *Storelodjan* ('Great Lodja'), *Tredjelodjan* ('No. 3 Lodja'), *Fjärdelodjan* ('No. 4 Lodja'), *Fiskelodjan* ('Fishing Lodja'), *Vinlodjan* ('Wine Lodja'), *Braxelodjan* ('Bream'), *Lindormslodjan* ('Serpent'), and *Lepelodja* ('Boozing Lodja').

Stålnäbben ('Steel Beak', 8)	Måns Eskilsson
Basiliscus (6)	Anders Bengtsson
Lilla bojorten ('Little Boyer')	Göran Göransson

Narva Squadron (Total strength: two pinnaces and one galley)

Commander	Captain Philip Trotz
Base	Stockholm
Ready for action	Mid April
Disbanded	Late June (when the *Lybska Salvator* was ordered into the little fleet)
Lybska Salvator ('Lübeck Salvator', 10)	Gabriel Eriksson
Kalmar Ängeln ('Kalmar Angel', 10)	Per Jonsson
Remus (6)	Philip Trotz

Lake Ladoga Squadron (Total strength: two pinnaces and 'a bunch' of lodja-type vessels)

Commander	Captain Lars Anfastsson (later Captain Tönnes Göransson)
Base	Kexholm

7

The Siege of Kalmar

On 1 May, King Christian's army consisted of three banners of national cavalry and 15 companies of foot, altogether approximately 400 horse and 3,900 foot.[1] The King decided not to wait for those units that were still on the way. Following his campaign plan, on this day, King Christian marched out from Christianopel to cross the border. At 4:00 p.m., his advance guard, consisting primarily of the cuirassiers of the Court Banner, encountered the first Swedish defence line, the Småland Banner, under Per Hammarskiöld. The Småland cavalry, mostly unarmoured harquebusiers, was pushed back with losses of several men. Hammarskiöld found it prudent to retreat to Kalmar. Meanwhile, the burghers of Kalmar evacuated women, children, and the elderly and then closed the gates.

King Christian spent the night in Hageby. The following day, his main force joined him. On 3 May, the King and the Court Banner reached Kalmar, soon followed by the rest of the army. Some Swedish cavalry immediately sallied out, but, following an inconclusive skirmish, they returned into the town. In the evening, the King ordered all men, whether commoners or nobles, to work throughout the night to build a defensive line of countervallation facing the town and castle. The walls were ultimately four ells (2.5m) high and wide. He also had trenches dug to enable his men to approach up to 12 fathoms (22.5m) from the town and castle walls.[2] King Christian's siege of Kalmar began on 4 May. He sent a trumpeter to demand the town's surrender. However, the demand was met with artillery fire, and Hammarskiöld led the Småland Banner on a sortie against the Danes. King Christian and the Court Banner met the Swedish cavalry head on. Hammarskiöld was again pushed back.

Kalmar Castle was originally a medieval castle, but had been extensively renovated and its defences modernised during the late 1540s and again from the 1570s onwards. Although Kalmar town lay on the mainland, Kalmar Castle was built on an adjacent island. In the early seventeenth century, Kalmar town lay closer to the castle than the new town built later, so the castle's close

---

1   Generalstaben, *Sveriges krig 1611–1632*, vol. 1, pp.142, 176, 584–85.
2   Abraham Kall (ed.), 'Mag. Ægidii Laurizens samlede Efterretninger om Krigen med Sverige i Aarene 1611 og 1612', *Nye Danske Magazin*, 2:2 (1806), pp.11–12.

THE KALMAR WAR

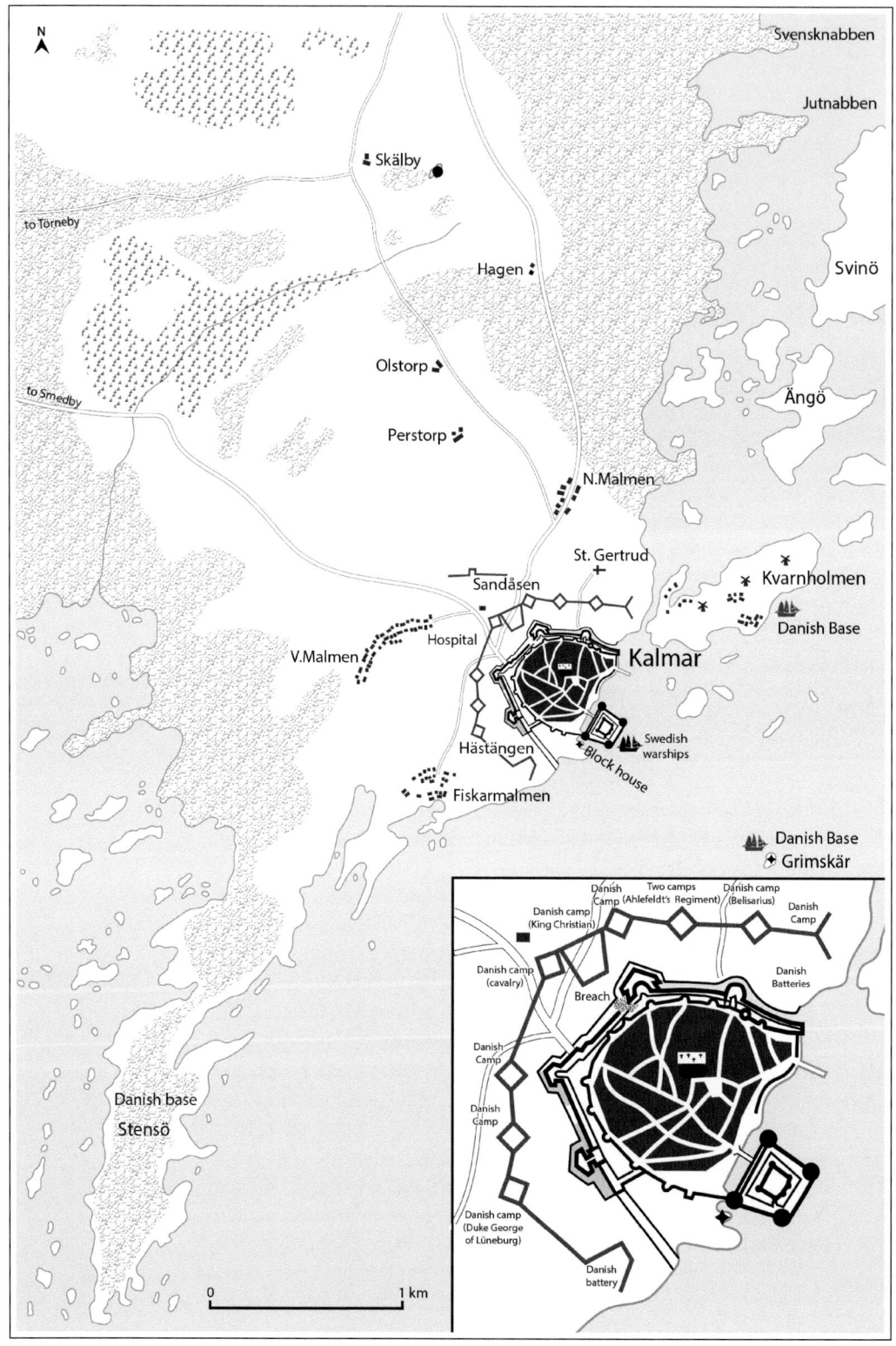

Map 5. The Siege of Kalmar, 1611

proximity protected the town from invading fleets. The town was fortified, but, although somewhat improved, the major part consisted of the old medieval town wall, eight metres high and two metres thick. A section of the southern wall remained incomplete; however, this was considered a minor problem since the castle could provide fire support to that sector. Kalmar town had possibly 50 cannons (including five of bronze, two of which were on loan from the navy's Kalmar Squadron, and 43 of iron). Considering the town's size, this was insufficient. Meanwhile, the castle had an artillery park of at least 93 bronze and 142 iron cannons.[3] There were apparently plans to transfer artillery from the castle to the town, but, if so, either time did not allow or the commandant chose not to reduce the defensive strength of the castle. Even so, the town's close proximity to the castle was a problem. If an enemy captured the town, it could use the buildings, or ruins thereof, as cover for an assault on the castle.

In comparison, the castle was both modernised and equipped with a strong artillery. The garrison consisted of five or six companies of foot to which was now added Hammarskiöld's Småland Banner. The garrison also had to defend the town, together with a few hundred burgher militia, who manned the town wall.[4] The Kalmar Squadron was in port, but the early arrival of the Danish naval blockade force prevented it from setting out.

We have seen that disgruntled Swedish exiles had led King Christian to believe that the Småland peasants feared King Charles, and that they would happily accept Danish rule if only Christian led an army there and the Danish soldiers treated them decently. Unfortunately for the Danes, the exiles, eager to promote themselves and their own interests, had greatly exaggerated. This quickly became obvious on the first day of the invasion, when Småland peasant levies stubbornly defended the roads from the cover of newly constructed timber obstacles (abatis). The peasant levies also ambushed Danish foragers and small units through the traditional means of guerrilla warfare.

The construction of timber obstacles was a time-honoured defensive practice of northern Europe. The timber obstacles consisted of barricades of trees felled to block roads and other approaches through existing forestland. They were quickly constructed by felling large number of trees in the same direction and typically on top of each other, with the branches deliberately left in place to entangle the tree trunks, making it all but impossible for men to climb through or above without first removing all the branches and usually the trunks as well. A dense line of timber obstacles was equally difficult to cross as the massive, barbed-wire defences of more recent centuries. To further confound an approaching enemy, the men built hidden passages camouflaged by natural, evergreen tree branches through the timber obstacles that allowed an unobstructed line of fire and even could be used as sally ports to attack intruders. Abatis was typically built in successive lines

---

3   Generalstaben, *Sveriges krig 1611–1632*, vol. 1, pp.182–84; Hedberg (ed.), *Kungl. Artilleriet: Medeltid och äldre vasatid*, pp.265, 284–85, a later study, claims 102 bronze and 183 iron cannons in the castle and five bronze and 34 iron cannons in the town, most of them small.

4   Generalstaben, *Sveriges krig 1611–1632*, vol. 1, pp.169–70, 185.

THE KALMAR WAR

so that the defenders could disengage and withdraw to the next line after disrupting and inflicting casualties on the advancing enemy.

The stubborn resistance of the Småland peasants was unwelcome news for the Danes. As could be expected, the invaders responded in kind, with looting, the murder of civilians, and the burning of peasant settlements along the road.

Yet there were also skilled professionals in the Danish army. Having gained theoretical and practical knowledge from the experiences of the sixteenth-century Italian Wars and the early sieges of the 1566 Dutch Revolt, it was they who led the construction of defensive lines of countervallation (i.e. facing the fortress) and, soon afterwards, circumvallation (i.e. facing the country) to protect themselves from sallies and the arrival of any Swedish relief force while they laid siege to the town and castle.

Soon, Admiral Erik Urne's warships and Captain Peder Nielsen's galleys cast anchor in an improvised port near the King's army. Nielsen based his galleys, soon known as the Kalmar Flotilla, first at Stensö Peninsula, on which the Danes built a depot from which they could maintain a supply line by sea, and later at Kvarnholm Island in May.

King Christian reaches Kalmar on 3 May 1611, as depicted in one of the tapestries celebrating events during the Kalmar War that King Christian ordered for display in Frederiksborg Castle in 1616. (Frederik Christian Lund, after Karel van Mander II)

Colonel Hammarskiöld led several sorties against the Danes but to no avail. On 6 May, Danish transports unloaded a siege artillery consisting of both 48-pounders and 24-pounders at Kalmar, altogether seven heavy cannons.[5] The last four of the expected Danish companies of foot arrived on the same day.[6] Apparently, plans had been made to ship more siege cannons, but a few had instead been dispatched to Bohus Castle in southern Norway.[7] On 7 May, the Swedish navy commander, Captain Christopher Olofsson, moved his ships in cover behind the castle in an attempt to protect them from artillery fire. (In June, the Swedes scuttled the ships so that they would not fall into Danish hands.) Soon yet, more Danish units arrived. The Fyn Banner rode in on 11 May, and the King's Life Banner, under Joachim von Bülow, joined the army on 14 May.[8] However, the army had only two mining engineers, known respectively as Bartholomæus and Valentin, and both were lost in action before the end of the month, which meant that the Danes had to abandon their mining operations.[9]

The Danish artillery managed to open a breach in the town wall. On 27 May, from about 1:00 a.m., Godske von Ahlefeldt's regiment of foot, and possibly other units, repeatedly attempted to storm the town of Kalmar. Lieutenant Colonel Godske von Ahlefeldt, who had set up the regiment, had been in Swedish service from 1601 to 1605, in which he served as commandant of Pernau, Estonia. Combat became ferocious, with not only Swedish soldiers and burgher militiamen but also women manning the defences. On Ahlefeldt's third attempt, at about 5:00 a.m., the Danes managed to break through. With the Danish infantry gaining control of the breach, other Danish units moved in, with the Court Banner in the vanguard. The storm culminated in slaughter. Total military losses during the storm were an estimated 100 Danish dead, including two captains (Caspar von Miltnitz and Melchior Rantzau), and possibly somewhat fewer Swedes.[10] The number of wounded is unknown but would not have been lower than the number of dead. Civilian casualties, however, seem to have been very high, particularly after the fall of the town.

After taking the town, the Danes turned their attention to the castle, preparing siege works. Kalmar Castle remained under arms even though the supply situation for the 400 defenders was poor. Those Swedes who had survived the fall of the town had withdrawn into the castle. There was little drinking water and only limited food supplies. The arrival of survivors from the town only exacerbated the supply problems.

---

5   Generalstaben, *Sveriges krig 1611–1632*, vol. 1, p.191.
6   Larsen, *Kalmarkrigen*, p.98.
7   This seems to have been standard procedure for siege artillery intended for the western front. In 1612, King Christian again sent siege artillery to Bohus Castle, which he then ordered to be delivered to his field army then laying siege to Elfsborg Castle. A few days later, the King also asked for alcohol to be sent from Bohus Castle, which functioned as a supply depot. King Christian to Steen Laxmand, 8 May 1612, *Norske Rigs-Registranter*, vol. 4, pp.464–65.
8   Larsen, *Kalmarkrigen*, p.98.
9   Larsen, *Kalmarkrigen*, p.99.
10 Wadén, *Berättande källor*, p.124.

THE KALMAR WAR

Above: Kalmar Castle today. (Photo: L. G. Foto)

Below: The defences of Kalmar town and Castle, 1610, as drawn by a contemporary but anonymous fortification officer. Note that a section of the southern wall remained incomplete. (Redrawn, from contemporary original, by Ludvig W:son Munthe, 1902)

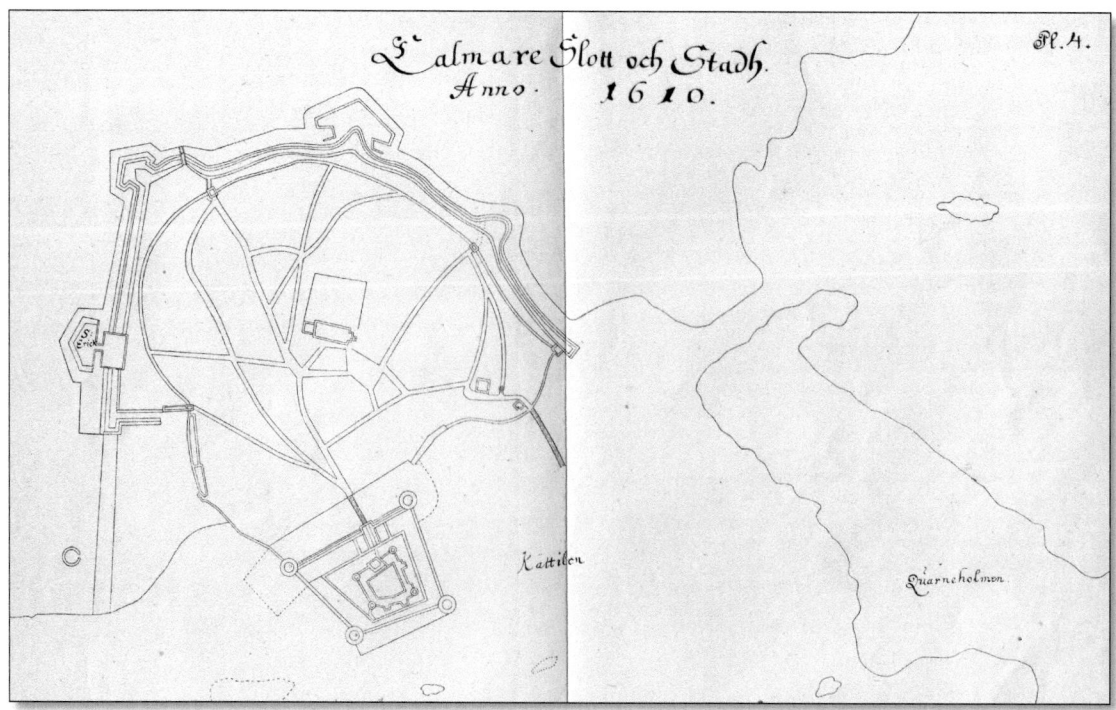

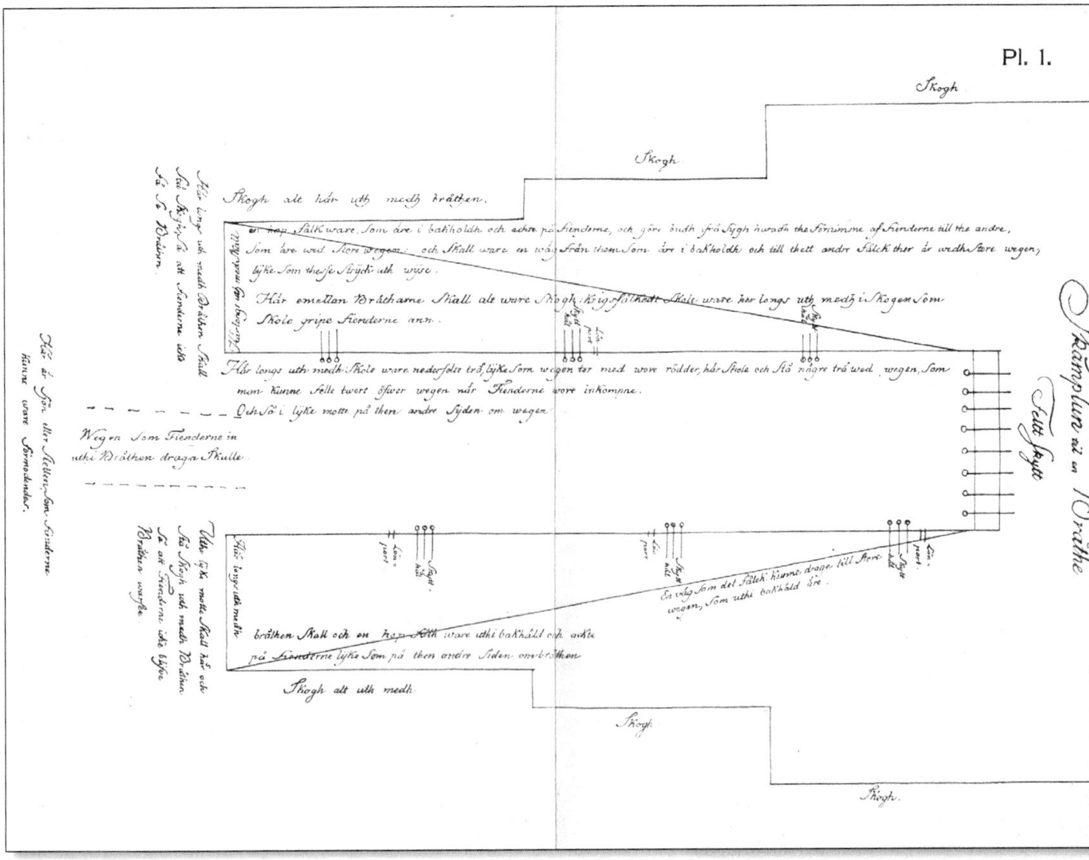

THE SIEGE OF KALMAR

Above: Swedish sapper's schematic plan for the construction of timber obstacles around a forest road, 1550s. The enemy was expected to approach along the road from the left side. Trees were felled to construct a wall along both sides of the road through which gun loopholes (Swedish: *skytthål*) and the occasional sally port (*lönnport*) allowed the defenders to attack the intruders. The felling of trees also opened up a slice of forestland on both sides of the road that allowed free movement for the defenders manning the timber obstacle and yet protected them from enemy observation. In a dense forest, the intruders could not see the timber obstacle until the last moment. If all went as planned, the intruders would only notice the ambush when they came under fire from the men manning the final line of gun loopholes in the abatis that directly blocked the road (on the right side). At this point, the remaining trees, which had been prepared in advance, would be felled directly over the enemy column of march, after which the defenders would engage the enemy through gun loopholes and sally ports. (Redrawn, from contemporary original, by Ludvig W:son Munthe, 1902)

Right: Pawel von Essen, military architect at Kalmar Castle. He participated in the siege and, after the war, assisted in the reconstruction of Kalmar town. In later sources, his personal name was given as 'Paul'. (Georg Günther Kräill, 1623)

THE KALMAR WAR

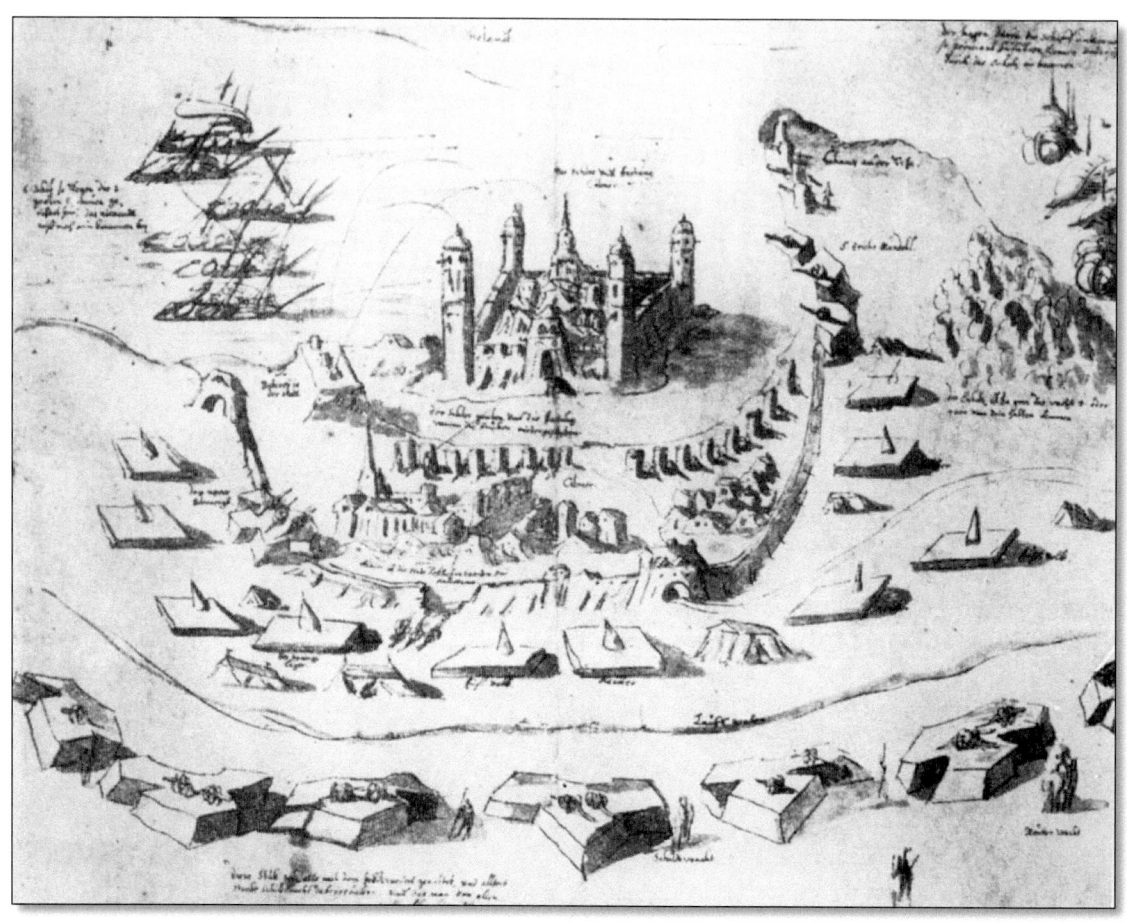

Above: Contemporary drawing of the siege of Kalmar Castle, probably made by somebody in the Danish camp as a pattern for a subsequent engraving. The Danes have successfully stormed the town, in which they take cover during the siege of the castle. Bottom: the Danish circumvallation defensive line protects against Swedish relief attempts. Left: the Swedish Kalmar Squadron, scuttled by their crews to avoid the warships from falling into Danish hands. Right: the Danish blockade fleet consisting of Admiral Erik Urne's squadron (five warships) and Captain Peder Nielsen's Kalmar Flotilla (around 10 galleys and yachts). Top: the island of Öland. (Herzog August-Bibliothek, Wolfenbüttel)

Facing page: Contemporary drawing of the siege of Kalmar, dated 3 June 1611. The drawing apparently shows the situation before the fall of Kalmar town but is believed to have been used to orient King Charles about the Danish defences. Top left: Borgholm Castle on the island of Öland. Left: Kvarnholm Island (Windmill Island), which became the new site of Kalmar town after the war. Centre: Kalmar Castle, providing cover for the Swedish Kalmar Squadron. (Swedish Military Archives)

THE SIEGE OF KALMAR

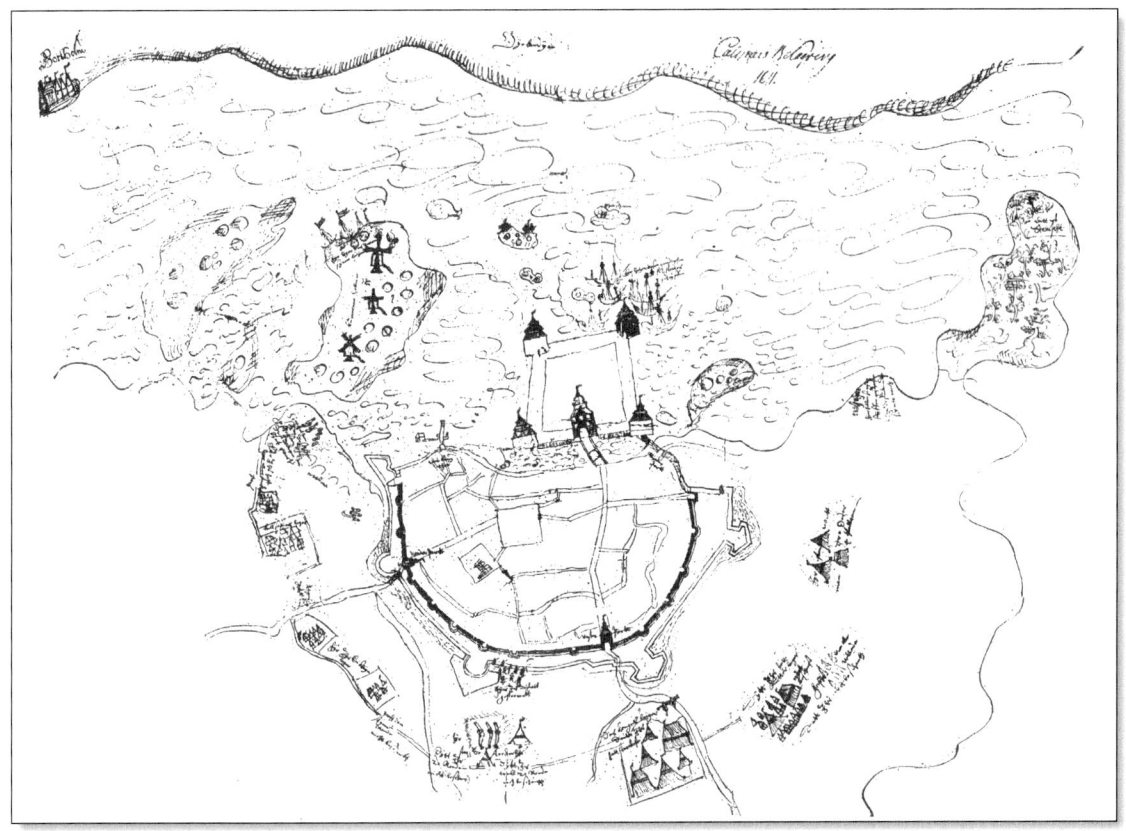

The Swedish Relief Army

King Charles's response to the Danish invasion had been slow, although somewhat more energetic than later historians sometimes have given him credit for. For sure, if he had followed his original intention to march out of Örebro around 20 April, a move soon postponed until 29 April and finally 7 May, he could have reached Kalmar in time to disturb, and quite likely prevent, the Danish storm of Kalmar town on 27 May. However, the Swedish King had been unwilling to acknowledge the inaccuracy of his assessment that Denmark would not attack, so preparations had been slow and insufficient. Perhaps King Charles's faulty assessment and stubborn refusal to act depended on more than just bad judgment. In poor health since a stroke two years previously, King Charles believed that he soon would die since he had foreseen his death in a comet.

King Charles moved out of Örebro with the main army on 9 May, marching south to meet the invaders. Dividing his army into two columns, one on each side of Lake Vättern (the western column under Gustavus Adolphus, the eastern under the King) to march faster, King Charles reached Jönköping on 18 May. Additional units from the Småland Army joined him along the way. King Charles soon led eight cavalry banners and 25 companies of foot,

THE KALMAR WAR

Duke John of Östergötland. (Portrait attributed to Holger Hansson, 1618)

altogether 1,330 horse and 4,640 foot.[11] Moreover, he expected reinforcements from Field Marshal Cruus on the western front, as well as the units commanded by his nephew Duke John of Östergötland. The King had ordered the Småland general levy to be raised and, furthermore, sent instructions to raise infantry companies throughout the country. The King commanded Admiral Bielkenstierna to join forces with the Nyköping Squadron at Älvsnabben, with orders to attack and disperse all Danish ships in the Kalmar Strait and between Öland and Gotland.

On 23 May, King Charles left Jönköping, having reinforced the garrison there with a couple of companies of foot. Three days later, he reached Vetlanda, where he added fresh conscripts from northern Småland to his army. On 28 May, he reached Högsby, where he learnt that Kalmar town had fallen the previous day.

King Charles continued the march by way of Ålem, and reached Ryssby on 9 June.[12] His army then consisted of nine banners of cavalry, and 21 national and four foreign enlisted companies of foot, altogether no more than 1,400 horse and 4,660 foot, or, in total, some 6,060 men.[13] The march continued while skirmishes took place between Swedes and Danes.

On or around 4 June, the Danes captured a Swedish courier who brought a message from King Charles to the commandant in Kalmar. Learning that King Charles was on the way to Kalmar and that he had reached Ålem on 2 June, Duke George of Brunswick-Lüneburg and Breide Rantzau immediately left with the intention to raid King Charles's camp at night. By then, King Charles had reached Ryssby. When the two Danish commanders successfully located the Swedish camp, they deemed the Swedish army too large to dare a surprise assault. Based on prisoner interrogations, Breide Rantzau claimed an exaggerated 10,000 Swedes. Moreover, the Swedish cannons were already deployed in position to defend the camp.

Meanwhile, the Danes had problems of their own. By this time, they lacked gunpowder, slow match, and even muskets. During the campaign, they had found that the issued muskets were so poorly made that one in 10 burst upon firing. To make sure that fresh supplies arrived, King Christian

---

11   Generalstaben, *Sveriges krig 1611–1632*, vol. 1, p.205.

12   In modern Swedish, the name 'Ryssby' means 'Russian village'. However, the name derived from 'Rydsby', an Old Swedish term for 'village in cleared lands' (i.e. recently cleared forestland). The name had already evolved into 'Ryzby' by 1336.

13   Generalstaben, *Sveriges krig 1611–1632*, vol. 1, p.211.

left the army on 10 June, sailing to Christianopel to bring reinforcements and to speed things up.

The Danes had built modern fortifications at Kalmar of the circumvallation type as the primary defensive line, facing north and west. They also utilised the walls of Kalmar town. This made it impossible to attack the Danish army in the field. Instead, the Swedes had to establish a camp of their own and lay siege to the Danish fortifications.

King Charles's advance guard reached Kalmar on 11 June, the day after King Christian left his army there. The same day, a cavalry skirmish took place.[14] The next day, King Charles and the main army arrived and offered battle. In response, the Danish cavalry made a sortie in force. The Danish cavalry force consisted of four banners: the Court Banner, the Zealand and Fyn Banners, and the King's Life Banner, under Joachim von Bülow. The Swedish cavalry, superior in numbers to the Danes, pushed them back easily, advancing until they came under fire from the well-fortified and essentially out-of-reach Danish artillery. Both sides exaggerated enemy losses and downplayed their own, so casualties are mostly unknown but were probably not high. Yet two of four Danish captains – Peder Basse and Joachim von Bülow – were wounded, and at least two Danish nobles fell.[15] The Danes made no further attempt to engage the Swedish army. King Charles established a camp at Perstorp, immediately outside Kalmar, intending to lay siege to the Danish fortifications. Knowing that King Christian had left the army, King Charles planned an assault on the night between 15 and 16 June. However, these plans were abandoned. Perhaps this was unwise since the Danes, by then, suffered shortages in gunpowder, ammunition, slow match, and food supplies. The departure of the Danish King had done nothing to ameliorate the mood in the exhausted Danish army, which had already been on campaign for a month and a half.

Duke George of Brunswick and Lüneburg. (Author's collection)

Meanwhile, at Sölvesborg, the Danish King had finally learnt that his field marshal, Sehested, had not marched on Jönköping according to the campaign plan but instead had abandoned the plan, marching north-west to lay siege to Elfsborg Castle. On 12 June, the King sent the aforementioned angry letter to Sehested, ordering him to abandon the siege if at all possible and instead march to Växjö in an attempt to force King Charles to divide his army in order to deal with two simultaneous threats. Sehested only received the letter on 22 June, and, by then, King Christian had changed his mind. He now wanted Sehested to continue with the siege of Elfsborg Castle but, at the

---

14 Wadén, *Berättande källor*, p.197.
15 Larsen, *Kalmarkrigen*, p.112.

same time, to send Gert von Rantzau together with his cavalry banner and infantry to march to join forces with the King.

At Kalmar, King Charles was faced with the double problem of reinforcing the castle and retaking the town. This was difficult since the Danish fleet patrolled the Kalmar Strait and the Danes held Kvarnholm Island, north of the castle, where the Danish galleys were deployed, protected by two cannons. The Swedes assembled boats, including five *lodja*-type rowing vessels from Öland, then, at dawn on 18 June, crossed to Kvarnholm Island, where they successfully took one cannon and spiked the other. Spiking a cannon was a method of temporarily disabling it by hammering a steel spike into the touch hole. However, the Danes built a pontoon bridge across the water to Kvarnholm Island and then sent Peder Hundemark's company of foot to hold the island. A couple of days later, Swedes under Admiral Bååt made another attempt to evict the Danes from Kvarnholm Island. Hundemark's infantry found themselves forced to retreat across the pontoon bridge. Bååt and his men pursued the Danes across the bridge, but, when confronted on the other side by the King's Life Banner of Horse, under Joachim von Bülow, and Blasius Belisarius's company of foot from Gert von Rantzau's regiment, they were pushed back. The pontoon bridge then collapsed because of the weight of so many men. The Swedes lost many men, especially when the Danes cut down those Swedes that remained on the Danish side. Then, the Swedish castle artillery opened fire, not distinguishing between Swedes and Danes in the evening light. Admiral Bååt, who had stayed until the very end, only saved himself by discarding his armour so that he could swim off the island. Kvarnholm Island remained in Danish hands. However, on 23 June, the Swedes nonetheless managed to bring a few hundred men under Captain Lars Brink into Kalmar Castle as reinforcements.[16]

To block the costal road between Christianopel and Kalmar, King Charles had a camp surrounded by six redoubts built at Ljungby, 15 km south of Kalmar. The camp was built by Colonel Johan (or Jean) van Monickhouen, a Dutchman in Swedish service since at least 1608 who was a qualified military engineer and siege specialist. First serving in Livonia, Monickhouen was one of few professional commanders from the eastern front who served in the Swedish theatre of war. Ordering Olof Hård's Småland infantry, Måns Stierna's Småland cavalry, and Jon Andersson's cavalry to man the Ljungby camp, King Charles also had peasant levies build abatis to block the road further. The fortified camp served its purpose: as long as it was manned, the Danes had to send supplies and reinforcements by sea, not land.[17]

On 25 June, Port Admiral Godske Lindenow's squadron reinforced the Danish army and fleet elements at Kalmar.

---

16 Generalstaben, *Sveriges krig 1611–1632*, vol. 1, p.219 and *Sveriges krig 1611–1632*, suppl. vol. 1, p.79.
17 Larsen, *Kalmarkrigen*, p.120.

THE SIEGE OF KALMAR

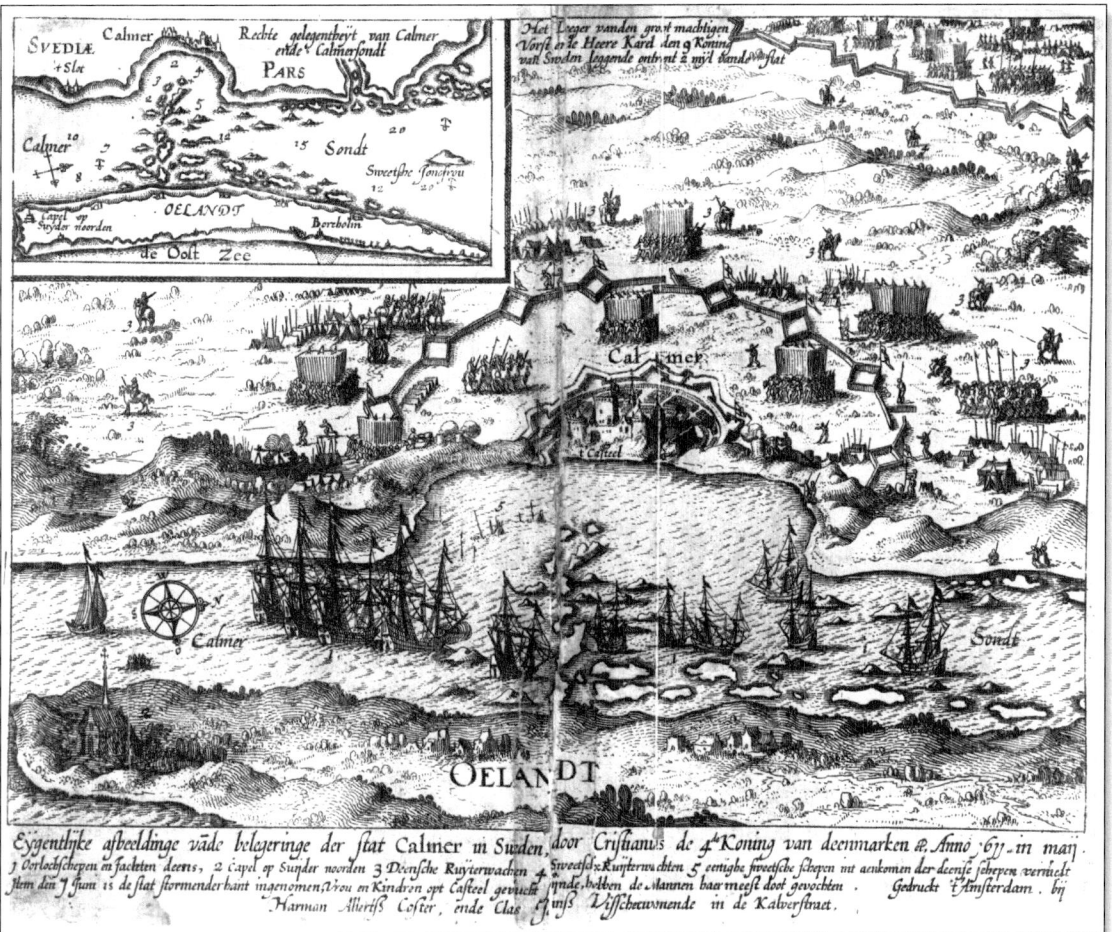

The siege of Kalmar, dated May 1611 but, in reality, showing the situation at some point after 11 June. Contemporary Dutch engraving, possibly based on drawings by the Dutch siege engineer Johan van Monickhouen. The print depicts the siege works after the fall of Kalmar town, as well as the geographical location of the events near the island of Öland (below). Centre left: the Danish blockade fleet, consisting of Admiral Erik Urne's squadron (five warships) and Captain Peder Nielsen's Kalmar Flotilla (around 10 galleys and yachts). Centre: Kalmar Castle and several scuttled Swedish warships. Top right: the Swedish camp after the arrival of King Charles. (Anon., *Eygentlijke afbeeldinge va[n] de belegeringe der stat Calmer* (Amsterdam: Herman Allertszoon Coster and Claes Janszoon Visscher, n.d. [c. 1611]))

Gustavus Adolphus's First Independent Command

Meanwhile, the Swedes had captured a courier with a letter from Jens Bjørnsen in Christianopel, which functioned as a major Danish supply depot. The letter was addressed to the town's *lensmand* and commandant, Jens Sparre, who had joined the Danish army at Kalmar. Bjørnsen requested reinforcements. Assuming that Sparre had not brought too many men with him, Christianopel may have had a garrison of 300 men.[18] Taking advantage of the fresh intelligence, King Charles sent Gustavus Adolphus with two cavalry banners (likely Måns Stierna's and Jon Andersson's cavalry banners from Ljungby) and a unit of sappers to Christianopel.

At 1:00 a.m., on 26 June, Gustavus Adolphus and his men reached Christianopel without being discovered. The watchmen at the gate were drunk, so a few Swedes managed to creep up to blow the gate with a petard. This allowed Gustavus Adolphus and his cavalry to charge into the town.[19] Jens Bjørnsen made a desperate attempt to hold the now open gate against the Swedes, killed a few Swedish cavalrymen, but was then himself struck down dead. Gustavus Adolphus ordered one of his banners to take control of the market square but let the other banner sack the town. Not inclined to show any more mercy than the Danes had displayed after capturing Kalmar town, the Swedes left the town sacked and burning in the morning, having killed all the men they could lay their hands on, as well as many women and children. It took several days before local peasants dared to approach the town and bury the dead. Young Gustavus Adolphus's first independent command turned into a brutal affair, much more so than what he would accept later in his career. One may wonder if the 16-year-old Prince planned to massacre the townsmen from the outset or merely lost control over his men, who certainly wished to take revenge for the sack of Kalmar.

Gustavus Adolphus took much booty, including the Danish war chest of 20,000 *Reichsthalers*. He then returned to the Swedish camp outside Kalmar with 28 captured Danish standards. According to one story, the proudly displayed Danish standards made the Swedish sentries panic, so some opened fire. One of Gustavus Adolphus's men lost his life in the friendly fire incident.[20] According to another, perhaps more credible story, the man died when fired upon from a Danish unit at Kalmar.[21]

It is hardly surprising if Gustavus Adolphus made a few mistakes during his first independent command. There is nothing to suggest that either of

---

18 Larsen, *Kalmarkrigen*, p.73.

19 After the event, Danish propaganda leaflets were distributed abroad, claiming that the intruders used treason to gain entrance into the town, but an eyewitness refuted this. Anon., 'Journal', p.689; Wadén, *Berättande källor*, pp.167–71.

20 The captured standards were brought to Stockholm for display in the Storkyrkan Church. However, in 1612, they were apparently quietly removed and distributed to newly raised units that needed flags. A later Danish account instead argues that the standards were returned after the war. Anon., 'Journal', pp.689–90. This seems unlikely.

21 Wadén, *Berättande källor*, p.86, citing the contemporary historian Johannes Messenius.

the two cavalry captains, or any other officer, functioned in the capacity of a mentor in military matters or tactics, which otherwise was customary for young princes. As far as is known, Gustavus Adolphus had to learn practical military skills on the job.

On 26 June, the same day that Gustavus Adolphus and his men returned to the camp, the Danish Court Banner and the King's Life Banner, under Joachim von Bülow, attempted to sally out. This time, the Swedes sent only two banners to meet them, intending to lure the Danes into a trap by arranging crossfire from an infantry unit and another banner. A Swedish noble of the Ribbing family fell in the ensuing skirmish.[22] However, the Danes realised the danger and soon returned into town.

---

22 Peder Hesselberg's diary, 29 June 1611. Holger Rørdam (ed.), 'To Dagbøger fra Kalmarkrigens Tid, 1611–1612', in *Historiske Samlinger og Studier vedrørende Danske Forhold og Personligheder især i det 17. Aarhundrede* (Copenhagen: G. E. C. Gad, 1891), p.293.

8

The Offensive Against the River Göta Älv Castles

We have seen that, in mid April, Swedish Field Colonel Jesper Matsson Cruus stood at Elfsborg with an army of three banners of cavalry and seven companies of infantry, altogether about 600 horse and 1,400 foot. Cruus was an experienced man who had already spent several years on the eastern front.

Meanwhile, there were only weak Danish garrisons, one banner of cavalry, and one foreign enlisted company of foot in nearby Halland. This would have presented a great opportunity to gain control of Halland, capture Halmstad, preempt the most likely Danish offensive against Småland, threaten the wealthy Danish province of Scania, and, moreover, possibly even preempt the Danish offensive against Kalmar, or at least reduce its strength. However, because of King Charles's general reluctance to believe in the reports about Danish mobilisation, he, even after the declaration of war, ordered Cruus to remain on the defensive and not initiate hostilities. As a result, Danish Field Marshal Sehested had ample opportunity to assemble his army without Swedish interference. This took time. As late as 16 May, he had only managed to assemble three-and-a-half cavalry banners and two companies of foot, altogether 580 horse and 640 foot. The supply difficulties remained unresolved. Captain Albert Skeel of the Ribe Banner informed the Council that neither beer nor bread was available.[1] Additional units began to arrive from 26 May onwards. By the end of the month, Sehested had gathered four-and-a-half national cavalry banners, three foreign enlisted cavalry banners, and 10 companies of foot, altogether 1,320 horse and 2,800 foot.[2] This meant that, henceforth, it was Cruus who was outnumbered, and, even had his orders allowed, he probably felt unable to go on the offensive.

On 31 May, the experienced military entrepreneur Gert von Rantzau spearheaded a Danish offensive towards Gullberg and Nya Lödöse with two banners of cavalry and seven companies of foot. Rantzau had been in Dutch

---

1 Larsen, *Kalmarkrigen*, p.115.
2 Generalstaben, *Sveriges krig 1611–1632*, vol. 1, pp.144, 222–23, 584–85; Norrie, *Kalmarkrigen*, p.22.

service, so we can assume that his men were trained in the Dutch model of warfare. The following day, Sehested followed Rantzau's advance guard with what has been described as '400 or 500 Danish cavalry and four companies of foot' but, in reality, must have been the rest of his army. They did not bring any siege artillery, possibly because they expected to get what they needed from Bohus Castle in Norwegian Bohuslän farther to the north. Perhaps to his surprise, Sehested almost immediately encountered Rantzau, who, having failed to make an impact on either Gullberg or, apparently afterwards, Elfsborg, for some reason had decided to retreat. Nonetheless, Sehested continued with the Danish army to Elfsborg Castle, which he reached the morning of 3 June.

The garrison at Elfsborg Castle, under Nils Silfverbielke, immediately sallied out with 150 men, but they could not push back Sehested's large force. Sehested, on the other hand, had no means to lay siege without artillery. Instead, he satisfied himself with plundering the surrounding countryside, capturing any cattle that had been abandoned or lost by local Swedes. While he busied himself with this campaign, he received additional reinforcements: Duke Philip of Glücksburg, who arrived with one cavalry banner, the rest of Rantzau's regiment, and Holger Rosencrantz's company of foot enlisted in the Dutch Republic.

On 7 June, Sehested returned across the border, building a fortified camp at Frölunda approximately 10 km south of the River Göta Älv Estuary. Two days later, he continued with five cavalry banners, 500 musketeers, and some additional infantry under the military professional Jørgen Lunge towards Nya Lödöse. On the road, the Aalborg Banner pushed back a Swedish cavalry force, estimated to have been 250 men strong.[3] However, Sehested still did not bring any artillery, so he soon abandoned the attempt and retreated to Frölunda.

On 11 June, Duke Philip of Glücksburg and Gert von Rantzau made a demonstration of their own against Elfsborg with their personal cavalry banners, the Ribe Banner, and some musketeers. The Swedes saw through their demonstration and refused to sally out. The Duke and Rantzau retreated.

The following day, Sehested ordered Daa's sailors across the River Göta Älv Estuary with orders to burn Gothenburg since the activities of the Dutch merchants there had strongly displeased King Christian. The fundamentally defenceless town had already, in May, been attacked by a Norwegian contingent from Bohus Castle. This time, the Danish sailors finished the job, thoroughly destroying the town. Sehested also learnt that Cruus had evacuated Nya Lödöse, withdrawing towards the north. Sehested immediately sent Albert Skeel, captain of the Ribe Banner, with his own men and Tessen von Parsow's and Jørgen Lunge's harquebusier companies to take the abandoned town. They were followed by Peter von Heinemark's company of foot. Although Skeel could not penetrate farther (on probably 13 June, he encountered four Swedish infantry companies behind a defensive line along a stream), the Ribe Banner and a company of foot was moved into Nya Lödöse to hold the abandoned town.

---

3   Generalstaben, *Sveriges krig 1611–1632*, vol. 1, p.224.

Sehested also received yet more reinforcements: Tessen von Parsow's regiment of foot (three companies) and Jørgen Grubbe's harquebusier cavalry company. Henceforth, Sehested led 10-and-a-half banners of cavalry and at least 15 (possibly 18) companies of foot, altogether 2,000 horse and 4,200 foot (as previously shown in Table 6). He led the entire army into Nya Lödöse.

At this point, on 22 June, Sehested received King Christian's order (of 12 June) to abandon the western campaign and instead march to Växjö. As a result, he immediately retreated to Kungsbacka, intending to march back through Halland before he entered Småland. Already at Varberg, he received the King's countermanding order to again attack Cruus – but first to send Gert von Rantzau with his regiment and cavalry to the King at Kalmar – and to send the Halland Banner, under Tage Krabbe, to hold Halmstad. Soon, yet more orders from King Christian followed. Intending to follow the flurry of rapidly changing orders, on 26 June, Sehested sent a corps (300 horse and 300 musketeers under Jørgen Lunge) towards Frölunda, but it soon encountered a Swedish unit the next day, failed to make an impact, and accordingly found it prudent to return to Varberg on 29 June with some captured cattle.

Cruus, meanwhile, received orders from King Charles (dated 12 June), who wished him to abandon the campaign and march to Kalmar. In a later instruction, the King countermanded the order, instead ordering Cruus to adjust his operation to Sehested's activities. Specifically, when Sehested moved to Kalmar (which King Charles now expected), Cruus should follow him through Halland and then shadow Sehested to Kalmar along the inland roads.

Then, reacting to Gustavus Adolphus's victory at Christianopel, King Christian again ordered most units to assemble at Kalmar. Sehested received the order on 29 June and, again following the King's orders, left four banners (the Halland, Aalborg, Aarhus, and Ribe Banners) to protect Halland. He brought the rest of his army in forced marches to Christianopel.[4] He set out on 1 July, marching by way of Halmstad, cutting across a corner of Småland, and then continuing along the coastal road to Christianopel. Cruus, however, marched along the more direct road through Värnamo, Växjö, and Långskruv to King Charles's camp at Ryssby.

---

[4] This means that he brought half of the Zealand Banner, five harquebusier cavalry companies (those of Duke Philip of Glücksburg, Duke Ernest Louis of Saxe-Lauenburg, Pentz, Parsow, and Grubbe), and eight companies of foot (his four companies of the King's Regiment, Parsow's three companies, and Lunge's independent company) with him on the march. Generalstaben, *Sveriges krig 1611–1632*, vol. 1, pp.226–27.

9

The Battle for Kalmar

King Christian had good reasons for ordering Sehested to bring the second Danish army to Kalmar.

By the end of June, the Swedish army at Kalmar had contained the Danish army inside the captured town. The newly built fortified camp at Ljungby prevented Danish communications with Christianopel. Still, the Danes enjoyed supremacy at sea and had a good port at Stensö Peninsula. Erik Urne's squadron and Peder Nielsen's Kalmar Flotilla were based at Kvarnholm Island, while Godske Lindenow's squadron was based at Stensö Peninsula.

On 30 June, the Swedish Inshore Fleet of 18 vessels under Anders Cordell arrived, with at least a company of foot on board (Lars Larsson Tacke's company of 264 men from Finland).[1] Peder Nielsen attempted to block their approach through the narrow strait at Svinö. However, Cordell received support from the land forces, and Nielsen had to return to Kvarnholm Island. On 1 July, the Swedes took up positions on Svinö Island, from which they attempted to engage the Danish ships at Kvarnholm Island with artillery fire. The following day, the Swedes landed on Stensö Peninsula. However, the Danes evicted them after four hours of combat.

On 7 July, King Christian arrived on Stensö Peninsula by sea. He brought Gert von Rantzau with most of his regiment of foot (six companies of 1,500 men) with him from Christianopel. The rest of the regiment (one company) arrived on 11 July. Tessen von Parsow's regiment arrived as well, or at least parts of it. Duke George of Brunswick-Lüneburg's regiment of foot (700 men) had already arrived on 29 May. This enabled the King to command more than three-and-a-half banners of cavalry and four regiments (altogether 25 companies) of foot, in total an estimated 650 horse and 6,400 foot. Because of this number, King Christian deployed Godske von Ahlefeldt's regiment of foot in Kalmar town while the four companies of the King's Regiment and the three companies of Duke George's regiment held the southern front down to Stensö Peninsula. This meant three regiments (17 companies) of foot, as well

---

1   Generalstaben, *Sveriges krig 1611–1632*, vol. 1, p.228.

as the cavalry, in readiness against King Charles's Swedes and another regiment (eight companies) that held the town and contained Kalmar Castle.[2]

The Danish reinforcements meant that King Christian now had more infantry than King Charles. Moreover, they were deployed behind strong defences. We have seen that the Danes had protected their camps in the modern manner by building defensive lines of circumvallation and countervallation. The Swedish main army could, accordingly, no longer expect to face the enemy in the open field. It is fair to conclude that the Danes enjoyed a superior position on land. King Charles had to put his hope in Cruus's men arriving before those of Sehested did so. This would enable him to attack before the Danes received yet more reinforcements.

On the afternoon of 8 July, Admiral Bielkenstierna arrived with the Swedish main fleet of 11 warships (the *Concordia*, *Samson*, *Svarta Hunden*, *Mjölkpigan*, *Röda Lejonet*, *Hollands Svanen*, *Josua*, *Tre Kronor*, *Ängeln*, *Draken*, and *Leoparden*). Joining forces with Cordell's inshore fleet, this gave the Swedes the advantage at sea. Urne commanded four warships at Kvarnholm Island while Lindenow commanded the remaining seven warships at Stensö Peninsula.[3] Since Ulfeldt remained at Gotland with the strongest Danish squadron, the two sides had about the same number of warships. Yet the Swedes counted on their inshore fleet to provide a decisive advantage.

There was no wind the following day, but, on 10 July, Bielkenstierna attacked Urne's squadron at Kvarnholm Island. Urne withdrew towards the south, receiving artillery fire from Kalmar Castle along the way, until he could join forces with Lindenow's squadron at Stensö Peninsula. Bielkenstierna ordered seven warships into the Kalmar roadstead to deny the Danes the use of the town's port. Another four were deployed in a forward position at Grimskär. On 13 July, King Charles asked Bielkenstierna to attack the Danish squadrons to the south, but Bielkenstierna first wished to increase his strength by salvaging the scuttled ships in the harbour, a work that he had already begun. He also managed to bring supplies into Kalmar Castle by sea.

King Charles and his commanders knew that Cruus and his men were not far away. They accordingly devised a plan to evict the Danes from Kalmar town. First, the field army would assault and penetrate the newly built Danish defences to push the Danes back into the town itself. At the same time, the defenders of Kalmar Castle would sally out to attack the town from their side. Meanwhile, the fleet would harass the Danes in the town through artillery fire. If the operation succeeded, the Danes would be squeezed from two directions between their own defensive lines: the circumvallation and the town wall.

On 14 July, King Charles sent Colonels Pierre De la Ville and Reinhold Taube with Captain Anders Gosen von der Maa into the castle to finalise

---

2   Generalstaben, *Sveriges krig 1611–1632*, vol. 1, p.229.

3   Generalstaben, *Sveriges krig 1611–1632*, vol. 1, p.229 and *Sveriges krig 1611–1632*, suppl. vol. 1, pp.81–82.

the battle plan.⁴ The same day, the King announced his intention to reinforce the castle garrison with 2,000 men and appointed Colonel Per Hammarskiöld commandant of the castle, instead of the previous and possibly less decisive commandant, Admiral Jacob Jacobsson Snakenborg Bååt, who formally was in command of the Kalmar Squadron.⁵ Command of Hammarskiöld's Småland Banner was, at the same time, transferred to Per Nilsson.

Late in the evening of 15 July, after darkness had fallen (which occurred at 9:20 p.m.), the promised reinforcements were secretly brought into the castle on yachts and rowing vessels. Their numbers were likely high, considering subsequent events, perhaps even as high as the 2,000 men that King Charles had promised. Some reinforcements were Swedish national troops.⁶ Others included 480 English and Scottish enlisted foot, as well as some 160 dismounted French cavalrymen under De la Ville.⁷ German infantrymen were reported as well. The reinforcements consisted of contingents from different companies temporarily brought together into new units, which was common practice on campaign when attrition reduced unit strengths. With the original garrison still fairly strong (106 horse and 864 foot as of 11 July), possibly some 2,800 men were available to sally out during the attack.⁸

Per Hammarskiöld. (Author's collection)

---

4   Pierre De la Ville de Dombasle was a professional officer who, until then, had served on the eastern front in the Swedish campaign in Muscovy. Reinhold Taube's regiment included the Drabant Company.

5   Bo Gustavsson Bååt, governor of Kalmar, had taken refuge in the castle but, despite his higher rank, played only a minor role in its defence. Incidentally, the two distant relatives Admiral Bååt and Governor Bååt did not yet use the family name 'Bååt' (Boat, from the family coat of arms), which was only assumed by their respective children.

6   The Swedish soldiers included Anders Håkansson's company and Christer Kock's company, both from Småland, which together counted 419 men. Generalstaben, *Sveriges krig 1611–1632*, vol. 1, p.232.

7   The English and Scots probably belonged to Ellingius's regiment but may have included a contingent of Scots and Irish from Patrick Rutherford's regiment. Colonel Patrick Rutherford (1577–1618) had served on the eastern front and was a good friend of Chancellor Oxenstierna. The French cavalrymen derived from De la Ville's regiment of horse, which apparently consisted of two companies, one under himself and the other under Captain Volais. The regiment possibly also included Victor Sim's Scottish cavalry company. The regiment's total strength was an estimated 260 horse.

8   Generalstaben, *Sveriges krig 1611–1632*, vol. 1, pp.233–34.

On 16 July, Cruus reached Kalmar with Swedish reinforcements: three banners of cavalry and seven companies of foot, altogether 576 horse and 1,470 foot when the march commenced, and they had not engaged in battle since. Together with other reinforcements, this increased King Charles's strength to an estimated 2,300 horse and 7,900 foot if the detachment at Ljungby, of unclear strength, and the Kalmar Castle garrison were included.[9]

King Charles then ordered an attack on the town. Preparations may have started well in advance because Danish sources relate how two Frenchmen 'deserted' from the Swedish army in order to insert themselves in the Danish King's Regiment. On 16 July, they attempted to set fire to the town with the help of gunpowder, apparently as a diversion ahead of the assault. The first attempt failed, but the second successfully ignited several houses. However, the Danes managed to extinguish the fire and capture the Frenchmen.[10]

At 1:00 a.m., on the night to 17 July, King Charles's men marched out of the camp, drawing up in battle formation outside the Danish circumvallation line, which was defended by Gert von Rantzau's regiment of enlisted professionals.[11] Sunrise took place at 4:45 a.m. Then, if not before, the Danes noticed the Swedes, who soon again retreated some distance. The deployment was a feint, intended to deflect attention from what happened in the castle. It is even possible that the Swedes applied some psychological warfare against the Danes to keep them awake during the night because a Danish record notes that a Swedish sentry, the previous day, had already told the Danish defenders that they would be dealt with tomorrow. Be that as it may, in the morning, the defenders of Kalmar Castle fired a Swedish salute (two cannon shots in rapid succession) and then sallied out in force. One Danish source claims this happened at 5:00 or 6:00 a.m., another at 9:00 a.m., but the later time seems more likely. The Swedish main army attacked as well. One column attacked the Danes in the north, in the sector defended by Lieutenant Colonel Blasius Belisarius, while the other attacked the north-western sector, defended by other units of Rantzau's regiment. Infantry attacked first, followed by cavalry that would be used to mop up remaining defences in case the infantry managed to break through the Danish defences. The Swedish columns charged two and three times, respectively, but failed to break through.

The castle garrison sallied out in two directions: one through a postern gate next to the south-western tower and the other through the main gate tower across the castle bridge. The first detachment, consisting of English, Scottish, and Irish soldiers under De la Ville, quickly took a Danish redoubt and then separated in several columns that moved into the town itself or the field between the circumvallation and the town wall. For a while, they were successful. One column attacked and took Söderport ('South Gate'), through which they entered the town. Another column advanced as far as

---

9   Generalstaben, *Sveriges krig 1611–1632*, vol. 1, pp.231–32.
10 Kall (ed.), 'Mag. Ægidii Laurizens samlede Efterretninger', p.20; Anon., 'Journal', p.694.
11 This was, incidentally, on the same day that the important Muscovite city of Novgorod surrendered to Jacob De la Gardie, the Swedish commanding general on the eastern front. It should be remembered that Sweden simultaneously fought on several fronts.

the Västerport ('West Gate') Bastion and took it, on which they raised two Swedish flags and re-aimed the cannons there against the Danes. A third column plundered the Danish supplies, apparently while waiting for other Swedes to arrive (if so, presumably the boat-borne detachment described below). However, soon the Danes struck back. Søren Bugge's company from the King's Regiment and the three companies from Duke George of Brunswick-Lüneburg's regiment countercharged, together with men from Peder Basse's Zealand Banner, the Scanian Banner, and even men from the supply train who took up weapons against the Swedes. As a result, most English and Scots of the first Swedish detachment remained outside the town.

The second detachment fought its way into the town across the castle bridge. Godske von Ahlefeldt's regiment was deployed in the town itself. Apparently, the second detachment expected support from the third column of the first detachment, but they wasted time plundering Danish supplies, which gave Ahlefeldt's men time to recover.

There seems to have been a third detachment as well, which attacked in boats commandeered by the castle Drabant Guard from the burghers who had taken refuge there.[12] If so, the plan may have been to attack the town's port, which would have formed the final component of a three-pronged attack. However, for one reason or another, the boats ended up at Kvarnholm Island. Perhaps their initial orders had been to meet up with the third column of the first detachment and the second detachment, which entered the town itself.

Suddenly, a fire broke out in the northern part of the town, apparently set by the Swedes in an attempt to deprive the Danes of their supply depot. This caused disorder among all participating units, with some even attempting to plunder or retrieve the loot from the burning houses.

King Charles had shipped across to the castle, from which he ordered the retreating sally parties to hold the captured parts of the contravallation line against the castle. King Charles stayed in the castle for about 13 hours, not only to observe and lead the battle but also to insert a newly appointed governor of Kalmar town, Christer Some of the Småland Army. He now replaced Bo Gustavsson Bååt as governor. Hammarskiöld then followed the King back to the mainland.

By late afternoon, the Danes still held the circumvallation line while the town remained contested. The Swedes still held the contravallation against the castle and retained the option to attack the port by boat. However, the conflagration spread, and soon the entire town was afire. The survivors on both sides withdrew.

It had been a hard-fought battle. On 18 July, neither side at first seems to have had the means to continue the struggle, and King Charles even suggested a short truce to bury the dead. King Christian brought the three companies of the King's Regiment into what remained of Kalmar town (one company was already there), taking up positions in the church and on the cemetery.

---

12   The burghers had apparently brought their belongings with them across the water, in the hope that the castle would offer some protection. The Drabant Guards, all enlisted abroad and without local connections, simply threw the goods into the sea so that they could embark soldiers into the boats.

Then, suddenly, everything changed. The transports carrying the infantry of Sehested's army arrived, landing at Stensö Peninsula (four companies of the King's Regiment, the three companies of Tessen von Parsow's regiment, and Jørgen Lunge's company). While Sehested's companies were understrength, they still constituted at least some 1,200 men.[13] His cavalry (half of the Zealand Banner and four cavalry banners) travelled overland, as did Sehested himself, but were not far away. In the evening darkness, Sehested's fresh companies attacked the Swedish positions in front of the castle. Although the Swedes counterattacked, the fresh companies turned the tide, and while fighting continued on 19 July, the Danes by the evening regained the contravallation

Though neither side had gained any ground, King Charles had failed to retake Kalmar, and following the arrival of Sehested's reinforcements, King Christian's army still enjoyed numerical superiority. Casualties had been heavy on both sides. The Swedes had already lost an estimated 1,000 men on the first, most intensive day of fighting. In total, Danish sources claimed about 1,600 Swedish casualties. Godske von Ahlefeldt was badly wounded, and two of his captains fell in the battle, as did so many of his men that ultimately the regiment was reduced to four companies. Joachim von Bülow was shot in the leg.[14]

The Danes were, however, successful at sea. On the evening of 19 July, Admiral Ulfeldt reached the northern part of the Kalmar Strait with the second squadron of the Danish main fleet (10 warships), and, two days later, he cast anchor off Kalmar. Meanwhile, Lindenow moved the two existing squadrons at Stensö Peninsula closer to the castle. Together, the two Danes surrounded the outnumbered Swedish main fleet of 11 warships. However, during the night between 21 and 22 July, Bielkenstierna broke through Ulfeldt's fleet, taking advantage of the fact that the Swedes knew the confined waters intimately. The outnumbered Bielkenstierna lost only one ship in the action, the *Mjölkpigan*, which accidently struck a rock. Yet, during the following days, the Danes, in Bielkenstierna's absence, took most of the small islands in the area, also capturing many vessels of the Swedish inshore fleet and the soldiers who manned it. On 27 July, Christer Some burned seven of the remaining 11 Swedish vessels at Kalmar Castle, which were now exposed to Danish attacks and no longer defensible.[15]

Previously, King Charles had retained superiority at sea in the vicinity of Kalmar. Now, the tables had turned, and King Christian controlled the Kalmar waters. In addition to everything else, this meant that King Charles was henceforth unable to bring in food and gunpowder supplies by sea.

The Fall of Kalmar Castle

King Charles's position was untenable. He had lost many men and consumed most of his gunpowder. He also had to expect an attack from the sea. On 23

---

13 Generalstaben, *Sveriges krig 1611–1632*, vol. 1, p.237.
14 Wadén, *Berättande källor*, pp.125–26, with references.
15 It will be recalled that the warships had already been scuttled. Wadén, *Berättande källor*, p.54.

July, King Christian marched out with his entire army to offer battle to the Swedish camp. Skirmishes took place, in which Duke George of Brunswick-Lüneburg was wounded, suffering a gunshot through the thigh. Lacking the men to confront the entire Danish army, King Charles refused battle, instead retreating under the cover of darkness during the night, establishing a new fortified camp at Ryssby, 20 km north of Kalmar. Cruus, with a rearguard of six cavalry banners, covered the retreat. Early the next morning, Cruus pushed back the first approaching Danish units. However, when the sun rose, it became obvious to everybody how few men Cruus had, so he retreated. The Danes did not pursue very far, finding the Swedish position at Ryssby too strong.

King Charles had no more reserves on land within reach of Kalmar. He hoped that Bielkenstierna's fleet would renew the offensive. When this did not happen, he removed Bielkenstierna from his position of command and instead appointed Jacob Gottberg new commander. Gottberg did sail south, but he was then pushed back in a minor engagement with Ulfeldt at the northern promontory of Öland.

By then, Christer Some's remaining garrison at Kalmar Castle still consisted of no less than 2,000 men (see Table 12).[16] Yet gunpowder supplies were limited since much had been consumed in the battle for Kalmar. Moreover, his large force soon consumed the available food supplies while the Danish blockade prevented any resupply attempts by sea. As if this was not enough, on 29 and 30 July, the Danes subjected the castle to intensive artillery bombardment. On 2 August, Some entered into negotiations with the Danes, and, suddenly and without warning the next day, Some surrendered Kalmar Castle. Through this act, the entire garrison, 104 cannons, and four small warships fell into Danish hands. Christer Some claimed a shortage of gunpowder, which, at least to some extent, was true. Yet his officers at first did not wish to surrender until they had fought off two or three Danish attempts to storm the castle and there was no hope of relief (a customary requirement before surrender was contemplated). However, Some pushed through the decision, appealing to the common soldiers who were easily persuaded to surrender in exchange for free departure. King Charles, and many later observers, concluded that Some's surrender was an act of treason. While it was obvious that Some could not have fought on for very long without the insertion of fresh supplies, which under the circumstances seemed unlikely, he could possibly have bound up the Danes for some time by prolonging the negotiations instead of giving in immediately. In hindsight, this would not have changed the strategic situation, yet Some could not know this. Perhaps Some's actions after the surrender constitute the most damning evidence against him. Christer Some did not wish to take his chances with the wrath of the usually vindictive King Charles.[17] Instead,

---

16 Not all the missing from the garrison were dead. Upon finding themselves outside the town after the battle, the surviving soldiers rejoined the main army. Anon., 'Journal', p.698.

17 After the surrender, those of Some's officers, primarily Nils Jönsson, who willingly had supported him in abandoning the castle were subsequently court-martialled and sentenced to death – even though all ultimately seem to have been pardoned.

he immediately went into Danish service, bringing with him the 24 Drabant Guards who as enlisted foreigners without local ties joined the Danish army.[18] King Christian rewarded Some with 1,000 *Reichsthalers* in cash and a ship for all his belongings, and soon also a rich estate in southern Holstein, Rohlstorf. Christer Some then sailed to Denmark, abandoning his wife in Sweden.[19] King Christian honoured the agreement of free departure with personal belongings and sidearms (but not their colours) for the other survivors of the Kalmar garrison, who were transferred to Öland and released.

Table 12. Kalmar Garrison under Governor Christer Some, late July 1611[20]

Province	Company	Strength
Enlisted	Drabant Guard of Foot	24
Småland	Nils Bryngelsson	352[21]
	Olof Svensson Hoffman	
	Olof Ingelsson	
Småland	Nils Bryntesson	873[22]
	Anders Håkansson	
	Per Jönsson	
	Erik Kock	
Västergötland	Nils Jönsson	231
Norrland	Matts Pålsson Slumpare	209
Unknown	Christer Kock	189
	Sailors	40
	Armed Servants	121
	Burgher Militia Survivors	Unknown
	Total	2,039

---

18 Barkman, *Kungl. Svea livgardes historia*, vol. 2, p.582, argues that available sources are too ambiguous to claim that the Drabant Guards joined the Danish army. Yet enlisted foreigners habitually, usually voluntarily but sometimes under compulsion, joined the victorious army to which they surrendered, so there is nothing implausible in this claim. As the official historian of the Life Guard, Barkman sometimes found it difficult to credit reports suggesting that the Guards had done less than sterling service.

19 Christer Some had no children. He subsequently treated the people of his new estate harshly. As a result, three of them murdered him on 19 October 1618.

20 Generalstaben, *Sveriges krig 1611–1632*, vol. 1, p.243, n.3.

21 The combined total strength of the separate companies of Nils Bryngelsson, Olof Svensson Hoffman, and Olof Ingelsson.

22 The combined total strength of the separate companies of Nils Bryntesson, Anders Håkansson, Per Jönsson, and Erik Kock.

The Battle for Öland

Danish reinforcements now arrived in the form of Sehested's cavalry and, around the same time (i.e. before 2 August), three fresh enlisted companies of foot: one for the King's Regiment, under Peter Ernst von Wulfen, and two for Duke George of Brunswick-Lüneburg's regiment, under Reinhold von Intima and Andreas Kitzleben.[23] With the arrival of these reinforcements, King Christian felt able to release the probably exhausted Zealand, Fyn, and Scanian Banners from the army.[24] By then, they had spent three months on active duty.

Late at night, on 29 July, King Christian marched out with most of his army towards the Swedish camp at Ryssby. He brought the Court Banner, the German cavalry companies, Rantzau's regiment, Parsow's regiment, and the much-reduced Ahlefeldt's regiment. The army reached Ryssby in the morning of the following day, no doubt in the hope of surprising the Swedes. However, Swedish patrols had noted the Danes, and the camp was strongly fortified. Nonetheless, over the next three days, King Christian made several attempts to attack the Swedes. Danish losses were significant. Among the wounded was apparently Captain Benedict Bernd von Hagen of Ahlefeldt's regiment, which suggests that this hard-worn regiment was again sent into action.

While these attempts failed, at this point, Christer Some suddenly surrendered Kalmar Castle. This gave King Christian new hope. He announced his intention to march along the coastal road to Stockholm, by which he hoped that King Charles would surrender. But first, he needed to conquer the nearby island of Öland, on which Borgholm Castle guarded the other side of the Kalmar Strait. The island served as the primary source of food supplies for Kalmar. During the operations around Kalmar, the governor of Öland, Johan Månsson Ulfsparre, had been able to supply Kalmar Castle with both gunpowder and food supplies by sea. Ulfsparre had both conscripts and peasant levies at his disposal. However, the island was only lightly fortified and, for reasons of geography, difficult to defend.

Although King Christian was uncertain whether he had enough men to take Öland, having gained Kalmar Castle and with King Charles in retreat, he decided to make the attempt. To maintain a Danish garrison in Kalmar for a substantial time, King Christian needed to also commandeer the resources of Öland. On 5 August, King Christian sent a trumpeter to Öland to demand the island's surrender. Christer Some had already written to Ulfsparre, advising him to surrender. The local officials of Öland said that they would meet with each other and Ulfsparre to discuss the issue, but, on 7 August, they already decided to surrender the island to King Christian. It was harvest time, and the peasants must have worried that extended combat would cost them the entire harvest. A group of 12 local representatives crossed the strait to swear loyalty to the Danish King. The same day, King Christian sent the four national companies of foot of the King's Regiment to the island.

---

23 Larsen, *Kalmarkrigen*, pp.135–36.
24 Generalstaben, *Sveriges krig 1611–1632*, vol. 1, p.247.

THE KALMAR WAR

Ulfsparre did not have enough men to confront them, so he withdrew into Borgholm Castle. The Öland levies dispersed and returned home.

On 8 August, King Christian personally crossed to Öland and prepared to lay siege to Borgholm Castle. Lacking the means to defend the castle, Ulfsparre agreed to surrender in return for free departure, which King Christian granted. On 12 August, representatives of the Öland population swore fealty to King Christian, who returned to Kalmar afterwards. He left a strong garrison under Christer Hansen and ordered the Öland peasants to house his soldiers, both horse and foot.

Model of Borgholm Castle, 1600. Above: facing the inland approach. Below: facing the sea. (Model by Christian Erlandsson, Borgholm Museum; author's photo)

A Challenge to Single Combat

After the fall of Öland, King Charles sent a letter to King Christian, challenging him to trial by combat.[25] Suggesting that single combat should conclude the war and decide its outcome, on 12 August, King Charles wrote:

> To avoid the shedding of yet more blood for your sake, enter into combat with Us on a plain field according to the commendable customs of the old Goths. Bring two of your noble knights with you [as seconds] without treasonous thought, and We shall meet you in our mere clothes, without any breastplate or armour, only with helmet on head and rapier in hand. If you do not join Us, We will not hold you as a brave king or soldier.[26]

King Christian, who, unlike King Charles, was a man in his prime, received the challenge on the way back from Öland. He scornfully turned it down in a letter that positively exudes insults (only some of which are translated here):

> We let you know that your frivolous and immodest letter was delivered by a trumpeter … With regard to the single combat to which you invite Us, it comes across to Us as particularly arrogant, since We know that in the eyes of God you already are defeated. So, it is better to pity you than to argue and fight with you, and it would serve you better to rest behind a good, warm oven than to fight or meet Us in single combat. You are in greater need of a good physician who can cure your brain. You should be ashamed, old fool, of attacking an honourable man, in the manner which you have learnt from old whores who defend themselves with curses and squabbles …[27]

King Christian then had the two letters translated into German and published for distribution on the Continent as part of his propaganda activities. He did not, however, translate the third letter in the exchange, which King Charles wrote in response to his Danish counterpart on 15 August and sent from Ryssby camp on 16 August. The third letter was, for King Charles, unusually statesmanlike in style and further noted that, for the Swedish King, the correspondence on this matter was now closed.

Later historians have generally interpreted King Charles's challenge as an act of despair and possibly madness. However, the custom of submitting to divine justice through trial by combat was alive in Sweden, even for royalty, and regarded as an act of honour. God would bestow victory to the combatant

---

25 Ingel Wadén, 'Skriftväxlingen mellan Carl IX och Christian IV efter Kalmar slotts fall 1611', *Personhistorisk Tidskrift*, 37 (1936), pp.52–64, which also includes the original text of the letters exchanged between the two monarchs. King Charles's original letter was signed on 12 August, but a concept seems to have been already prepared on 11 August. King Christian's original letter seems not to have survived into the present, but contemporary copies exist.
26 Wadén, 'Skriftväxlingen', pp.61–62.
27 Wadén, 'Skriftväxlingen', pp.62–63.

with the just cause. While still a young man and in rebellion against his elder brother, King Erik, Charles was himself challenged to single combat by the King to decide the outcome of his revolt.

For one reason or another, King Christian did not share this belief. He was physically fitter, stronger, and much younger than his adversary and had participated in combat several times, so his refusal to fight is unlikely to have resulted from cowardice. Perhaps he thought that the time had passed for such old-fashioned gestures. Or perhaps he still hoped that an offensive against Sweden's capital Stockholm would give greater gains than ending the war here and now. Regardless, there would be no single combat between the two kings.

Mediation

Soon after, the first attempt of mediation took place. Representatives from the Dutch Republic, which lost trade revenues because of the Danish blockade of Swedish ports, first visited King Christian and then King Charles. The Dutch may also have been concerned over the war between Protestant countries at a time when Catholicism and especially Habsburg power were growing stronger. King Charles, in his camp outside Kalmar, told the Dutch mediators that he was willing to initiate negotiations to end the war. However, King Christian brusquely terminated the attempt to make peace by informing the mediators that he did not recognise the Dutch Republic and was only willing to negotiate with the King of Spain.[28] Christian clearly regarded the war as already won.

Yet the Danish army at Kalmar no longer was as strong as it had been. There had been losses from combat. In addition, rampant disease was taking its toll of the men. With the customary deployment of soldiers to the fleet, the disease spread to the sailors as well. Officers died, too, including Field Marshal Sehested, who died from illness in Kalmar Castle. Soon, the 'Kalmar disease' grew into a greater threat to the cohesion of the Danish invasion force than King Charles's army. Danish records list numerous casualties from the epidemic, and the situation did not improve over time. The King accordingly reorganised the army as needed. The four national companies of the King's Regiment were reduced to three. The sorely depleted Godske von Ahlefeldt's regiment was reformed as two companies, which then were added to the King's Regiment. He also received reinforcements, including a company of French dragoons under Jean Dupuis. On 20 August, the Danish army consisted of 10 banners of horse and four regiments of foot.

---

28 The Dutch diplomats did not enter the King's comment into their official report since this would have effectively precluded any further negotiations. However, after the war, the comment was published in Emanuel van Meteren's Dutch history. Wadén, *Berättande källor*, p.287, with sources.

THE BATTLE FOR KALMAR

Table 13. King Christian's Field Army, 20 August 1611[29]

Horse		
Origin	Banner	Companies
Denmark/Germany	Court Banner	1
Germany	The King's Life Banner	1
Zealand	Zealand Banner	1
The Duchies	Duke Philip of Glücksburg's Company	1
Germany	Duke Ernest Louis of Saxe-Lauenburg's Harquebusier Company	1
Germany	Gert von Rantzau's Harquebusier Company	1
Germany	Jørgen Grubbe's Harquebusier Company	1
Germany	Tessen von Parsow's Harquebusier Company	1
Germany	Marquard von Pentz's Harquebusier Company	1
France	Jean Dupuis's Dragoon Company	1
	Total	10
Foot		
Origin	Unit	Companies
Dutch Republic/Germany/Denmark	The King's Regiment	12
Germany	Gert von Rantzau's Regiment	10
Germany	Duke George of Brunswick-Lüneburg's Regiment	6
Germany	Tessen von Parsow's Regiment	3
Germany/Dutch Republic	Jørgen Lunge's Company	1
	Total	32
	Grand Total	42

Having reformed his army, King Christian wanted to continue the advance to the north according to his original intentions. He left Andrew Sinclair (1555–1625), a naturalised Danish noble originally from Scotland, as commandant in Kalmar Castle, with his own Scanian company of foot from the King's Regiment as garrison, four other companies in Kalmar town, and two companies on Öland. Then, the King prepared to march north along the coastal road, accompanied and supported by Nielsen's Kalmar Flotilla with 500 men from the warships. His army had an impressive strength. Unfortunately, King Christian now lacked the cash to pay his men, which produced some turbulence since a great majority were enlisted foreigners.[30]

---

29 Generalstaben, *Sveriges krig 1611–1632*, vol. 1, p.251.
30 Generalstaben, *Sveriges krig 1611–1632*, vol. 1, p.251; Norrie, *Kalmarkrigen*, p.27.

Ryssby

On 19 August, King Christian sent Gert von Rantzau with his cavalry banner against the Swedish camp at Ryssby. Rantzau soon found himself surrounded, barely escaping with his life but losing 13 men dead or wounded in the skirmish. The following day, two Swedish banners made a reciprocal raid against the Danes, this time with more success than Rantzau had achieved.

Later the same day (20 August), King Christian again moved against the Swedish camp at Ryssby with his entire army. He hoped that the Swedes would march out, but they failed to take the bait. Both sides suffered casualties in the ensuing skirmishes. On 23 August, the Swedish cavalry captain Daniel Wagner fell into Danish captivity. However, the Swedish camp was simply too strongly fortified. The Danes accordingly retreated to Kalmar. With the Swedish army at Ryssby, King Christian realised that his dream to continue the offensive towards the north was unrealistic. He accordingly decided that the campaign was concluded for the year and appointed Gert von Rantzau to be in charge of Kalmar and Öland with three banners of cavalry and 13 companies of foot (three of which were stationed on Öland). The rest were ordered to return home, and, on 11 September, the King rode to Christianopel followed by six banners (the Court Banner, Zealand Banner, and four German cavalry companies). Then, his men moved into winter quarters in Blekinge and Scania while the King, in late September, sailed home with the main fleet.

King Charles had no intention of going into winter quarters. He ordered the fleet to assemble at Älvsnabben, from which it would go on the offensive against the Kalmar Strait. In fact, pushed by the King's numerous urgent dispatches, Admiral Gottberg had already attempted to reconquer the strait. This had failed, and he had lost the warship *Röda lejonet*. Gottberg accordingly returned to Älvsnabben. No more substantial fleet actions took place during the rest of the year.

The Swedish army was exhausted, too. On 19 September, King Charles reluctantly issued the first orders to go into winter quarters. Those Swedish units that were not ordered into winter quarters were sent home. Field Marshal Cruus resumed command in Västergötland while Nils Sternskiöld received command in Småland.

Musketeer. Only those who carried heavy muskets of the modern type would use a fork rest. (Jacob de Gheyn II, *Wapenhandelinghe van Roers, Musquetten ende Spiessen*)

Reconquest of Öland

While King Christian prepared to return to Copenhagen with the main fleet, Gustavus Adolphus prepared to retake Öland together with Per Hammarskiöld, who knew the island well. By some accounts, he was born there. Gustavus Adolphus gathered three banners of cavalry and seven or eight companies of foot. The cavalry included Hammarskiöld's old unit, the Småland Banner, currently commanded by Per Nilsson, and Victor Sim's cavalry company. The infantry included the Drabant Company under Anders Larsson, Gertorm Yggesson's Småland company, Nils Assersson Mannerskiöld's Östergötland company, and probably Olof Olsson's Västmanland company. The corps included infantry that had recently arrived from Finland as well, including Erik Olsson's and Bryngel Torstensson's companies, both conscripted in Finland, and Robert Sim's Scottish company.[31] Contemporary sources note that the total strength of this army was 2,000 men.[32]

Gustavus Adolphus and his men arranged to cross the Kalmar Strait to Öland with the so-called 'little fleet' under Captain Erik Kyle, which would set out from Skäggenäs, a small peninsula some 15 km north of Kalmar. Before the crossing, Gustavus Adolphus established contact with local peasants, who promised to assist.

Gert von Rantzau learnt of the operation on 25 September, apparently from observing the Swedish warships in Skäggenäs, so he led three companies of foot of his own regiment (under Valentin Rosworm, Christopher Luppert, and Jørgen Baroldt, respectively) across the strait to Öland. As a result, Öland was now defended by two Danish cavalry units (the enlisted harquebusier companies of Jørgen Grubbe and Tessen von Parsow, who had handed over command to Franz Ernst von Dalwig) and five companies of foot (the three from Rantzau's regiment and those respectively under Mathias Kochheim and Søren Bugge of the King's Regiment).[33]

Rantzau probably informed King Christian. Yet, the following day, the Danish main fleet returned to Copenhagen with King Christian aboard. Later the same day, in the evening of 26 September, Gustavus Adolphus crossed the strait, landing near Stora Rör, 18 km south of Borgholm Castle. It was a flawless operation, and local peasants met him on the shore with horses. He surprised and dispersed two Danish companies at Räpplinge on the way to Borgholm. The rest sought refuge in Borgholm Castle. Rantzau attempted to return to the mainland by sea to bring reinforcements, but unfavourable winds swept his yacht eastwards to Gotland, not Kalmar, which delayed the Danish response. Gustavus Adolphus and his corps easily mopped up the remaining Danes on the island. On 7 October, Borgholm Castle surrendered to Gustavus Adolphus, who marched in on 8 October, installing Hammarskiöld as commandant. Most of the Germans in the Danish companies enlisted in the Swedish army, while Gustavus Adolphus

---

31 Generalstaben, *Sveriges krig 1611–1632*, vol. 1, pp.253–54, n.3.
32 Wadén, *Berättande källor*, p.98, with references.
33 Generalstaben, *Sveriges krig 1611–1632*, vol. 1, p.253; Larsen, *Kalmarkrigen*, pp.150–51.

had the others shipped to Kalmar, after they had sworn not to fight Sweden for three months. Hammarskiöld received the three banners of cavalry, the Drabant Company, and four other companies of foot to defend the island. The peasant representatives who had crossed the strait to swear fealty to King Christian were brought to trial and executed for treason.

This was Gustavus Adolphus's second independent command. It seems likely that he received some advice from the more experienced Hammarskiöld during the operation, but, as in the raid on Christianopel, there is nothing to suggest that Hammarskiöld, or any other officer, functioned in the capacity of a mentor in military matters or tactics.

Gustavus Adolphus then returned to his father at Ryssby. During December and January, Danes from Kalmar raided Öland several times. However, they did not attempt to reconquer the island.

10

The West Coast

When Field Marshal Sehested left Halland, he left the three Jutland banners (Aarhus, Aalborg, and Ribe) and the Halland Banner of cavalry to stiffen the peasant levies who were expected to guard and defend the border. The Aarhus and Aalborg Banners garrisoned Varberg, while the Ribe and Halland Banners garrisoned Halmstad.

In mid July, the commandant of Elfsborg Castle, Nils Silfverbielke, who now commanded four companies of foot, moved north into the Norwegian part of the nearby island of Hisingen. He devastated the area unopposed since the garrison at Bohus Castle did not move out to protect the peasants. He then turned south, storming and taking Kungsbacka in the province of Halland on the night of 17 July. The small garrison was cut down, and the town looted and burnt. Learning of the raid, the Captains Knud Brahe of the Aarhus Banner and Ulrich Sandberg of the Aalborg Banner set out, but they were too late. Silfverbielke had already returned to Elfsborg.

In early September, King Charles ordered Jöran Claesson Uggla to safeguard the border with Norway and the town of Nya Lödöse (north-east of Elfsborg) with his Västergötland companies of foot, reinforced with two banners of cavalry.

Silfverbielke then resumed the cross-border raiding. He crossed the border into Halland north of Kungsbacka. By chance, both Knud Brahe and Ulrich Sandberg, with their respective Aarhus and Aalborg Banners, were then in the vicinity – only 7 km south of Kungsbacka. A peasant sought them out, asking for help, and, by then, the smoke from burning farmsteads was already visible. Riding north, they located the Swedish raiders, reportedly 600 men, both horse and foot, at Vallda Church. The raiders were moving north with a large number of captured cattle. Not expecting the 200 Danes to attack their larger number, the Swedes continued the march to the north. Even so, Brahe and Sandberg charged the Swedes. The Danes were cuirassiers, and the Swedish cavalry almost certainly harquebusiers. The Swedish cavalry countercharged, but their captain fell in the battle, and the cavalrymen dispersed. The Danes then charged the Swedish infantry. They broke, too, and Silfverbielke fell into captivity. Skirmishes continued long into the night. The local peasants joined in the search for fleeing Swedes, many of whom were hunted down and killed.

In September, King Christian sent additional reinforcements to Halland: the Fyn and Scanian Banners. Since the Crown had also raised 2,000 Norwegian peasants at Bohus Castle, King Christian wanted his western army to go on the offensive against Nya Lödöse or any other Swedish territory within reach. However, the peasant levies were untrained, and their officers were unwilling to go on the offensive against the more experienced and properly trained Swedish regulars. As a result, the King's plan to go on the offensive was abandoned. On 19 November, the Scanian and Halland Banners were sent home. They were replaced by enlisted cavalry banners.

The Skagerrak and Kattegat saw little naval activity during the summer since Jørgen Daa maintained the blockade of the River Göta Älv Estuary and the Swedish squadron in the area was too small to risk battle. King Charles repeatedly sent orders to the squadron to break through the Danish blockade and sail to Amsterdam, where additional ships could be hired and soldiers enlisted.

When Sehested marched towards Kalmar, Daa asked for reinforcements since he feared attacks by Swedish inshore vessels manned by soldiers. The only result was that the commandant at Bohus Castle was instructed to send a couple of skerry boats in case of need. In late October, Daa reported that the Swedes were putting their warships in order. King Christian sent a warship to support Daa, with orders to take or at least burn the Swedish ships. On the night to 27 November, nine Danish longboats rowed towards Elfsborg. Captain Jens Munk, Daa's second-in-command, managed to board two of the Swedish ships, the *Hector* and *Blå Ormen*. However, the inlet was blocked with barriers of tree trunks chained together, so he could not bring them out to sea. He set the *Hector* on fire, but then the Elfsborg artillery forced him to retreat. This enabled the Swedes to extinguish the fire.

In early December, Daa received orders to go into port for the rest of the winter.

11

Norway and Lapponia

We have seen that the mobilisation that King Christian ordered in Norway failed miserably. Many soldiers, both cavalry and infantry, never showed up for muster. The companies of foot that assembled in Akershus refused to fight the Swedes, whom they believed to be superior in training and experience. Other units, although possibly less outspoken, were no more willing to go on the offensive than those in Akershus. As a result, the only offensive that southern Norway managed to carry out was a simple raid into Dal.

Yet the rumours of the Norwegian mobilisation did have an impact. The men of Dal refused to fight elsewhere, fearing an imminent invasion. Besides, the situation remained serious in northern Norway. The two Norwegian provinces of Jämtland and Härjedalen formed a wedge into the Swedish heartland, which might enable a determined Norwegian force to rapidly penetrate all the way to the Baltic shore, capturing the primary north–south highway and thus not only severing Swedish communications between the north and south but also effectively cutting Sweden in half.

In 1607, King Charles had already appointed Baltzar Bäck governor of Lapponia ('Norrland', i.e. Northern Lands) as part of his plan to gain supremacy in the far north. In response to King Christian's declaration of war, in May 1611, the King ordered Bäck to invade and conquer the Norwegian province of Jämtland with those units that, in an unrelated plan, had been intended for an operation in 1610 to conquer Kola Castle (the strongest fortress on the Kola Peninsula, known in Sweden as 'Kolahus') as part of the ongoing war in Muscovy.[1] These units were normally deployed in the coastal towns on the shore of the Gulf of Bothnia, the northernmost arm of the Baltic Sea.

At the same time, the King ordered the governor of Dalecarlia, Carl Bonde (1581–1652), to move into Härjedalen with peasant levies from the

---

1   On 3 October 1609, King Charles ordered Bäck to raise 500 men in northern Sweden and another 500 men in northern Finland, all of them good skiers, and then conquer Kola Castle, which, he argued, belonged to Sweden. Muscovy maintained a strong garrison in Kola, consisting of no less than 500 arquebusiers (*streltsy*) and nine artillerymen in the mid seventeenth century. Johan E. Waaranen (ed.), *Samling af urkunder rörande Finlands historia 3 (1609-1611)* (Helsinki: Finska Litteratur-Sällskapet, 1866), pp.47–49.

THE KALMAR WAR

Kola Castle. Although populations were small in the Arctic North, military operations still took place there in times of war and conflict. (Gerrit de Veer, 1598)

Swedish province of Dalecarlia under Colonel Jacob Tomasson. Levies had to be used since few, if any, regular units were available there.

The King also sent an open letter to the peasants of the two provinces, urging them to renounce Danish rule. The Jämtland population had been Swedish subjects in the past, remained under the Church jurisdiction of the archbishop of Uppsala in Sweden, and still felt affinity to Swedish customs. The King had some hope that they would welcome liberation.

Farther north, King Charles ordered the governor of Västerbotten to assemble 500 men and advance towards the Norwegian fortress in northern Lapponia, Vardøhus. However, logistics failed, so the operation was ultimately abandoned.

On the Norwegian side of the border, the *lensmand* and governor of Trondheim, Jämtland, and Härjedalen, Steen Bille, had indeed already in March received orders to raise 2,000 infantry and lead them into Sweden no later than June. In May, King Christian ordered an incursion into Dalecarlia to prevent the Dalecarlians from sending reinforcements to King Charles at Kalmar.[2] A raid into Dalecarlia indeed took place the next month because, on 22 June, a Swedish letter mentioned the incursion of Norwegian soldiers.[3] Yet Bille was perhaps not the best choice for a commander to lead an army all the way to the Baltic shore – the daring plan that worried the Swedes. A scholar, former diplomat, and translator of hymns without a military background,

---

2   Larsen, *Kalmarkrigen*, p.127.
3   'Från gamla ofredsår', *Julbok för Västerås stift*, 9 (1914), p.131.

Bille announced the plans to a large number of local officials, and rumours of the planned invasion soon spread to Sweden.

As instructed, Bille conscripted men whom he organised into four companies of foot from, respectively, Namdalen, Fosen, Søndmøre, and Romsdalen. Bille personally remained in Trondheim because of ill health, but, in July, he nonetheless sent the raised men (essentially an all-infantry force) under Jens Bielke and Hans Basse into Jämtland to prepare for incursions into northern Sweden from this province and Härjedalen. Reinforced by two Jämtland companies of foot under Johan Vesling and Henning Jönsson, Bielke and Basse sent a few raiding parties into Swedish Medelpad. However, the men of the four Trondheim companies had been raised along the coast, not in Jämtland. When the coastal companies moved into Jämtland, problems soon emerged between them and the Jämtland companies, which made cooperation difficult. The Jämtland men felt badly treated by Copenhagen and refused not only to cross the border into Sweden but also to provide food supplies to the Trondheim men.[4]

Needing no further prompting, Bäck reacted quickly. In mid July, Bäck moved into Jämtland with a small Swedish expeditionary force consisting of four companies of foot from Norrland, a company of Poles who had gone into Swedish service, a company of locally raised men, and a banner of cavalry from Finland, as well as some artillery under four artillerymen. He also brought a fortification engineer, apparently a Scot known only as 'Master William' (Wellam).[5] By then, Bielke seems to have abandoned the Norwegian command. His second-in-command, Basse, had no more supplies. Their men, inexperienced and torn by internal divisions, were unwilling to fight. After two weeks of skirmishing, on 15 August, the Norwegians felt compelled to retreat, effectively abandoning the two provinces. Bäck accordingly occupied the entire province of Jämtland without difficulties, and the population swore fealty to the Swedish Crown. Bäck built a redoubt on an island named Frösö, a stronghold henceforth known as Frösö Redoubt. It played little role during this war but would gain an importance in subsequent seventeenth-century campaigns.

The governor of Dalecarlia, Bonde, was slower to act, reportedly because the Dalecarlians expected a major incursion from Norway, which ultimately never took place. However, in time, a force of Dalecarlian levies and 100 cavalry under Oluf Ingemarsson moved into Härjedalen. It was, in effect, a pincer operation, with Swedish expeditionary forces advancing from both the south and east. However, communications and geography did not yet allow for this degree of coordination. Moreover, the population in Härjedalen, unlike that of Jämtland, remained hostile to the Swedish invaders. This caused resistance, for which reason the Dalecarlian levies retaliated, plundering the locals without mercy. Unfortunately for the Swedish cause, Bäck's men behaved in the same manner in friendly Jämtland. The Swedish commanders

---

4   H. Stålhane, 'Baltzar-fejden', *Östersunds-Posten*, 92 (18 June 1898), 93 (20 June 1898), 96 (25 June 1898), 97 (27 June 1898), 98 (28 June 1898).

5   Generalstaben, *Sveriges krig 1611–1632*, vol. 1, p.255.

treated the peasants badly, won no loyalty to the Swedish cause, and only caused deep resentment against the Swedish presence. The invasion and the ensuing hostilities became known locally as the 'Baltzar War' (*Baltzarfejden*), after the personal name of Baltzar Bäck. Although Bäck had to bear much of the blame for the mistreatment of the peasants, King Charles, in an angry moment, had ordered him to kill all 'Jutes' (by which he meant Danes) in the theatre. Nonetheless, Bäck sent a few raiding parties across the mountains in the direction of Trondheim, but he lacked the resources to make any real impact there.

12

Invasion of Ösel

It was inevitable that the war between Denmark and Sweden also spread across the Baltic Sea. Sweden held Estonia, while the nearby island of Ösel, whose bishop had submitted to Danish rule in 1559, belonged to Denmark since the Nordic Seven Years' War.

By this time, Ösel was ruled by a Danish *lensmand* and governor, Claus Maltesen Sehested (1558–1612), the younger brother of Field Marshal Sehested. As part of his military preparations, before the outbreak of war, King Christian ordered Governor Sehested to remain vigilant and make sure that his castle, Arensburg, was well defended. Claus Sehested accordingly requested a few hundred experienced soldiers to stiffen his defences. However, the Council of the Realm replied from Copenhagen that King Christian did not have the men to support Ösel, so the Governor would have to make do with what he had, making full use of the Ösel nobility and the burgher militia. The Council also, somewhat overconfidently, declared that there was no cause for concern because King Charles had brought all his soldiers to Sweden. Unfortunately for Claus Sehested, this was incorrect. Sure enough, on 6 May, King Charles sent orders to the governor of Reval in Estonia, Anders Larsson of Botila (d. 1613), to occupy Ösel. Larsson received the order in July, after which he assembled men and carried out the invasion. Although Larsson's men looted, burned, and occupied Ösel, they lacked the men and artillery to take Arensburg, so Sehested remained safe, although no longer in control of his territory. Some Ösel nobles defended their island against the Swedes, while others preferred Swedish rule and swore fealty to King Charles. Governor Anders Larsson's son Lars participated in the invasion but fell in battle.

The war between Denmark and Sweden also took a heavy toll on the Baltic Sea trade. Although the Danes mostly enjoyed supremacy in the southern Baltic Sea, all Danish warships were fully occupied against their Swedish counterparts. The Danish Crown accordingly re-equipped numerous merchantmen as privateers. The privateers habitually inspected any non-Danish merchantmen, bringing the suspect ones and their cargoes to Copenhagen. In total, some 60 merchantmen were brought to Copenhagen during the war. About a third were eventually released and awarded the right to sell their goods wherever they wanted, as long as it was not in a Swedish port. The rest were deemed to have been taken as legitimate prizes.

The Death of King Charles

The summer campaign season ended in disappointment on both sides. King Christian could console himself with the conquest of Kalmar Castle, one of Sweden's key strongholds. On the other hand, his plan to continue the offensive into the Swedish heartlands had been unachievable. The war, no doubt, turned out to be harder fought than he had expected.

In contrast, King Charles had little with which to console himself. The Ryssby camp remained manned during the winter and was indeed extended further. Having ordered some units into winter quarters, on 16 October, King Charles and Gustavus Adolphus set out by sea, bound for Nyköping. On the way, the King's condition deteriorated rapidly, and he could no longer speak. Perhaps it was another stroke. Having arrived in Nyköping, the King died from natural causes on 30 October.

Gustavus Adolphus inherited the Swedish throne at age 16. Technically, he should not have inherited ruling power before he came of age at 18, and, even then, he was supposed to share power with the Queen Dowager, Duke John, and other members of a regency government until he turned 24. The political turmoil of recent years and the ongoing wars put the succession at risk. Duke John, the son of the late King John, could have challenged the succession had he wanted to and had he gained the support of the nobility. Such a deal might have been possible because the nobility, including Axel Oxenstierna, wanted to limit the monarch's power through constitutional means. King Charles had been a harsh and cruel ruler, and nobody wanted more of the kind.

Hoping to take advantage of the uncertainties regarding the Swedish succession, King Christian wrote to Andrew Sinclair, his commandant in Kalmar. He instructed Sinclair to inquire whether King Christian could not offer his candidature to the Swedish throne himself. However, even had the Nyköping parliament been willing, the Danish King no longer had the military power to lay claim to the throne with some level of credibility. He had sent home most national troops, closed the contracts with many enlisted units, and prepared no further enlistment until the next year.

Duke John renounced his claim to the throne at the parliament in Nyköping in December. Meanwhile, Gustavus Adolphus and Axel Oxenstierna rapidly learnt to trust one another. On 26 December, parliament recognised Gustavus Adolphus as King of Sweden. Moreover, in a demonstration of trust, the Estates vowed that they were willing and prepared to continue the war, with additional conscription, levies, and taxation as needed. No coercion was involved or needed. In the final account, Gustavus Adolphus was the only candidate to the throne who was acceptable to all four Estates. The young man had already proven himself. Henceforth, he had to shoulder overall military command as the ruler of Sweden.

13

The Winter Campaign

Both sides prepared for new operations during the winter of 1611/1612, when the frozen ground and ice-covered rivers allowed easy transportation. The Danish field army was, in January 1612, deployed as follows:[1]

- Bohus Castle (commanded by Steen Laxmand): one company of foot (Lukas Klüsemann's company from the King's Regiment)
- Halland (to be led by King Christian): seven banners of cavalry (Fyn Banner, Aarhus Banner, Aalborg Banner, Ribe Banner, Duke George of Brunswick-Lüneburg's harquebusiers with quarters in Halmstad, Benedict Bernd von Hagen's banner with quarters in Kungsbacka, and Halland Banner, subject to immediate recall) and five companies of foot (Duke George of Brunswick-Lüneburg's regiment with quarters in the Halland fortresses)[2]
- Scania (commanded by Breide Rantzau): nine banners of cavalry (Court Banner with quarters in Ystad, Zealand Banner with quarters in Ystad, the King's Life Banner, under Bülow, with quarters in Villand District, Duke Ernest Louis of Saxe-Lauenburg's harquebusier company with quarters in Sölvesborg, Gert von Rantzau's banner with quarters in Åhus Castle, Pentz's harquebusiers with quarters in Vä, Dalwig's harquebusiers with quarters in Landskrona, Rabe Philip Bogreben's harquebusiers with quarters in Landskrona, and Scanian Banner, subject to immediate recall) and possibly only one company of foot (Lunge's regiment with quarters in Sölvesborg and Åhus Castle)[3]
- Blekinge: two banners of cavalry (Andreas Flotow's Schleswig Banner with quarters in Ronneby and Duke Philip of Glücksburg's presumably harquebusiers with quarters in Ronneby), one dragoon

---

1 Generalstaben, *Sveriges krig 1611–1632*, vol. 1, p.263; Larsen, *Kalmarkrigen*, p.176.
2 The Halland Banner was sent home on 19 November, with instructions to be ready for immediate recall.
3 The Scanian Banner was sent home on 19 November, with instructions to be ready for immediate recall.

company (Eustachius de Carmissin's dragoons with quarters in Christianopel),[4] and two or three companies of foot (Duke George of Brunswick-Lüneburg's regiment with quarters in Christianopel and Gert von Rantzau's regiment with quarters in Christianopel)
- Kalmar (commanded by Andrew Sinclair): 11 companies of foot (six companies of the King's Regiment, four companies of Gert von Rantzau's regiment, and one company of Lunge's regiment).

King Christian sent men to enlist more units on the Continent, where he had hoped to raise 1,000 horse and 15,000 foot (although the actual outcome did not reach this target).[5] By this time, essentially all Danish fortifications had been put in order, and many had upgraded defences.

By January 1612, the Swedish field army's deployment was planned as follows:[6]

- Mariestad, Västergötland (commanded by Duke John): one or two banners of cavalry (one or two Uppland Banner(s)) and four companies of foot (three Dalecarlian companies and one Uppland company)
- Bogesund, Västergötland (commanded by Field Marshal Cruus): four banners of cavalry (Ducal Life Banner, Småland Banner, and two Östergötland banners), three companies of foot (three Östergötland companies), and Västergötland levy
- Småland (commanded by Admiral Bååt): contingent of unknown strength, to be supported by two companies of Patrick Rutherford's regiment of enlisted Scots and Irishmen
- Jönköping Castle, Småland (Steen Claesson Böllja as governor and Colonel Olof Hård as commandant): contingent of unknown strength
- Vimmerby, Småland: one company of foot (one Uppsala company)
- Ryssby fortified camp, Småland (commanded by Colonel Nils Stiernskiöld): contingent of uncertain strength, including but not limited to three banners of cavalry (Måns Stierna's banner, Abel Svenske's banner, and Erik Jönsson's banner (probably)) and eight to 11 companies of foot (three Västmanland companies of foot (certainly), Göran Hansson's Dalecarlian company (certainly), Sven Pjeske's Södermanland company (probably), Hans von Akern's Hälsingland company (probably), Jöns Didriksson's company (probably), Robert Sim's Scottish company (probably), Olof Hoffman's Småland company (possibly), Sven Krååk's Småland company (possibly), and Håkan Knutsson's Småland company (possibly))

---

4   Jean Dupuis had died on 17 October, so Eustachius de Carmissin assumed command of the dragoons.
5   Generalstaben, *Sveriges krig 1611–1632*, vol. 1, p.260.
6   Generalstaben, *Sveriges krig 1611–1632*, vol. 1, p.261; Bertil Broomé, *Nils Stiernsköld*. 1950. Stockholm University, PhD, pp.71–72.

The winter campaign began in January 2012. First out was Steen Laxmand, commandant of Bohus Castle, who sent part of his garrison on a raid into Västergötland. They took some plunder but were then chased back by Swedish cavalry.[7] On the Swedish side, Niels Stiernskiöld was tasked with gathering intelligence on the situation in Kalmar and 'by day and night' forwarded his reports to the King. Gustavus Adolphus already wanted to carry out a surprise attack on Kalmar in the second half of January in case Stiernskiöld found any opportunity for such an endeavour. In this role, Stiernskiöld essentially functioned as a staff officer; he was a veteran of the wars on the eastern front against the Commonwealth and Muscovy who, in 1610, was so badly wounded when a cannon that he was about to fire exploded that, for three years, he could only walk with crutches.

A heavy responsibility had been laid on the young King's shoulders. It is obvious from his requests for advice to his mother, Duke John, and the Council of the Realm that the young King keenly felt the lack of experienced advisors. Henrik Horn, who accompanied the King as the representative of the Council, wrote to Chancellor Oxenstierna that it was regrettable that Gustavus Adolphus had so few experienced commanders with him. Despite orders to this extent, neither Reinhold Taube nor De la Barre had joined the King. Horn, who was a civilian without military background, pointed out that the only experienced commanders presently with the King were Stiernskiöld and a Scotsman, Captain (possibly Gilbert) Wauchope. Both were quite young, which worried Horn. The old soldier Admiral Bååt was elsewhere in Småland, so he was not available.[8]

In mid January, Gustavus Adolphus travelled from Nyköping to Västervik and then onwards to Ryssby. He ordered Admiral Bååt to assemble the Småland levy at Ryssby no later than 22 January. However, on 20 January, Stiernskiöld notified Gustavus Adolphus that Kalmar now was so strongly fortified that a surprise attack was out of the question. He had also learnt that the Danes planned another attack on Öland. Gustavus Adolphus accordingly abandoned the plan against Kalmar. Instead, he began to plan for an attack on the apparently more vulnerable Blekinge.

However, while still on the road, Gustavus Adolphus received news from Böllja in Jönköping that Danish units were on the way there. The King accordingly ordered Böllja, Cruus, and Duke John to delay the Danish offensive through the construction of abatis. As for himself, the King planned to force the Danes to retreat by carrying out a diversionary raid through Blekinge.

On 21 January, Duke John reached Jönköping. A week later, he joined forces with Field Marshal Cruus south of Falköping. Cruus had earlier moved into Bohuslän for some raiding, but, upon hearing of the Danish King's march into Halland (more on which later), he abandoned the venture.

---

7   Larsen, *Kalmarkrigen*, p.176.
8   Henrik Carlsson Horn was only five years older than Stiernskiöld but may have felt like an old man in comparison to young Gustavus Adolphus and the commanders in his immediate entourage. Broomé, *Nils Stiernsköld*, pp.74–75.

THE KALMAR WAR

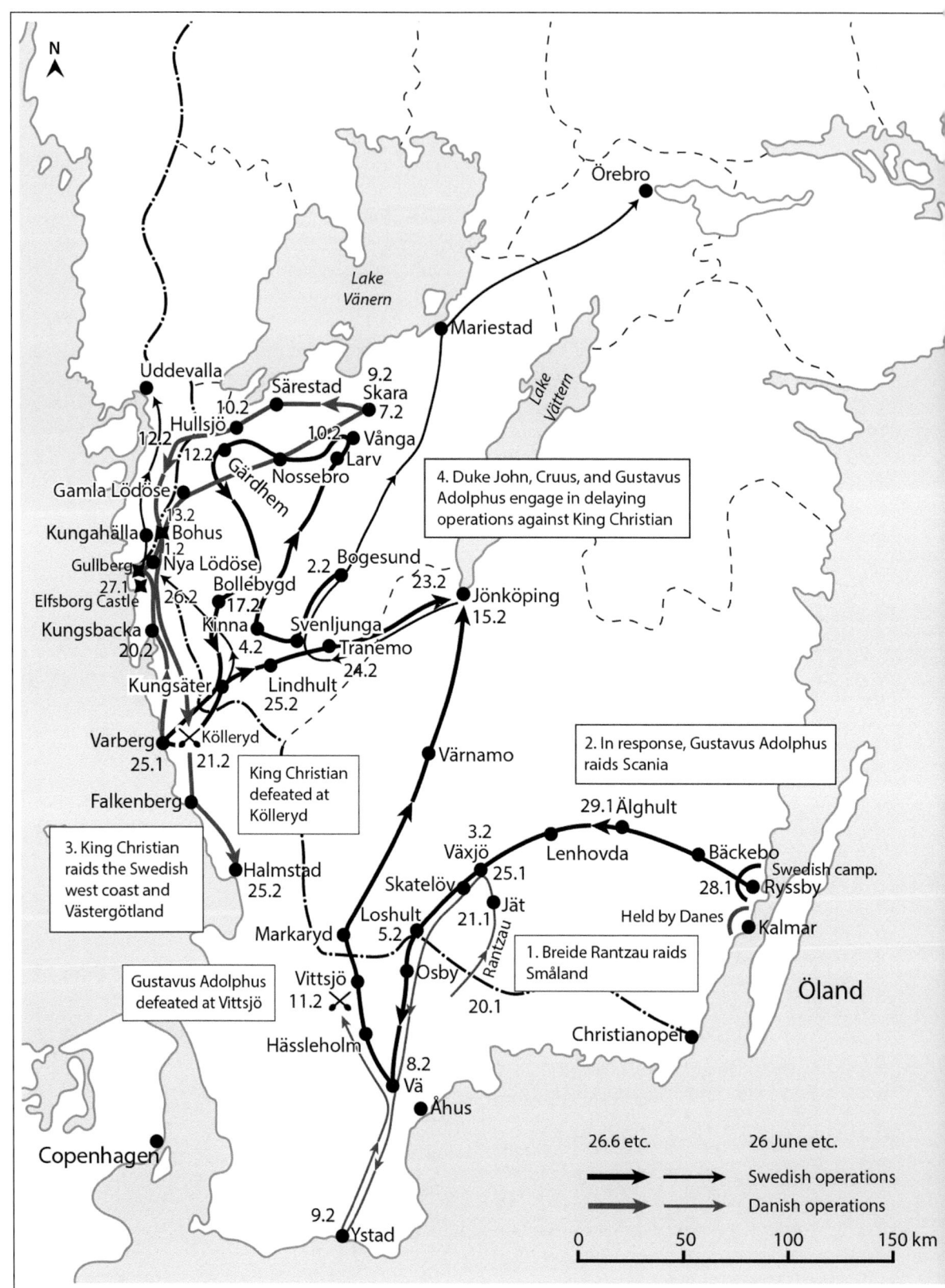

THE WINTER CAMPAIGN

Left: Map 6. Operations in the winter of 1612

Below: Gullberg Castle, as depicted in King Christian's victory medal from 1612, and a reconstruction of the castle based on the medal. (Reconstruction after Lars Gahrn).

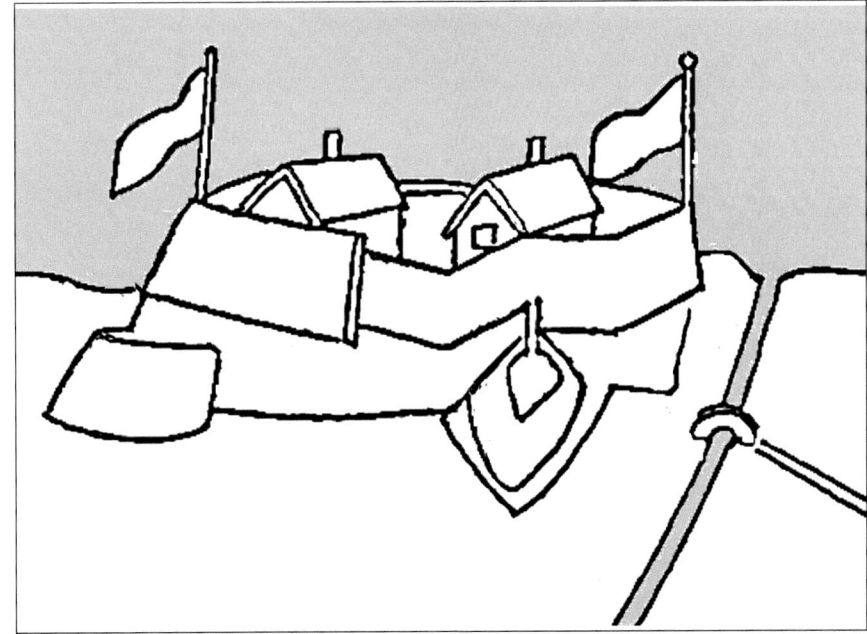

Assault on Gullberg Castle

This time, King Christian focused his attention on the western front. Sehested was no longer with him: the Marshal, as previously noted, had died of the Kalmar disease. On 15 January, King Christian marched into Halmstad with a couple of companies of foot as reinforcements. There he received a letter from the Swedish Council of the Realm, written on 1 January. It was an offer to negotiate peace as long as King Christian agreed to return Kalmar and his other conquests. This proposal annoyed King Christian to the extent that he later wrote to Gustavus Adolphus that the suggestion itself necessitated a resumption of the war (Latin: *renovatio armorum*).[9] King Christian also sent a raiding party, the Ribe Banner under Lieutenant Knud Gyldenstjerne, into south-western Småland.

Meanwhile, the Danish army assembled at Varberg. By 21 January, it consisted of five national cavalry units (the Fyn, Halland, Aarhus, Aalborg, and Ribe Banners), Duke George of Brunswick-Lüneburg's enlisted harquebusier cavalry company, parts of Duke George's regiment (five companies, respectively under the Duke himself, Ernst von Botner, Anthonius Freudemann, Adam von Köten, and Marquard Rantzau), and the King's Regiment (the newly raised Life Company under Thomas Nold and a company under Mathias Kochheim). Total strength has been estimated as approximately 2,500 men.[10] By then, Danish raiding parties had already entered Swedish territory. On 25 January, King Christian personally led the Danish main army on an 80 km forced march to Gullberg Castle, the nearest of the River Göta Älv castles. The King hoped to conquer the castle by surprise.

Gullberg Castle was a small castle on a high cliff that controlled the main road from Halland to Elfsborg Castle farther to the west.[11] Construction had begun in 1568 as a replacement for an old medieval castle. The stronghold was small, only two block houses surrounded by walls, yet modern. King John had it built to secure Nya Lödöse. Gullberg Castle was again upgraded in the early 1600s, immediately before the Kalmar War.

The Danes reached Gullberg Castle at 2:00 a.m. on 26 January.[12] Although a sudden thaw made the streams difficult to cross, the Danes immediately attempted to storm Gullberg. Having no siege artillery and, at this point, probably no infantry, they attempted to rely on the moment of surprise. In a

---

9   Kristian Erslev (ed.), *Aktstykker og Oplysninger til Rigsraadets og Stændermødernes Historie i Kristian IV's Tid* (Copenhagen: Nielsen & Lydiche, 1883), vol. 1, p.208.
10 Generalstaben, *Sveriges krig 1611–1632*, vol. 1, p.263; Larsen, *Kalmarkrigen*, p.176.
11 Gullberg was built on the rock that currently hosts the late seventeenth-century round tower and bastion known as Lejonet ('The Lion') in modern-day Gothenburg.
12 Widekindi, *Then fordom Stormächtigste*, p.39. Widekindi based his account on Krakow's own report. Wadén, *Berättande källor*, pp.60–77. Other details derive from Krakow's daughter Cecilia Krakow's account. Young Cecilia witnessed the assault. Wadén gives her account little credit, but it contains nothing implausible and much of an eyewitness character. See also Lars Gahrn, 'Gullbergs försvar 1612 – Ett 400-årsminne', *Lars Gahrn skriver* (2011), <https://larsgahrnskriver.wordpress.com/2011/12/01/gullbergs-forsvar-1612-ett-400-arsminne/>, accessed 23 June 2023.

sudden night attack, the French petardier Julien Grandfond managed to blow the castle's outer gate with a petard. However, the approximately 300 defenders had reinforced the entrance, so, even with the outer gate blown, the Danes could not penetrate in force. A few Danes did manage to enter the castle's cookhouse, however. During the combat, the commandant of Gullberg, Mårten Krakow, accidentally fell off his horse, breaking his left leg, which put him out of combat since he, in 1603, had already lost his lower right leg in action in Livonia (oral tradition tells that he also lost a hand in battle). The resolute Lady Emerentia Pauli, Krakow's wife, then assumed command of the defences, bringing the womenfolk of the castle into battle alongside the men. Under her leadership, Krakow's men, aided by their womenfolk, killed the Danes who had entered and repulsed five attempts to storm the castle in six hours. The total Danish casualties were estimated as between 150 and 200 men.[13]

Having failed to take Gullberg, King Christian sent a messenger to Lady Emerentia, requesting a ceasefire for retrieving the dead Danes in the castle for burial. Probably suspecting a ruse, the bellicose Lady responded that, since God had let her slay all the intruders, she would certainly also see to their burial. Lady Emerentia added that the Danes had turned up at her gate without warning – if they cared to return for dinner, she would prepare a better meal for them. Realising that Gullberg was too hard a nut to crack, King Christian abandoned the assault.

The Danes instead turned east, moving on to the town of Nya Lödöse. They did not encounter any resistance because the burghers had fled.[14] King Christian put a Danish garrison of two companies from Duke George of Brunswick-Lüneburg's regiment into the town.

On 29 January, King Christian advanced towards Elfsborg Castle with the intention of destroying the six Swedish warships put up there for the winter. The warships were stationary, frozen into the ice and thus vulnerable to attack, even though the Swedes had prepared defensive works in the form of palisades and open-water channels cut into the ice. King Charles ordered a bronze culverin onto the ice to open fire on the ships. The single culverin had likely been found abandoned in Nya Lödöse because there is no information that the Danes had brought any other artillery. However, the warships could respond with significantly more powerful return fire from the shipboard artillery, so the single Danish cannon was soon neutralised, tumbling into the water as the ice cover on which it was deployed broke up. King Christian thus abandoned the attempt, and, the next day (30 January), he and his men were already back in Nya Lödöse. The King may have planned to move against Elfsborg Castle itself, but, lacking siege artillery, he abandoned any such plans. Instead, King Christian decided to move into the province of Västergötland to ravage Swedish territory there.

The same day (30 January), the King ordered the all-cavalry raiding parties of Lieutenant Knud Gyldenstjerne and Captain Benedict Bernd von Hagen, then at Björkris, north of Kungsbacka (in Danish Halland), across the border

---

13 Generalstaben, *Sveriges krig 1611–1632*, vol. 1, p.270; Wadén, *Berättande källor*, p.224.
14 Anon., 'Journal', p.725.

into the Swedish province of Västergötland as a vanguard. On 1 February, King Christian led the rest of the army to Bohus Castle and, from there, to Gamla Lödöse, burning a manor house and all villages along the road. The next day, he continued towards Skara, which he burned on 7 February, with the cathedral the only building left standing. The single Swedish infantry company that had garrisoned Skara wisely withdrew ahead of the arrival of the Danish army.

Raids and Counterraids in Småland and Scania

But what about the news from Böllja in Jönköping about a major Danish offensive in Småland? Before King Christian set out towards Gullberg Castle, he had sent a raiding party, the Ribe Banner under the aforementioned Knud Gyldenstjerne, into south-western Småland. Gyldenstjerne burned four villages and a manor house, after which he returned to Halmstad on 21 January. At the same time, the King sent the Aarhus Banner, under Lieutenant Jørgen Skeel, and the aforementioned Benedict Bernd von Hagen's German banner with orders to attack the enlisted French cavalry that guarded the Swedish border. The outnumbered French cavalry, under De la Barre, heard of the planned attack in advance and abandoned the border. As a result, Skeel and Hagen only managed to burn their abandoned quarters.

It was the intrusion of Gyldenstjerne's raiders that had made Böllja report a major Danish offensive. In reality, as we have seen, King Christian assembled troops for an offensive against Gullberg Castle and the River Göta Älv Estuary. Meanwhile, in January 1612, Breide Rantzau brought together, without the Swedes noticing, a corps of mostly cavalry, an infantry company, and Anders Bille's Scanian levies in Allbo, in Scania, on the southern border with Småland, altogether an estimated 1,500 to 2,000 men:[15]

- Cavalry: cuirassiers (Court Banner, Zealand Banner, Scanian Banner, King's Life Banner under Bülow, and (possibly) Schleswig Banner under Flotow) and harquebusiers (Gert von Rantzau's harquebusier company, Duke Ernest Louis of Saxe-Lauenburg's harquebusier company, Marquard von Pentz's harquebusier company, Franz Ernst von Dalwig's harquebusier company, and Rabe Philip Bogreben's harquebusier company)
- Infantry: Jørgen Lunge's company
- Levies: Anders Bille's Scanians.

He broke into Småland on 21 January, burning and ravaging.

Arriving at Ryssby late on 24 January, Gustavus Adolphus received conflicting reports about the aforementioned Danish offensives into Småland by Gyldenstjerne, Skeel, Hagen, and Breide Rantzau. A Swedish banner of

---

15 Individual unit strengths remain unknown. Gert von Rantzau and Jørgen Lunge were personally absent from their respective units. Generalstaben, *Sveriges krig 1611–1632*, vol. 1, p.263; Larsen, *Kalmarkrigen*, pp.179–80.

cavalry under Erik Jönsson sent on a reconnaissance mission to Christianopel had been defeated and possibly wiped out.[16] Another report claimed that Breide Rantzau and his men marched towards Växjö in Småland, from which they intended to continue towards Jönköping. These reports were true but had nothing to do with Gyldenstjerne's raid into south-western Småland. According to the reports, Rantzau had, around 21 January, defeated and dispersed a unit of Småland levies and burnt Växjö and Kronoberg Castle, located on an island near Växjö. However, these reports were exaggerated. Certainly, Rantzau had moved into Småland towards Växjö, burning and devastating everything in his path. He also reached Kronoberg Castle, marching across the ice, on 24 January, but his men only succeeded in burning the castle's barn. The next day, temperatures rose, the ice began to melt, and Rantzau ordered a retreat back to Scania by way of Loshult. He then went into his old quarters at Allbo.

Based on the reports of Rantzau's intrusion, on 28 January, Gustavus Adolphus set out from Ryssby towards Växjö with Colonel Nils Stiernskiöld and at least four horse and eight infantry companies, altogether an estimated 2,500 to 3,000 men, with some artillery.[17] The number may have been smaller. Henrik Horn, who accompanied the King, estimated the number as approximately 2,000. He also noted that Hans von Akern remained at Ryssby, assuming command there in Stiernskiöld's absence. If Akern's men also remained at Ryssby, this may explain the difference in estimated numbers.[18]

[See Table 14, **Field Army under Gustavus Adolphus and Nils Stiernskiöld, January 1612**, end of chapter]

Arriving at Växjö on 3 February, Gustavus Adolphus sent orders to Duke John and Cruus to protect Västergötland from King Christian's army at Elfsborg. As for himself, the Swedish King followed in the tracks of Rantzau, crossing the border into Scania on 5 February without encountering any resistance. Now, it was the Swedish King who burned and looted but on Danish territory. Crossing the River Helgeå, he apparently left his artillery and most or all foot in a bridgehead at Osby. Then, he continued towards the west with what seems to have been an all-cavalry force, reaching Farlev the following day. He continued to the little town of Vä, which he burned on 8 February.[19] Whatever may have happened in Christianopel in the previous year, this time, the devastation caused by Gustavus Adolphus was surely deliberate. In a letter to Duke John, he noted that, altogether, his raiding party had devastated 24 parishes. The King continued, 'We have ravaged, laid waste, burned, and killed just everywhere we wanted'.[20] This was an exaggeration that probably can be attributed to youthful enthusiasm.

---

16 Larsen, *Kalmarkrigen*, pp.192–93.
17 Generalstaben, *Sveriges krig 1611–1632*, vol. 1, p.264.
18 Broomé, *Nils Stiernsköld*, p.75.
19 Vä was located south of modern-day Christianstad, which was founded in 1614 as a more secure replacement for Vä and nearby Åhus Castle.
20 Gustavus Adolphus to Duke John, 13 February 1612.

Gustavus Adolphus mentioned, in the same letter, that he had hoped to take Åhus Castle, near Vä, but it was too strongly garrisoned. Åhus Castle was also defended by a newly erected wall built in the previous year. The same day that Gustavus Adolphus burned Vä, he also withdrew from Lillö Castle at River Helgeå, which was defended by the resolute Lady Beate Huitfeldt (1554–1626), who refused to surrender. Nor did his men attack Hovdala Castle, held by Sivert Grubbe (1566–1636), one of the Danish King's most trusted men. Gustavus Adolphus led a raiding party without the infantry and artillery necessary for a siege. Moreover, the Swedes, as usual, lacked slow match in sufficient quantities to continue the expedition. As a result, the King decided to join forces with Duke John and Cruus and retreated towards Markaryd.

Modern historians sometimes fail to understand that the violent raiding undertaken by both sides in the war was not a pointless endeavour but rather the outcome of a deliberate strategy. In the context of early modern warfare (as well as those of previous centuries), raiding was a deliberate strategy to gain specific military objectives, not merely random looting. Raiding and looting constituted the chief means to make sure that the devastated territory could not be used as a base area for subsequent enemy attacks on one's own territories. This objective was best accomplished by devastating towns and villages – and the associated agricultural industry that produced food supplies – on the enemy side of the border, thus denying the enemy the resources and supplies that were vital to launch an invasion. In addition, large-scale raiding and looting constituted the logical outcome of a deliberate strategy to win the war by applying pressure on the enemy in the ongoing or expected peace negotiations. Most early modern rulers understood that war was best waged to gain specific strategic objectives, not to engage in a fight to the death for religious faith or radical ideologies (even if such factors were occasionally used to mobilise the population). Finally, and of no less importance, raiding and looting formed a means to feed and thus retain the army when logistics broke down, which commonly happened. Although King Christian still dreamt about conquering Stockholm, it very soon became apparent to commanders on both sides that neither party in the war was strong enough decisively to defeat the other. This meant that the best option was to maintain not only a defensive strategy but also one that actively prevented the other side from launching a full-scale invasion in the first place.[21]

The strategy of violent raiding was not a new development. Border populations had a good idea of what would happen when war broke out. It was not a coincidence that, as we have seen, the Norwegian peasants in Bohuslän moved their cattle and cultivated fields away from the border when they sensed the risk of war.

---

21 For the inhabitants of the border region, this strategy spelled disaster and caused all sorts of human suffering. However, from a military point of view, the strategy was rational and, we should remember, not unlike the deliberate destruction of the enemy's strategic resources that took place in later centuries (including the extensive campaigns of strategic bombing by air forces in modern times that are also aimed primarily at production facilities, that is, industrial and civilian targets).

THE WINTER CAMPAIGN

Meanwhile, Rantzau was in Ystad. He gathered six banners of cavalry: the Court Banner, Zealand Banner, Scanian Banner, the King's Life Banner, under Joachim von Bülow, and Marquard von Pentz's two German banners. Altogether, he probably amassed some 600 horse.²² The Scanian Banner was commanded by Captain Anders Bille (1578–1633), a Scanian nobleman who knew the terrain well. Rantzau's men then set out to follow the Swedish King's corps. Bille also raised peasant levies in Göinge. They seem to have joined Rantzau's corps west of Vittsjö. Rantzau and Bille aimed to carry out a surprise attack on the young Swedish King.

The result was a famous battle even the very fundamentals of which are difficult to clarify. Different contemporary sources indicate two different locations for the battle, which is described as taking place at Vittsjö, Osby, or both.²³ There is good reason to conclude that Rantzau's and Gustavus Adolphus's men simultaneously fought the battle(s) in two separate locations, with contingents that formed part of the same command but, because of previous events, found themselves separated.

Anders Bille.
(Author's collection)

The Battle of Vittsjö

On 11 February, Gustavus Adolphus let his men rest in Vittsjö, forming a rearguard while the bulk of his force, under Stiernskiöld, continued towards the north. The road north from Vittsjö (to Markaryd) crossed a small stream, Dragsån (modern day Verumsån or Vieån), between two lakes (nowadays three: modern-day Lakes Öresjön, Pickelsjön, and Vittsjön). The stream was only a few metres broad and less than a metre deep at the crossing place, which was an old ford but, by this time, had been dignified with a small bridge. The ruins of a redoubt remain in place, but it is unclear if these are

---

22   Generalstaben, *Sveriges krig 1611–1632*, vol. 1, p.267; Larsen, *Kalmarkrigen*, p.183.
23   Wadén, *Berättande källor*, pp.170–78, 222–23, argues that only one battle was fought and that it took place at Vittsjö. Generalstaben, *Sveriges krig 1611–1632*, vol. 1, p.268, follows Wadén. However, on this issue, Wadén'a arguments do not seem conclusive. The fact that some sources mention a place called 'Osby' (or 'Wosbye', 'Risby', or something similar) and others one called 'Vittsjö' (or 'Widtsöe') does not preclude but does seemingly support two separate locations. Moreover, two locations make more logical sense since it is hard to reconcile the confined geography at Vittsjö with the large-scale operations described by the sources. The account of the battle(s) offered here should be regarded as tentative.

the ruins of a stronger Danish redoubt built later during the Kalmar War or, even yet, another built as a defensive measure against Swedish intrusions during the Thirty Years' War. The village of Vittsjö was possibly already burned, and, if it was not, it may have consisted of only three farmsteads, so the Swedes may have made camp in and around the twelfth-century church and cemetery. We do not know how many men remained with the King.

Meanwhile, Anders Bille advanced from the south in two columns. We do not how many men he led, presumably only his banner and the levies that he had raised. Bille's force presumably constituted the vanguard of Rantzau's army. There is nothing to suggest that Rantzau himself, or his entire army, was in the area. Bille ordered a pincer movement. The first column, the peasant levies, he may have ordered around Lake Öresjön to block the Swedes from the north. The other, the Scanian Banner, which he led himself, advanced towards Vittsjö from the south. According to one story, Bille approached along a small secondary road that was covered with snow and, for this reason, had gone unnoticed by the Swedes, who had posted patrols only on the main roads. According to another, possibly more apocryphal story, Bille ordered his men to bring evergreen tree branches to hide their movements. When darkness fell (different sources suggest a time between 4:00 and 5:00 p.m.; sunset took place at 5:20 p.m.), Bille attacked the small Swedish camp. The Danes surprised and cut down the sentries and then charged. The surviving Swedes fled towards the north. Some escaped across the stream, but they were attacked by the levies coming from the north, who reportedly killed many Swedes. Others fell into captivity. Gustavus Adolphus managed to reach his horse, but it went through the ice near a prominent rock in the middle of the stream, since known as the 'King's Rock' (Swedish: *Kungsstenen*). He was saved by the Uppland cavalryman Thomas Larsson and the noble Per Banér, both of the Life Banner. In the struggle, Banér himself went through the ice, but he was in turn saved from the water by his younger brother Nils Banér (who ultimately fell in battle in Muscovy). The Danes captured the King's horse, saddle, and pistols. Since the stream was very shallow, it was probably the Danes, not the water, that was the greater danger. Thomas Larsson gave Gustavus Adolphus his own horse. Both Larsson and Banér were well rewarded by the King.[24]

---

24 Lauritz Weibull, 'Gustaf II Adolfs räddare vid Vittsjö', *Scandia*, 16:1 (1944), pp.90–95. The King immediately gave the soldier Larsson his silver belt. Later, he also awarded Larsson the farmstead Igelsta in Romfartuna, which remained in the possession of his descendants for seven generations. Ebbe Schön, *Kungar, krig och katastrofer: Vår historia i sägen och tro* (Fourth edition, Stockholm: Hjalmarson & Högberg, 2011), pp.96–97. Banér was rewarded, too, in the form of a knighthood and the return of a land grant previously lost by his family. Incidentally, a descendant of the soldier Larsson was, until the late twentieth century, customarily invited to speak during the celebration of the anniversary of the battle. However, by then, identitarian Scanian newspaper reporters routinely criticised any attempt to mention Gustavus Adolphus's name during the anniversaries. Instead of celebrating a bloodthirsty king and enemy of Scania, they argued, focus should lie on the death of the common soldiers who perished in the battle.

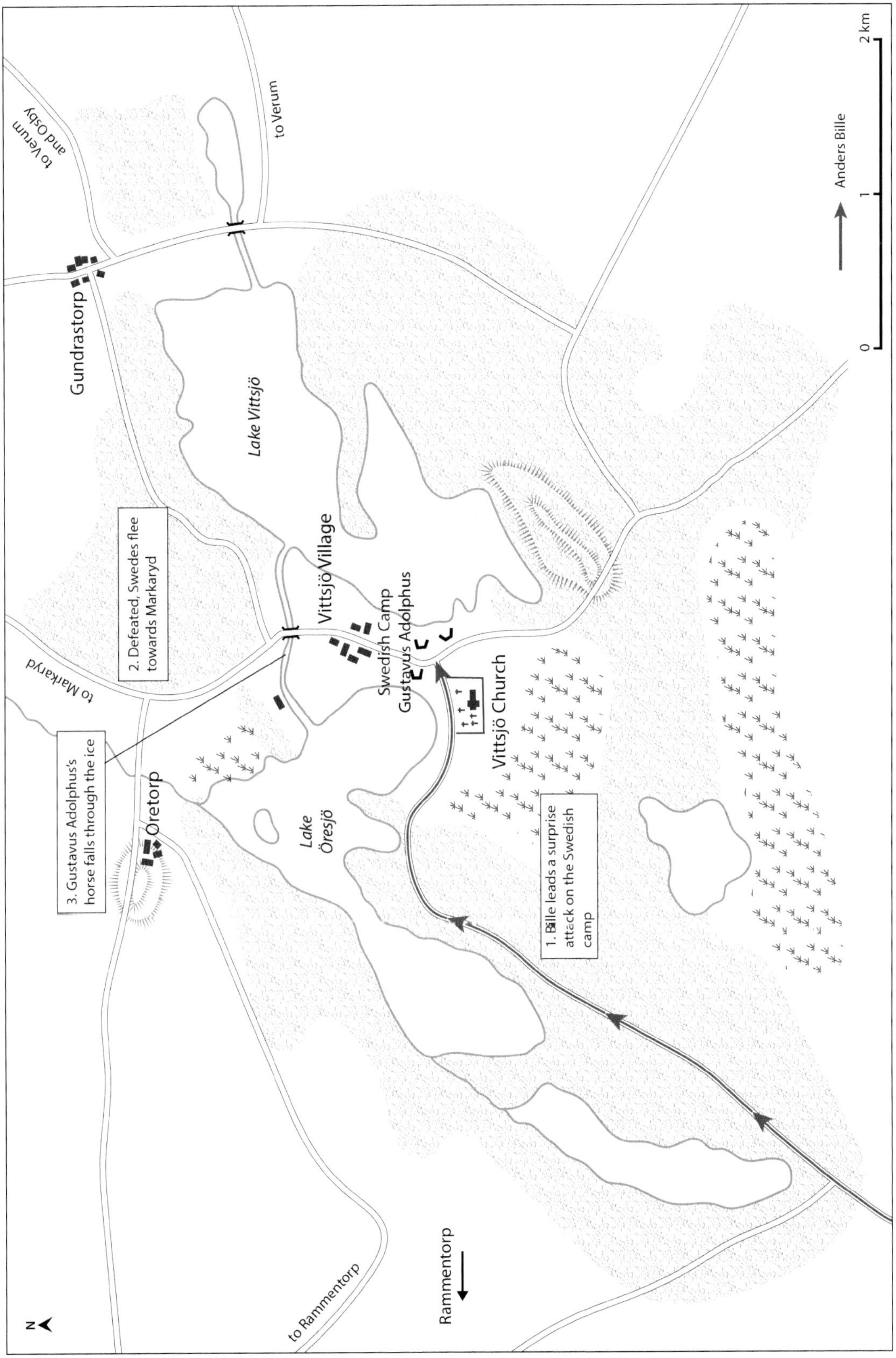

THE WINTER CAMPAIGN

Map 7. Battle of Vittsjö, 1612.

Numerous legends quickly grew around the incident, and many question marks remain about the course of events. Neither side could have consisted of more than a few hundred men at most. The battle was essentially a skirmish. So much is certain that Bille carried out a successful surprise attack at night, that the Swedes fled or perished, and that Gustavus Adolphus barely escaped with his life. In the letter to Duke John, the King estimated that he had lost 300 men, but this number almost certainly referred to the total number of lost and dispersed men, not only the fallen. A mass grave has been found near the site of battle, but it was never properly excavated. The number of dead was, at the time, estimated as 120 men.[25] Losses included several officers, including the cavalry captain Abel Svenske. Others fell into Danish captivity, among them the captain of the King's Life Banner, Herman Wrangel (unless he was captured the days before, near Vä) – a Livonian who, in the coming years, would make a name for himself as a field marshal – and, if at Vittsjö and not Osby, the German captain von Lobwitz. The King and the survivors then made their way to Markaryd.

While Bille surprised the Swedish King at Vittsjö, Rantzau surprised the Swedish bridgehead at Osby, approximately 25 km east of Vittsjö. The Danes again, possibly, bypassed the Swedes, attacking from the north. Rantzau reportedly took several cannons and cut down much of the Swedish infantry. Losses again included many officers, among them the Scottish Captain Robert Sim and the captain of the Dalecarlian company, Göran Hansson. Rantzau's men captured the German Captain Tideman Schrou and an officer known as 'Thomas Bingley'. The Danes pursued the surviving Swedes as they set off towards the north to join Gustavus Adolphus and Nils Stiernskiöld, who hurriedly formed a defensive line with any men still available along the old border.

Neither Bille nor Rantzau made any attempt to cross the old border. In effect, they were satisfied with their victories and, no doubt, realised the Swedish King's main army remained undefeated somewhere around Markaryd. On the Swedish side, the King ordered Stiernskiöld to command the border defences. As for himself, he continued to Jönköping, where he arrived on 13 February. He sent three disrupted companies of foot, two from Västmanland and one from Södermanland, farther north to be reorganised and brought up to strength again with fresh replacements.

The Battle of Kölleryd

When King Christian led his army towards Skara, Duke John and Field Marshal Cruus stood at Bogesund (modern-day Ulricehamn), farther to the south. Together, they still controlled a few banners of cavalry, several companies of Scots and Irish foot from Rutherford's regiment, and probably a few national infantry companies. We cannot, with any certainty, identify the units under their command nor their total manpower, but the corps is

---

25 Generalstaben, *Sveriges krig 1611–1632*, vol. 1, p.268.

unlikely to have exceeded 2,000 men.[26] King Christian commanded an all-cavalry corps of seven banners, perhaps about 1,500 men. His corps consisted almost certainly of the Fyn, Halland, Aalborg, Aarhus, and Ribe Banners, together with the presumably harquebusier companies of Duke George of Brunswick-Lüneburg and Captain Benedict Bernd von Hagen.[27] However, neither Duke John nor Cruus, at first, had any means of knowing that the Danish King was outnumbered. Instead, they feared that their numbers were too small to confront King Christian, whom they moreover believed was on the way to Jönköping. As a result, they made no attempt to confront the Danish army, instead contenting themselves with defending and blocking the roads to Jönköping with abatis and other field fortifications.

However, by 2 February, Duke John and Cruus realised that the Danish offensive only was a plundering expedition into Västergötland, not a general offensive against Jönköping. The Swedes may have planned to take advantage of the Danish King's absence to carry out a raid of their own against Varberg. However, upon the road, they heard about King Christian's diminished numbers, so they marched north-west in order to confront the Danish King. Weather was deteriorating, with snow and winter storms, but, on 9 February, King Christian began the retreat towards the west. It is quite possible that the Danish King, realising his lower numbers, had decided to avoid Duke John's and Cruus's army. Meanwhile, King Christian sent Claus Daa with the Aalborg Banner to raid and reconnoitre the lands on the Danish army's left (south) flank, presumably to secure the retreat. At the village of Vånga, Daa stumbled onto two Swedish cavalry banners, advance units of Duke John's and Cruus's army, which was then approaching from the south. Receiving assistance from the Halland Banner, Daa managed to repulse the Swedish cavalry, retaining the field of battle. Nonetheless, Duke John and Cruus moved to intercept the Danish army. Several skirmishes followed between the Danish rearguard and the Swedish vanguard. According to a Danish report, a Danish unit ended up behind the Swedish army, which allowed it to plunder the Swedish supply train while still on the march. Be that as it may, to avoid battle, King Christian took the precaution of crossing the River Göta Älv into Norwegian territory on 12 February. Having failed to intercept, Duke John and Cruus henceforth marched on a parallel road as King Christian retreated to the south, essentially shadowing the Danish army.

While King Christian tarried in Norwegian Bohuslän, Duke John and Cruus found themselves entering Danish Halland unopposed. On 20 February,

---

26 Larsen, *Kalmarkrigen*, p.188, suggests at least 4,000 men (eight banners and around 20 companies of foot), which seems exaggerated.

27 Larsen, *Kalmarkrigen*, p.188, notes seven banners; Generalstaben, *Sveriges krig 1611–1632*, vol. 1, p.271, suggests 'not much over 1,500 men' since King Christian had already left his infantry units at Nya Lödöse. Seven banners would seem to equal about 1,500 men. There is reason to believe that the Danish King's army, by this time, had shrunk considerably from attrition. Both sides habitually overestimated enemy strength, often to a very large degree, which, at least to some extent, can be explained by the fact that their intelligence and reconnaissance capabilities were underdeveloped in comparison to later in the century.

they took and burned the unfortified Varberg Town. They Swedes did not attempt to take Varberg Castle, a modern fortress next to the town with the same name.[28] Duke John and Cruus then prepared to return to Sweden.

However, by then, King Christian was on his way south, riding with Duke George of Brunswick-Lüneburg and seven banners of cavalry. On 21 February, Duke John and Cruus accordingly deployed their men in a pass at Kölleryd. The Swedish musketeers deployed on the hill sides of the pass while the cavalry blocked the pass itself. The Danish cavalry was tired from the long ride, but King Christian immediately ordered a charge. Swedish musket fire disrupted the Danish cavalry charge, with the Danes fleeing in disorder. The Swedish cavalry then charged the Danes, completing the victory. Several legends detail stories from the battle.[29] According to one that modern scholarship generally attributes to the eighteenth century, King Christian's horse got stuck in a bog during the pursuit. Realising that the King was in danger of being captured by the pursuing Swedish cavalry, the 56-year-old Christian Barnekow, a scholar and diplomat, gave up his horse to the King, with the words 'I give my horse to the king, my life to the enemy and my soul to God.' The aged Barnekow then attempted to run alongside the fleeing horse by holding on to a stirrup yet was soon so exhausted that he had to let it go. Trying to recover his breath and possibly taking cover by a rock, he was then cut down by a Swedish soldier. Another story describes the end of the 23-year-old noble Steen Rosensparre. Before the battle, another Dane warned him, 'Be careful, remember that you are the last of your line!' Rosensparre then replied, 'You are right, that is a beautiful thought; an honourable name takes precedence over anything.' Half an hour later, he had fallen.

Other notable Danish casualties included Franciscus (Frants) von Rantzau, the elder brother of Breide and Gert von Rantzau, and several other leading nobles. Total Danish casualties were between 130 and 250 according to Danish accounts or, possibly less likely, between 300 and 400, as reported by Swedish sources.[30]

The similarity between the near-capture of King Christian at Kölleryd and the near-capture of Gustavus Adolphus at Vittsjö, within 10 days of each other and while both led raiding parties in enemy territory, is striking and emphasises the inferior intelligence and reconnaissance capabilities available to both sides. It is equally striking that neither side managed to gain any decisive advantage of their respective victory.

The surviving Danes took refuge in Varberg Castle. When the Swedes had departed, King Christian reorganised defences in Halland and then travelled home to Copenhagen by way of Halmstad and Scania.

---

28 Varberg Town was then located approximately four kilometres north of Varberg Castle. The town was moved to its current location only in 1613.

29 In Danish historiography, the fighting at Kölleryd is known as the Battle of Skillinge, after Skällinge Parish. The number of men on either side is uncertain.

30 Wadén, *Berättande källor*, p.140, with sources; Generalstaben, *Sveriges krig 1611–1632*, vol. 1, pp.272–73.

Cruus then continued to Nya Lödöse. On the morning of 27 February, he had his artillery (several cannons) open fire. The town was garrisoned by two enlisted German infantry companies from Duke George of Brunswick-Lüneburg's regiment and 300 Norwegian peasant levies. Faced with artillery fire, the Danish garrison soon surrendered. Cruus spared the captured Continental soldiers (200 of whom immediately went into Swedish service), but the Norwegians who had also formed part of the garrison were killed almost to a man in revenge for previous massacres, real and alleged, and the destruction of Skara. Cruus then continued into the Norwegian province of Bohuslän, which he thoroughly ravaged. Among the burned towns were Kungahälla and Uddevalla. Reaching as far as Frederiksstad in Norway, he also burned 544 tax-paying farmsteads and 40 'abandoned' farmsteads (i.e. farmsteads that, for one reason or another, lacked the means to pay taxes). By tradition, border wars in this region were devastating, and Cruus took revenge for previous Danish raids and massacres by slaughtering and burning well beyond what the Danes and Norwegians, neither of whom had been lenient, had accomplished. In Bohuslän, Cruus's campaign was later referred to as the 'Scorching War' (*Brændefejden*).

The winter campaigns only ended when the spring thaw made the roads impassable. The Swedish commanders went to Stockholm for the funeral of the late King Charles.

Both sides also began to prepare for the summer campaign. Sweden had few reserves left. Småland and Västergötland had already been thoroughly devastated, and no tax payments could be expected from them. Gustavus Adolphus sent emissaries to the north German towns as well as to the Dutch Republic in an attempt to secure loans, but he seems not to have achieved any real results.[31] In March, the young King's newly appointed Lord High Chancellor, Axel Oxenstierna, laconically summarised Sweden's position with the words that 'all our neighbours are our enemies' and 'we have absolutely no friends … and if some existed, we cannot expect any help or relief from them'. He then continued with a lengthy and detailed description of the fundamentally derelict state of the kingdom.[32] Oxenstierna did not exaggerate. Sweden was at war with all its neighbours. Danish armies had conquered or devastated Swedish core territories. The economy was in shambles, and most inhabitants ruined. It was all but impossible to raise new taxes to fund the ongoing wars.

---

31 Sweden could only negotiate a defence treaty with the Dutch Republic in 1614, after the end of the war.

32 Axel Oxenstierna, in the name of the Council of the Realm, to the Queen Dowager Christina, 25 March 1612. Axel Oxenstierna, *Rikskansleren Axel Oxenstiernas skrifter och brefvexling* (Stockholm: Vitterhets- historie- och antiqvitets-akademien, 1896), vol. 1, part 2, pp.42–48. While the intention of the letter was to persuade the Queen Dowager, who was exempt from taxation, to contribute funds and supplies to the war effort, there is no reason to doubt the sincerity of Oxenstierna's description of the state of the realm.

Tables

Table 14. Field Army under Gustavus Adolphus and Nils Stiernskiöld, January 1612[33]

Horse		
Unit	Captain	Strength[34]
Life Banner (cuirassiers)	Herman Wrangel	
Cavalry banner (harquebusiers)	Knut Håkansson Hand	
Cavalry banner (harquebusiers)	Abel Svenske	
Dragoon company	Robert Halswell	
Likely part of the army but unconfirmed		
Cavalry banner (enlisted French harquebusiers)	De la Barre[35]	
	Total	600–700
Infantry		
Province/Origin	Company	Strength[36]
Hälsingland	Hans von Akern (personally absent)[37]	
Dalecarlia	Göran Hansson	
Västmanland	Hans Campbell	
Västmanland	Lars Fordel	
Småland	Sven Trulsson Spinke	
Enlisted Scots/Irish	William Morgan	
Enlisted Scots	Robert Sim (Syme?)	
Enlisted Germans	Tideman Schrou	
Likely part of the army but unconfirmed		
Enlisted Germans (possibly cavalry harquebusiers)	Hans Jürgen(?) von Lobwitz	
	Total	1,700–1,800
	Grand Total	2,500–3,000[38]

---

33 Generalstaben, *Sveriges krig 1611–1632*, vol. 1, p.265; Broomé, *Nils Stiernsköld*, p.75.
34 Individual unit strengths remain unknown.
35 When, or if, De la Barre joined the army is unknown.
36 Individual unit strengths remain unknown.
37 There is reason to believe that Hans von Akern remained at Ryssby, possibly his company as well.
38 Information on the artillery and its strength is unknown and thus not included.

14

Summer Campaign

Although not everything had gone his way, King Christian retained the initiative as summer approached, and with it the expected summer campaign.

Realising that he needed more men, this time, King Christian aimed to raise an army of some 4,200 cavalry, 400 dragoons, and approximately 20,500 foot. He already had men under arms corresponding to about 3,000 cavalry (16 banners), 200 dragoons, and 3,500 foot, and the rest, he argued, could be had by enlisting men in Germany, the Dutch Republic, and England. Ultimately, King Christian failed to raise the desired numbers. Horse, in particular, was difficult to obtain. Yet, by the end of winter, the King controlled, as a combined total of garrisons and field units, approximately 3,200 cavalry, 200 dragoons, and 17,600 foot – 21,000 men in total.[1] To this must be added the Norwegian army, which could be expected to bind significant Swedish forces along the common border and, with a little luck, even invade the Swedish core territories.

King Christian's significant host would be divided into two field armies, one in the west and one in the east. King Christian would personally take command of the western army, which consisted of 11 cavalry banners, one dragoon company, four regiments of foot (together consisting of 32 infantry companies), and two independent companies of foot, altogether an estimated 10,250 men (2,250 horse and 8,000 foot).

He gave Field Marshal Gert von Rantzau command of the eastern army, which consisted of six cavalry banners, one dragoon company, three regiments of foot (together consisting of 25 companies), and four independent companies of foot, altogether an estimated 8,120 men (1,320 horse and 6,800 foot).[2]

Varberg and Halmstad would each have a garrison of 500 men, while Laholm only would have 50. Bohus Castle would have 300. Christianopel retained a garrison of two companies. The Danish Crown raised four companies of peasant levies as infantry to protect the Scanian border. In the

---

1   Larsen, *Kalmarkrigen*, p.199; Generalstaben, *Sveriges krig 1611–1632*, vol. 1, p.276; Norrie, *Kalmarkrigen*, p.35.
2   Generalstaben, *Sveriges krig 1611–1632*, vol. 1, pp.260, 263, 277.

same way, the Crown raised a company of 400 peasant levies to protect the Blekinge border (this company was ultimately incorporated into the field army). In both Scania and Halland, their respective cavalry banners of the retinue of nobles were designated to support the levies as reserves for border protection. In case the Swedes would enlist units in Germany or the Dutch Republic that would attempt to invade Jutland or Zealand from the south or by sea, the Crown raised levies (*landeværn*) for home defence by means of a quota that local peasants and burghers had to fulfil.[3]

King Christian's plan for the 1612 summer campaign is believed to have been similar to the one agreed upon, but never implemented, in the previous year, that is, an offensive along the Baltic seaboard towards the Swedish core territories in the north. As noted, it was easier to march along the coast because then the navy could provide logistical support, including the transportation of supplies. As in the previous year, we do not know for sure how King Christian intended to carry out the campaign, so a certain level of conjecture is required to reconstruct his strategy.

Possibly learning from the events of the previous year, this time, the King apparently envisaged an initial offensive into Västergötland and Småland before the general advance north would follow from Kalmar. This can be deduced from the fact that King Christian personally assumed command of the offensive into Västergötland while he gave Field Marshal Gert von Rantzau command on the eastern front. As in 1611, he also allocated a higher share of cavalry to the western army, destined for the Västergötland front. In the west, the King wanted first to lay siege to, and take, Gullberg, Elfsborg, and the other settlements alongside the River Göta Älv Estuary. In the east, the first objective was the conquest of the Ryssby fortified camp and the reconquest of Öland.

Having conquered the castles on the River Göta Älv, and possibly after also defeating any Swedish relief army, King Christian probably expected to continue towards Jönköping and the east to join forces with Rantzau at Ryssby, the conquest of which might need the combined Danish field armies.[4] The Danish army could then follow the coastal road towards the north and the Swedish heartlands, where the navy could meet up with fresh supplies at Västervik and Norrköping.

Possibly, as an alternative, King Christian envisaged that Rantzau first would advance from Kalmar towards Jönköping. If attacked from both directions, Jönköping would surely fall, which would enable an offensive towards the Swedish heartlands along the old highway known as the 'Hola Forest Way' (*Holavedsvägen*), which ran through the wild Holaveden ('Deep Forest'), a dark and desolate region east of Lake Vättern that marked the border between Småland and southern Östergötland. If this barrier could be overcome, the navy could meet up with fresh supplies at Norrköping.

King Christian seems to have planned no naval activities beyond the necessary transportation of men, weapons, and supplies in support of the

---

3   Generalstaben, *Sveriges krig 1611–1632*, vol. 1, p.277; Larsen, *Kalmarkrigen*, p.194.
4   Generalstaben, *Sveriges krig 1611–1632*, vol. 1, p.275.

overland offensives and, we can assume, the provision of a safeguard against any Swedish naval operations.

Aware of, or anticipating, King Christian's plans, early in the year (24 March), Gustavus Adolphus already ordered Baltzar Bäck to leave a garrison in Jämtland and Härjedalen and, with the rest of his men (the Polish banner and six companies of foot), to march to Stockholm, where units from Uppland and Södermanland also assembled. The King ordered the infantry company in Västervik to stay in place since this port was at risk from the Danish fleet. He also ordered the retinue of nobles to assemble at Örebro, where they King would meet them.

In addition, Gustavus Adolphus anticipated offensives from Norway into Dal and Värmland. He accordingly ordered the conscripted infantry there to remain in place.[5] Ultimately, no such offensive materialised, and, in early April, the King ordered the units to join the main field army.

In anticipation of the departure of the Swedish fleet, on 8 April, Gustavus Adolphus imposed sanctions on those German mercantile centres that provided supplies to Denmark and paid the Sound Toll to the Danish Crown.[6] In the previous year, the Swedish Crown had lacked the means to reciprocate the Danish blockade of Sweden. Perhaps this year might be different.

Gustavus Adolphus had ordered the Swedish main fleet in Stockholm to set out against the Danish fleet in the Baltic and, in particular, support operations on Öland, which he considered most at risk. However, it always took time to equip a fleet, especially under northern winter conditions, so it was only on 17 April that the first two Swedish ships, the *Hollands Svanen* and *Hollands Ängeln*, under Captain Lars Bubb, were ready to set out. At that time, there were six Danish warships already in the Baltic. Richard Clerck set out from Stockholm with a squadron of eight warships (the *Concordia*, *Meerman*, *Draken*, *Justitia*, *Gula Lejonet*, *Leoparden*, *Mercurius*, and *Vita Falken*) and the pinnace *Lybska Salvator* bound for Älvsnabben, the customary Swedish naval summer base in the southern Stockholm Archipelago, only at the end of May.[7] He then set out to sea on 7 June. By then, we will see that Admiral Jacob Beck was in command of the entire Danish main fleet in the southern Baltic from its new base at Kalmar. In face of this massive Danish superiority in numbers, Clerck had to take cover in the waters around Gotland and Gotska Sandön, which meant that he was unable to support the ongoing army operations. Clerck's squadron sailed around Gotland without encountering any Danish warships and then returned to Älvsnabben on 13 June.

But much happened before then. In April 1612, King Christian mustered his army. On 28 April, Colonel Jørgen Lunge, now with a regiment of his own, and Captain Joachim von Bülow of the King's Life Banner advanced from Ängelholm to Elfsborg with 11 cavalry banners and approximately 2,000 foot. Altogether, their army may have consisted of some 4,000 men. On

---

5   Generalstaben, *Sveriges krig 1611–1632*, vol. 1, pp.260–81.
6   Kall (ed.), 'Mag. Ægidii Laurizens samlede Efterretninger', pp.38–39; Anon., 'Journal', p.733.
7   Generalstaben, *Sveriges krig 1611–1632*, suppl. vol. 1, p.108.

2 May, King Christian set sail from Helsingør in the Danish Strait towards Elfsborg. In mid May, about half of an enlisted English regiment of foot raised by Peregrine Bertie, Lord Willoughby (fl. 1585–1624), a naturalised Englishman from Cleves, arrived at Elfsborg. The remaining men of the regiment arrived by the end of the month.[8] At about the same time, the end of May, it appears that Gert von Rantzau, too, had assembled his army in the Kalmar area.

The warships of the Danish fleet set out to sea when they had finished preparations and not as a united fleet (see Table 15). In an ominous order, King Christian instructed Admiral Ulfeldt not to take any prisoners but to instead kill all enemies.[9] First out, already in late March, was Jørgen Daa with a squadron of warships bound for the River Göta Älv Estuary with orders to prevent the Swedish squadron there from setting out to block the waterway for Danish vessels. In effect, Daa was expected to preempt a proper Swedish naval defence of the waterways, which would have enabled the Swedes to supply their various castles by sea.

[See Table 15, **Danish Fleets and Squadrons, Spring 1612**, end of chapter]

Gustavus Adolphus had already ordered the Elfsborg Squadron, six warships, to be ready to set out to sea (see Table 16). However, when Daa arrived with his squadron, only three Swedish ships were ready for combat. It was obvious to the Swedish King that this was insufficient. On 9 April, he ordered the crews and cannons to be sent to Stockholm and the warships to be cleared of gear and scuttled to deny them to the Danes.

[See Table 16, **Swedish Fleets and Squadrons Deployed for Participation in the Kalmar War, Spring 1612**, end of chapter]

Siege of Elfsborg

Soon after Daa's Skagerrak Squadron set out, two additional Danish warships, the *Penitens* and *Sankt Michael*, left port but with orders to patrol the Baltic Sea. About a week later, Admiral Jacob Beck set out with another four warships (the *Lybske David*, *Jupiter*, *Markatten*, and *Sankt Peder*) to blockade Kalmar and Öland and to support Rantzau's operations there. In early May, another four warships (the *Mælkepige*, *Lindormen*, *Sankt Anna*, and *Justitia*) were sent to reinforce Beck's squadron. Soon after, Admiral Ulfeldt followed them on the *Argo*.[10] Admiral Ulfeldt assumed command of the fleet. Yet another seven warships were ready to set out in mid May. By then, the Danish fleet in the Baltic consisted of 18 warships – the entire Danish main fleet. In the end of May, the Baltic fleet was reinforced with yet

---

8   Generalstaben, *Sveriges krig 1611–1632*, vol. 1, pp.277–78.
9   Larsen, *Kalmarkrigen*, p.246.
10 Generalstaben, *Sveriges krig 1611–1632*, suppl. vol. 1, pp.106–07.

another three warships, Lindenow's squadron, which had transported King Christian to Elfsborg but now returned.

When the Danish fleet arrived in the Kalmar Strait, the Swedes ordered all Småland units, except for two cavalry banners and Halswell's dragoon company, to redeploy from Jönköping, their customary central base, to Ryssby. Their task was to switch positions with the Dalecarlia infantry, which was shipped across the strait to Öland. The Swedish King advised the commanders at Ryssby that they should not defend the fortified camp to the end. If the Danes gained the advantage, they could surrender the camp in return for free departure. It was more important to maintain an efficient and mobile field army than fighting to the end in one fixed location.

Admiral Bååt again received command in Småland (with eight companies of foot), while Stiernskiöld was ordered to Elfsborg to take command there with reinforcements that Gustavus Adolphus had ordered from the province of Närke. We will see that neither Stiernskiöld nor the reinforcements arrived at Elfsborg in time.

Elfsborg Castle was defended by Olof Stråle (1578–1648), a diplomat and administrator more than a soldier, with reportedly 400 infantrymen, 10 artillerymen, 39 bronze cannons, and some iron cannons.[11] His second-in-command was Captain Gustav Hansson. The two Swedes were assisted by a recently arrived, professional German officer, Captain Hans Otto, who had been in Danish service until he surrendered on Öland. Numbers are uncertain. Altogether, Elfsborg's garrison consisted of two or three companies of foot. Stiernskiöld had orders to assume command from Stråle, who had complained that the castle was indefensible. However, he did not get there in time before the Danes arrived.

Modernised and extended after the conclusion of the Nordic Seven Years' War and then again during the 1600s, Elfsborg Castle was a strong fortress.[12] The entire fortress covered a distance of 370 m from east to west and 150–200 m from north to south, which made Elfsborg a large castle in Scandinavia.[13] Based on a citadel built according to the *trace italienne*, with outer defences in the form of a moat and bastions, Elfsborg Castle was built on a rock, from 15–20 m in height, with steep cliffs facing the south and west. The north side sloped down towards the estuary. However, the castle had

---

11 Perhaps his garrison counted slightly more men: Elfsborg and Gullberg Castles together were said to be defended by two or three companies, which suggests a total of some 1,000 men. Elfsborg was the larger castle, so Stråle possibly had more men at his disposal in the initial stages of the siege. However, it is just as likely that the companies were understrength. Broomé, *Nils Stiernsköld*, p.78, suggests 200 men from various units. Generalstaben, *Sveriges krig 1611–1632*, vol. 1, p.285; Hedberg (ed.), *Kungl. Artilleriet: Yngre vasatiden*, p.181.

12 The first modernisation project was undertaken by the Flemish architect Hans Hendrik van Paesschen, who already projected the first bastions at Elfsborg in 1559 or 1561, before he left Swedish service and instead went to work on Bohus Castle for King Frederick II of Denmark. Work continued in 1577–1578 under Johan (Giovanni) Baptista Pahr.

13 In comparison, Bohus Castle covered an area of 290m by 200m, while Varberg Castle covered 300 m by 175 m.

THE KALMAR WAR

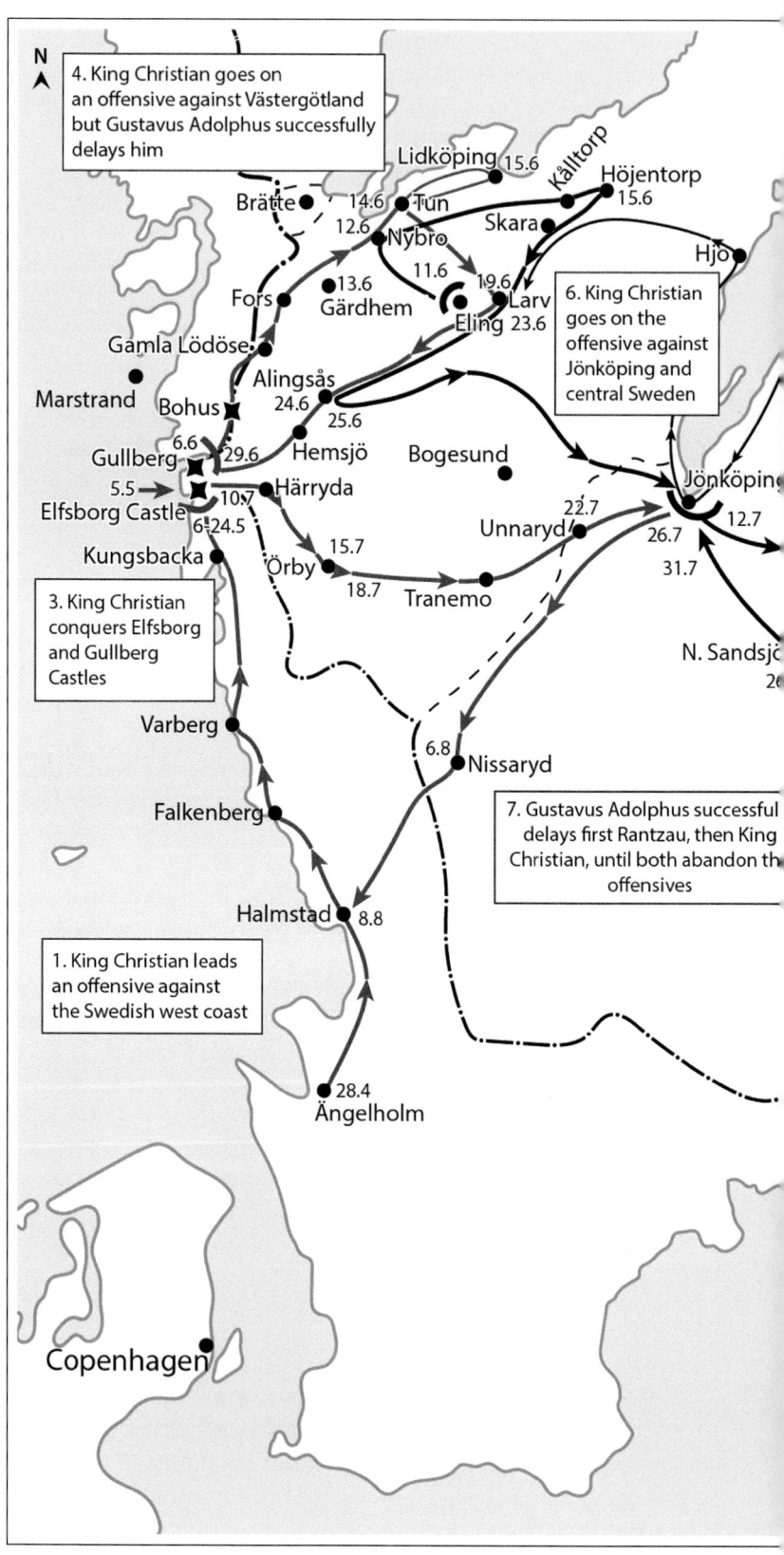

SUMMER CAMPAIGN

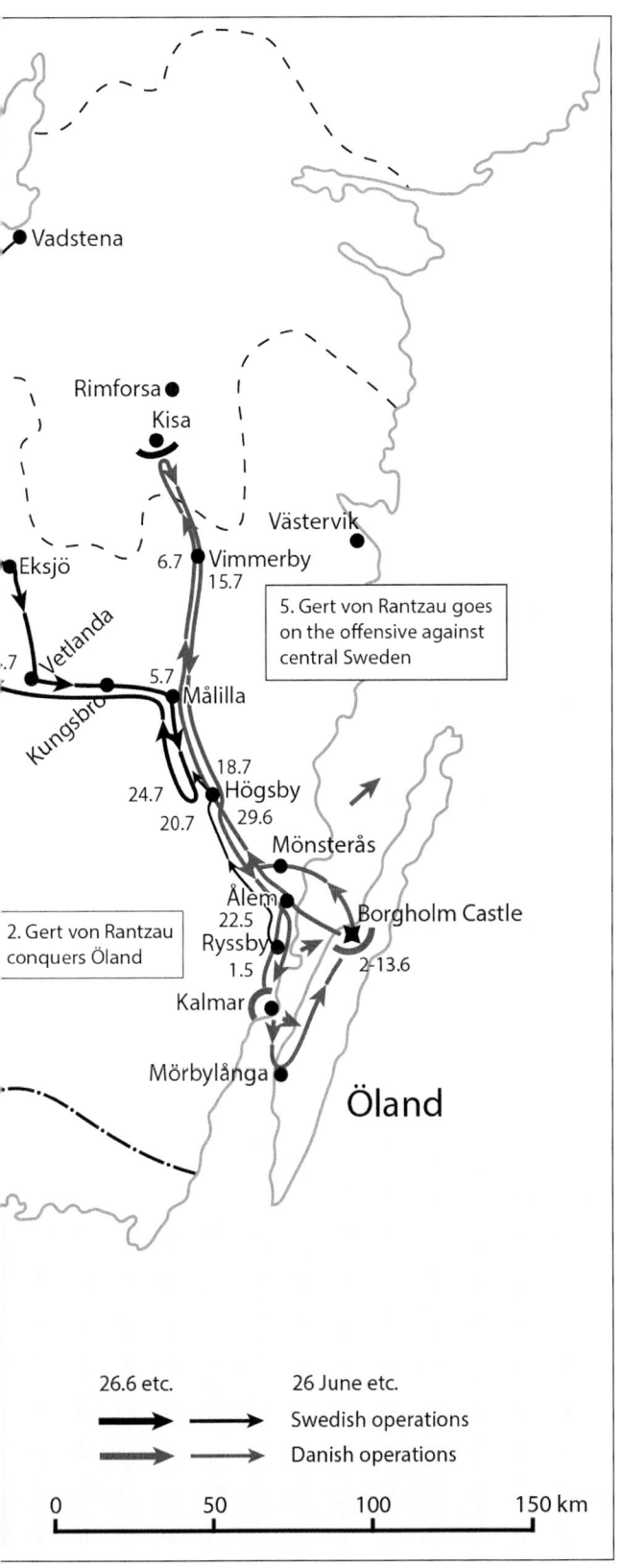

Map 8. Operations in the summer of 1612

THE KALMAR WAR

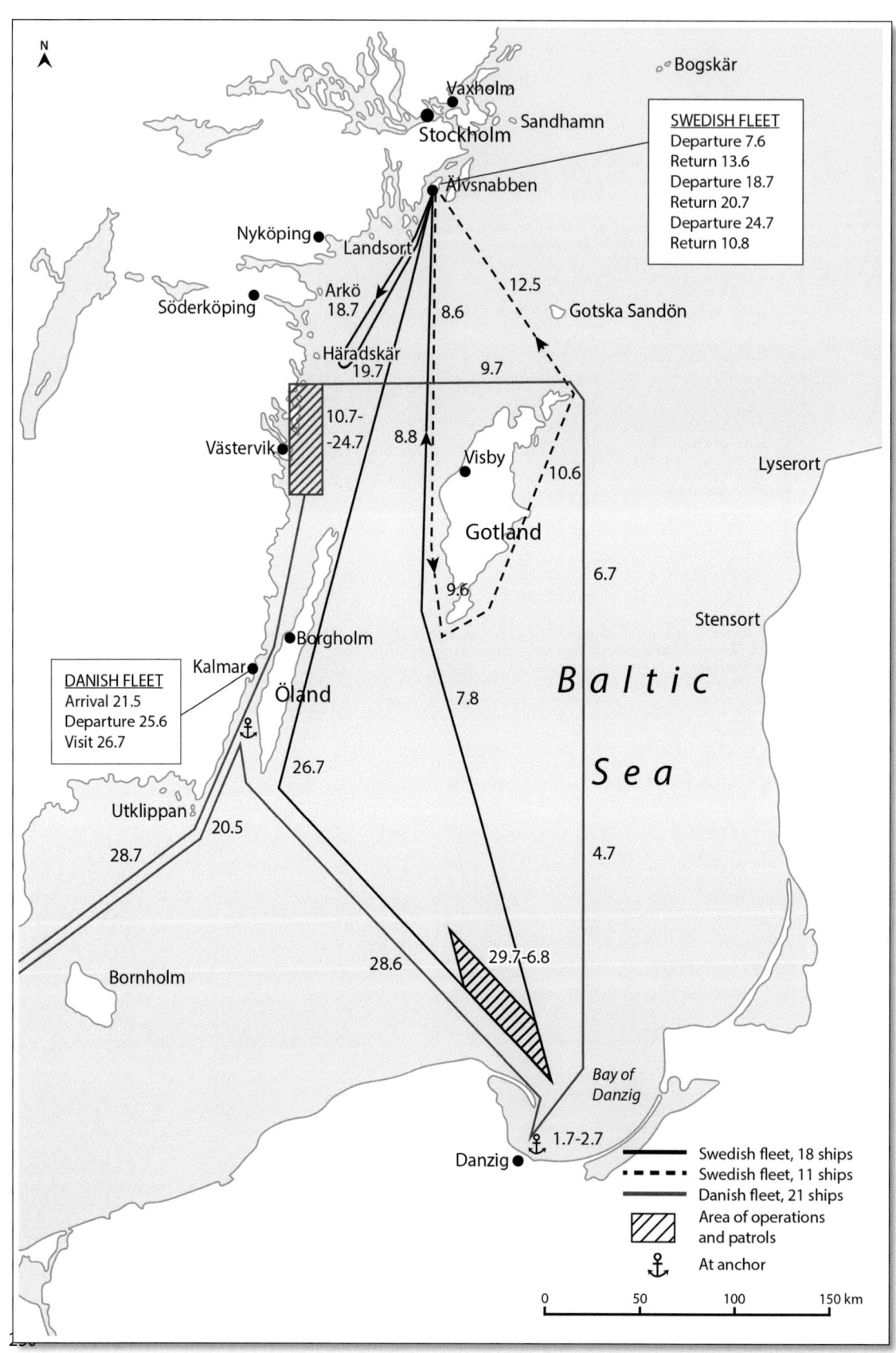

serious weaknesses. The towers were built of wood, which could not sustain attacks by fire. The moat contained some water, but water depth depended on rain and perhaps local wells, was very shallow, and, as we will see, easy to overcome by a determined attacker. Beyond the moat, only wooden palisades protected the outer courtyard. Another weakness was that the east side of the citadel rock was easy to climb. Moreover, to the east of the castle, at a distance of some 200m, there was a lower rock, known as '*Skinnareklippan*' (Skinner's Rock). An outpost consisting of a block house with a couple of cannons had been built there, from which a defender could cover the warships at anchor in the little estuary harbour below the castle. However, if an attacker gained control of Skinner's Rock, he was already within musket range of the castle, and his men could take cover in the block house. The castle defences were upgraded from 1609 onwards according to the Spanish–Dutch system. During the renovation, a new bastion was built to protect the citadel from Skinner's Rock in case the latter fell to enemy action. The main gate into the castle was located in the wall between the citadel and the rock. Elfsborg was also vulnerable from an area of low hills to the south and south-west of the castle. Siege artillery positioned there might be able to lay down a devastating fire on the castle.

Preparing for the campaign against Elfsborg, Jens Munk landed sailors and soldiers from the warships who, in a series of actions, secured those islands that, if Swedish artillery deployed on them, could threaten the arrival of Danish ships.

On 2 May, King Christian set sail, on the *Victor*, from Helsingør in the Danish Strait with Lindenow's squadron of the main fleet towards Elfsborg. The squadron was accompanied by transports, for, three days later, the King disembarked four companies of foot near Elfsborg Castle. They were joined by the four companies of foot that, since February, had waited at Bohus Castle, upstream. Jens Munk's landing party of 200 sailors were sent ashore to dig trenches. The King encouraged them with wine from the Rhine and beer from Rostock.[14] The same day that he arrived, King Christian personally reconnoitred the enemy stronghold. Establishing a fortified camp south-west of the castle, the Danes began to lay siege works. Moreover, on the night between 7 and 8 May, the Danish King sent two warships, one of them the *Makrelen*, to take up positions in the estuary between Elfsborg and Gullberg Castles, which cut communications between the two strongholds. Siege artillery as well as the necessary tools were disembarked from the fleet. Yet more siege equipment and probably artillery arrived from Bohus Castle. Ultimately, the Danes deployed 14 siege cannons at Elfsborg. Danish units took up positions at Mölndal to prevent Swedish relief efforts from the south. On 8 May, the Danes managed to open a canal that emptied the castle's moat of water. Over time, yet more units arrived, including Jean Bouvier's French dragoon company, which had gone into Danish service in April.[15] On

Facing page:
Map 9. Naval operations in May–August 1612

---

14 Larsen, *Kalmarkrigen*, p.204.
15 Jean Bouvier is called 'Jean de Bouin' in Swedish sources. Having returned to France, Bouvier later described the war to the author Julien Peleus, who seems to have been greatly impressed by

12 May, the Danish siege batteries were ready for action. The following day, the Danes took the outlying defences on Skinner's Rock, smashing the gate of the block house with a petard. This allowed for the deployment of cannons there, which exposed the entire castle to effective Danish artillery fire. With the arrival of the final units of Lord Willoughby's enlisted English regiment of foot, by the end of May, King Christian's army reached a strength of an estimated 10,200 men (2,300 horse and 7,900 foot), divided into 11 banners of cavalry, one company of dragoons, and 34 companies of foot.

[See Table 17, **King Christian's Western Army at Elfsborg Castle, May 1612**, end of chapter]

Following two-days' artillery bombardment, King Christian demanded that Stråle surrender the castle. Biding for time, Stråle asked for a two-week armistice, which the Danish King refused. Danish sappers, tunnelling, undermined the walls. On 17 May, they exploded a mine under one of them. Violent fighting later the same day took place around Skinner's Rock, which a Swedish sally force regained. The Danish sentries had not been diligent, as a Danish source later concludes. However, probably within hours, the Danes again gained the outworks in a counterattack. Soon, Danes under Jens Munk placed mines also at the walls next to the moat.

On the night to 22 May, the Danes commenced an intensive artillery bombardment of Elfsborg Castle. From 6:30 to 9:30 a.m., the Danish artillery concentrated fire on a widening breach in the south-western section of the wall. Jean Bouvier's dragoons then stormed Skinner's Rock, reportedly under the personal command of King Christian. The petardier Grandfond managed to break open the gate to the Skinner's Rock block house. The Swedes there retreated, after which Elfsborg Castle's position was untenable. The Danes offered Stråle the opportunity to surrender, but he again refused. The artillery bombardment resumed. Meanwhile, King Christian ordered four English companies of foot to storm Elfsborg at 7:00 p.m., but they were pushed back. There may have been a second assault, led by Duke George of Brunswick-Lüneburg's regiment and the King's Regiment. Surviving sources are unclear on this point since enlisted English companies existed in these two regiments as well. If there was a second assault, it was again repulsed. In any case, Albert Skeel, the captain of the Ribe Banner, reported that the attempt(s) cost the Danes 200 men. However, the Swedes also lost many men.

Among other defensive weapons, the Swedes used incendiaries like the incendiary wreath, a wreath of flammable materials such as straw, tow, or oakum soaked in pitch or tar, no less than 40 cm in diameter, at times wrapped around an iron frame for stability, and enclosed in sailcloth. Unfortunately for the Swedes, some incendiaries accidently set a Swedish wooden tower on fire, after which defence became impossible. Stråle had suffered a thigh wound, and some 100 to 150 defenders had fallen. When King Christian again demanded the castle's surrender, Stråle asked for respite until 8:00 a.m.

'le brave Bouvier'.

the following day (23 May). The next morning, he agreed to surrender in return for free departure with personal belongings, weapons, colours, and full military honours.

The following day, Stråle and his remaining 250 to 300 men, the wounded and ill included, marched off to join Swedish forces elsewhere. A German master artilleryman named Hans Jonas, who had deserted from the Danish army at Kalmar, was recognised by his former comrades, who pulled him out of the Swedish column. There were rumours that he had tried to shoot King Christian. The unfortunate man was immediately executed for treason by the wheel and quartering.[16] Neither Hans Otto nor the other Germans who had gone into Swedish service on Öland suffered this fate. They departed, bound for home, having agreed not to serve Sweden anymore. Stråle was later court-martialled for having surrendered too easily.[17]

The Danes soon restored the castle and installed a garrison under the aforementioned Albert Skeel. King Christian then turned on Gullberg Castle. On 28 May, he sent Lunge's regiment against the castle. The next night, Lunge's regiment took some of the outer earthworks, and, either on this day or the following, when the King himself arrived, the Danes commenced an artillery bombardment. On 31 May, King Christian demanded the surrender of Gullberg. No longer defended by Lady Emerentia and Mårten Krakow, who had been transferred elsewhere earlier in the month, the new commanders of Gullberg – Rasmus Tordsson, Tomas Est, and Paul Wulf, captain of an Östergötland company – accepted to surrender in exchange for free departure with their personal belongings and one of their colours. They marched out on 1 June. King Christian first had Gullberg Castle garrisoned, but, later in the month, he ordered it demolished. Having conquered the River Göta Älv Estuary and seen the Swedish Elfsborg Squadron scuttled, he felt sufficiently secure to order a part of Daa's squadron to the Baltic Sea. The remaining warships were ordered to hunt for Swedish privateers, several of which operated along the western seashore.

The Danes also set out to salvage the six scuttled Swedish warships. The *Hektor*, *Blå Ormen*, *Krabban*, and *Lamprellen* were salvaged before the end of June. The *Jonas* was badly damaged but could be salvaged later. The *Fransiscus*, which was the most badly damaged, could not be raised.[18]

---

16   The unfortunate Hans Jonas absconded from the Danish army and joined the garrison at Kalmar Castle on 6 May 2011. Anon., 'Journal', p.680. Since Hans Jonas greatly feared the revenge of King Christian, the castle commandant, Christer Some, ultimately sent him to the Swedish camp at Ryssby so that he would not risk capture if the castle fell. Wadén, *Berättande källor*, p.48, n.6, with references.

17   The court process, which was characterised by legal irregularities and included testimonies from both Swedish and Danish officers, took years to reach a verdict. In 1619, Stråle was sentenced to death for handing over the castle prematurely and for various related offences. Fortunately for Stråle, Gustavus Adolphus was not his father. Despite being displeased with the circumstances of Stråle's surrender, the King pardoned him and changed the sentence into a fine.

18   The likely remnants of the *Fransiscus* were found in an archaeological excavation in 2005.

THE KALMAR WAR

Above: Somewhat imaginary but likely reasonably accurate reconstruction of Elfsborg Castle, as it may have appeared in 1612, as seen from the south. (Gothenburg City Museum; photo: dagjoh)

Below: Elfsborg Castle after numerous improvements, mid to late seventeenth century. Although the defences would have been less elaborate in 1612, this illustration, as seen from the south, gives a better view of the site. This drawing also depicts the small, sheltered port east of the stronghold, located between the castle and (not depicted) the vulnerable Skinner's Rock, and it depicts the protected channel that provided access to the River Göta Älv, north of the site. (Erik Dahlbergh)

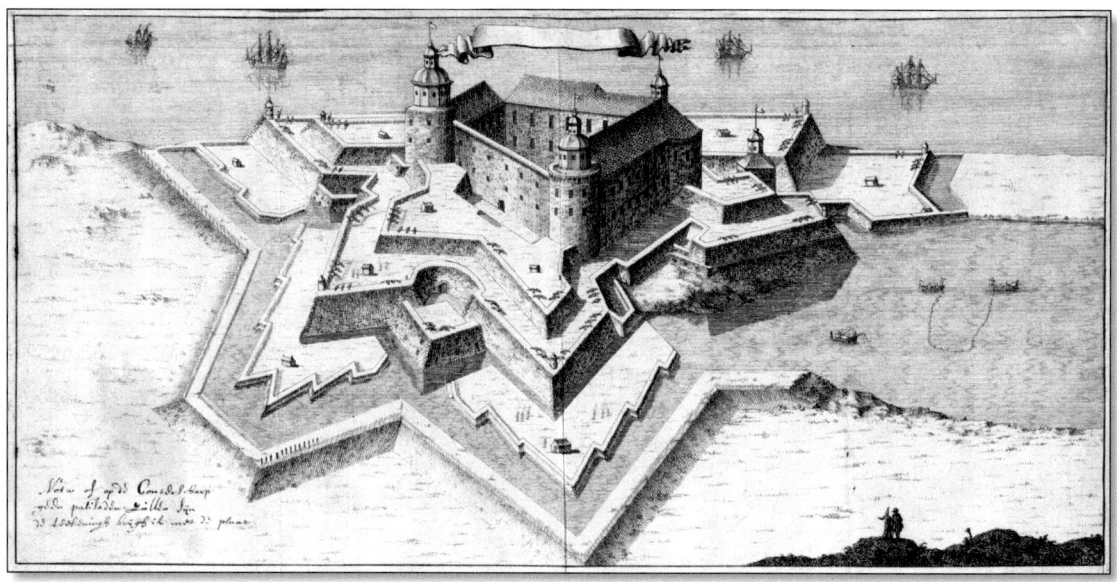

SUMMER CAMPAIGN

Above: The siege of Elfsborg Castle, 1612. Although still often reprinted, the depiction is inaccurate. The print fails to show the water-filled moat and the small port attached to the castle, which is represented too far inland. While the drawings of soldiers are contemporary, the illustration as a whole was based on an earlier print of a previous siege of Elfsborg Castle ('Elseburg') that took place during the Nordic Seven Years' War. Moreover, the original print depicted two actions in the same print: the siege of Elfsborg Castle and a naval battle off Öland. When the print was redrawn in 1612, the artist failed to separate the two (for further details, see Ingel Wadén, 'Ett kopparstick över Elfsborgs belägring 1612', Rig, 20:3 (1937), pp.147–55). Contemporary writers realised the mistake, so when the depiction was reprinted in Gottfried's famous Inventarium Sueciae, it was indeed included in the section describing the previous war. Because of the spelling employed in some versions of the print ('Elsenburg'), the stronghold is sometimes inaccurately identified as Helsingborg. (Georg Keller?)

THE KALMAR WAR

It seemed to King Christian that there were no longer any Swedish armed units in Västergötland. He accordingly revised (we must assume) his campaign plan. Instead of going on the offensive towards Jönköping and onwards to the north from there or along the eastern seashore, the Danes would proceed straight north through Västergötland. If no more organised Swedish defences remained there, there was no need to wait further. On 6 June, King Christian marched north into Västergötland with 10 cavalry banners, one dragoon company, and 30 companies of foot. However, because of the poor road, he left his artillery behind.[19] He marched along the River Göta Älv by way of Bohus Castle and Gamla Lödöse towards Lidköping.

Incendiary wreath (Swedish: *stormkrans* or *beckkrans med blånor*, the former term meaning 'assault wreath'). (Author's collection)

King Christian IV, as conqueror of Elfsborg Castle. The depiction of the castle shows the gate tower, which collapsed on 22 May 1612. (Silver medal by Thomas Borstorff, 1612; photo: Gabriel Hildebrand, Economy Museum – Royal Coin Cabinet/SHM, Stockholm)

---

19 Generalstaben, *Sveriges krig 1611–1632*, vol. 1, p.290.

Tables

Table 15. Danish Fleets and Squadrons, Spring 1612[20]

Skagerrak Squadron (Total strength: five warships)	
Commander	Admiral Jørgen Daa
Base	Copenhagen and Kalundborg, Zealand
Ready for action	Mid March
Disbanded	Late May (part remained on station)
Sorte Hund ('Black Dog', 12)	Steffen Sørensen
Makrelen ('Mackerel', 6?)	Oluf Normand
Røde Løve ('Red Lion', 6)	Anders Nolk
Turtelduen ('Turtledove')	Claus Pofvelsen
Heringnæs (18)	Jens Munk

Main Fleet[21] (Total strength: 21 warships)	
Commander	Admiral Mogens Ulfeldt
Base	Copenhagen
Ready for action	Early April (first squadron), mid May (second squadron), and early May (third squadron)
Disbanded	Late July

First Squadron	
Commander	Jacob Beck
Lybske David ('Lübeck David', 22)	Jacob Beck
Penitens (14)	-
Sankt Michael ('St Michael', 20)	-
Jupiter (16)	John Cunningham (also known as Hans Köning or König)
Markatten ('Guenon', 16)	Johan Mortensen
Sankt Peder ('St Peter', ex-Swedish *Sankt Per*, 12)	Peter Jacobsen

Second Squadron[22]	
Commander	Gabriel Kruse

---

20 The captain of each vessel is, when known, given after the ship's name. When known, each ship's number of cannons in 1611 is given in parentheses, sometimes after a translation of the ship's name. Generalstaben, *Sveriges krig 1611–1632*, suppl. vol. 1, pp.282–83.

21 From mid August to late September, the main fleet was reinforced with another 15 warships, including almost certainly the *Krokodillen*, *Forloren Søn*, *Spes*, *Josaphat*, *Røde Løve* (ex-Swedish *Röda Lejonet*), and most of the Skagerrak Squadron, including the Swedish prize ships taken at Elfsborg. King Christian assumed personal command of the main fleet, with the *Victor* as his flagship.

22 Probably included four other warships: the *Tre Kroner* ('Three Crowns', 64?), *Concordia* (23?), *Gideon* (34?), and *Enhjørning* ('Unicorn', 18?).

THE KALMAR WAR

Argorosa (38)	Gabriel Kruse
Lindormen ('Serpent', 16)	Gert Johansen Blok
Sankt Anna ('St Anna', 36)	Johan Diriksen Vagebund
Argo (44) [Flagship]	-
Justitia (37)	Willum Petersen Spition
Mælkepige ('Milkmaid', ex-Swedish *Mjölkpigan*, 18)	Sten Willumsen
Gabriel (22)	Claus Petersen
Trøst ('Consolation')	Erik Høg
Third Squadron[23]	
Commander	Godske Lindenow
Victor (37)	Godske Lindenow
Leoparden ('Leopard', 20)	Envold Stygge
Raphael (18)	Jacob Claussen

Table 16. Swedish Fleets and Squadrons Deployed for Participation in the Kalmar War, Spring 1612[24]

Main Fleet (Total strength: 17 warships and two pinnaces)	
Commander	Grand Admiral of the Realm Göran Gyllenstierna
Bases	Stockholm
Ready for action	Late May (first squadron) and mid June (second squadron)
Disbanded	Early October
First Squadron	
Commander	Admiral Richard Clerck
Draken ('Dragon', 16)	Junker Nobis
Justitia (16)	Erik Bertilsson
Meerman (14)	Anders Svensson
Gula Lejonet ('Yellow Lion', 16)	-
Leoparden ('Leopard', 16)	Johan von Bergen
Concordia (28)	Lars Bubb
Lybska Salvator ('Lübeck Salvator', 10) [Pinnace]	Lars Torstensson
Mercurius (12)	Jacob Bülow
Vita Falken ('White Falcon', 12)	Daniel Andersson

---

23 After transporting King Christian and units of his army to Elfsborg, this squadron joined the main fleet in late May.

24 Fleet elements remained on the eastern front as well. The captain of each vessel is, when known, given after the ship's name. When known, each ship's number of cannons in 1612 is given in parentheses, sometimes after a translation of the ship's name. Generalstaben, *Sveriges krig 1611-1632*, suppl. vol. 1, pp.280–81.

Hollands Svanen ('Dutch Swan', 16)	Lars Mattsson
Hollands Ängeln ('Dutch Angel', 16)	Anders Påvelsson

Second Squadron	
Commander	Admiral Hans Bielkenstierna
Tre Kronor ('Three Crowns', 40)	Alexander Foratt
Svarta Hunden ('Black Dog', 26)	Peter Fransson
Spegeln ('Mirror', 30)	Måns Eskilsson
Oraniebom (28)	Anders Nilsson
Smålands Lejonet ('Småland Lion', 40) [Flagship]	Nils Olsson Hinseberg
Jägaren ('Huntsman', 10)	Lars Persson
Danska Stjärnan ('Danish Star', 18)	-
Samson (20)	Jacob Gottberg and Per Andersson

Stockholm Squadron (Total strength: three pinnaces, one praam, and one boyer)	
Base	Stockholm
Ready for action	Late August
Disbanded	Mid October
Basiliscus (6)	-
Finken ('Finch', 8)	-
Angelus	-
Nya byggningen ('New Construction')	-
Stora bojorten ('Great Boyer')	Göran Göransson

Elfsborg Squadron (Total strength: six warships)	
Base	Elfsborg Castle
Ready for action	Although not disbanded in the previous autumn, only half were ready for action in early April.
Disbanded	Although all crews scuttled their own ships rather than seeing them fall into Danish hands, the Danes salvaged all ships except the *Franciskus* after the fall of Elfsborg Castle.
Hector	-
Blå Ormen ('Blue Snake')	-
Franciskus	-
Krabban ('Crab')	-
Lamprellen ('Lamprey')	-
Jonas ('Jonah')	-

Table 17. King Christian's Western Army at Elfsborg Castle, May 1612[25]

Cavalry		
Unit	Banners/Companies	Strength[26]
Court Banner	1	300*
Fyn Banner (retinue of nobles)	1	150*
Aalborg Banner (retinue of nobles)	1	393[27]
Aarhus Banner (retinue of nobles)	1	
Ribe Banner (retinue of nobles)	1	
The King's Life Banner (under Joachim von Bülow)	1	200*
Duke George of Brunswick-Lüneburg's Harquebusier Company	1	200*
Jacob Prenger's Harquebusier Company (Duke George's second cavalry unit)	1	176
Cornelius Post's Harquebusier Company	1	229
Benedict Bernd von Hagen's Harquebusier Company	1	200*
Franz Ernst von Dalwig's Harquebusier Company	1	200*
Total	11	2,048*

Dragoons		
Unit	Companies	Strength
Jean Bouvier's French Dragoon Company	1	240
Total	1	240

Infantry		
Unit	Companies	Strength
The King's Regiment	4	1,200*
Duke George of Brunswick-Lüneburg's Regiment	7	1,800*
Jørgen Lunge's Regiment	7	1,400*
Peregrine Bertie Lord Willoughby's Regiment	14	3,130
John Selby's Company	1	200*
Johan Kaufmann's Company	1	200*
Total	34	7,930*
Grand Total		10,200*

25 Generalstaben, *Sveriges krig 1611–1632*, vol. 1, p.286; Larsen, *Kalmarkrigen*, pp.199–201.
26 Asterisk indicates estimated strength.
27 The combined total strength of the separate Aalborg, Aarhus, and Ribe banners.

15

Gustavus Adolphus's Response

The Swedish position had grown very difficult. Hitherto preoccupied with the Danish invasion, Gustavus Adolphus fully knew that he must also consider the situation on the eastern frontier, where decisive action at this point might result in significant gains that, in the long term, would also reinforce the Swedish position versus Denmark. On 26 May, Gustavus Adolphus wrote to Duke John, asking him to assume command in the war against Denmark and Norway so that he could sail to Finland to assume command in Muscovy.[1] First, however, the King wanted to see the situation in Västergötland province for himself. This was a wise decision. Arriving at Mariestad on 7 June, Gustavus Adolphus learnt that both Elfsborg and Gullberg Castles were in Danish hands. Meanwhile, the Danish fleet dominated the southern Baltic Sea. Two Danish armies stood on Swedish soil, one in the west and the other in the east. Gustavus Adolphus had to postpone the voyage to the eastern front. He would not gamble the homeland for the chance to gain Muscovy.

Gustavus Adolphus knew that he could not stop the Danes if they operated as a united force. His only recourse was to prevent the reunification of the Danish armies. Rantzau's Kalmar army was again engaged on Öland. King Christian's army was the more urgent threat.

When King Christian moved into Västergötland, he had to divide his army into three columns for logistical reasons.[2] On the road, he learnt that Cruus, and soon Gustavus Adolphus, also operated farther east. This did not deter the Danish King, who probably reckoned that his army was stronger than anything the Swedes could raise in the region.

This opened an opportunity for Gustavus Adolphus. While he could not outfight the united Danish army, he could deal with it when divided into columns. He switched to a harassing and delaying strategy. He ordered local peasants to build abatis to block the roads. At least one enterprising local freebooter, Gisle Andersson, received a patent to raise young men eager for plunder who were then free to attack anybody who spoke out in favour of the

---

1 Henrik Horn to Duke John, 26 May 1612, and Gustavus Adolphus to Duke John, 30 May 1612, both cited in Petri, *Kungl. Första livgrenadjärregementets historia*, pp.397–98.

2 Larsen, *Kalmarkrigen*, p.209.

Danes and take their belongings and to raid Danish territories if they could.[3] By manoeuvring around the Danish army, Gustavus Adolphus managed to delay it until Danish supplies began to run out. Albert Skeel again complained, this time in a letter to his wife Birte (Berte), that he and his men suffered from a shortage of beer. Moreover, the presence of the Swedish army compelled King Christian to gather his columns into one. This made it yet more difficult to find supplies. The enlisted units complained, being close to mutiny. In the end, King Christian had to retreat. By the end of June, he had returned to Gullberg.

On 13 June, at Gärdhem, King Christian learnt from captured prisoners that the Swedish King stood at Nybro with 10 cavalry banners and 10 companies of foot (a good estimate: Gustavus Adolphus had eight cavalry banners and 11 companies of foot at the time).[4] King Christian had been right: the Swedes were too few to confront the Danish army directly. Gustavus Adolphus withdrew. When King Christian reached Nybro on 14 June, he found the Swedish camp abandoned. Yet, by then, King Christian faced problems of another kind. The supply situation had not improved, and disease had begun to spread within his army. He abandoned the attempt to find the Swedish army, instead establishing a camp at Tun on Lake Vänern. Although he, on 15 June, led his cavalry and 500 musketeers all the way to Lidköping, he found the town abandoned so then ordered a general retreat south towards Alingsås.[5]

Patrick Rutherford's regiment of Scots and Irish foot had indeed stayed in Lidköping during the winter. Most of the time, they had been unwilling to march out since, in their opinion, they were paid too little and too infrequently. However, by this time, Rutherford's men had joined forces with Gustavus Adolphus's field army. The same day that King Christian marched into Lidköping, the Swedish army moved into Höjentorp, north-east of Skara, farther to the east. At the same time, Duke John was on his way, too, with additional reinforcements from the direction of Vadstena. Duke John had expected to catch up with the Swedish King at Jönköping, but, learning of the events in Västergötland, he had then rounded Lake Vättern and instead marched on Skara.

Suddenly, it was the Danish King who was pursued by his Swedish counterpart, not vice versa as previously. The aggressive pursuit of Gustavus Adolphus resulted in several skirmishes between his vanguard and the Danish rearguard. Meanwhile, King Christian continued the retreat. He left Alingsås on 24 June, and, the following day, the Swedish King marched into the town. King Christian retreated all the way to Gullberg, where his army established a camp on 29 June. Realising that, even with the reinforcements currently available to him, the Swedish field army was too weak to regain the River Göta Älv Estuary, Gustavus Adolphus abandoned the pursuit of the Danish King,

---

3 Larsen, *Kalmarkrigen*, p.212.
4 Generalstaben, *Sveriges krig 1611–1632*, vol. 1, pp.291–92; Petri, *Kungl. Första livgrenadjärregementets historia*, p.400.
5 Generalstaben, *Sveriges krig 1611–1632*, vol. 1, p.293.

reversing course towards Jönköping, where he moved in on 2 July. Three days later, Duke John joined him there with his men.

The Fall of Ryssby

The Swedish King had ordered Admiral Bååt again to resume command in eastern Småland. Before Bååt managed to assemble the Småland units, which he was expected to rely upon as a reserve, the Danish commandant in Kalmar, Andrew Sinclair, sent Major Peter von Heinemark and Captain Holger Rosencrantz, with their respective companies of the King's Regiment, against the fortified Swedish camp at Ryssby.

Bååt was already preparing to abandon the camp when the Danes arrived early in the morning of 1 May. The Swedish camp was divided by the Stream Thorsbäck, which by this time had greatly expanded by the melting snow. Heinemark and Rosencrantz assaulted and took the part of the camp south of the Thorsbäck, after which Heinemark waded across the cold stream, the water now reaching his armpits. When the Swedes in a redoubt north of the stream refused to surrender, he and his men stormed it. By all accounts, there was only a skeleton garrison in Ryssby, so the Danes took the camp without further difficulties.

The reason was that Bååt and most Swedes had withdrawn to Ålem, where he had built and fortified a new camp. Presumably, the Ryssby camp was too large to defend with the men then available to Bååt. From Ålem, Bååt sent raiding parties against Ryssby and Kalmar. Bååt was greatly outnumbered: even had he managed to assemble his three banners and eight companies of foot, they likely counted 2,000 men at most – a fourth of Rantzau's army.[6]

It had taken longer for Gert von Rantzau than for King Christian to gather his troops for the summer offensive since he first had to assemble the newly enlisted German units in the ports of Wismar, Warnemünde, and Heiligenhafen. Having finally arrived in Kalmar, Gert von Rantzau accordingly decided to push Bååt and his men out of the new camp as well. On 22 May, Rantzau led the army out of Kalmar. He also sent three cavalry banners on a flank march with orders to attack Ålem in the rear. Bååt, however, continued the delaying action, retreating to Högsby, where he secured to road to Jönköping. Unwilling to continue farther, Rantzau returned to Kalmar.

Back to Öland

Instead of allowing himself to be drawn farther inland, Rantzau wanted to carry out King Christian's order to reconquer Öland. As we have seen, their plan was probably that Rantzau would take Ryssby and Öland while King Christian took Elfsborg Castle, after which the two would join forces for the invasion of the Swedish heartland. Öland was defended by Per Hammarskiöld,

---

6   Generalstaben, *Sveriges krig 1611–1632*, vol. 1, p.284.

who had few men at his disposal to defend the entire island: his old Småland Banner of cavalry, one Öland company, two Småland companies, two Dalecarlian companies, one Finnish company, and the peasant levy.[7]

Hammarskiöld had proven himself a nuisance to the Danes more than once. On 29 April, boats from Öland set out to capture a Danish boyer from Ystad, loaded with beer and bound for Kalmar. In response, three Danish yachts from Kalmar, with 140 soldiers, set out to give chase. Ultimately, they managed to retake the boyer with its precious cargo.

By the end of May, Rantzau's entire army and the Danish main fleet had assembled at Kalmar. Rantzau drew up an ambitious plan, according to which landings would take place at night in three locations on the Öland coastline: in the north, at Färjestaden just across the strait from Kalmar, and in the south. Having landed, they would establish bridgeheads, after which the main force would be shipped across the strait under the artillery cover of the main fleet to Mörbylånga, where the main bridgehead would be established. The plan was carried out during the night between 30 and 31 May, and, the following morning, the main force was shipped across the strait, including the siege artillery.

Hammarskiöld had prepared a strong redoubt at Färjestaden. However, with the Danish main bridgehead in another location and under cannon fire from the Danish warships, he had to evacuate the redoubt, withdrawing into another fortified position about 10 km south of Borgholm Castle. On 1 June, Hammarskiöld deployed his available men (the Småland Banner, three companies of foot, perhaps six light cannons, and the levies), with the soldiers in the centre and the peasant levies on the flanks.[8] The Danes, superior in numbers, attacked his centre. The Swedes repulsed the first Danish charge, but, in their second charge, the Danes managed to disperse the outnumbered Swedish cavalry and separate them from the infantry. Rantzau thereby also managed to separate the Swedish units from Borgholm Castle, which the Danes now surrounded. During the same night, the Danes began to build a siege artillery battery at Borgholm, but the Swedish counterfire from the castle delayed them so that it was only during the night of 6–7 June that the Danes managed to deploy their 24-pounders. Within days, Rantzau brought in an additional four heavy cannons. On 2 June, Rantzau also sent a trumpeter to demand the castle's surrender. Hammarskiöld refused. The artillery fire caused significant damage. Hammarskiöld and his men repaired the damages to tower and walls as well as they could, but the damage increased faster than they could repair it. On 12 June, there was a breach in the wall big enough 'to drive through with four carts in a line'.[9]

At this point, Hammarskiöld let the Danes know that he was ready to discuss terms of surrender. The Danish side, at first, claimed that it was too late to surrender since the wall was already breached. Nonetheless, on 13 June, another trumpeter arrived, offering the Swedish soldiers the chance

---

7 Generalstaben, *Sveriges krig 1611–1632*, vol. 1, pp.283, 296.
8 Generalstaben, *Sveriges krig 1611–1632*, vol. 1, p.297.
9 Hammarskiöld's report, cited in Generalstaben, *Sveriges krig 1611–1632*, vol. 1, p.297.

GUSTAVUS ADOLPHUS'S RESPONSE

Rantzau's men land on Öland, 31 May 1612, as depicted in one of the Frederiksborg Castle tapestries celebrating events during the Kalmar War. (Frederik Christian Lund, after Karel van Mander II)

to surrender but not extending this courtesy to Hammarskiöld. The Swedes refused to give up their commander, threatening to set fire to the gunpowder depot and blow the entire castle. Rantzau then gave in, offering free departure to all, with their personal belongings, as long as they swore an oath not to raise arms against the Danish Crown for three months. Hammarskiöld agreed and surrendered the castle. However, the Danish soldiers attempted to massacre the 500 Swedish survivors as they departed and plundered their belongings. Apparently, only 200 survived. Because of the plundering, Hammarskiöld later announced that the oath they had sworn was no longer valid.

On 20 June, the Danish army returned to Kalmar, leaving Christian Friis with five companies of foot to garrison the island.[10]

By the end of June, Rantzau's field army consisted of some 8,000 men, but some units were tied up as garrisons in Kalmar and on Öland. Probably, only an estimated 6,500 men were available for the field army.

---

10   Generalstaben, *Sveriges krig 1611–1632*, vol. 1, p.298.

Table 18. Gert von Rantzau's Eastern Army at Ålem, late June 1612[11]

Cavalry		
Unit	Banners/Companies	Strength[12]
Zealand Banner (retinue of nobles, under Christer Hansen)	1	202
Schleswig Banner (under Andreas Flotow)	1	200*
Duke Ernest Louis of Saxe-Lauenburg's Harquebusier Company	1	max. 200
Gert von Rantzau's Harquebusier Company	1	200*
Rabe Philip Bogreben's Harquebusier Company	1	200*
Marquard von Pentz's Harquebusier Company	1	200*
Total	6	1,200*

Dragoons		
Unit	Companies	Strength
Eustachius de Carmissin's Dragoon Company (formerly under the late Dupuis)	1	120*
Total	1	120*

Infantry[13]		
Unit	Companies[14]	Strength
Duke Ernest Louis of Saxe-Lauenburg's Regiment	7*	
Gert von Rantzau's Regiment	10–11*	
Michael von Wustrow's Regiment	10*	
Marquard von Pentz's Companies	2*	
Jens Sparre's Company	1	
Georg Hartwig von Veltheim's Company	1	
Total	31*	6,800*
Grand Total		8,120*

---

11 Generalstaben, *Sveriges krig 1611–1632*, vol. 1, p.299; Larsen, *Kalmarkrigen*, pp.199–201.
12 Asterisk indicates estimated strength.
13 Five unidentified infantry companies of those listed remained detached as an occupation force on Öland.
14 Asterisk indicates estimated number of companies.

16

The Overland Offensive Towards the Swedish Heartland

Rantzau had done well, but he had heard nothing from King Christian for some time. Assuming that the overall strategy still entailed an offensive towards the north along the Baltic coast, Rantzau arranged with Admiral Ulfeldt that the fleet should sail north, take the town of Västervik, and assemble cargo ships with food supplies there as a means of supplying the marching army. Rantzau himself would then finally embark upon the long-planned offensive towards the north with the field army.

On 25 June, Rantzau marched out for the offensive towards the north, while the Danish main fleet set out bound for Danzig. Admiral Ulfeldt responded to a false rumour that Sweden and the Commonwealth had signed a peace treaty and that the Swedish main fleet had sailed to Danzig to embark enlisted units now released from service. The Danish fleet arrived in Danzig on 1 July, but, having ascertained that the rumour was false, soon departed the following day. The fleet then sailed north, circled Gotland, and, on 10 July, reached the seas off Västervik.

Concerned that Bååt still operated in his flank, Rantzau decided not to take the coastal road but instead to first march along the main road by way of Högsby and Målilla to Vimmerby, from which there was a trail to Västervik. Although the main road was superior to the coastal road, Rantzau probably did not know that the continuation to Västervik was only suitable for men and horses, not carts. We have seen that the Swedes frequently suffered from poor intelligence collection, but Danish intelligence was no better. This was also evident from the fact that, by then, Rantzau was out of communication with King Christian and the Danish army on the western front. Rantzau wrote to the King that he hoped to receive orders in Vimmerby. If not, Rantzau would act according to the circumstances. Rantzau finally sent a message to King Christian that he would now march west towards Jönköping. When King Christian received the message, he likewise moved towards Jönköping.

Rantzau reached Högsby on 29 June. His men quickly dispersed the Swedish corps there, who were under Colonel Jesper Andersson Cruus (Swedish cavalry and infantry, Halswell's English dragoons, and levies). Andersson and his men quickly retreated to Admiral Bååt, who was based north of Västervik. The Danes learnt from Swedish captives that Bååt had three banners of cavalry and 500 infantry. However, Rantzau then waited for a few days to gather supplies, in the meantime fortifying a position on both sides of the small River Em. The march continued on 2 July, with an advance guard of cavalry and 1,000 musketeers since the latter were more useful for combat in the Swedish forestland than the pikemen.[1] This was a wise decision because, soon, the advance guard encountered a line of abatis built by Swedish levies, who also harassed the Danes with constant attacks from small bands and snipers. Colonel von Wustrow was wounded by a well-aimed shot, and Captain von Veltheim had his horse shot under him (and ultimately fell in a later engagement on the way back to Högsby). The Danish musketeers managed to bypass the defences so that the march could continue. Soon, they encountered yet another line of abatis, this time between a stream and a cliff. Again, the musketeers managed to get through or around the defences, at which time the Swedish defenders withdrew. Yet it took time to clear the road, and Rantzau reached Målilla only on 5 July.

By then, Gustavus Adolphus had already moved into Jönköping. He assembled at least eight cavalry banners (including his Life Banner), 16 infantry companies (including six in Rutherford's regiment, six in Taube's regiment, one of which may have been the Drabant Company, and three from Västmanland and Närke), and Duke John's approximately 1,000 men. Altogether, the King's army in Jönköping consisted of an estimated 4,000 men.[2] On 5 July, Gustavus Adolphus sent a message to Hammarskiöld, ordering him to send his cavalry to the King's army and then to use the infantry and levies to delay the Danish offensive, hitting them in the flanks and rear. By then, Hammarskiöld held the coastal road north, presumably with the survivors from Öland. Meanwhile, Duke John set out to defend Östergötland by erecting a line of abatis at Kisa.

The Swedish disposition was not strong, but it controlled plenty of territory. Ahead of Rantzau's direction of march stood Duke John and his Östergötland soldiers. Gustavus Adolphus and his units operated along Rantzau's left flank, while a few of Admiral Bååt's Småland companies of foot remained in Rantzau's rear. Hammarskiöld controlled the coastal road with a weak corps. Rantzau had more men, but he faced opposition on all sides.

Yet, if King Christian advanced towards Jönköping, as the Danes clearly had planned, it would be the Swedes who were surrounded. Gustavus Adolphus must have realised that, if the two Danish armies converged on Jönköping, the Swedish position would turn disastrous. In response to such an outcome, Gustavus Adolphus called out the general levy of peasants. They initiated an effective guerrilla war against the advancing Danes. They blocked roads, destroyed bridges, and prepared abatis in strategic positions to harass the enemy. They removed everything of value and hid any remaining food

---

1 Generalstaben, *Sveriges krig 1611–1632*, vol. 1, p.301.
2 Captain Patrick Learmonth (d. 1613) commanded a company in Rutherford's regiment. Generalstaben, *Sveriges krig 1611–1632*, vol. 1, p.301; Barkman and Lundkvist, *Kungl. Svea livgardes historia*, vol. 3, part 1, p.198, n.1.

supplies. The King also called out the nobility, ordering them to Jönköping as a focus for defences. However, in the end, he was greatly disappointed in their turnout, ultimately threatening the nobility with loss of privileges if they did not live up to their responsibilities.

On 6 July, Rantzau reached Vimmerby, having marched through a desolate territory. All food had been removed by the Swedish levies, and there was nothing left of value to loot to encourage the soldiers. They found the town of Vimmerby as abandoned and empty as the other settlements that they had passed through. It became clear to Rantzau that any supplies must be sent by sea, through Västervik. We have seen that Ulfeldt's fleet moved into Västervik on 10 July, bringing in the agreed-upon supply vessels.

Meanwhile, Rantzau sent a column to the neighbouring town of Eksjö, but conditions were no better there. He also sent a column to Västervik. The detachment sent to Västervik returned with some supplies from Ulfeldt's fleet but only after eight days instead of the expected two. The supplies were insufficient. Since the trail to Västervik could only be traversed by packhorses, they had not been able to bring everything that was needed. Besides, soon afterwards (before 13–14 July), Hammarskiöld and his men, reinforced by local levies, attacked Västervik. The town caught fire during the attack, so the Danish supply vessels there abandoned the port. Hammarskiöld also attempted, but failed, to take the strongly fortified Stegeholm Castle, which by then was also held by the Danes.

It was not only Hammarskiöld who did his best to wrestle Västervik out of Danish hands. The Swedish Stockholm main fleet, 17 warships and two pinnaces under Grand Admiral of the Realm Göran Gyllenstierna, set out from Älvsnabben on 18 July. Sailing south towards the seas off Västervik, where the Danish main fleet was then operating, the excursion turned out to be a brief one. The voyage was interrupted by a severe storm, which damaged several ships, including Gyllenstierna's flagship. Already on 20 July, the fleet returned to Älvsnabben for repairs. Meanwhile, Ulfeldt's fleet continued to operate off Västervik until 24 July.

The Swedish King now seem to have planned an envelopment of Rantzau's army before it received additional support from King Christian.[3] Duke John would attack from the north, while Gustavus Adolphus would advance by way of Eksjö against Vetlanda. His men would also build a new line of abatis across Rantzau's road back to Kalmar. Reaching Vetlanda on 14 July, Gustavus Adolphus learnt that King Christian was on the way towards Jönköping. Would the Swedes be caught between the anvil and the hammer? Displaying the coolness that he later would become known for, Gustavus Adolphus realised that, because of the poor quality of the Swedish road network, the Danish King would be unable to bring any siege artillery to Jönköping. It would accordingly take time for the Danes to reduce the Swedish town. For

---

3   Axel Oxenstierna to Johan De la Gardie in Åbo and Jacob De la Gardie in Novgorod, 23 July 1612, based on Gustavus Adolphus's instructions in Jönköping on 12 July, in Axel Oxenstierna, *Rikskansleren Axel Oxenstiernas skrifter och brefvexling* (Stockholm: P. A. Norstedt, 1896), vol. 1, part 2, pp.74–75; Petri, *Kungl. Första livgrenadjärregementets historia*, p.405.

once, the young King must have been satisfied with the poor state of his country's internal communications! Meanwhile, the Swedish King would continue the envelopment operation against Rantzau. Gustavus Adolphus no doubt hoped to first destroy Rantzau's army and then King Christian's before the two managed to join forces.

The Swedish King had assessed the situation correctly. Because of the lack of supplies, Rantzau's men were close to mutiny. On 15 July, the Swedish King reached Repperda, from which he sent one cavalry banner and 200 foot on a reconnaissance mission against the Danes. After probing the situation at Kisa, where Duke John had built an abatis line, Rantzau had ordered a general retreat, moving south. His men had now retreated to Vimmerby. The men under Gustavus Adolphus followed the retreating Danes, harassing them and engaging in minor battles on several occasions. Swedish units inflicted casualties on the Danes first at Målilla and then at Emmenäs, where they took 115 captives.[4] However, on 18 July, Rantzau reached Högsby, which meant that he had managed to slip out of the Swedish envelopment and again had a free line of communications with Kalmar, to which he continued the retreat.

Gustavus Adolphus continued the pursuit until Högsby, which he reached on 20 July. With Rantzau having escaped the Swedish envelopment, the Swedish King then turned back to relieve Jönköping.[5] He also gave a patent to another Småland freebooter to raise men to ravage and plunder at will in Danish Scania and Blekinge.[6]

In one of the engagements, the pursuing Swedes had destroyed two Danish units, Rantzau's life banner of horse and the harquebusier company of Duke Ernest Louis of Saxe-Lauenburg (known as the 'Duke's Life Banner'). These losses, together with the mutinous feelings among the enlisted soldiers, caused Rantzau to dissolve Duke Ernest Louis's and Wustrow's regiments when he finally reached Kalmar. The men were instead transferred into Rantzau's own regiment and that of Marquard von Pentz. This part of the Danish campaign plan to take Jönköping and then bring the war into the Swedish heartlands had failed utterly.

King Christian did not fare much better. He set out from Gullberg on 10 July. His army then consisted of about 10 cavalry banners, one dragoon company, and some 20 companies of foot. He left behind, under the command of the experienced Jørgen Lunge, the Fyn Banner, the English foot who suffered badly from disease, and the siege artillery. From this onwards, the experienced military entrepreneur Jørgen Lunge came to dominate Danish

---

4   Katarina Harrison Lindbergh, *Kalmarkriget 1611–1613* (Lund: Historiska Media, 2022), p.142.
5   Barkman and Lundkvist, *Kungl. Svea livgardes historia*, vol. 3, part 1, pp.200–01, notes that the existing road network actually did not enable an envelopment of Rantzau's army if the avowed intention was to destroy it. The Swedish army still lacked both good maps, even of its own country, and the capacity to produce accurate tactical intelligence on enemy armies. We must assume that Gustavus Adolphus, at least to some extent, improvised his strategy day by day and not pretend that every decision was a stroke of genius. Nonetheless, the strategy that Gustavus Adolphus executed was a sound one, and it neutralised Rantzau's army for several weeks.
6   Larsen, *Kalmarkrigen*, p.228.

military affairs on the western front. He certainly proved a more determined western commander than the King's men in Norway. While King Christian set out, he sent orders to the Norwegians in Bohuslän to go on the offensive towards Brätte in Västergötland, where the River Göta Älv flowed out from Lake Vänern. The Norwegians did indeed set out from Uddevalla and entered Dal. However, again, logistical problems hampered the raid, and, ultimately, most of the Norwegians abandoned the venture and returned home. Not so Lunge, whom King Christian had given command at Elfsborg Castle. He set out towards the north as well, and, when the Norwegians deserted, he moved into Brätte, compelling the locals to swear loyalty to King Christian.[7]

Meanwhile, King Christian marched on by way of Härryda, Örby, Tranemo, and Unnaryd, after which he followed the River Nissan. On 23 July, he finally reached Jönköping. The levied peasants who guarded the approach to Jönköping abandoned their positions as the large Danish army approached. However, the defenders burned the outskirts of Jönköping to deny cover to the Danes.

Uncertain of what happened elsewhere, King Christian ordered Albert Skeel to ride farther south-east into Småland with 100 men from his Ribe Banner, Corfitz Rud's Fyn Banner, and the King's Life Banner. Units were now understrength, and men from different companies were increasingly often mixed when greater numbers were required. Skeel and his men soon reached Rogberga Church, which they plundered. They also managed to capture four Swedes, whom the Danes interrogated for information. However, when Skeel wanted to return to Jönköping on 26 July, he found the road back blocked by abatis. The local game warden, Mickel Jönsson of Tenhult, had raised the levy against the Danes. Skeel and his men managed to break through but at the loss of several men and horses. His horse shot under him, Skeel had to run in his heavy cuirassier armour for some distance before one of his men managed to rein in a stray horse whose rider had already fallen.[8]

On 24 July, the day after King Christian arrived at Jönköping, news about his arrival and, yet more importantly, his lack of siege artillery reached Gustavus Adolphus. Having already seen off Rantzau, Gustavus Adolphus now set out towards Jönköping. He also sent orders to his various commands: to Duke John to meet him at Jönköping and to the Småland levies to prepare abatis to block the Danish King's line of retreat. In short, Gustavus Adolphus planned to rely on the same efficient tactics against King Christian that he had already used against Rantzau. The town and castle of Jönköping were defended by Göran Månsson Stierna and Sten Claesson Böllja, who had received orders to defend the town until the end. It never came to this. Three days later, King Christian learnt from captured Swedish prisoners that Rantzau had retreated to Kalmar. By then, his men already faced shortages in supplies and rising rates of disease. Disappointed, King Christian ordered a

---

7   Lunge employed so harsh methods that his campaign remained in local memory as the 'Lunge War' (Swedish: *Lungefejden*). Larsen, *Kalmarkrigen*, pp.240–41.

8   Albert Skeel to his wife Birte, 26 July 1612, cited in Kall (ed.), 'Mag. Ægidii Laurizens samlede Efterretninger', pp.51–52.

general retreat south to Halmstad, which he reached on 8 August. He handed over command to Duke George of Brunswick-Lüneburg. The King then returned to Copenhagen.

Meanwhile, some 4,000 to 6,000 soldiers were enlisted in England on behalf of the Danish cause, and, during the summer, the first of these reinforcements arrived to support King Christian's army. Unfortunately for the Danes, they arrived too late to take active part in the hostilities.[9]

Gustavus Adolphus reached Jönköping with the Swedish field army on 31 July. By then, both the King and many of his men suffered from similar diseases as the Danes.

Although King Christian had conquered Elfsborg Castle in the west and Borgholm Castle on Öland in the east, the rest of the summer campaign had been unsuccessful. Again, he had been unable to move his armies into the Swedish heartland.

Gustavus Adolphus, on the other hand, seems to have learnt from his experiences. The record of his previous raids and battles, whether successes such as Christianopel or failures such as Vittsjö, was spotty, as could be expected of a novice junior commander. He had displayed bravery and the ability to command men in his close vicinity, but he had not always given evidence of the steadiness expected of a senior commander. However, during the summer campaign of 1612, the young King began to display a higher degree of confidence in his own abilities than previously. He successfully operated multiple units on the inner lines of the theatre, ably employing them to contain first one, then the other, of the two Danish armies, which were both numerically larger than his own forces. It is telling that both Rantzau and King Christian ultimately drew the conclusion that they had to retreat in the face of the advancing Swedish King, despite his inferior numbers, or risk the destruction of their armies. Perhaps they remembered how, in 1604, the Danish Council of the Realm had advised against an invasion of Sweden, which, they maintained, was by nature easy to defend: '… if the country's enemies invade in strength, they will lack supplies; if the invasion force is weak, they will be defeated'.[10] That the campaign became one of logistics instead of glorious battle only shows that Gustavus Adolphus had understood what was crucial in military operations. The young Swedish King had learnt to assess his own sources of intelligence, limited as they were, as well as the capabilities of his men and those of his enemies in a realistic manner. Until then, the young King operated as a junior officer, not a general. He had already proven that he was a leader of men. In the summer campaign of 1612, the 17-year-old Gustavus Adolphus matured into a commander of armies.

---

9 Steve Murdoch, 'Diplomacy in Transition: Stuart-British Diplomacy in Northern Europe, 1603–1618', in A. I. Macinnes, T. Riis, and F. Pedersen (eds), *Ships, Guns and Bibles in the North Sea and the Baltic States, c.1350–c.1700* (East Linton: Tuckwell Press, 2000), pp.104, 113, n.90.

10 Erslev (ed.), *Aktstykker*, vol. 1, p.128.

17

The Naval Expedition Towards Stockholm

We have seen that the Danish fleet returned to Copenhagen in late July. By chance, this was the time when the Swedish main fleet again set from Älvsnabben, on 24 July. Again commanded by Grand Admiral Gyllenstierna, it sailed south to Öland, although staying in the open sea on the east side of the island. It then turned south-east towards the bay of Danzig, where it operated from 29 July to 6 August, searching for its Danish counterpart. The only prizes gained were a few merchantmen.[1] Then, Gyllenstierna gave up the search and turned north again, returning to Älvsnabben on 10 August. As in the Danish fleet, the Swedish one now suffered from diseases.

Back in Copenhagen, King Christian had apparently given up on the previous strategies. This time, he would entrust the task to the navy, in which he had put much effort and money and of which he was rightly proud. On 11 August, King Christian set out with the Danish main fleet (36 ships) from his capital. In Kalmar, from 16 to 20 August, he embarked several units of Rantzau's army, according to a Swedish source some 1,000 musketeers, in addition to those he already had embarked in Copenhagen.[2] Learning that the Swedish fleet was last heard sailing towards Danzig, the King decided to follow it there, apparently hoping to inflict a crushing defeat on the enemy to give him uncontested supremacy at sea. The fleet then circled Öland and sailed to Danzig, where it cast anchor from 24 to 25 August. The Swedes had long ago returned towards the north. Then, the King sailed towards Stockholm. This time, he would attack the centre of Swedish power by sea.

There were two main sea lines of communications through the Stockholm Archipelago that led into the capital city from the Baltic Sea. Both entered from the north. The western route was protected by Vaxholm Castle, a round stone tower on a small island that blocked the sailing channel. The eastern route was less strongly fortified and defended, but, since the days of King

---

1 Swedish warships apparently also took the Danish warship *Stjernen* (with 22 cannons), which carried Swedish prisoners to Copenhagen. Wadén, *Berättande källor*, p.293.
2 Generalstaben, *Sveriges krig 1611–1632*, vol. 1, p.310.

THE KALMAR WAR

Vaxholm Castle, as seen by a Dutch delegation, 1616. Oddly, the landscape depicted in this print does not at all resemble that surrounding Vaxholm Castle, which protected the western route into Stockholm. Instead, by coincidence or design, the landscape in the print is almost a perfect match for the landscape along the eastern route. This poses awkward questions because the present citadel in this location, a similarly round castle named Fredriksborg Castle, is generally believed only to have been built a century after the Kalmar War. Was it perhaps built upon an earlier castle that has been forgotten? (Anthonis Goeteeris)

Facing page:
Map 10. Naval operations in August–September 1612

Gustavus I, attempts had been made to block it by the scuttling of superseded ships in the sailing channel.[3]

On 31 August, the Danish fleet encountered units of the Swedish fleet in the Stockholm Archipelago. Skirmishes between Danish and Swedish longboats followed, but the Swedes, under Gyllenstierna, withdrew to Vaxholm Castle, which barred the inlet to Stockholm. King Christian's strategy seems bizarre at first: instead of pushing on, he merely raised a memorial on one of the islands to commemorate his victory. Meanwhile, Swedish inshore boats and gunners repeatedly attacked the Danish fleet. King Christian ordered Peder Nielsen to take a longboat from each ship with which to engage the Swedes. This turned into a rowing battle between Danes under Nielsen and Swedes under Johan van Monickhouen, who recently had arrived in Stockholm with an enlisted Dutch regiment (more on which later). Having more firepower (both muskets and falconets), Nielsen managed to repulse the Swedes, who withdrew. Nielsen landed on the island from which the Swedes had departed, took eight or 10 prisoners, and captured three pyrotechnical devices with which the Swedes had launched attacks on the Danish ships at night.

---

3   The estuary in the north was by tradition named 'Trälhavet' ('Thrall Sea'), possibly in memory of the slave trade prevalent there in the Viking Age. The western route, west of Rindö Island, was called 'Kodjupet' ('Cow Deep'), which derives from the older form 'Koggdjupet' ('Cog Deep'), so named after the medieval ship type cog. The eastern route, between Rindö and Värmdö Islands, was known as 'Oxdjupet' ('Ox Deep'), presumably as a popular name invented to relate to the supposed 'Cow Deep'.

THE NAVAL EXPEDITION TOWARDS STOCKHOLM

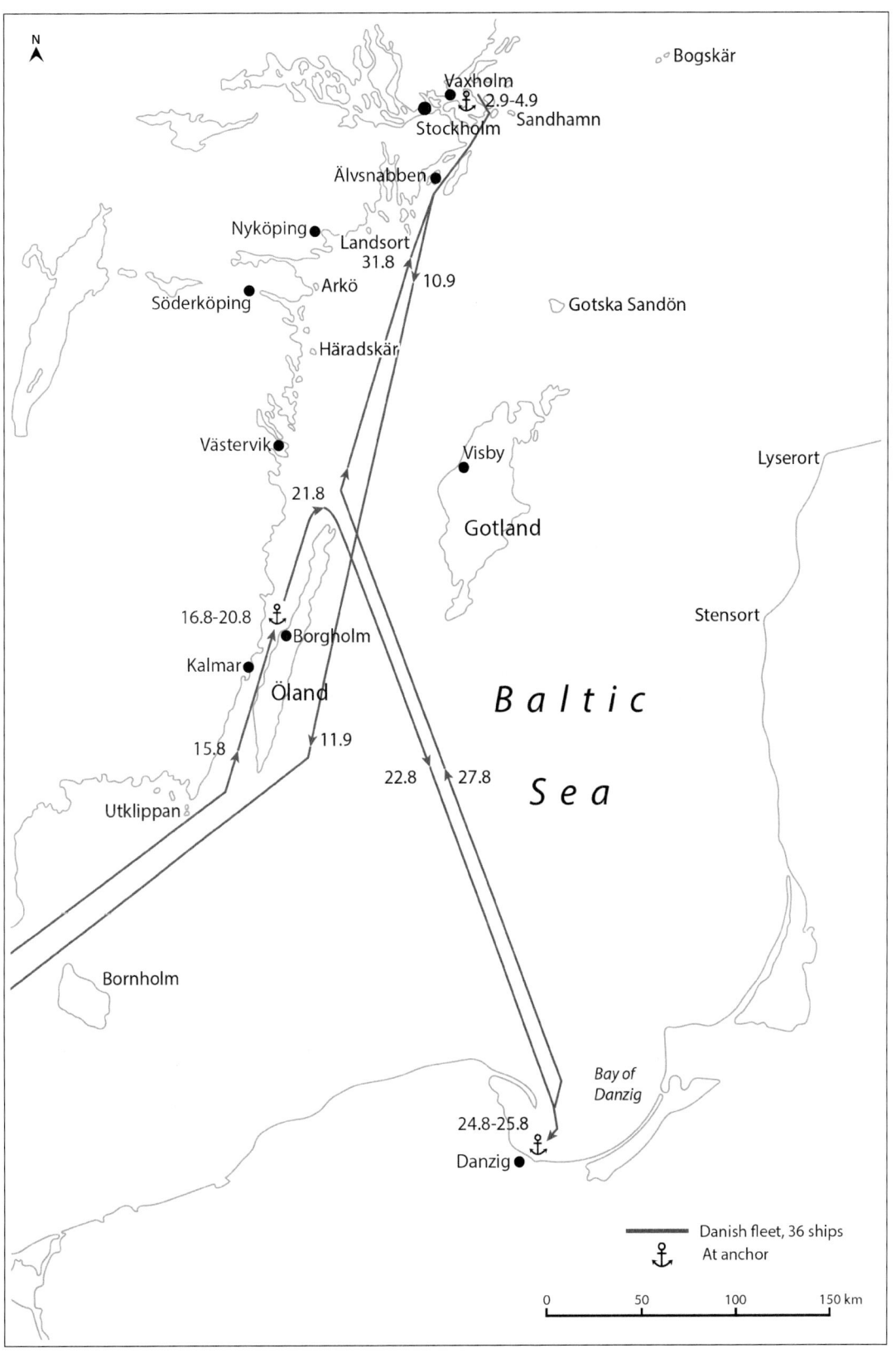

On 2 September, King Christian's fleet finally reached Vaxholm Castle. Since May 1612, Vaxholm was defended by a garrison of some 50 men under the one-legged Mårten Krakow and his wife, Emerentia Pauli, who did not intend to let the Danish fleet reach Stockholm. Nor did Gustavus Adolphus. Having received news of the Danish fleet, he rushed from Jönköping towards Stockholm, where he arrived at 3:00 a.m. on 9 September after covering the 340 km in a three-day ride. At 5:00 a.m., the King continued his ride towards Vaxholm. The defences of Stockholm were hastily improved. Warlike levies were called from Dalecarlia and set out on forced marches towards the capital.

These efforts were unnecessary. On 4 September, King Christian gave up the attempt. The endeavour was doomed from the start. While his fleet was strong, the ambition to conquer Stockholm with only the soldiers brought on the fleet must have seemed hopeless to professionals. After Monickhouen's arrival with fresh Dutch infantry, the regular Swedish army units alone at Stockholm encompassed no less than 2,500 men.[4] King Christian was not a fool, but he was vain and not always realistic in his plans. Perhaps he hoped that a mere show of strength would make the Swedish capital surrender. If so, this would at least provide the arguments that he needed to negotiate a fruitful peace treaty. Abandoning the campaign and, in reality, the war, the Danish fleet set out on its voyage back to Copenhagen. The Danes now learnt, the hard way, the Swedish lesson of setting sail out of Stockholm. For several days, contrary winds delayed and slowed down the voyage out of the Stockholm Archipelago. This gave Monickhouen the opportunity to attack the Danish fleet on 8 September with 500 men embarked on boats and burners. However, the Danes (by some accounts due to the vigilance of King Christian himself) discovered the attempt, which accordingly failed. The Danes only lost a yacht.[5]

On 10 September, the Danish fleet returned to the south. King Christian left the fleet on Bornholm on 13 September, handing over command to Ulfeldt. He was back in Copenhagen on 17 September. The war was over for King Christian – for this time, that is.

Not so for his fleet. Soon afterwards, intelligence arrived that 24 ships from Lübeck were ready to sail from Travemünde with supplies to Sweden. These were merchantmen that Gustavus Adolphus had been eagerly awaiting. King Christian ordered Gabriel Kruse, with a squadron of nine small warships then in the port of Slite on Gotland, to prevent the Lübeck merchantmen from reaching Sweden. First planning to cruise between Bornholm and Rügen, he soon concluded that the nights were now too dark to prevent an incursion. Instead, he decided to sail to Warnemünde to strike at the source of the problem. Some of his captains worried over this breach of neutrality, but Kruse pointed out that they had been to Danzig already without complaints. He then sent Captain Peder Jacobsen with a small ship to Travemünde.

---

4   Generalstaben, *Sveriges krig 1611–1632*, vol. 1, p.310.
5   Generalstaben, *Sveriges krig 1611–1632*, vol. 1, p.311 and *Sveriges krig 1611–1632*, suppl. vol. 1, p.120.

THE NAVAL EXPEDITION TOWARDS STOCKHOLM

Above: Vaxholm Castle, after further improvements later in the seventeenth century. At the time of the Kalmar War, the round castle was less imposing but similar in size and shape and built on an island, as depicted here. (Erik Dahlbergh)

Right: The original tower of Vaxholm Castle as depicted in a nineteenth-century Navy assessment

THE KALMAR WAR

Above and right: King Christian IV, as the victor of the Kalmar War. The proud text 'CALMAR CEDE MAIORI' translates to 'Kalmar, Yield to the Greater One'. (Silver medal by Thomas Borstorff, 1612; photo: Gabriel Hildebrand, Economy Museum – Royal Coin Cabinet/SHM, Stockholm)

Having located the Lübeck merchantmen at the Travemünde roadstead, Kruse ordered an attack. Combat ensued, during which the Lübeck captains deliberately grounded their ships and then brought heavy cannons ashore to fire at the Danes, who in turn returned the fire from farther out at sea. The next day, Kruse fired a Danish salute (i.e. three cannon shots in rapid succession) and then sailed towards Rügen. However, on the way, he met Admiral Lindenow with several warships, who ordered him to attack again. Lindenow also assumed command of the Danish squadrons. The Lübeck ships had returned to sea. However, then, a boat with a trumpeter from the mayor and council of the city arrived. Negotiations ensued, and the two sides agreed that Lübeck would not ship any more supplies to Sweden that year.[6] This action concluded the naval war of 1612.

It is unclear if the Lübeck merchants held this promise. On 7 and 14 October, Admiral Clerck received orders to sail to Germany with 11 Swedish warships and a contingent of soldiers to convoy merchantmen with supplies on their way to Sweden. Whether this voyage actually took place is uncertain. Kruse soon returned to Denmark, so the expedition, if it took place, would not have been noticed by the Danes.

---

6   Generalstaben, *Sveriges krig 1611–1632*, suppl. vol. 1, pp.120–21.

18

Operations into Norway

We have seen that, having taken control of Jämtland and Härjedalen, Governor Baltzar Bäck allowed his men to institute a reign of terror in the occupied provinces. The situation improved slightly after the death of King Charles. On 31 January 1612, Gustavus Adolphus sent an angry letter to Bäck, ordering him to cease any unnecessary violence and instead protect the people now under his rule. Unfortunately, the new monarch was far away, so Bäck continued to oppress the locals.

This did not mean that Gustavus Adolphus was unaware of the need to also maintain a northern strategy. On 12 March, he wrote an open letter to the Norwegians, encouraging them to throw off Danish rule. Later in the month, he sent emissaries with the letter and proclamations along these lines into Norway. Considering Sweden's difficult strategic situation at the time, it seems likely that Gustavus Adolphus regarded the open letter more as an attempt to sow dissent than as a serious proposition. Certainly, the letter found little acceptance on the other side of the border. The Norwegian response was to move into Värmland and Dal to ravage these provinces. Some combat also took place much farther to the north, in Lapponia, where the local Lapps (Sami) seem to have been the primary targets, presumably to prevent them from paying taxes to Swedish officials.

Besides, in the summer, Gustavus Adolphus again ordered Bäck to withdraw most of his men from the occupied provinces since soldiers were more urgently needed elsewhere, not least to protect the capital of Stockholm. In early autumn, Bäck assembled his men and returned to Sweden.

Yet two more Swedish incursions into Norway took place but from the west, not the east. In July and August 1612, two contingents of enlisted men, one from the Dutch Republic and the other from Scotland, landed at separate locations in northern Norway. With the fall of Elfsborg Castle, they had no way to reach Sweden except through Norwegian territory. The original plan seems to have been for the two contingents to first sail to Shetland to combine their units, as well as those under another Scotsman who remained in Amsterdam, Captain John Halkett, into one united expeditionary force. But, if so, the two commanders soon abandoned the plan because neither sailed to Shetland. Halkett, as far as is known, remained in Dutch service.

THE KALMAR WAR

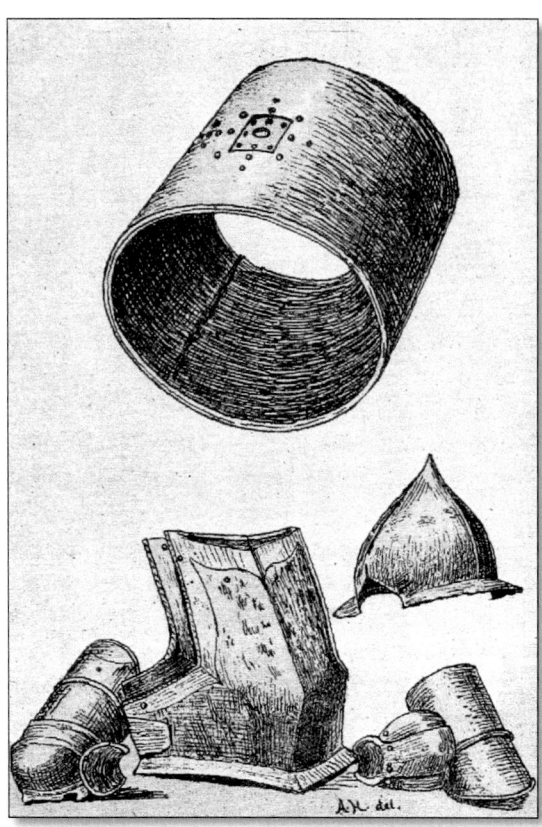

Remnant of Scottish drum and armour alleged to have belonged to members of Captain Ramsay's company. (Nineteenth-century drawing of items in Copenhagen National Museum

Colonel Johan (Jean) van Monickhouen (d. 1614) had travelled to the Dutch Republic in December 1611 to enlist soldiers. At first, the Dutch Republic opposed any enlistment on behalf of Sweden, but, eventually, they ignored such enlistment as the war went on. Monickhouen set sail on 14 July 1612 with four ships and possibly 800 men, apparently accompanied by camp followers.[1] He sailed into the Trondheim Fjord, (by luck, skill, or superior force) evaded the naval patrols, and landed his men at Stjørdal on 19 July. The local peasants mobilised but kept their distance from the well-armed Dutch soldiers. They then began to march eastwards to Sweden towards Åre and Frösö in Jämtland, from which they planned to continue south into Sweden. Gustavus Adolphus instead wanted them to first march south from Trondheim and only enter Swedish territory in Värmland or Västergötland. However, the Dutch preferred to march straight towards Stockholm. They reached the city on 31 August, just as King Christian threatened it from the archipelago, which made the Dutch soldiers very welcome. In early September, Monickhouen led the aforementioned attempt to attack the Danish fleet with 500 men embarked on boats and burners.

Sir James Spens (1571–1631) had enlisted in Scotland in the winter of 1611/1612. His endeavour had suffered from difficulties from the very beginning. Already before the war broke out, Danish soldiers with peasant garb over their armour had penetrated Swedish territory, where they attacked and robbed Spens to prevent him from carrying out his task.[2] Next, when he was on route to the British Isles, other Danish soldiers had detained him for three days. Moreover, in 1603, King James VI of Scotland had simultaneously become 'James I of England', an act of state that established the Union of the Crowns of Scotland and England. Unfortunately for Spens, King James of Scotland and England was married to Anne of Denmark, King Christian's elder sister. For this reason, King James forbid Swedish recruitment in Scotland. Nonetheless, Spens had excellent connections and, through Colonel Andrew Ramsay (who did not personally participate in the ensuing expedition), successfully enlisted three companies of foot: one under the Colonel's brother, Captain Alexander Ramsay, another under Captain George Sinclair, and the third under Captain George Hay. Each company consisted of 100 men. Captain Ramsay, who technically held the rank of lieutenant colonel for his brother, was on good terms with King James, so he presumably felt safe to ignore the ban on recruitment for the Swedish cause.

1 Generalstaben, *Sveriges krig 1611–1632*, vol. 1, p.309.
2 Larsen, *Kalmarkrigen*, p.89.

OPERATIONS INTO NORWAY

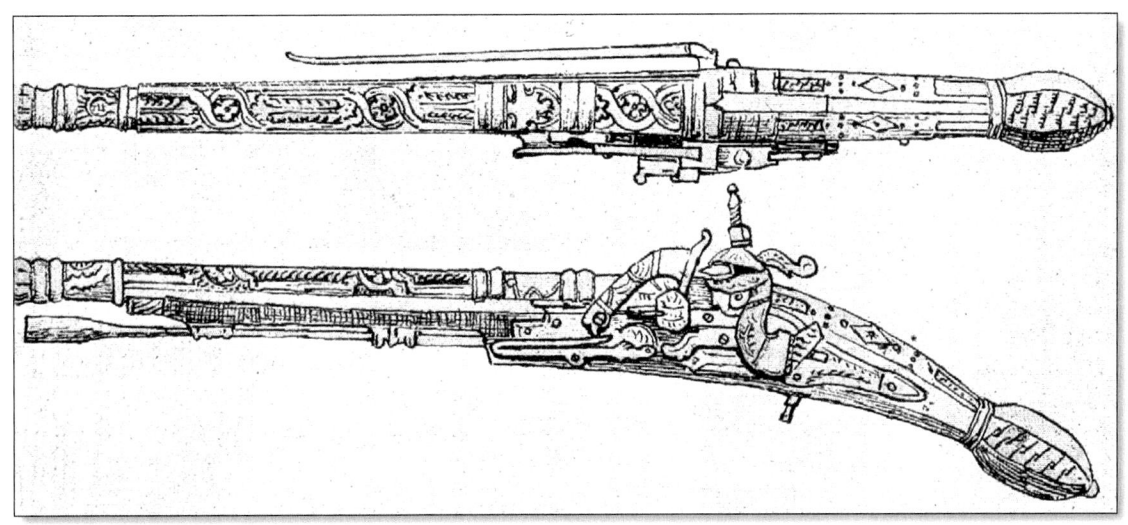

Pistols traditionally alleged to have belonged to Captain George Sinclair. (Nineteenth-century drawing of items in Copenhagen National Museum)

Altogether, the Scots were about 300 men.³ Some were experienced soldiers, including Lieutenant James Moneypenny, who previously had been in both Danish and Swedish service and accordingly functioned as interpreter, and Henry Bruce, who had fought in Dutch, Spanish, and Imperial armies.

With two ships, the Scots sailed into Molde Fjord, south of Trondheim, from which they planned to march south-eastwards into Sweden, probably aiming for Värmland. They landed on 19 August. Less fortunate, or intimidating, than Monickhouen's Dutchmen, the Scotsmen found themselves blocked at Kringen by 405 local peasant levies under *Lensmænd* Laurits Haga and Peder Ranklev. According to local tradition, the Norwegians prepared a trap of tree trunks and rocks above the trail on which the Scotsmen travelled. Other peasants gathered to prevent the Scotsmen from retreating whence they came. When the Scotsmen marched into the trap on 26 August, the peasants released the tree trunks and rocks, which then thundered down the slope and into the Scottish ranks. Then, the Norwegians attacked. Most Scotsmen were killed or drowned in the river when they tried to escape. It is possible that not all of the Scotsmen were fully armed since Ramsay had pressed convicted criminals into his ranks, perhaps intending to arm them only upon joining a larger Swedish formation. Be that as it may, Norwegian levies knew how to fight, especially when their homes were at risk. The snaplock weapons of the Norwegians were more advanced and, in poor weather, certainly more efficient than the matchlocks presumably carried by the Scots. The entire

---

3 Generalstaben, *Sveriges krig 1611–1632*, vol. 1, p.309. When first King Christian, in a letter to his brother-in-law King James, and then Sir Robert Anstruther, the British ambassador, described the incident, Anstruther reported 300 Scotsmen. King Christian to King James, 18 October 1612; Sir Robert Anstruther to King James. The National Archives (TNA) SP 75/5, fols 23–24, 29d. The Norwegian official report claimed a total of 550 Scottish dead after the battle, a highly exaggerated figure – clearly Copenhagen understood this. Captain Ramsay told his Norwegian interrogators that another four ships with men would follow, but the Norwegians already knew that King James had taken steps to prevent their departure.

battle lasted only an hour and a half and resulted in the surrender of 134 Scotsmen who survived the ambush. By their own report, the Norwegians lost six men while another 10 or 12 were wounded but recovered. Unsure of what to do with so many captives, the peasants moved the captives away from the site and then massacred them, sparing only 18 men. Three surviving officers – Captain Ramsay, Lieutenant Moneypenny, and Henry Bruce, who styled himself 'captain' – were sent to Akershus Castle. The surviving common soldiers were used for forced labour or ultimately sent to Elfsborg for enlistment into an English company in Lunge's regiment.[4] The three officers, together with another surviving officer named James Scott (since he was not described as a captain, perhaps a lieutenant), were sent onwards to Copenhagen and ultimately returned to Britain, where they were released. Captain Ramsay, a favourite at court, blamed his brother for the unfortunate venture, landed on his feet, and remained in good standing with King James.[5]

Ramsay's failure did not mean Swedish plans for offensives into Norway went unheeded. In early September, Oluf Ingemarsson sent 300 men from Jämtland towards Norway. However, they soon found that Norwegian levies guarded the border in great numbers. Outnumbered, they aborted the raid.[6]

---

[4] National Archives of Norway (NRA) Danske Kancelli, Innlegg og henlagte saker, eske 5, DK B 160, 17 September 1612 (EA-3023/Fccb/L0001) and Danske Kancelli, Norske henlagte saker, 3 October 1612 (EA-3023/Jaa/L0001).

[5] Thomas Michell, *History of the Scottish Expedition to Norway in 1612* (London: T. Nelson and Sons, 1886) remains the most comprehensive history of the Scottish expedition and includes English translations of most relevant archive documents.

[6] Larsen, *Kalmarkrigen*, p.240.

19

The Treaty of Knäred

The Dutch Republic and the Union of the Crowns of Scotland and England had important financial interests in the Baltic Sea trade. Although King James sympathised with Denmark, neither maritime power wished to see Denmark acquire full control of the Baltic.[1] In July 1612, Dutch and British mediators met King Christian and Gustavus Adolphus. Neither ruler was particularly interested in mediation. Yet, after the summer 1612 campaign season, both monarchs had mellowed – King Christian in particular, who, after his return to Copenhagen after the failed expedition to Stockholm, was finally running out of funds for the enlistment of foreign troops. Peace negotiations accordingly began in earnest in autumn 1612, which ended the Kalmar War before a decisive victory could be attained by either party.

Both sides agreed to send emissaries to Knäred, near Laholm, and to maintain a truce in the area for as long as negotiations continued. Each party would be accompanied by 50 cavalry: the Danes by the Halland Banner and the Swedes by a composite unit of men from several banners under Måns Stierna.

The negotiations were mediated by the Dutch Republic and the Union of the Crowns of Scotland and England. A key participant was the aforementioned Scotsman, Sir James Spens, who had personal interests in Sweden. Meanwhile, his close relative, Sir Robert Anstruther, negotiated on behalf of Denmark. Neither of the two wished for complete Danish dominance. Moreover, both men also had to consider Anglo–Scottish relations. Enmity between Scots and English ran deep, and hostilities abroad between soldiers of the two nations might yet cause unrest at home. Large numbers of Scots served in the Swedish army, while, in 1612, recruitment

---

1   The Union of the Crowns meant that, henceforth, the previous English diplomatic focus on France, Spain, and the Dutch Republic was subordinated to the demands of the Stuart alliance with Denmark and the interests of the vast Scottish mercantile communities in Norway, Sweden, and the Commonwealth (Poland and Prussia). After 1603, all Jacobean ambassadors to Denmark, Sweden, and the Commonwealth hailed from Scotland. Meanwhile, King James retained the previous, solely English focus on the Muscovy trade (which engaged many London-based, but hardly any Scottish or other English, merchants). Murdoch, 'Diplomacy in Transition', pp.106–07.

THE KALMAR WAR

Gustavus Adolphus, 1616. (Author's collection)

was underway in England for the Danish army. This worried Spens and Anstruther. In July 1612, Anstruther wrote to Spens that, if peace could not be concluded before Scots and English soldiers in the two armies came to blows, then this would 'breed a graite inconvenience betuix the contries of England and Scotland, and it is to be feared at if there be a day of battell, at then the English and Scots will cout on [an]others throths'.[2] In short, the mediators were not disinterested observers; they had real incentives to engineer peace between the two hostile Scandinavian monarchs.

Denmark and Sweden agreed upon the Treaty of Knäred on 19 January 1613. The representatives signed on 20 January, and King Christian signed on 26 January.[3]

Neither side was satisfied with the outcome. Denmark had proven the stronger power, and Sweden had to accept harsh terms to end the war. Territorially, the treaty was essentially a return to the status quo. Sweden returned Jämtland and Härjedalen (and those unfortunate Jämtland peasants, who, after the Swedish occupation of the province, had initially sworn fealty to the Swedish Crown, were soon severely punished by King Christian). Denmark returned Kalmar and Öland.[4] However, Sweden had to ransom Elfsborg Castle and the surrounding lands for a shocking 1,000,000 *Reichsthalers*, and, until this huge ransom was paid, Elfsborg and Sweden's one access point to the North Sea remained under Danish control. The treaty further stipulated that, if Sweden did not pay the ransom by 20 January 1619, the territory would pass to Denmark for all eternity. King Christian IV expected that Sweden could not raise such a huge amount and that he would be able to retain Elfsborg. However, Gustavus Adolphus and Chancellor Oxenstierna managed to raise the funds, not only through the introduction of extraordinary emergency taxation but also through massive exports of copper and loans secured from the Dutch Republic. The Elfsborg ransom was paid in four instalments, mostly in cash, but Denmark also accepted 97 tons of copper to alleviate her unbecoming shortage of bronze cannons. As a result, Denmark returned Elfsborg to Sweden in January 1619.

As for other terms, Sweden abandoned its claims on the Sonnenburg Castle on Ösel. Sweden also abandoned its claim on the coast of the Arctic North (Lapponia), north of the Titisfjord Estuary. If the Swedish King wanted

---

2 Anstruther to Spens, 18 July 1612, cited in Murdoch, 'Diplomacy in Transition', p.104.
3 Rydberg and Hallendorff (eds), *Sverges Traktater med främmande magter*, vol. 5, part 1, pp.211–23.
4 Before returning Borgholm, the Danes removed everything of value, including doors and windows.

to resume the title 'King of the Lapps', this had to henceforth encompass only the Lapps on Swedish territory, not those on Norwegian territory.

Both monarchs retained the right to use the three crowns that once had symbolised the Kalmar Union in their banners but without any right to rule over the other. Sweden retained the right to not pay the Sound Toll. If Gothenburg was rebuilt, its privileges must not be allowed to interfere with Danish rights in the Danish Strait. The trade through Riga and Courland would be free for Danish ships, as well as ships of other nations (by which was primarily meant the Dutch Republic, Scotland, and England), with the important caveat that trade would not be free when Sweden laid siege to Riga in the ongoing war with the Commonwealth.

Finally, both sides also agreed to ransom POWs, who ranged from nobles and officers to priests and commoners taken on Öland for forced labour at the naval shipyard at Bremerholm in Copenhagen.

King Christian may have hoped to gain the Swedish throne and thus recreate the Kalmar Union, but, if so, this was beyond his power.[5] Moreover, the idea of a recreated Kalmar Union had little support in either Denmark or Sweden, or indeed among neighbouring countries, since it would have created a formidable Nordic state that, by default, would gain maritime supremacy in the entire Baltic.

Gustavus Adolphus, c. 1616. (Gold medal, dated to 1614–1618, Gustavianum, Uppsala)

The Legacy of the Kalmar War

The Swedish concessions to Denmark were considerable, and, had Sweden not been able to ransom Elfsborg Castle, Denmark would have made a significant territorial gain as well. Of course, the ransom was paid on time, and the other concessions would, within a generation, be of less importance than the Danish negotiators and King Christian might have hoped for. Ultimately, the able policies of Gustavus Adolphus and Chancellor

---

5   King Christian included the possible subjugation of Sweden among his political goals but was open to the less ambitious objective of using military force merely to bring the Swedish King to order (Latin: *redigere in ordinem*). Both the nineteenth-century Larsen, *Kalmarkrigen*, p.71, as well as more recent works such as Ole L. Frantzen and Knud J. V. Jespersen (eds), *Danmarks krigshistorie: 700-1814* (Copenhagen: Gad, 2008), vol. 1, p.191, argue that King Christian wanted to gain the Swedish throne for himself and thus revive the Kalmar Union. Yet others, including Askgaard, *Christian IV*, p.97, contend that King Christian's political goals were less ambitious. Ultimately, we cannot know how far the Danish King would have gone had he been able to achieve a decisive victory.

Oxenstierna raised Sweden to a great power status. Sweden eclipsed Denmark as the leading power in the Baltic. It is probably fair to say that the later achievements of Gustavus Adolphus derived from the lessons he had learnt from his experiences during the Kalmar War. Meanwhile, Denmark's victory contained the seeds of the country's undoing as a great power. Success in war tends to encourage complacency, while defeat encourages the adoption of new strategies, industries, tactics, policies, and, indeed, ideas.

The losses in the Kalmar War showed Gustavus Adolphus that the Swedish army was obsolete and needed thorough modernisation. Gustavus Adolphus was particularly disappointed with the Swedish cavalry and, most of all, with the retinue of nobles, which had underperformed badly. Henceforth, the Swedish King trusted his infantry, and he made an infantry-based Swedish variant of the Dutch model of warfare the new standard for all his units, whether national or enlisted abroad.

Gustavus Adolphus's views on the importance of infantry can be found in his *Organisation of Soldiers*, which was written in 1619 or possibly 1620. In this work, the King explained the primacy of the infantry and linked this view to the old Scandinavian tradition of calling out the nation at arms. 'The infantry I mention first,' Gustavus Adolphus wrote, 'since after God, the entire nation's prosperity hinges on them.' He then explained that only the infantry could handle operations in the vast forestlands of the kingdom, man the warships and defend the sea lines, on which the nation's prosperity depended, and defend and attack fortified sites. In short, the kingdom needed its infantry to be of good quality and in sufficient numbers, for which conscription was required.[6]

The navy, too, had underperformed. In the southern Baltic and on the west coast, Danish fleets had consistently bested their Swedish counterparts. It was hardly a coincidence that Danish armies had achieved their greatest successes at Kalmar and Elfsborg, where they benefited from naval support and shipborne logistics. Inland, Danes and Swedes had fought on significantly more equal terms, and results had been less spectacular. Gustavus Adolphus accordingly initiated a programme to build better and larger warships with two full gundecks and armed with heavier guns than the ubiquitous 12-pounder, which was the most common naval cannon. In 1618, naval shipbuilding was centralised and, although still handled by private entrepreneurs, consolidated into two naval shipyards – the navy yard in Stockholm and a private yard in the town of Västervik.[7]

Gustavus Adolphus and Axel Oxenstierna also realised the need for better intelligence. Tactical intelligence – in the form of individual scouts,

---

6   Gustavus Adolphus, 'Krigsfolks-Ordning', in C. G. Styffe (ed.), *Konung Gustaf II Adolfs skrifter* (Stockholm: P. A. Norstedt & Söner, 1861), pp.5–6. Beginning with references to the military practices of the ancient Jews, Assyrians, Persians, Greeks, and Romans and of Dark Age and Medieval Scandinavians, Gustavus Adolphus intended this as a major treatise on warfare but only found time to complete the first part, on conscription.

7   Fredholm von Essen, *Lion from the North: The Swedish Army during the Thirty Years War* (Warwick: Helion & Company, 2020), vol. 2, p.203.

cavalry or dragoon patrols, reconnaissance missions, prisoner interrogation, and so on – had not performed very well during the war. This problem was the same at sea. Swedish and Danish fleets set out in search of each other, but chance determined if they actually met. Gustavus Adolphus and Oxenstierna established a military engineering corps in 1613. Its responsibilities included producing reliable maps in all theatres of operations. Henceforth, talented officers produced large numbers of maps, often under difficult circumstances such as on undercover missions or in territories with hostile populations. From the 1620s onwards, Swedish army commanders usually had reliable tactical and strategic information available for decision making. Naval intelligence improved, too.[8]

In short, the defeat in the Kalmar War was the catalyst that prompted Gustavus Adolphus to reform the Swedish army, which in turn set Sweden on the path to become a regional great power in the subsequent Thirty Years' War. At the same time, the enormous effort to raise the extra taxes to pay the Elfsborg ransom prompted Chancellor Oxenstierna to reform the revenue system, something that was equally important for modernising the country.

King Christian had raised the Sound Toll for the duration of the war. Dutch mercantile interests had objected, but King Christian dismissed their protests. Worried by this development, after the war, the Dutch Republic entered into a defensive alliance with Sweden in 1614, which ultimately would prove very beneficial for Sweden's political and industrial development and for Dutch access to Baltic markets.

Other changes took place as well. In 1621, Gustavus Adolphus granted town privileges to a new mercantile town, built on a more easily protected site on the south side of the River Göta Älv Estuary, immediately downstream of the demolished Gullberg Castle, as a replacement for Gothenburg, which King Christian had destroyed. The new town, also known as Gothenburg, formed the core of the modern city of the same name. The new town ultimately subsumed whatever then remained of Nya Lödöse, a neighbourhood that soon became known as Gamlestad ('Old Town').

Likewise, Kungahälla, on the Norwegian side of the River Göta Älv (south-west of modern-day Kungälv) and burned by the Swedes in 1612, was moved to the island already occupied by Bohus Castle and renamed 'Kungälv' in 1613. The same year, Varberg Town was moved to a closer and more secure position next to Varberg Castle.

The location of Kalmar town had been problematic due to its proximity to Kalmar Castle. The Crown began to consider relocating the town, but

King Christian IV, as the victor of the Kalmar War. He would never surpass this victory. (Silver medal commemorating the conquest of Gullberg Castle, probably by Thomas Borstorff, 1612)

---

8   Fredholm von Essen, *Lion from the North*, vol. 1, pp.224–33.

THE KALMAR WAR

Gustavus Adolphus, 1618. The 'Lion from the North' as he would become known in the Thirty Years' War and to posterity. (Gold medal, Economy Museum – Royal Coin Cabinet/SHM, Stockholm)

the burghers were reluctant to move. When an accidental fire destroyed the town in 1647, there was no longer any incentive to delay relocation, and Kalmar town was moved to Kvarnholm Island, some distance away from the castle.

In 1614, King Christian attempted to introduce a standing national army of 4,000 men, based on two permanent, conscripted border regiments, the Scanian and Jutland Regiments. Henceforth, these were known as the 'national regiments'. The reform began with a royal letter from 17 November 1614 that proclaimed a 'military formation ... of a certain number of infantry soldiers to be held for now and all time in the realm'.[9] Their task was to defend the respective northern and southern Danish borders. Although at first intended as mere independent companies, a plan that remained as late as June 1615, the two were soon established as permanent regiments. A decree dated 17 December 1615 ordered each to be commanded by a colonel supported by a full regimental staff. The Jutland Regiment would have an establishment strength of 2,000 men, while the Scanian Regiment was planned as 1,600 men. In addition, the plan envisaged 200 men on Fyn and 200 on Zealand.[10] The two regiments were not exclusively conscripted on Jutland and Scania, but conscripts from the islands were sent to one or the other based on geographical proximity. Moreover, the colonels in these regiments did not have the authority to appoint captains. These were instead appointed by royal command. The King firmly enforced his right to appoint or dismiss officers of the rank of captain and up. The men of the regiments were raised from 4,000 farmsteads held by peasants on Crown land, who were henceforth exempted from other kinds of taxation in return for providing and paying a soldier when mobilisation was ordered. This put the soldiers on a similar standing to that of an enlisted soldier.

While not strictly speaking a standing army, it was at least a dedicated mobilisation force with permanent institutions and salaried officers (although some posts, like that of quartermaster, so far remained empty). Henceforth, they were able to function in the manner of an enlisted regiment but under the direct authority of the King. It seems that the immediate inspiration for this reform was Sweden, which maintained some permanent units to reinforce the levy. In particular, the Swedish system of providing cavalrymen to national units was in many ways similar.

The two permanent Danish regiments were linked to the rapid construction of border fortresses then underway. New fortresses were built:

---

9   Lind, *Hæren*, p.39.
10 Lind, *Hæren*, pp.39–40.

Christianstad, founded in 1614 as a replacement for the unfortunate Vä on the Swedish border, and Glückstadt, founded in 1617 on the River Elbe. The fortifications around Copenhagen were greatly improved, too.

In a similar manner, a permanent army was also envisaged for Norway. It would be based on 1,500 men in southern Norway (*søndenfjelds*) and 600 in the north (*nordenfjelds*).[11] However, the King's plans for Norway ultimately failed. Most Norwegian peasants were freeholders. They were also less well monitored and controlled than Danish peasants on Crown lands, which made them less willing to serve in return for the exemption from taxes, which they might be able to evade anyway. King Christian's increasing focus on Continent affairs also seems to have made the Crown neglect Norwegian affairs. In Norway, national regiments were first established only in 1628.

Meanwhile, state poverty remained a persistent problem in Sweden. During the war, King Christian had relearnt the old lesson that the Swedish core territories lacked the means to sustain a large invasion army. Gustavus Adolphus had learnt the same lesson. Sweden still lacked the food supplies and revenues to support its own army. For this, he needed financial subsidies from abroad, to move the army out of the country to live off another monarch's territory, or both. Abroad, he could raise money by the then prevailing system of asking for contributions. A contribution (German: *Kontribution*) was an impost in money or kind levied under the threat of force. The concept seems to have derived from, and absorbed elements of, the old custom of demanding money to ransom property that, under the then prevailing law of war, could be looted or burned (*Brandschatzung*).[12] Foreign subsidies being unavailable, and with the Swedish Crown already at war with King Sigismund of the Polish–Lithuanian Commonwealth, Gustavus Adolphus chose to move his army overseas into enemy territory: first, Muscovy, and then, the Commonwealth.[13]

---

11 Lind, *Hæren*, p.40.
12 F. Redlich, 'Contributions in the Thirty Years' War', *Economic History Review*, New Series, 12:2 (1959), pp.247–54.
13 On these wars, see Fredholm von Essen, *Sweden's War in Muscovy* and *Lion from the North*, vol. 1.

Colour Plate Commentaries

Figures

Plate A
Swedish cuirassier, retinue of nobles
The retinue of nobles provided most of the few cuirassiers that Sweden had. This cuirassier wears full armour: a burgonet, gorget for the neck, and three-quarter armour that covers the entire upper body and both arms, as well as the front half of the upper legs. On the Continent by this time, cuirassiers customarily wore armour that reached down to and included the knees, but contemporary Swedish depictions (almost exclusively found on grave memorials) do not show this additional level of protection. Although the Continental style was in the process of reaching Sweden, it clearly had not yet become common there. In a similar manner, this cuirassier wears a breastplate of the peascod-belly or goose-belly type, which was already falling out of fashion on the Continent. Even in Sweden, professional soldiers mostly wore blackened armour if they expected to use firearms. Yet this noble cuirassier, armed with wheellock pistols and a rapier, apparently remains committed to the old school of shining armour, which was kept alive within the nobility.

Plate B
Swedish dragoon, Robert Halswell's Company
At the time of the Kalmar War, the Swedish military establishment employed dragoons, but there were no national dragoon units. Instead, Sweden enlisted dragoon units abroad. Captain Robert Halswell's company was raised in England. Dragoons used the same muskets as other infantry, in this case, a matchlock musket. They wore helmets but no breastplates. Dragoons were mounted on horseback but fought on foot, so they wore shoes, not riding boots and spurs. A dragoon would carry a rapier or similar sidearm. This dragoon is armed with a cutlass, a cheap cutting sword that might be straight or, in this case, slightly curved. Some dragoons may have been equipped with axes as well.

Plate C
Swedish guardsman, Drabant Guard
This guardsman is dressed in the uniform issued for the 1607 coronation of King Charles. At the time, guardsmen were issued garments of yellow and blue woollen cloth, with a dozen glass buttons for decoration. Drabant officers

COLOUR PLATE COMMENTARIES

instead wore garments of yellow and blue silk, with silver buttons. Musicians wore blue, with silver buttons and knitted stockings. Other guardsmen wore sewn stockings. The colour of the stockings is unknown, so, in this reconstruction, we conjectured them as white. New garments were regularly issued, but the same basic uniform, in yellow and blue, remained in use for more than a decade. During the coronation, guardsmen wore helmets plated in silver with decorations in the form of small blue and yellow flags and carried gilded halberds for added splendour. Similar, but more utilitarian, arms and armour were used in the field. The Drabant-style halberd with a concave cutting edge was introduced from Germany in the 1570s and known under this name from 1582 onwards. As a sidearm, this guardsman carries a swept-hilt rapier. The Drabant Guard is believed to have worn grey woollen casacks and grey hats for daily dress at the outbreak of the Kalmar War.

Pikeman. (Jacob de Gheyn II, *Wapenhandelinghe van Roers, Musquetten ende Spiessen*)

Plate D
Swedish pikeman, Hans Mattsson's Dalecarlian Company

Pikemen were expected to wear a full set of armour consisting of both breastplate and backplate, gorget, and tassets to protect the upper thighs. This man never received the gorget. A pikeman would also wear a helmet. The cabasset seems to have been the most common type, but this pikeman wears a burgonet, an older style that, no doubt, remained in use in remote areas. Pikemen were issued rapiers or cutlasses as sidearms, but, because of shortages, some instead had to carry an axe, which would have been suspended from the belt. This was particularly common in remote areas such as Dalecarlia. This pikeman has also armed himself with a good-quality dagger, perhaps a leftover from an earlier war. The Crown regularly distributed cloth for garments to common soldiers, which meant that the men of a given unit commonly presented a uniform appearance, with garments of the same style and colour. Blue cloth was easy to obtain, so blue garments were particularly common in remote areas such as Dalecarlia, the north, and Finland.

Plate E
Swedish musketeer, Per Månsson's Västergötland Company

Unlike the provincial pikeman in Plate 4, this musketeer carries a full set of up-to-date arms and equipment. The Västergötland army was well armed since it was close to the mercantile centres of Gothenburg and Nya Lödose with their trade links to the Dutch Republic. He carries an imported, Dutch 10-bore (19.7 mm) matchlock musket with fork rest, with a rapier as a

THE KALMAR WAR

Musketeer. (Jacob de Gheyn II, *Wapenhandelinghe van Roers, Musquetten ende Spiessen*

sidearm. His dress, too, is up to date for an infantryman, which makes him fundamentally indistinguishable from a Continental soldier. Brown cloth seems to have been distributed to at least one Västergötland company.

Plate F
Swedish infantry under-officer, Östergötland Ducal Arquebusier Company

An under-officer might have the means to provide his own garments but, unlike officers, would have received his arms from the Crown or, in this particular case, from Duke John of Östergötland, the youngest son of the late King John and cousin of Gustavus Adolphus. Duke John maintained his own small ducal army, which was similar to the Crown army yet differed in certain ways. For instance, Duke John maintained his own Drabant Guard, life banner of horse, and a dedicated arquebusier company of some repute, commanded by Captain Mårten Hemmingsson. This well-to-do under-officer of the ducal arquebusier company wears a gorget as a symbol of rank, which is also enhanced by his armament: a Drabant-style halberd of the modern German type with a concave cutting edge. He could have worn a helmet and a cuirass for added protection, with tassets to protect the upper thighs if serving in a pike unit. However, this arquebusier under-officer prefers a hat and buff coat, which would provide at least some level of protection against slashing weapons. He carries a rapier as sidearm.

Plate G
Swedish artilleryman, Ordnance Corps

Artillery personnel were enlisted among semi-civilian professionals, who in the sixteenth century wore civilian dress each according to his choice. However, at some point in the early seventeenth century, the custom emerged among Swedish artillerymen of wearing grey woollen garments. This eventually became the common practice for artillerymen in the Swedish army. It may be assumed that grey clothes were deemed more suitable to the rough work of servicing the cannons, in the same way that blackened armour, somewhat earlier, became the norm for soldiers armed with firearms. Or perhaps the practice emerged when artillerymen assigned to warships received their share of the grey woollen cloth customarily distributed to sailors. Artillerymen might serve either on land or at sea. As a long-term professional, this artilleryman almost certainly served on the eastern front in Livonia or Muscovy in the early 1600s, perhaps at sea as well. He would have kept a rapier and perhaps an arquebus or musket at hand for protecting himself and his cannon if the need arose.

COLOUR PLATE COMMENTARIES

Plate H
Enlisted Scottish musketeer, Alexander Ramsay's Company

Although numerous Scots already served in the Swedish army and for this reason were dressed and armed in much the same manner as other Swedish soldiers, fresh recruits from Scotland often retained aspects of their daily dress at home. During the Kalmar War, Sweden made great attempts to raise fresh enlisted soldiers in Scotland. However, the Danish blockade made it difficult for foreign enlisted units to travel to Sweden. One of the very few who attempted the journey was Captain Alexander Ramsay, who, with a few companies of men, made it to Norway, where he landed with the intention to march to Sweden. This Scottish musketeer belongs to the trained core of Ramsay's contingent, which also included untrained men and convicts pressed into service. Although still dressed in the Scottish manner, he brings a 10-bore matchlock musket with a fork rest. He carries a rapier or long cutlass with a *tessak*-style hilt as a sidearm. Both musket and sidearm were probably delivered from the Dutch Republic, where much of the initial planning for the recruitment of men and expedition to Scandinavia took place among Scotsmen already in place.

Plate I
Danish officer 'of the House'

This officer is a professional soldier 'of the House' who received waiting pay from the Crown until King Christian ordered the army to mobilise and called upon him to raise a company. The men 'of the House' typically served for many years in a military capacity, so they can be said to have constituted the core of a standing army or at least of a permanent military establishment. While waiting, this officer served in foreign armies to gain experience and additional income. As a result, he wears serviceable three-quarter armour and is armed with a rapier and wheellock pistols in the manner of a cuirassier. However, he wears a helmet of the cabasset type, which provides better visibility than the types of helmets customarily employed by cuirassiers. His partiality towards the practical cabasset instead of a traditional cuirassier helmet is another result of his previous foreign military service.

Plate J
Danish cuirassier, Scanian Banner, retinue of nobles

On the surface, there is little to distinguish this member of the Danish retinue of nobles from his Swedish counterpart, illustrated in Plate 1. This cuirassier, who just as well instead might be a member of the Court Banner, wears the same breastplate of the peascod-belly or goose-belly type that already was going out of fashion on the Continent. Like his Swedish counterpart, he wears three-quarter armour and is armed with a rapier and wheellock pistols. However, he has adopted knee-length cuisses, the additional protection that reached down to and covered his knees that his Swedish counterpart lacks, as well as steel gauntlets. Although this Scanian cuirassier presently wears a burgonet, he is also far more likely to own a visored helmet that he might use in battle instead of the more comfortable but less protective burgonet. This cuirassier is also far more likely to own a real heavy warhorse than his

Swedish counterpart. This man carries red and yellow plumes and sash as a field sign since these were the colours of the House of Oldenburg. If he had derived from Jutland, he would already be expected to wear a 'cuirassier coat' (i.e. a casack) over his armour in the colour of his unit.

Plate K
Danish serving cavalryman, Scanian Banner
Every cuirassier of the retinue of nobles and Court Banner would bring along at least one serving cavalryman (*svend*). Although expected to fight in the same unit as his master, the serving man's horse might be smaller, and he customarily was supplied with cheaper and less comprehensive arms and armour. This *svend* is fortunate to wear a solid burgonet and half armour in the form of a shot-proof breastplate, backplate, and spaulder-style shoulder and arm defences. Yet he lacks cuisses to protect the thighs and iron gauntlets. Nonetheless, he is lucky because most serving cavalrymen received only a 'simple', non-shot-proof breastplate since these were significantly cheaper. Similar to his master, this serving cavalryman is armed with a rapier and pair of wheellock pistols. Little is known of how the serving cavalrymen formed up in battle, but we can assume that they comprised the rear ranks in a cuirassier unit.

Plate L
Danish harquebusier cavalryman, Gert von Rantzau's Harquebusier Company
This harquebusier carries a 16-bore (16.8 mm) wheellock arquebus as his primary armament. The cavalry arquebus is hung from a swivel attached to a bandolier across the left shoulder. It can be fired without unhooking from the bandolier. On his right side, the harquebusier carries a special leather strap from his belt with a powder horn, priming flask, ammunition pouch, and wheellock spanner. As additional armament, a harquebusier might also carry one or two wheellock pistols on his horse and certainly a sidearm of some kind. Similar to some other Danish cavalrymen, this man carries a sidearm referred to as a 'cavalry cutlass' instead of a rapier. Although little is known about this weapon, the cavalry cutlass was presumably a cheap cutting sword shorter than a rapier. A Danish harquebusier was supposed to wear a helmet as well as a breast- and backplate. This harquebusier is not so fortunate. He wears a morion to protect his head but lacks other armour. He is probably a fresh recruit enlisted by Gert von Rantzau in Holstein. Other harquebusiers in Danish service might be professional soldiers enlisted in Germany.

Plate M
Danish pikeman, Holger Rosencrantz's Company of the King's Regiment of Foot
The King's Regiment of Foot was mostly officered by Danes, but the common soldiers included both conscripts from Denmark and enlisted soldiers from the Dutch Republic and Germany. This is a Dutch pikeman from Holger Rosencrantz's company. Rosencrantz was a Danish noble, but the men he commanded were mostly Dutch professionals. In comparison to the Swedish provincial pikeman in Plate 4, this Dutch pikeman is armed and equipped in

the up-to-date style that had already become standard on the Continent. For protection, he wears both breastplate and backplate, gorget, tassets to protect the upper thighs, and helmet. In addition to the pike, his primary weapon, he carries a rapier as sidearm.

Plate N
Danish arquebusier, Peder Hundemark's Company of the King's Regiment of Foot

Peder Hundemark's company consisted of conscripts from Copenhagen and Scania. As one of only three companies of national infantry in the Danish army, we can assume that they received their arms and equipment from the Copenhagen Armoury. This arquebusier carries a 16-bore matchlock arquebus with fork rest, with a rapier as a sidearm. Few arquebusiers wore armour by this time, but armour was still distributed on occasion, and it seems likely that any available infantry cuirasses and helmets would be used to equip the newly raised conscripts of the King's Regiment of Foot. The men had previously trained for the brief period of one month in the Dutch model of warfare before they were discharged. In early 1611, they were recalled to duty but this time for war. King Christian had high hopes for these companies, but, in reality, their lack of experience caused major problems in the early stages of the war. Later, with increased experience and the infusion of additional enlisted soldiers from the Continent, the companies of the King's Regiment performed well. It is unlikely that many men still wore cuirasses in the later stages of the war.

Plate O
Norwegian arquebusier, Akershus Castle garrison company

Since most conventional military units based in Norway were sent from Denmark, there were few Norwegian army regulars. At the outbreak of war, such men were limited to a handful of castle garrisons. This Norwegian arquebusier belongs to the garrison company of Akershus Castle, near Oslo. He is armed with a 16-bore matchlock arquebus, which is sufficiently light to operate without a fork rest. Since this arquebusier is a professional soldier, he carries a rapier as a sidearm instead of the cheaper but obsolete *tessak* (cutting sword), which was distributed among Norway's levies. Regarding both armament and dress, he is indistinguishable from any enlisted Continental soldiers who might be sent to Norway.

Plate P
Norwegian levied irregular

This irregular is a mere farmhand, so both his dress and armament could be regarded as poor, possibly even archaic, when compared to what a more well-to-do peasant freeholder would wear and carry. Regardless, this should not be interpreted as an inability to fight. Norwegian levies could, when they wanted, be very efficient fighters. Regulations required that each owner of a full farmstead must own a long arquebus with gunpowder and shot, a *tessak* (cutting sword), and an axe. Poorer peasants could dispense with the *tessak* or the axe but must nonetheless own a long arquebus. Those with least land, or those who were employed by another peasant, needed only an iron-reinforced 'halberd' (presumably a poleaxe) and an axe. Farmstead workers could bring a hunting spear and a *tessak*, or a spear and an axe if very poor. When engaged in hand-to-hand combat, a poleaxe of the type carried by this irregular is a deadly weapon. Norwegian levies would fight to protect their homes, and most were not averse to going on cross-border raids in search of plunder.

Flags

Plate Q

1. Småland cavalry cornet
Descriptions in Laurentius Bojerus's poem *Carolomachia* suggest that Swedish cavalry units already flew cornets with the coat of arms of their respective province. The provincial coats of arms already played an important heraldic role and they certainly appeared on banners later in the century. The Småland cavalry is described as flying a cornet with a standing lion carrying a crossbow, which is illustrated in this reconstruction.

2. Västergötland infantry colour
Following the pattern suggested in the poem *Carolomachia*, the colours of Västergötland infantry companies can be reconstructed as displaying a proud lion on a bicolour field, which based on later banners can be assumed to have been black and yellow. We do not know if Swedish provincial colours already included a laurel wreath but this seems likely.

3. Södermanland infantry colour
Again based on a description in Bojerus's poem *Carolomachia*, the Södermanland infantry companies flew colours which displayed a black griffon, which the poet described as terrible in countenance.

Plate R

4. Finland infantry colour
The Finland infantry companies (which later became known as the Åbo and Björneborg regiment) carried colours decorated with a standing bear wielding a sword. According to Bojerus, the colour also displayed a star, although two stars is more likely since this was included in the contemporary coat of arms.

5. Nyland Cavalry Cornet
The Nyland cavalry from Finland (later to be known as Nyland and Tavastehus regiment) flew a cornet with a helmet crowned with two flags (presumably blue with a cross of yellow or white – that is, heraldic gold or silver)

Further Reading

Few modern works, and none in English, describe the Kalmar War in more than general terms. Unsurprisingly, the most comprehensive military history of the war remains *Danska och ryska krigen*, published by the Swedish General Staff in 1936. This, the first volume of the multivolume *Sveriges krig 1611-1632*, published from 1936 to 1939, remains a key modern reference work to the wars of Gustavus Adolphus. It is unlikely that we will ever again see a military history project with this magnitude of funding, access to archival resources, military and academic expertise, and, not least, time for research. This work contains many valuable archive documents relating to the Swedish army under Gustavus Adolphus and is reliable in its use of official records including orders of battle, casualty lists, and logistical inventories. However, its conclusions on tactics and strategy cannot always be taken for granted due to bias in favour of Gustavus Adolphus and extrapolation from developments that took place much later.

The existence of such assumptions often becomes clear from the second key reference work: the multivolume *Kungl. Svea livgardes historia*, by Bertil C:son Barkman and others, which describes the history of the Swedish Royal Life Guard. Although this work covers a far longer period of time than the General Staff's work and, since it focuses on the Life Guard, does not cover every incident of the war, it updates and often provides a better reading of the sources than *Danska och ryska krigen* (in which Barkman was indeed involved). Publication started in 1937 and was not concluded until 1983. Some additional information is provided by other regimental histories, the most useful of which is the multivolume *Kungl. Artilleriet*, by Jonas Hedberg and others, which describes the history of the Royal Artillery. Publication began in 1975 and apparently reached its conclusion in 2011. Among other regimental histories, Gustaf Petri's first volume of *Kungl. Första livgrenadjärregementets historia* is particularly good on the Östergötland Ducal Army and further includes much else of interest.

The military narratives of the Kalmar War should be read in conjunction with Ingel Wadén's various works, in particular *Berättande källor till Calmarkrigets historia* (1936), which attempt to clarify the reliability and mutual dependence of the various surviving sources from the period. Wadén's highly critical (sometimes perhaps overly critical) analysis of existing sources provides a much-needed corrective on traditional historiography's interpretations of chronology and events.

In comparison, more recent *general* works in Swedish on the wars under King Charles and Gustavus Adolphus are most often derivative and contain little new analysis, although particular aspects have been the subject of often excellent articles and monographs. The beautifully illustrated *Gustav II Adolf och hans folk*, by Göte Göransson, should be mentioned since it includes a wealth of information on events and dress at the time, including those relating to military matters. Published in 1994, it was the result of years of research into primary sources.

Among works in Danish, Axel Larsen's *Kalmarkrigen* (1889) pioneered a very detailed and, in many ways, excellent description of the war. However, in some respects, it was overtaken by the research carried out later at the Swedish General Staff. One of the few later works that deal with the Kalmar War with a focus on military history is J. W. Gordon Norrie's *Kalmarkrigen* (1978). Although printed without notes and in an edition that, on the surface, looks somewhat amateurish, Norrie used many sources in his research, which he prepared in 1965 as a military history of the Kalmar War for the Army Staff's Section for Military History (*Hærstabens Militærhistoriske sektion*). Gunner Lind's *Hæren og magten i Danmark 1614-1662* (1994) is an indispensable academic study on the Danish and Norwegian armies, though it focuses on trends, not details, and concentrates on a later period. In comparison, the multivolume general military history *Danmarks krigshistorie* (2008) provides only a general history of the war, with few details.

Bibliography

Archival Sources

National Archives of Norway (NRA)
Danske Kancelli, Innlegg og henlagte saker, eske 5, DK B 160, 17 September 1612 (EA-3023/Fccb/L0001)
Danske Kancelli, Norske henlagte saker, 3 October 1612 (EA-3023/Jaa/L0001)

The National Archives (TNA)
SP 75/5, fols 23–24
SP 75/5, fol. 29d

Contemporary Sources and Compilations

Andersen, Halvor, 'Kong Christian den Fjerdes Artickle for det Danske Krigsfolk eller Landsknegte, dateret 10 April 1611 tilligemed hans Krigs-Ordning eller Rytter-Ret, samt Ridder-Ret, uden Aar og Dag, begge af Cancelliets Arkiv (Siellandske Register No. 15 Folio 334 a. til 360 a.)', *Danske Magazin*, 2:3 (1810), pp.161–197 [Included in which is a copy of King Christian IV's Articles of War of 1611]

Anon., *Eygentlijke afbeeldinge va[n] de belegeringe der stat Calmer* (Amsterdam: Herman Allertszoon Coster and Claes Janszoon Visscher, n.d. [*c.* 1611])

Anon. [Ernst Werckman], 'Journal über alles des Jenige, so sich in dem so genannten Calmarschen Krieg zugetragen', in H. Rørdam (ed.), *Monumenta Historiæ Danicæ. Historiske kildeskrifter og bearbejdelser af dansk historie, især fra det 16. Aarhundrede* (Copenhagen: G. E. C. Gad, 1887), pp.671–762 [Werckman was a secretary in King Christian's German Chancellery during the Kalmar War who compiled a history from various sources]

Anon., *Samlinger til det norske folks sprog og historie* (Christiania: Samfund, 1835), vol. 3

Becke, Berthold von der, *Soldaten-Spiegel: Historische Anweisung welcher Gestalt ein Guarison oder Vestung nicht allein mit aller jhrer Notturfft vnnd Zugehörung wohl zu versorgen hohen vnd nidern Aemptern recht anzuordnen* (Frankfurt am Main: Johann Spieß und Johann Jacob Porschen, 1605)

Bojerus, Laurentius, *Carolomachiae liber* (Vilnius: Jesuit Academy, 1606), vol. 3

Breen, Adam van, *De Nassausche Wapen-Handelinge, van Schilt, Spies, Rappier, ende Targe* (The Hague: Aert Meuris, 1618)

Bricka, Carl F. (ed.), 'Eske Brocks Dagbog for Aaret 1611', *Danske Magazin*, 4:5 (1881), pp.125–45 [Eske Brock was a Danish war commissar during the Kalmar War]

Bricka, Carl F., Fridericia, Julius A., and Skovgaard, Johanne C. E. (eds), *Kong Christian den Fjerdes egenhændige Breve* (Copenhagen: Selskabet for Udgivelse af Kilder til dansk Historie, 1887–1947), vols 1–8

Brock, Eske, 'Udtog af Eske Brocks Almanak for 1612', *Magazin til den Danske Adels Historie*, 1 (1824), pp.8–30

de Londoño, Sancho, *El discurso sobre la forma de reduzir la disciplina militar, a meyor y antiguo estado* (Brussels: Rutger Velpius, 1589)

Erslev, Kristian (ed.), *Aktstykker og Oplysninger til Rigsraadets og Stændermødernes Historie i Kristian IV's Tid* (Copenhagen: Nielsen & Lydiche, 1883), vol. 1

'Från gamla ofredsår', *Julbok för Västerås stift*, 9 (1914), pp.127–40

Gheyn II, Jacob de, *Die Reitschule oder Übungen der Kavallerie* (Amsterdam: C. J. Visscher, 1599–1600)

Gheyn II, Jacob de, *Wapenhandelinghe van Roers, Musquetten ende Spiessen* (Amsterdam: Robert de Baudous, 1608) [First published in 1607]

Geyn [Gheyn] II, Jacob de, *Waabenhandling Om Rør, Musketter oc Spedser* (The Hague: Publisher unknown, 1607)

Gottfried, Johann Ludwig, *Inventarium Sueciae* (Frankfurt am Main: Friedrich Hulsius, 1632)

Gustavus Adolphus, 'Krigsfolks-Ordning', in C. G. Styffe (ed.), *Konung Gustaf II Adolfs skrifter* (Stockholm: P. A. Norstedt & Söner, 1861), pp.1–61

Gyllenhjelm, Carl Carlsson, 'Egenhändiga anteckningar af Carl Carlsson Gyllenhjelm rörande tiden 1597–1601', *Historiska Handlingar*, 20 (1905), pp.258–395

John of Nassau, 'Grefve Johans av Nassau relation angående kriget i Livland 1601–1602', *Historiska Handlingar*, 20 (1905), pp.396–438

Kall, Abraham (ed.), 'Mag. Ægidii Laurizens samlede Efterretninger om Krigen med Sverige i Aarene 1611 og 1612', *Nye Danske Magazin*, 2:2 (1806), pp.9–56 [Lauritzen was a priest in Ribe during the Kalmar War who compiled a variety of documents]

Kancelliets Brevbøger vedrørende Danmarks indre Forhold (Copenhagen: Rigsarkivet, 1885–2005), vols 1–39

Lange, Christian C. A. (ed.), *Norske Samlinger* (Christiania: Feilberg & Landmark, 1860), vol. 2

Moltke, L. (ed.), 'Rigsraad Eske Brocks Dagbøger for 1604, 1609, 1619 og 1622', *Danske Samlinger*, 2:2 (1872–1873), pp.256–300

Norske Rigs-Registranter (Christiania: Det norske historiske kildeskrift-fond, 1861–1891), vols 1–12

Oxenstierna, Axel, *Rikskansleren Axel Oxenstiernas skrifter och brefvexling* (Stockholm: P. A. Norstedt & Söner/Swedish National Archives (Riksarkivet, RA), 1888–2018), multiple vols and databases

Peleus, Julien, *L'Histoire de la derniere Guerre de Suede* (Paris: François Pomeray, 1622) [Peleus was a councillor and historian in Paris who interviewed French participants in the Kalmar War]

Roberts, Henry, *The Most Royall and Honourable Entertainement, of the Famous and Renowmed King, Christiern the Fourth, King of Denmarke, &c* … (London: William Barley, 1606)

Rørdam, Holger (ed.), 'To Dagbøger fra Kalmarkrigens Tid, 1611–1612', in *Historiske Samlinger og Studier vedrørende Danske Forhold og Personligheder især i det 17. Aarhundrede* (Copenhagen: G. E. C. Gad, 1891), pp.289–319 [Contains two Danish diaries, one by Peder Hesselberg of the Court Banner and the other by Christian Friis of Kragerup, the captain of an enlisted company in the King's Regiment.]

Rydberg, O. S., and Hallendorff, C. (eds), *Sverges Traktater med främmande magter* (Stockholm: P. A. Norstedt & Söner, 1903), vol. 5, part 1

Schildknecht, Wendelin, *Harmonia in fortalitiis construendis, defendendis & oppugnandis* (Stettin: Johann Valentin Rheten, 1652)

Secher, V. A., *Corpus Constitutionum Daniæ: Forordninger, recesser og andre Kongelige Breve, 1558–1660* (Copenhagen: Gad, 1897), vol. 4

Ufano, Diego, *Artillerie, ou vraye instruction de l'arttillerie et de ses appurtenances* (Rouen: Jean Berthelin, 1628) [The first French edition was published in 1614 by Johann Theodor de Bry]

Ufano, Diego, *Tratado de la artilleria y uso della, platicado por el capitan Diego Ufano en las guerras de Flandes* (Brussels: Juan Momarte, 1613)

Vedel Simonsen, Lauritz Schebye (ed.), *Bidrag til Lænsmanden paa Dronningborg, Rigsraad Eske Brocks, Levnetsbeskrivelse; indeheldende hans egenhændige Dagbog for 1613* (Odense: Vedel Simonsen, 1843)

Vedel Simonsen, Lauritz Schebye (ed.), *Bidrag til Lænsmanden paa Dronningborg, Rigsraad Eske Brocks, Levnetsbeskrivelse; med hans egenhændige Dagboger for 1608 og 1612* (Odense: Vedel Simonsen, 1842)

Waaranen, Johan E. (ed.), *Samling af urkunder rörande Finlands historia 3 (1609–1611)* (Helsinki: Finska Litteratur-Sällskapet, 1866)

Wallhausen, Johann Jacobi von, *Kriegskunst zu Fuß* (Leeuwarden: Claude Fontaine, 1630) [First published in 1615]

Wallhausen, Johann Jacobi von, *Kriegskunst zu Pferdt* (Frankfurt-am-Main: Johann Theodor de Bry, 1616)

Widekindi, Johan, *Then fordom Stormächtigste, Högborne Furstes och Herres Herr Gustaff Adolphs den Andres och Stores Sweriges, Götes och Wändes etc. konungs Historia, och Lefwernes Beskrifning, Then Första Deel* (Stockholm: Niclas Wankijf, 1691) [A history of Gustavus Adolphus based on archive documents, some of which are now lost]

Databases

Bruzelius, Lars, *The Maritime History Virtual Archives*, <http://www.bruzelius.info/Nautica/Nautica.html>, accessed 23 June 2023

Murdoch, Steve, and Grosjean, Alexia, *The Scotland, Scandinavia and Northern European Biographical Database* (SSNE), <https://www.st-andrews.ac.uk/history/ssne/>, accessed 23 June 2023

Riksarkivet (Swedish National Archives), *Svenskt biografiskt lexikon* (SBL), <https://sok.riksarkivet.se/SBL/>, accessed 23 June 2023

Later Studies

Ahnlund, Nils, *Gustav Adolf den store* (Stockholm: Aldus/Bonniers, 1963)

Alhaug, Knut Olav, *Angrepet på Kalmar 1611. Militæradministrative forhold under Kalmarkrigens oppløp og innledende fase*. 2018. University of Bergen, Master Thesis

Alm, Josef, *Arméns eldhandvapen förr och nu* (Stockholm: Kungl. Armémuseum, 1953)

Alm, Josef, *Blanka vapen och skyddsvapen från och med 1500-talet till våra dagar* (Stockholm: Rediviva, 1975) [First published in 1932]

Alm, Josef, *Eldhandvapen 1: Från deras tidigaste förekomst till slaglåsets allmänna införande* (Stockholm: Rediviva, 1976) [First published in 1934]

Alm, Josef, 'Flottans handvapen', in *Sjöhistorisk Årsbok 1953–54* (Stockholm: Föreningen Sveriges Sjöfartsmuseum i Stockholm, 1954), pp.67–147

Artéus, Gunnar, *Till militärstatens förhistoria: Krig, professionalisering och social förändring under Vasasönernas regering* (Stockholm: Probus, 1986)

Askgaard, Finn, *Christian IV: 'Rigets væbnede Arm'* (Copenhagen: Tøjhusmuseet, 1988)

Barkman, Bertil C:son, *Kungl. Svea livgardes historia: 1560–1611* (Stockholm: Stiftelsen för Svea livgardes historia, 1939), vol. 2

Barkman, Bertil C:son, and Lundkvist, Sven, *Kungl. Svea livgardes historia: 1611–1632* (Stockholm: Stiftelsen för Svea livgardes historia, 1963), vol. 3, part 1

Barkman, G. B. C:son, *Gustaf II Adolfs regementsorganisation vid det inhemska infanteriet: En studie över organisationens tillkomst och huvuddragen av dess utveckling mot bakgrunden av kontinental organisation* (Stockholm: Meddelanden från Generalstabens krigshistoriska avdelning, 1931)

Bellamy, Martin, *Christian IV and His Navy: A Political and Administrative History of the Danish Navy 1596–1648* (Leiden: Brill, 2006)

Bellander, Erik, *Dräkt och uniform: Den svenska arméns beklädnad från 1500-talets början fram till våra dagar* (Stockholm: P. A. Norstedt & Söner, 1973)

Blom, Otto, *Kristian Den Fjerdes Artilleri, Hans Tøihuse og Vaabenforraad* (Copenhagen: C. C. Lose, 1877)

Broomé, Bertil, *Nils Stiernsköld*. 1950. Stockholm University, PhD

Brzezinski, Richard, *The Army of Gustavus Adolphus (2): Cavalry* (London: Osprey Publishing, 1993)

Delbrück, Hans, *History of the Art of War, Volume IV: The Dawn of Modern Warfare* (Lincoln: University of Nebraska Press, 1990)

Ericson, Lars, and Sandstedt, Fred, *Fanornas folk: Den svenska arméns soldater under 1600-talets första hälft* (Stockholm: Armémuseum, 1982)

Fagerlund, Rainer, 'De finska fänikorna under äldre Vasatid: Forskningsläge och problem', *Turun historiallinen arkisto*, 38 (1982), pp.94–116

Frantzen, Ole L., and Jespersen, Knud J. V. (eds), *Danmarks krigshistorie: 700–1814* (Copenhagen: Gad, 2008), vol. 1

Fredholm von Essen, Michael, *Charles X's Wars. Volume 1 – Armies of the Swedish Deluge, 1655–1660* (Warwick: Helion & Company, 2021)

Fredholm von Essen, Michael, 'Early Eighteenth Century Naval Chemical Warfare in Scandinavia: A Study in the Introduction of New Weapon Technologies in Early Modern Navies', *Baltic Security and Defence Review*, 13:1 (2011), pp.122–51

Fredholm von Essen, Michael, *Muscovy's Soldiers: The Emergence of the Russian Army 1462–1689* (Warwick: Helion & Company, 2018)

Fredholm von Essen, Michael, 'On the Trail of Rocketry: The Enigma of Scandinavian Naval Pyrotechnics in the Sixteenth to Eighteenth Century', *Arquebusier*, 30:6 (2008), pp.24–39

Fredholm von Essen, Michael, 'On the Trail of Rocketry 2: Early Eighteenth-Century Gas Warfare and Other Norwegian Innovations in Naval Pyrotechnics', *Arquebusier*, 32:1 (2010), pp.2–5

Fredholm von Essen, Michael, *Sweden's War in Muscovy, 1609–1617: The Relief of Moscow and Conquest of Novgorod* (Forthcoming: Helion & Company, 2023)

Fredholm von Essen, Michael, *The Lion from the North: The Swedish Army during the Thirty Years War* (Warwick: Helion & Company, 2020), vols 1–2

Gahrn, Lars, 'Gullbergs försvar 1612 – Ett 400-årsminne', *Lars Gahrn skriver* (2011), <https://larsgahrnskriver.wordpress.com/2011/12/01/gullbergs-forsvar-1612-ett-400-arsminne/>, accessed 23 June 2023

Generalstaben, *Sveriges krig 1611–1632* (Stockholm: Generalstaben, 1937), suppl. vol. 1: *Sveriges sjökrig 1611–1632*

Generalstaben, *Sveriges krig 1611–1632* (Stockholm: Generalstaben, 1936), vol. 1: *Danska och ryska krigen*

Glete, Jan, 'Naval Power and Control of the Sea in the Baltic in the Sixteenth Century', in J. B. Hattendorf and R. W. Unger (eds), *War at Sea in the Middle Ages and Renaissance* (Woodbridge: Boydell Press, 2003), pp.217–32

BIBLIOGRAPHY

Glete, Jan, *Navies and Nations: Warships, Navies and State Building in Europe and America, 1500–1860* (Stockholm: Almqvist & Wiksell International, 1993), vol. 1

Glete, Jan, 'Vasatidens galärflottor', in H. Norman (ed.), *Skärgårdsflottan: Uppbyggnad, militär användning och förankring i det svenska samhället 1700–1824* (Lund: Historiska Media, 2000), pp.37–49

Göransson, Göte, *Gustav II Adolf och hans folk* (Location unknown: Bra Böcker, 1994)

Hamilton, Henning, *Afhandling om krigsmaktens och krigskonstens tillstånd i Sverige, under Konung Gustaf II Adolfs regering* (Stockholm: Kongl. Vitterhets Historie och Antiquitets Academiens Handlingar 17, 1846)

Hansen, Svend Aage, *Adelsvældens grundlag*. 1964. Copenhagen University, PhD

Hauge, Thomas, 'Galeier i den dansk-norske marine', *Norsk Tidskrift for Sjøvesen*, 69 (1954), pp.351–71

Hazelius, Kim, *De kallades snapphanar: Friskyttar, rövare & bondeuppbåd* (Bjärnum: Bokpro, 2006)

Hedberg, Jonas (ed.), *Kungl. Artilleriet: Medeltid och äldre vasatid* (Stockholm: Militärhistoriska Förlaget, 1975)

Hedberg, Jonas (ed.), *Kungl. Artilleriet: Yngre vasatiden* (Stockholm: Militärhistoriska Förlaget, 1985)

Hocker, Frederick M., *Vasa: A Swedish Warship* (Stockholm: Medström, 2011)

Höglund, Lars-Eric, *Från Karl Knutsson till Kristina: Svenska fälttecken och beklädnad från senmedeltid till trettioåriga kriget* (Karlstad: Acedia Press, 2012)

Jägerhorn, Sebastian, *Hårdast bland de hårda: En kavalleriofficer i fält* (Stockholm: Medström, 2018)

Jakobsson, Theodor, *Lantmilitär beväpning och beklädnad under äldre Vasatiden och Gustav II Adolfs tid* (Stockholm: Generalstaben, 1938; published separately and as suppl. vol. 2 in Generalstaben, *Sveriges krig 1611–1632*)

Larsen [Liljefalk], Axel, *Kalmarkrigen. Et Bidrag til de nordiske Rigers Krigshistorie* (Copenhagen: G. E. C. Gad, 1889)

Larsen [Liljefalk], Axel, *Kampen om Kalmar 1611* (Copenhagen: Det krigsvidenskabelige Selskaps Forlag, 1884)

Larsson, Stefan, *Slagfält Kalmar: En glimt av belägringen 1611* (Kalmar: Länsstyrelsen i Kalmar län, 2016)

Lind, Gunner, *Hæren og magten i Danmark 1614–1662* (Odense: Odense Universitetsforlag, 1994)

Lindbergh, Katarina Harrison, *Kalmarkriget 1611–1613* (Lund: Historiska Media, 2022)

Lundkvist, Sven, 'Verklighetsuppfattning och verklighet: En studie i Gustav II Adolfs handlingsramar', in R. Sandberg (ed.), *Studier i äldre historia tillägnade Herman Schück 5/4 1985* (Stockholm: Festschrift, 1985), pp.227–41

Madsen, Emil, 'Om Fodfolket i de danske Hære i det 16de Aarhundrede', *Dansk Historisk Tidskrift*, 7:1 (1897–1899), pp.165–215

Madsen, Emil, 'Om Rytteriet i de danske Hære i det 16de Aarhundrede', *Dansk Historisk Tidskrift*, 7:1 (1897–1899), pp.414–60

Michell, Thomas, *History of the Scottish Expedition to Norway in 1612* (London: T. Nelson and Sons, 1886)

Munthe, Ludvig W:son, *Kongl. Fortifikationens historia 1: Svenska fortifikationsväsendet från nyare tidens början till inrättandet af en särskild fortifikationsstat år 1641* (Stockholm: P. A. Norstedt & Söner, 1902)

Murdoch, Steve, 'Diplomacy in Transition: Stuart-British Diplomacy in Northern Europe, 1603-1618', in A. I. Macinnes, T. Riis, and F. Pedersen (eds), *Ships, Guns and Bibles in the North Sea and the Baltic States, c.1350–c.1700* (East Linton: Tuckwell Press, 2000), pp.93–114

Norrie, J. W. Gordon, *Kalmarkrigen 1611-1612* (Copenhagen: Sixtus, 1978)

Östergren, Stefan, *Sigismund: En biografi över den svensk-polske monarken* (Location unknown: Fredestad, 2005)

Petri, Gustaf, *Kungl. Första livgrenadjärregementets historia 1: Östgötafänikorna till och med år 1618* (Stockholm: P. A. Norstedt & Söner, 1926)

Redlich, F., 'Contributions in the Thirty Years' War', *Economic History Review*, New Series, 12:2 (1959), pp.247–54

Schön, Ebbe, *Kungar, krig och katastrofer: Vår historia i sägen och tro* (Fourth edition, Stockholm: Hjalmarson & Högberg, 2011)

Seitz, Heribert, *Svärdet och värjan som armévapen* (Stockholm: Kungl. Armémuseum, 1955)

Skenbäck, Urban, *Sjöfolk och knektar på Wasa* (Stockholm: Statens sjöhistoriska museet, 1983)

Stålhane, H., 'Baltzar-fejden', *Östersunds-Posten*, 92–93, 96–98 (18–28 June 1898)

Svensson, S. Artur (ed.), *Svenska flottans historia* (Malmö: Allhem, 1942), vol. 1

Wadén, Ingel, *Berättande källor till Calmarkrigets historia*. 1936. Lund University, PhD

Wadén, Ingel, 'Ett kopparstick över Elfsborgs belägring 1612', *Rig*, 20:3 (1937), pp.147–55

Wadén, Ingel, 'Samtida bilder över belägringen av Kalmar stad och slott år 1611', *Rig*, 19 (1936), pp.85–106

Wadén, Ingel, 'Skriftväxlingen mellan Carl IX och Christian IV efter Kalmar slotts fall 1611', *Personhistorisk Tidskrift*, 37 (1936), pp.52–64

Wagner, Eduard, *European Weapons & Warfare 1618-1648* (London: Octopus Books, 1979)

Weibull, Lauritz, 'Gustaf II Adolfs räddare vid Vittsjö', *Scandia*, 16:1 (1944), pp.90–95

Other titles in the From Retinue to Regiment series:

No 1 *Richard III and the Battle of Bosworth* Mike Ingram

No 2 *Tanaka 1587: Japan's Greatest Unknown Samurai Battle* Stephen Turnbull

No 3 *The Army of the Swabian League 1525* Doug Miller

No 4 *The Italian Wars Volume 1: The Expedition of Charles VIII into Italy and the Battle of Fornovo* Massimo Predonzani & Alberici Vincenzo, translated by Irene Maccolini

No 5 *The Commotion Time: Tudor Rebellion in the West, 1549* E.T. Fox

No 6 *The Italian Wars Volume 2: Agnadello 1509, Ravenna 1512, Marignano 1515* Massimo Predonzani & Alberici Vincenzo, translated by Rachele Tiso

No 7 *The Tudor Arte of Warre Volume 1: The Conduct of War from Henry VII to Mary I, 1485–1558* Jonathan Davies

No 8 *The Ethiopian–Adal War 1529–1543: The Conquest of Abyssinia* Jeffrey M. Shaw

No 9 *The Ōnin War: A Turning Point in Samurai History* Stephen Turnbull

No 10 *One Faith, One Law, One King: French Armies of the Wars of Religion 1562–1598* T J O'Brien de Clare

No 11 *The Italian Wars Volume 3: Francis I and the Battle of Pavia 1525* Massimo Predonzani & Alberici Vincenzo

No 12 *On the Borderlands of Great Empires: Transylvanian Armies 1541–1613* Florin Nicolae Ardelean

No 14 *The Art of Shooting Great Ordnance: A History of the Development, Manufacture and Use of Artillery, 1494–1628* Jonathan Davies

No 15 *The Italian Wars Volume 4: The Battle of Ceresole 1544 – The Crushing Defeat of the Imperial Army* Massimo Predonzani & Simon Miller

No 16 *The Men of Warre: The Clothes, Weapons and Accoutrements of the Scots at War 1460–1600* Jenn Scott

No 17 *The German Peasants' War 1524–26* Douglas Miller

No 18 *The Tudor Arte of Warre Volume 2: The conduct of war in the reign of Elizabeth I, 1558–1603: Diplomacy, Strategy, Campaigns and Battles* Jonathan Davies

No 19 *The Kalmar War 1611–1613: Gustavus Adolphus's First War* Michael Fredholm von Essen

About the author

Professor Michael Fredholm von Essen is an historian and former military analyst who has published extensively on the history of Eurasia and lectured, during conferences or as visiting professor, around the world. He has published a large number of books, including *The Goths 1–2* (Society of Ancients, 2021–2022); *Afghanistan Beyond the Fog of War* (NIAS Press, 2018); *Transnational Organized Crime and Jihadist Terrorism: Russian-Speaking Networks in Western Europe* (Routledge, 2017); numerous articles in *Slingshot*, the journal of the Society of Ancients, and *Arquebusier*, the journal of the Pike and Shot Society; and many books for Helion & Company.

About the artist

Sergey Shamenkov graduated from the Academy of Arts in Lviv. He is a sculptor, author and illustrator who specialises in uniformology, military and costume history. His principal area of interest is the study of the Swedish army of Charles XIIth. When not painting, he is involved in re-enactment, depicting Ukrainian and Swedish units of the 17th and 18th centuries.